# MYTH & MYSTERY

# MYTH&
# MYSTERY

## An Introduction to the Pagan Religions of the Biblical World

## Jack Finegan

This book is a gift from the
RICHARD GRAY FAMILY to
Bethany College

**BAKER BOOK HOUSE**
Grand Rapids, Michigan 49516

**Library of Congress Cataloging-in-Publication Data**

Finegan, Jack, 1908–
    Myth and mystery : an introduction to the pagan religions of the
biblical world / Jack Finegan.
      p.  cm.
    Includes bibliographical references.
    ISBN 0-8010-3555-4
    1. Religions.  2. Mediterranean Religion—Religion.  I. Title.
BL96.F56  1989
291'.093—dc20                                89-38823
                                                          CIP

Bust of the Graeco-Egyptian deity Sarapis, portrayed
as a majestic robed and bearded figure much like
Zeus, with the Roman *modius* or corn-measure on his
head, suggestive of fruitfulness. The figure is in the
Museum of Graeco-Egyptian Antiquities in Alexandria,
and was found near the so-called Pompey's Pillar,
which may once have belonged to the nearby Temple
of Sarapis.

# Contents

# List of Tables

# Acknowledgments

I have written both the present book and a chapter on ancient religions in *An Introduction to the World's Religions*, edited by Joseph Bettis, to be published by Macmillan–Scribner. I thank Joseph Bettis, editor of the *Introduction to the World's Religions*, and Allan Fisher, Editor of Academic and Reference Books, Baker Book House, for their permission, respectively, for me to publish both works, the larger and the smaller, at the same time.

J. F.
*Pacific School of Religion*

# Introduction

Both Jews and Christians believe that their Scriptures can speak to them directly and immediately at any time and place, including the present. But in addition to such timeless and universal aspects of the Bible, it is also true that the Jewish Scriptures (commonly called the Old Testament) and the Christian Scriptures (commonly called the New Testament) originated in the ancient world, a world distant from our own in both time and place. It is therefore a needful part of Bible study to learn as much as possible about that world out of which the Bible has come. Relevant fields of research include biblical languages, biblical chronology, biblical archeology, and investigation of the religious environment of the biblical world. It is with the last area that the present book is concerned.

The religions here dealt with are all ancient religions in the sense that they originated in what to us is ancient time; and, with two exceptions, are now religions of the past. Although some of them were once very widespread (notably Manichaean religion) and very long-enduring (notably Egyptian religion), they have now ceased to exist as continuing communities of faith, even if many of their ideas still live on in various places. The two exceptions are the Mandaean religion, which has persisted into modern times among a small group centered in southern Iraq and southwestern Iran, and Zoroastrianism, which is still influential in India, the United States, and elsewhere. Concerning these two it is interesting to note in connection with the Bible that the Mandaeans consider themselves to stand in the line of tradition from John the Baptist, and that Zoroastrian teachings very possibly influenced Cyrus the Great, the one foreign king whom the Bible (Isa. 45:1) speaks of as the "anointed" of the Lord.

All of the religions here in question are often called "pagan." As to this term, in the Hebrew Scriptures the word גּוֹיִם *(gôyim)* is the name for all the "nations" of the earth (Gen. 10:32), but can also mean especially the "heathen" that are antagonists to Israel (Ps. 79:1). In the Greek Septuagint the word is translated by ἔθνη, "nations," and the same Greek word is used by Josephus for the non-Jewish "foreign nations" (*Antiquities* 13.196). In the Christian Scriptures ἔθνη is the term used to designate all non-Christians other than the Jews. In the Revised Standard Version it is translated variously in accordance with the context, thirty-seven times as "nations," eighty-nine times as "Gentiles," three times as "heathen" (1 Cor. 12:2; 1 Thess. 4:5; 3 John 7), and two times as "pagans" (1 Cor. 5:1; 10:20). In turn in the Vulgate and in ecclesiastical Latin the corresponding terms for the non-Jew and the non-Christian are *gentilis* and *paganus*. Finally, in common usage "pagan" has come to mean that which is not Jewish, Christian, or Islamic.

In itself the word *pagan* may imply only contrast and not opposition, but in particular cases it may also convey a critical judgment of religious and moral character. In view, however, of the profound and persistent human response to reality which is designated by the word *religion*, it seems appropriate to try first to appreciate all that is good in the pagan religions and indeed to recognize that in biblical thought itself there is not only opposition to, but in not a few cases sympathy for and even appropriation of the religious ideas of the environing world.

As to human response to reality, it is evident in the study of the cultures here involved that all these ancient peoples dealt in practical ways with the natural world as such and, in not a few cases, attained such knowledge of the natural world as, at least in some of its elements (e.g., in astronomical observations), may be called scientific.

At the same time among all of these ancient peoples belief is also found in a power or powers in control of or manifest in various aspects of the natural world and human life. This belief may be explained as rational speculation based on analogy with human life and human society. Human institutions are organized and supervised by human beings. Similarly, it is reasonable to suppose, the various aspects of the cosmos must have been arranged by and be in the charge of a living being or beings; and because of the greater magnitude of the whole and its everlasting continuance, this being or these beings must be both greater than human and immortal.[1]

But it also seems evident that, at least upon occasion, the peoples in question were not engaged in speculative thought as to how the universe is run, but were involved in experience of the power or powers as having a wholly other, sacred, or "numinous" (from Latin *numen*,

---

1. For this explanation in regard to Mesopotamia, see Samuel Noah Kramer, review of *The Intellectual Adventure of Ancient Man* by Henri Frankfort et al., *JCS* 2 (1948): 40–49.

"divine force or spirit") quality, that is, as evoking that feeling of awe which is the characteristic religious response, a mingling of fear and attraction.[2] This experience with the wholly other can be expressed only by using comparisons or metaphors drawn from what is here present.[3] Such comparison often results in visualization of the power or powers in anthropomorphic (sometimes theriomorphic or even mixed) form.

The perception of the power or powers as wholly other, sacred, or numinous also means that the experience is normally tinged with a sense of mystery. Thus in the presence of the divine reality even the prophet Zarathushtra asks wonderingly, "Tell me truly, Who fashioned light and darkness?" and continues with many other such questions. As for the meaning of "mystery," the Greek noun μυστήριον is derived from the verb μυέω, which means "to shut [the mouth]" and thus suggests being silent as in the presence of the inexpressible.

The sense of mystery can lead in turn to the rise of myth, a connection which is suggested already in the Greek, where the word for "myth" is μῦθος, which is derived from the same verbal root (μυ) as the word for "mystery." Myth may be defined as a form of symbolic thought in which intellect, imagination, and emotion combine to communicate a perceived truth. A myth is not, then, in the first instance, a fanciful tale, but a symbolic or poetic expression of that which is incapable of direct statement. Thus even the prophet Zarathushtra, for example, tells picturesquely of a "bridge" of separation which is yet to be crossed in the future.

Closely related to myth but distinguishable from it is the epic tale, the distinction lying in the fact that here, while deities may still figure in the account, the chief actors are represented as being (at least originally) human. Yet again, the account may be called a legend if it supposedly goes back to some actual historical event, remembered however dimly. It is of course not to be forgotten that the myths and related traditions were kept alive in ritual and cult, and reflected in architecture and art.[4] In some instances both written records and corresponding monuments are available to us.

The ancient religions with which we have here to deal rest, then, upon theological and mythological ways of thought which, to a greater or lesser degree, they all share; in their individual configuration, however, they are very distinctive, although in various places and times borrowings, equivalences, and syncretisms will be observed.

2. Mircea Eliade, *Traité d'histoire des religions*, 23–24; G. van der Leeuw, *Religion in Essence and Manifestation*, 1.48.

3. For metaphor as the means of communicating the sense of the numinous, see Thorkild Jacobsen, *The Treasures of Darkness: A History of Mesopotamian Religion*, 3–5.

4. For the close relationship between myth and rite, as seen for example in Egypt, see C. J. Bleeker, *Egyptian Festivals: Enactments of Religious Renewal*, 11–12.

# Abbreviations

| | |
|---|---|
| *AEHL* | *Archaeological Encyclopedia of the Holy Land,* ed. Avraham Negev (New York: Putnam, 1972) |
| *AJA* | *American Journal of Archaeology* |
| *AJSL* | *American Journal of Semitic Languages and Literatures* |
| *AM* | *Asia Major: A British Journal of Far Eastern Studies* |
| *AMI* | *Archaeologische Mitteilungen aus Iran* |
| *ANEP* | *The Ancient Near East in Pictures Relating to the Old Testament,* by James B. Pritchard (2d ed.; Princeton: Princeton University Press, 1969) |
| *ANET* | *Ancient Near Eastern Texts Relating to the Old Testament,* ed. James B. Pritchard (3d ed.; Princeton: Princeton University Press, 1969) |
| *ARAB* | *Ancient Records of Assyria and Babylonia,* ed. Daniel David Luckenbill (2 vols.; Chicago: University of Chicago Press, 1926–1927) |
| *ATR* | *Anglican Theological Review* |
| *BA* | *Biblical Archaeologist* |
| *BAR* | *Biblical Archaeology Review* |
| *BASOR* | *Bulletin of the American Schools of Oriental Research* |
| *BR* | *Bible Review* |
| *BSOAS* | *Bulletin of the School of Oriental and African Studies* |
| *CAH* | *Cambridge Ancient History* (Cambridge: Cambridge University Press, 1924ff.; CAH³ = 1970–) |
| *CBQ* | *Catholic Biblical Quarterly* |
| *CHI* | *Cambridge History of Iran* (Cambridge: Cambridge University Press, 1968–) |
| *EB* | *Encyclopaedia Britannica* (24 vols.; 1966 edition) |
| EPRO | Études préliminaires aux religions orientales dans l'empire romain |

| | |
|---|---|
| GCS | Die griechischen christlichen Schriftsteller der ersten [drei] Jahrhunderte |
| HERE | *Encyclopaedia of Religion and Ethics*, ed. James Hastings (12 vols.; Edinburgh: T. & T. Clark, 1910–1922) |
| HTR | *Harvard Theological Review* |
| IDB | *Interpreter's Dictionary of the Bible*, ed. G. A. Buttrick (4 vols.; Nashville: Abingdon, 1962) |
| IDBS | *Interpreter's Dictionary of the Bible: Supplementary Volume*, ed. K. R. Crim (Nashville: Abingdon, 1976) |
| IEJ | *Israel Exploration Journal* |
| IIJ | *Indo-Iranian Journal* |
| JAAR | *Journal of the American Academy of Religion* |
| JAOS | *Journal of the American Oriental Society* |
| JASPR | *Journal of the American Society for Psychical Research* |
| JBL | *Journal of Biblical Literature* |
| JCS | *Journal of Cuneiform Studies* |
| JEA | *Journal of Egyptian Archaeology* |
| JMS | *Journal of Mithraic Studies* |
| JNES | *Journal of Near Eastern Studies* |
| JPOS | *Journal of the Palestine Oriental Society* |
| JTS | *Journal of Theological Studies* |
| LCL | Loeb Classical Library |
| NBD | *New Bible Dictionary*, ed. J. D. Douglas et al. (Grand Rapids: Eerdmans, 1962) |
| NG | *National Geographic* |
| NHS | Nag Hammadi Studies |
| NT | *Novum Testamentum* |
| PR | *Parapsychology Review* |
| PWRE | *Paulys Realencyclopädie der classischen Altertumswissenschaft*, ed. G. Wissowa (Stuttgart: J. B. Metzler, 1893–) |
| RAAO | *Revue d'assyriologie et d'archéologie orientale* |
| RSR | *Religious Studies Review* |
| RSV | Revised Standard Version |
| RV | *Reallexikon der Vorgeschichte*, ed. Max Ebert (15 vols.; Berlin: Walter de Gruyter, 1924–1932) |
| SC | Sources Chrétiennes |
| TU | Texte und Untersuchungen |
| UF | *Ugarit-Forschungen* |
| VT | *Vetus Testamentum* |
| WM | *Wörterbuch der Mythologie*, ed. H. W. Haussig (Stuttgart: Ernst Klett, 1965–) |
| ZÄS | *Zeitschrift für ägyptische Sprache und Altertumskunde* |
| ZDMG | *Zeitschrift der Deutschen Morgenländischen Gesellschaft* |

# 1

# Mesopotamian Religion

## History and Language

In the valley of the Tigris and Euphrates rivers, which the Greeks called Mesopotamia,[1] the first people known to us from their own written records are those who lived in the lower part of the valley and called their land Sumer, for which reason we call them Sumerians. They were perhaps not the first people in the valley, for many of the early settlements bear non-Sumerian names, and the Sumerians may have derived much from otherwise unknown predecessors, but, in the lack of other evidence, who those predecessors were can only be a matter of surmise. The Sumerians themselves refer to a sacred land called Dilmun (probably to be identified with the island of Bahrain), "where the sun rises," and this suggests that they came into Mesopotamia from somewhere in the East. As to the time involved, the beginnings of Sumerian civilization are believed to be as early as the middle of the sixth millennium B.C.[2] It was probably the Sumerians who, by the fourth millennium, invented cuneiform, the wedge-shaped form of writing which remained in use thereafter for some three thousand years. As for the Sumerian language, it is found in its most classic form in the inscriptions of Gudea, governor of Lagash (2143–2124 B.C.).

Since some of the non-Sumerian substrate words found in the Sumerian language are similar to words found in Semitic languages, it is probable that Semitic people were among the predecessors of the Sumerians; at any rate by around 2600 Semitic-speaking nomads came from the west and settled in the upper part of Lower Mesopotamia. The capital of the empire which their king Sargon (2371–2316) soon

1. Martin A. Beek, *Atlas of Mesopotamia.*
2. *CAH*[3] 1.1.289.

established was a city probably not far from present-day Baghdad, called Agade in Sumerian (Akkadian, Akkade; Hebrew, Accad; see Gen. 10:10), and from this they themselves are called Akkadians and their language is Akkadian, the oldest known form of the widespread family of Semitic languages.

The Akkadians soon adopted from the Sumerians the cuneiform manner of writing as well as much of the Sumerian way of life; thus there emerged a Sumerian/Akkadian civilization, and all of Lower Mesopotamia became known as Sumer and Akkad (and later as Babylonia). By around 1900 the Sumerians were fully absorbed by the Akkadians, and the Sumerian language ceased to be spoken popularly although it continued for centuries as a language of literature and cult alongside the Akkadian. The Akkadian language, which was in use down into the first century A.D., developed into two chief dialects, the Babylonian of the south, found already in classic form in the time

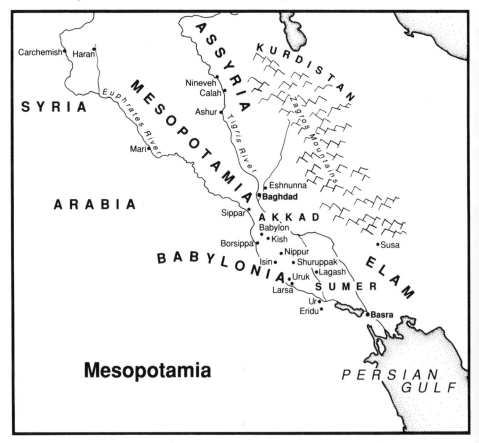

of Hammurabi (1792–1750 B.C.), and the Assyrian of the north, written, for example, by Ashurnasirpal II (883–859). The Late Babylonian of the Chaldean kings (e.g., Nebuchadnezzar II, 604–562) was influenced by Aramaic, the latter known from the beginning of the first millennium B.C., and much used as the language of international correspondence (see table 1).[3]

## Sources

The chief categories of the Sumerian/Akkadian documents which have been recovered in archeological excavations at many Mesopotamian sites are temple archives; economic, administrative, legal, and school texts; literary compositions in the form of myths, epic tales, hymns, lamentations, and proverbs; royal annals; historical chronicles; letters; collections of omens and incantations; and medical, mathematical, and astronomical texts. In these written records we find a large number of references to deities and many mythologies; back thereof we may surmise and to some extent discern a long development. Along with the written materials there are also many artifacts and architectural monuments, and it is from all of these that we endeavor to understand what we can of the thoughts, beliefs, and practices of the Mesopotamian people.[4]

TABLE 1
### Languages of the Middle East

| Non-Semitic | Semitic | | |
|---|---|---|---|
| | *Northeast Semitic* | *Northwest Semitic* | *Southwest Semitic* |
| Sumerian | Akkadian Babylonian Assyrian (collectively called Assyro-Babylonian) | Canaanite Ugaritic Amorite Eblaite Hebrew Phoenician Aramaic Syriac | Arabic Ethiopic |

3. A. Falkenstein, *Das Sumerische*; Arthur Ungnad, *Grammatik des Akkadischen*; Kaspar K. Riemschneider, *Lehrbuch des Akkadischen*; Sabatino Moscati, ed., *An Introduction to the Comparative Grammar of the Semitic Languages*.

4. Samuel Noah Kramer, *Sumerian Culture and Society: The Cuneiform Documents and Their Cultural Significance*.

The Mesopotamians—like other ancient peoples—looked upon and dealt with the natural world as exactly that, that is, as a world of material entities. There is an example in the Sumerian words *an* (Akkadian, *anu* or *anum*), which means "above" and therefore signifies the sky or the heaven, and *ki*, which means "below" and therefore signifies the earth. Thus when it is said, in the introduction to the Sumerian epic "Gilgamesh, Enkidu, and the Netherworld" (a text from the end of the third millennium, found at Nippur), that *an* and *ki* were originally united and then were separated, it is plain that the two are here designations of the actual physical realms of the sky and the earth. A medical text of the same date and provenance describes the rather elaborate chemical procedures by which various medicines were prepared from plant, animal, and mineral sources, and prescribes the external and internal application of those medicines without any suggestion of magic spells or incantations. In many Sumerian texts considerable knowledge of both geometry and mathematics is seen; in mathematics both the sexagesimal and decimal systems of notation were in use. In astronomy, observations of the moon are recorded from the time of the Third Dynasty of Ur (c. 2000 B.C.), and observations of Venus from the time of King Ammisaduqa (1646–1626) of the First Dynasty of Babylon. By the time of King Nabonassar (747–734) of Babylon astronomical knowledge provided an adequate basis for the very accurate Babylonian lunar calendar, which was also adopted by the Assyrians, Achaemenians, and Jews. The Mesopotamians also dealt with the material world in practical ways, including agriculture, irrigation, architecture, and metallurgy.[5]

## Sacred Powers

Like other ancient peoples, the Mesopotamians experienced a sense of the numinous in much of their environment; they believed in sacred power or powers in, or in charge of, various aspects of the natural world. As the force and will in a particular phenomenon the numinous might take its name from and be perceived in terms of that visible reality. Thus the power that was in the raincloud was seen as Imdugud, a great black bird floating in the sky with outstretched wings; it had the head of a lion and the voice of thunder. From probably very early time, however, the numinous was conceived not only in nonhuman but

5. Samuel Noah Kramer, *Sumerian Mythology*, 37–38; idem, *History Begins at Sumer*, 60–64; D. Opitz, "Stern, Sternkunde," in *RV* 12.422–36; A. Sachs, "Babylonian Observational Astronomy," in *The Place of Astronomy in the Ancient World*, ed. F. R. Hodson, 43–50; R. J. Forbes, *Studies in Ancient Technology*.

also in human form, and not only as in the phenomenon but as separate from it and in control of it. As such the power was a living being, like a human person but superhuman and immortal; in short, a personal god or goddess. Thus the words *an* and *ki* which originally meant the sky and the earth, became the names *An* and *Ki* meaning, respectively, the god who is on high, and the goddess who is in the earth.[6]

The Sumerian designation for "god" is *dingir,* a term of uncertain derivation, while the Akkadian term is *ilu.* The latter is the generic Semitic name for "god" or "deity," found in Hebrew as *el.* The plural is *ilanu* ("gods") and, like the Hebrew *elohim,* is not only used for a plurality of deities, but can also be applied to a particular god in the sense of the highest god, the fulness of the divine. Often used as part of a god's name or in connection with a deity is the Sumerian *en,* which means "lord" in the sense of an owner and manager, while *nin* is of similar connotation but is used mostly with feminine personages. The corresponding titles found widely in the Semitic world are *baal* and *baalat,* familiar also in the forms *Bel* and *Belet,* "lord" and "lady."

In its root meaning the Semitic *ilu/el* probably connotes power (e.g., the "cedars of El" are the "mighty cedars," Ps. 80:10 RSV). This power is numinous in character (in Gen. 28:17 Jacob, experiencing what he understands to be "the house of El," says, "How awesome is this place!"). To return to a Sumerian example, Ningirsu, the tutelary deity of Lagash, is the god whose power is in the thunderstorm (appropriately Imdugud is his symbol) and who sends the annual flood of the Tigris. Gudea of Lagash, in building a temple for the god, prays with a sense of the fearsome might of the deity, yet with a desire to come near to him for guidance:

O my master, Ningirsu, lord who sends the awesome waters . . .
Warrior whom none can challenge. . . .
O my master, your heart, the onrushing waters of a breach in a dike,
      not to be restrained,
Warrior, your heart, remote like the heavens,
How can I know it?[7]

In connection with the gods the Sumerian plural word *me* (pronounced "may"; Akkadian, *mu*) is often used; etymologically it may mean "being" and suggest normative ways of being or patterns of behavior. The gods rule in accordance with these universal standards.

---

6. Thorkild Jacobsen, *Toward the Image of Tammuz and Other Essays on Mesopotamian History and Culture,* 16–17.

7. Thorkild Jacobsen, in *EB* 2.972. For Ningirsu, see also Jean Nougayrol, "Ningirsu Vainqueur de Zu," *RAAO* 46.2 (1952): 87–97, esp. 87 n. 1.

It is also often said that the gods, or at least the chief gods, meet in an assembly and arrive at their decisions by vote, which is probably a reflection of a sort of primitive democracy in the early Sumerian cities. The creative work of the gods, like the command of a king, is often accomplished by the utterance of a word or the pronunciation of a name. This doctrine of the creative power of the divine word became widespread throughout the ancient Middle East (cf. Gen. 1:3, etc.).[8]

It is of course true that any attempt to reconstruct the religion of the ancient Mesopotamian world not only is dependent upon what texts and artifacts have actually been found—certainly only a fraction of what was once in existence—but also has to do with a period of several thousand years, within which at any given time the same concept may be variously and inconsistently attested. It is held, as a broad overview, that in the fourth millennium, when life in the small Mesopotamian villages and towns was relatively peaceful, the powers were worshiped primarily as providers of the essentials for economic survival; in the third millennium, when enormous walls were built around great cities, the gods were seen as rulers from whom protection against enemies might be sought; in the second millennium, when the welfare of the individual assumed greater importance, the deities were pictured as parents with whom a close personal relationship was possible; and in the first millennium, when the times were disturbed by invasions and by both foreign and civil wars, the image of the warrior was more frequently applied to the gods, and the myths reflected cruelty and brutality.[9]

Associated at the outset with the localities where they were first worshiped, the various Mesopotamian deities were soon brought together in family groups and eventually came to constitute a very numerous pantheon, the chief figures in which were generally recognized throughout the Sumerian/Akkadian realm.[10] For example, in the many inscriptions of Gudea of Lagash, whose prayer to Ningirsu we have cited, nearly seventy deities are named, some of them recognizable as local gods of early settlements, some of them obviously brought together as the individual settlements were united in the city-state of Lagash, and some of them major figures worshiped throughout the land.[11] Altogether the total number of deities whose names have been found in the Sumerian/Akkadian texts is more than three thousand.[12]

8. Kramer, *History Begins at Sumer*, 77–79. For the concept of *me* see Thorkild Jacobsen, review of Kramer's *Sumerian Mythology*, in *JNES* 5 (1946): 139 n. 20; Gertrud Farber-Flügge, *Der Mythos "Inanna und Enki" unter besonderer Berücksichtigung der Liste der m e*, 116–64.

9. Thorkild Jacobsen, *The Treasures of Darkness: A History of Mesopotamian Religion*.

10. John Gray, *Near Eastern Mythology*, 12–63.

11. A. Falkenstein, *Die Inschriften Gudeas von Lagaš*, vol. 1, *Einleitung*, 55–115.

12. Antonius Deimel, *Pantheon Babylonicum*, 30 and passim. See also J. J. M. Roberts, *The Earliest Semitic Pantheon*.

Systematized lists of the main gods were drawn up. The oldest such list presently known was found at Tell Fara (ancient Shuruppak) and dates from about 2600. It begins with six chief deities of the Sumerian pantheon—An, Enlil, Inanna, Enki, Nanna, and Utu—and also includes the deified rulers Lugalbanda and Gilgamesh, both of whom appear in the Sumerian King List as kings of Uruk. A list which is attributed to the Kassite period (soon after Hammurabi, 1792–1750) and was later widely accepted is known as *An: Anum.* As the name indicates, it gives the name of the deity in Sumerian and the equivalent in Akkadian; it also gives the family relationships and the chief city of the deity. Of the main figures the list names An, Enlil, Beletili, Ea, Sin, Ishtar, Ninurta, and Nergal.[13]

In Akkadian texts of the Old Babylonian period (the time of Hammurabi) we also hear of two groups of gods: the Igigi and the Anunnaki. In most instances there seems to be no difference between the two designations; in some cases the Igigi are gods of heaven, the Anunnaki gods of the earth and the underworld. It may be that originally Igigi was a group designation in the more cosmically oriented Akkadian religion, Anunnaki a name in the more chthonian Sumerian religion.[14]

Of the six chief deities of the Sumerian pantheon named in the list from Tell Fara, An, Enlil, and Enki are cosmic gods in charge of, respectively, the realms of the sky, the atmosphere, and the earth and its waters.

An (from the Sumerian word *an,* "above, sky, heaven"; Akkadian, Anu or Anum) is the lord of heaven and the highest deity in the Sumerian pantheon. Himself the son of Anshar and Kishar (the gods of the horizons of heaven and earth), his wife is Ki, the goddess of earth; and he is the father of numerous gods and the creator of various demons. His chief center of worship is the city of Uruk and its temple Eanna (from the Sumerian words *e,* "house," and *anna,* "heaven"). An is not portrayed personally in the iconography, but his symbol is a horned crown, which is shared with Enlil and Enki.[15]

Enlil (from the Sumerian words *en,* "lord," and *lil,* "wind") is the lord of the atmosphere and the son of An. The two are mentioned together in the prologue of the Code of Hammurabi, but actually Enlil is much more prominent in Sumerian thought. Being in control of the

---

13. For the Sumerian/Akkadian deities and the lists of the gods, see Dietz Otto Edzard, "Mesopotamien. Die Mythologie der Sumerer und Akkader," in *WM* 1.1.38–139, esp. 75, "Götterlisten." For hymns to the gods, see A. Falkenstein, *Sumerische Götterlieder.* For the symbols of the deities, see E. Douglas Van Buren, *Symbols of the Gods in Mesopotamian Art.*

14. Burkhart Kienast, "Igigū und Anunnakkū nach den akkadischen Quellen," in *Studies in Honor of Benno Landsberger on His Seventy-Fifth Birthday,* ed. H. G. Guterbock and T. Jacobsen, 141–58.

15. For An, see Herman Wohlstein, *The Sky-God An-Anu.*

atmosphere, Enlil sends the beneficent rain but also the destructive storm. He is also the creator of the pickax (Akkadian, *marru*), an indispensable instrument for the Mesopotamian farmer and builder. Among the epithets of Enlil are Great Mountain (Sumerian, *Kur-gal*) and Father of the Gods. The chief center of worship of Enlil is Nippur, where his temple, like himself, was called Great Mountain. Like An, Enlil is symbolized by the horned crown.

Enki (from the Sumerian words *en*, "lord," and *ki*, "below"; Akkadian, Ea), himself the son of Nammu the goddess of the primeval sea, is the lord of what is below, that is, of the earth and of the waters which are under the earth and in its springs and rivers. Since water makes the earth fruitful, renders clay plastic, and serves to cleanse, Enki is the manager of the productivity of the earth, the god of artists and craftsmen (his chief epithet is Nudimmud, which means "he who shapes"), and the god of ritual ablutions and purification from the pollution of evil; he is also the god of wisdom. His chief center is Eridu, supposedly the oldest city of Sumer. In the iconography he sits upon a throne, and two streams of water (presumably the Tigris and Euphrates) flow from his shoulders or from a vase which he holds; like An and Enlil he has the horned crown for his emblem.

Next are three celestial deities, Inanna, Nanna, and Utu, who are associated, respectively, with the planet Venus, the moon, and the sun.

Inanna (the Sumerian name goes back to the form Ninanna, from *nin*, "lady" or "queen," and *anna*, "heaven"; Akkadian, Ishtar), the queen of heaven, is associated with the planet Venus as the morning and evening star. She is the goddess of love, being always young and beautiful, and is yet again a warrior goddess dangerous to her enemies and the enemies of Sumer. In her many-faceted character Inanna is the chief feminine deity of the Sumerian pantheon, and as identified with the Akkadian Ishtar (Hebrew, Ashtoreth; Greek, Astarte) is widely known throughout the Semitic world. She is variously the daughter of An or Enlil or Nanna; An exalted her to be the Venus-star and his own consort. Her central cult place is Uruk, where she shares the sanctuary Eanna with An. In the iconography, as the goddess of love she is naked, but she may also be robed. As the astral deity rays extend from her back, and her symbols are both a bundle of reeds and an eight-pointed star.[16]

Nanna (Akkadian, Sin; earlier, Suen) is the moon-god, and as such illuminates the night and measures time. He is the son of Enlil and

---

16. William W. Hallo and J. J. A. Van Dijk, *The Exaltation of Inanna*; Samuel Noah Kramer, *From the Poetry of Sumer*, 71–97; Diane Wolkstein and Samuel Noah Kramer, *Inanna: Queen of Heaven and Earth*; Tikva Frymer-Kensky, "Inanna—The Quintessential *Femme Fatale*," review of Wolkstein's *Inanna*, in *BAR* 10.5 (Sept.–Oct. 1984): 62–64.

Priests march in procession and present gifts to the goddess Inanna, on a tall alabaster vase from ancient Uruk in Mesopotamia. The vase is in the Iraqi Archaeological Museum in Baghdad.

Ninlil; his wife is Ningal ("great queen"), and their children are Inanna (in one view) and Utu. The chief cult centers of Nanna are Ur in Lower Mesopotamia and its sanctuary Ekishnugal, Haran in northwestern Mesopotamia (both Ur and Haran are associated with Abraham in Gen. 11:31), and Tema in Arabia. The symbol of Nanna is the crescent of the moon, with the ends turned up, which may have suggested the heavenly ship on which the moon-god traveled, as Inanna also did upon occasion. Nanna is also represented as a bull whose horns resemble the moon crescent; such a bull's head with beard of lapis lazuli adorned a harp found at Ur.

Utu is the sun-god. Under his Akkadian name Shamash he is very widely known in the whole Semitic world (e.g., Beth-shemesh is "the house of the sun god"; see Josh. 15:10, etc.). As the god whose light penetrates everywhere, he is judge and defender of justice. At night he descends into the sea and passes through the underworld, where he dispenses light, food, and drink to the deceased; in the morning he rises again over the eastern mountains. In family relationships Utu/Shamash is son of Nanna/Sin, and brother of Inanna/Ishtar. His sacred cities are Sippar and Larsa. He is depicted with rays extending from his back; his symbol is the sun disk. In Ezekiel 8:16 a number of men in Jerusalem are evidently engaged in cult practice related to Shamash, for they are standing with their backs to the temple and their faces toward the east, worshiping the sun.

Several other important deities are mentioned in the *An: Anum* list: Beletili, Ninurta, and Nergal.

Beletili ("mistress of the gods") is the Akkadian title of the mother goddess or goddesses, who are known by various individual names. One of these is the Sumerian Ninhursaga, who is the "lady of the foothills," perhaps a reference to the ranges east of Mesopotamia thought of as the residence of the gods. Ninhursaga (as well as Ninlil) is considered a wife of Enlil, and their son is Ninurta ("lord of the earth"), the god of the thunderstorm, who is probably identical with the above-mentioned Ningirsu ("lord of Girsu," a city in the territory of Lagash).

Nergal is the god of the underworld, and on earth is also responsible for the scorching summer sun and for fever and plague. He is the son of Enlil and Ninlil, or otherwise the son of the mother goddess Beletili. His wife, who shares with him the rule of the netherworld, is Ereshkigal. The latter is sister and underworld rival of Inanna. Namtar ("fate") is son of Ereshkigal, and serves as her vizier and messenger. As for the realm of the dead, it is pictured as a city with seven walls and seven gates.[17]

On one occasion Inanna visited her sister Ereshkigal in the underworld, and Inanna's consort Dumuzi also went thither and returned. As a result of his visit, however, Dumuzi was not free to remain on earth, and he and his sister Geshtinanna alternated living in the netherworld. Evidently Dumuzi is a god of dying and reviving vegetation. Like Lugalbanda and Gilgamesh the name of Dumuzi appears in the Sumerian King List, once as Dumuzi, a shepherd, king of Badtibira, and once as Dumuzi, a fisherman, king of Uruk; so it is probable that the god was originally an actual legendary ruler. In Hebrew his name is rendered as Tammuz, and it is for his experience of death that the women at the north gate of the temple in Jerusalem engage in cultic lamentation (Ezek. 8:14).[18]

17. *ANET*. 103–4, 507–12; Egbert von Weiher, *Der babylonische Gott Nergal*.

18. Anton Moortgat, *Tammuz: Der Unsterblichkeitsglaube in der altorientalischen Bildkunst*; Jacobsen, *Toward the Image of Tammuz*. 73–106.

Eventually two deities emerged as very prominent national gods, namely, Marduk in Babylonia and Ashur in Assyria.

The familiar name of Marduk is derived from the Sumerian Amar-Utu ("calf of [the sun-god] Utu"); in the prologue of the Code of Hammurabi, however, he is called the firstborn of Enki. Marduk was the god of the city of Babylon, and it was probably when Babylon rose to supremacy under Hammurabi (1792–1750) and his successors that Marduk also attained to supreme place among the gods. In the Akkadian epic *Enuma elish* the chief theme is how Marduk gained the supremacy. For this reason it seems probable that the epic dates from this time, that is, the Old Babylonian period in the early second millennium B.C., although some opinion would assign the work to the Middle Babylonian period (c. 1100 B.C.).[19] In the last native dynasty of Babylon, the Chaldean, Nebuchadnezzar II (604–562) affirms in grateful prayer that it is Marduk who has entrusted him with kingship over all people.[20] In Hebrew Marduk appears as Merodach, and is frequently referred to by his title Bel (Isa. 46:1; Jer. 50:2; 51:44; and the apocryphal addition to Daniel, Bel and the Dragon). In Babylon the temple of Marduk was Esagila ("house whose top is lofty"), and the adjacent temple tower (ziggurat) was Etemenanki ("house of the terrace-platform of heaven and earth"). The symbol of Marduk is the pickax (Akkadian, *marru*), and his emblematic animal is a composite serpent-dragon (with a name derived from the Sumerian *mush-hush*, "fire-red dragon").

The consort of Marduk is Sarpanit (also Sarpanitu, Sarpanitum, "silver-gleaming"), and their son is Nabu (Nebo in Hebrew). The cult center of Nabu was at Borsippa, near Babylon, and in the spring festival of the New Year the image of Nabu was brought from Borsippa to Babylon to be carried in sacred procession together with that of Marduk (see Isa. 46:1). Nabu himself is the god of the planet Mercury, the god of wisdom, and the patron of scribes, with the stylus of the scribe as his emblem.

From the fourteenth century B.C. onward Marduk was worshiped not only in Babylonia but also in Assyria, and his son Nabu attained such prominence that the inscription on a statue of Nabu set up at Nimrud (Calah) under Adad-nirari III (810–783) ends, "Wait on Nabu; do not trust in another god."[21] When the Assyrian king Sargon II (722–705) took over the rule of Babylon (709), he "grasped the hand

---

19. *ANET*, 60–72—see p. 60 for the date in the Old Babylonian period; W. G. Lambert, "A New Look at the Babylonian Background of Genesis," *JTS* 16 (1965): 285–300—see p. 291 for the date in the Middle Babylonian period.

20. Jacobsen, *Treasures of Darkness*, 239.

21. *ARAB* 1.264, §745.

of the great lord Marduk" (a ceremonial gesture to signify the assumption of the kingship of Babylon).[22] But Sennacherib, who destroyed Babylon in 689, strongly opposed the worship of Marduk; in fact, during his reign Assyrian scribes replaced the name of Marduk in their copies of *Enuma elish* with the name of the Assyrian god Ashur.

The god Ashur (also Assur) bears the same name as the oldest Assyrian capital (both the god and the city are mentioned in literary sources from the third millennium B.C.), and it is from this name that the name of Assyria is derived. As in the case of Marduk and Babylon, the rise of Ashur to great prominence paralleled the rise of the city to political supremacy. From the thirteenth century onward Ashur is assimilated with Enlil, and assumes Enlil's titles such as Great Mountain and Father of the Gods. He is also later equated with Anshar, the father of An, and it is as Anshar-Ashur that he replaces Marduk in the Assyrian version of *Enuma elish*. The great temple tower of Ashur in the city of Ashur was Ekursagkurkurra ("house of the mountain of the lands"). In Assyrian iconography the sun disk, which was the symbol of Shamash, and the winged sun disk, which came originally from Egypt, are probably the symbols of Ashur, as is also the special form of the winged sun disk in which the lower part of the human body of the god spreads out into the tail of a bird.[23]

That the Assyrians felt a personal relationship with the deity is evident from the standard Old Assyrian term *god of the fathers*. We hear, for example, of "Ashur, the god of your fathers," and "Ilabrat [the Assyrian messenger-god], the god of our fathers." Similar phraseology is found at the same time (second millennium B.C.) among Assyrian traders in Cappadocia and under Amorite rulers at Mari, and may be compared with the usage in Genesis 26:24; 28:13; 31:5, 53; and Exodus 3:15.[24]

## Temples and Festivals

We have already referred to various Mesopotamian cult places and festivals. The sacred site was the temple, and the most characteristic feature of the architecture was the temple tower known as a ziggurat (Akkadian, *ziqquratu,* from *zaqaru,* "to be high"; hence the top of a mountain), a lofty pyramidal structure built in successive stages. It

22. *ARAB* 2.36, §70.
23. *ANEP.* figs. 536, 706. For the relation of the god Ashur to the city of Ashur, see W. G. Lambert, "The God Aššur," *Iraq* 45.1 (Spring 1983): 82–86.
24. Jacobsen, *Treasures of Darkness,* 159.

had outside staircases and a shrine at the top, and was surrounded by other temple buildings. We know the locations of more than two dozen ziggurats in Mesopotamia. The best preserved is at Ur, built by Ur-Nammu (2112–2095). The most famous, now almost completely destroyed, was at Babylon, dating from the time of Hammurabi (1792–1750), rebuilt by Nebuchadnezzar II (604–562), and remembered in biblical tradition as the tower of Babel (Gen. 11:1–9).[25]

The most important celebration was the New Year, which began with the month Nisanu in the spring and was marked at Babylon by a festival of some twelve days' duration, the festival in which the gods Marduk and Nabu joined in procession and other ceremonies took place. The climax probably saw the statues of Marduk and his consort Sarpanit taken to the shrine on the summit of the ziggurat where, according to Herodotus (1.181–82), the ceremony of the sacred marriage was enacted.[26]

## Mythology

It is most of all in the myths and epic tales that we not only learn of the doings of the gods, but also discern some of the major topics with which Mesopotamian religious thought was concerned, topics which range from the creation of the universe and humankind to the great flood and to the problem of death.[27]

Concerning the creation of the universe, the Sumerian epic tale, "Gilgamesh, Enkidu, and the Netherworld," begins with a passage in which we read of the ancient days:

When heaven had been moved away from the earth,
When earth had been separated from heaven,
When the name of man had been fixed—
When An had carried off heaven,
When Enlil had carried off earth,
When Ereshkigal had been carried off into the netherworld as its
    prize. . . .[28]

Likewise in the Sumerian myth, "The Creation of the Pickax," we read that Enlil moved heaven away from earth, and earth away from heaven,

25. *ANEP*, figs. 746–47; André Parrot, *The Tower of Babel.*

26. Samuel Noah Kramer, *The Sacred Marriage Rite: Aspects of Faith, Myth, and Ritual in Ancient Sumer.*

27. Gray, *Near Eastern Mythology.*

28. Kramer, *Sumerian Mythology,* 37; idem, *The Sumerians,* 200; idem, *From the Poetry of Sumer,* 23–24.

and afterward brought into existence the pickax, an instrument the usefulness of which the poem describes at length.[29]

Thus the conception is that there was a primeval time when the previously united heaven and earth were separated and the universe was established in its threefold form of heaven, earth, and netherworld beneath the earth, the realms, respectively, of An, Enlil, and Ereshkigal. It was naturally understood that Enlil, the god in charge of the atmosphere between heaven and earth, accomplished their separation. Human beings evidently came into existence by the utterance of the name of man. The pickax, the instrument so essential for work in the fields and the building of cities, was provided at this time.

In a Sumerian poem on "The Creation of Man," Nammu, the goddess of the primeval sea, entreats her son Enki to "fashion [servants] of the gods," whereupon Enki leads forth a group of "fashioners," and says to Nammu:

> O my mother, the [creature] whose name you uttered, it exists;
> Bind upon it the . . . of the gods;
> [Mix] the heart of the clay that is over the abyss;
> The good and princely [fashioners] will [thicken] the clay.[30]

Here humankind is made of clay, and there is thus a measure of agreement with Genesis 2:7, where man is made "of dust from the ground."

The "Epic of the Flood," which is found in both Sumerian and Akkadian forms, also contains accounts of the creation of humankind. In the incompletely preserved Sumerian version, several of the chief deities are responsible for the creation of human beings and animals:

> After An, Enlil, [and] Ninhursag
> Had created the black-headed people,
> Animals multiplied everywhere,
> Animals of all sizes; the quadrupeds were placed as a fitting ornament
>     of the plains.

"The black-headed people" is usually a reference to the inhabitants of Sumer and Akkad; here the context may suggest humankind as a whole. The text goes on to say that a god, not specifically named, then founded the five antediluvian cities, Eridu, Badtibira, Larak, Sippar, and Shuruppak (which are also the first cities named in the Sumerian King List), and assigned each to the care of its guardian god. After that, although the text is incomplete, we hear of a destructive storm

29. Kramer, *Sumerian Mythology*, 51–53; idem, *From the Poetry of Sumer*, 25–26.
30. Kramer, *Sumerian Mythology*, 70.

and flood which a certain Ziusudra ("life-day prolonged"), warned by some of the gods, survived by riding it out in a huge boat.[31]

The Akkadian version of the "Epic of the Flood" is called by the name Atrahasis, this being the title (meaning "exceeding wise") given to the Sumerian Ziusudra. Here we are told the fuller story at length. At the outset the gods grow weary of all the work that they have to do, and it is for this reason that they resolve to create humankind to be their servants. Enki/Ea calls upon Nintu, the birth-goddess, to fashion man to bear the yoke, so the gods can be free:

> You are the birth-goddess, creatress of mankind,
> Create Lullu [man] that he may bear the yoke,
> Let him bear the yoke assigned by Enlil,
> Let man carry the toil of the gods.

Nintu asks for clay, so that she may create humans. Enki suggests the slaughter of one of the gods, from whose flesh and blood Nintu may mix clay, so that "god and man may be thoroughly mixed in the clay." This was done, and Nintu was soon able to announce to the assembly of the gods the completion of her task:

> You commanded me a task, I have completed it. . . .
> I have removed your heavy work,
> I have imposed your toil on man.
> You raised a cry for mankind,
> I have loosed the yoke, I have established freedom.

As the story goes on, humankind becomes numerous and disturbs the gods. The gods undertake first to restrict the excessive growth by plague and then by drought, and finally to annihilate humanity by a flood. Enki manages to warn Atrahasis, who builds a great boat and survives the flood.[32]

Yet another account of the creation of the universe is contained in the Akkadian myth Enuma elish, although the central theme of this work is the supremacy of Marduk and his city Babylon. The account begins at a time when neither heaven nor earth had been named, but two beings were in existence, Apsu (Sumerian, Abzu) the primeval fresh-water ocean, and Tiamat ("sea") the primeval salt-water ocean. From the mingling of their waters came the origin of the gods and of all things. The deities were Lahmu and Lahamu, Anshar and Kishar,

---

31. W. G. Lambert and A. R. Millard, Atra-ḫasīs: The Babylonian Story of the Flood, 141–45.
32. Ibid., 43–103; Isaac M. Kikawada, "The Double Creation of Mankind in Enki and Ninmah, Atrahasis I 1–351, and Genesis 1–2," Iraq 45.1 (Spring 1983): 43–45.

Anu, and others down to Marduk, son of Ea (Enki). Eventually the
doings of the gods became so annoying to their parents that Apsu
announced his intention of destroying them. Ea, however, discovered
the plan and was able to fetter and slay Apsu. To avenge Apsu, Tiamat
then created a host of gruesome monsters and prepared to wage war
against the gods. Marduk stepped forward as the champion of the gods
and in fierce combat succeeded in slaying Tiamat. At this point a brief
portion of the myth describes creation. Marduk divided the dead body
of Tiamat into two parts. "Half of her he set in place and formed the
sky therewith as a roof." Next he established the earth, the residences
of the gods, and the constellations. Kingu, the leader of the hosts of
Tiamat, was slain; and with the blood of his arteries the gods fashioned
humankind. The service of the gods was laid upon mankind, while the
gods themselves molded bricks for a year and labored to construct
Esagila, the temple tower of Marduk at Babylon. Finally the gods
gathered at a festive banquet and sang the praises of Marduk, con-
ferring upon him fifty names which signify the power and attributes
of the various Babylonian gods.[33]

The problem of death is the theme of the Akkadian "Epic of Gilgamesh," in which there is also an account of the great flood.[34] Gilgamesh, a legendary king of Uruk, has a friend named Enkidu who
is his faithful companion in adventures and difficulties. When Enkidu
dies, Gilgamesh is saddened and bewildered, and undertakes a haz-
ardous journey across untraversed mountains and the waters of death
to find Utnapishtim ("day of life"; the Sumerian Ziusudra), who survived the flood and attained immortality in the land of Dilmun. Advised to abandon a hopeless quest and instead to devote himself to
merriment by day and by night (cf. Eccles. 9:7–9), Gilgamesh utters
his plaint:

> [How can I be silent?] How can I be still?
> [My friend whom I love has turned] to clay!
> [Must I too, like] him, lay me down,
> [Not to rise] again for ever and ever?

Reaching Utnapishtim, Gilgamesh hears from him the story of the
flood, but as to achieving the object of his journey is only given direc-
tions for obtaining the plant of long life. In the end Gilgamesh suffers
the loss of even this to a serpent and returns disconsolate. In a few

33. E. A. Speiser, in *ANET*, 60–72; Alexander Heidel, *The Babylonian Genesis*.
34. Speiser, in *ANET*, 73–97; Alexander Heidel, *The Gilgamesh Epic and Old Testament Parallels*; Jeffrey H. Tigay, *The Evolution of the Gilgamesh Epic*.

fragmentary lines at the close of the epic Gilgamesh surveys the walls of Uruk; perhaps the thought that his city will endure brings some consolation. Nevertheless, death, the ultimate tragic element in life, must be accepted.

As to what lies beyond this inevitable fate of all humankind, it was the general Mesopotamian belief that the dead go to a shadowy underworld which is ruled by Nergal and Ereshkigal. In the texts which narrate the descent of Inanna/Ishtar to the netherworld, the goddess is described as going to the Land of No Return,

> To the dark house . . .
> To the house which none leave who have entered it,
> To the road from which there is no way back,
> To the house wherein the entrants are bereft of light,
> Where dust is their fare and clay their food,
> [Where] they see no light, residing in darkness . . .
> [And where] over door and bolt is spread dust.[35]

In Tablet XII of the "Epic of Gilgamesh" (and also in "Gilgamesh, Enkidu, and the Netherworld") Gilgamesh calls up the spirit of his deceased friend Enkidu and asks him to tell what the land of the dead is like. Enkidu is reluctant to do so, saying that if he does, Gilgamesh will "sit down and weep." The text which follows is badly preserved, but in it Enkidu refers to the various fates of different people in the underworld: one who died a sudden death "lies upon the night couch and drinks pure water"; the father and mother of one who was killed in battle "raise up his head, and his wife [weeps] over him"; the spirit of one whose corpse was cast out upon the steppe "finds no rest in the netherworld"; and one "whose spirit has no one to tend it" is reduced to eating crumbs of bread and street garbage.[36] From this it is evident that proper burial and the continuing concern of living family members were considered of importance for the welfare of those who had passed into the beyond.

It was also believed that the sun after setting continues its journey in the underworld, and that the moon spends its "day of sleep" (the twenty-eighth or twenty-ninth day of the lunar month) down there. In this connection a Sumerian funeral dirge (in a document preserved in the Pushkin Museum, Moscow) describes the sun-god Utu as illuminating the netherworld, and speaks of both Utu and the moon-god Nanna as judging the dead there:

35. *ANET*, 107.
36. Ibid., 98–99; Kramer, *Sumerians*, 205

Utu, the great lord [?] of Hades,
After turning the dark places to light, will judge your case [favorably];
May Nanna decree your fate [favorably] on the "Day of Sleep."[37]

If the suggested readings ("favorably") are correct, the expectation was that the spirit would continue in some degree of happiness. From the Mesopotamian intuition of the transcendent, then, at least some illumination fell into death's dark shadow.

## Society

Along with the development of Mesopotamian religion there were significant developments in human society. These were usually seen as standing in some relationship to the transcendent world of the deities. Not a few firsts in recorded history have been identified in the Sumerian texts; these firsts occur in such fields as government and politics, education and literature, philosophy and ethics, and law and justice.[38] In government, for example, there was an assembly of free men. When Gilgamesh, king of the city-state of Uruk (c. 3000 B.C.), received some kind of threat from Agga, last ruler of the first post-diluvian dynasty at Kish, Gilgamesh consulted "the convened assembly of the elders," and they advised submission. But when he consulted "the convened assembly of the men" (probably those who bore arms), they said to fight for independence, and this pleased Gilgamesh. The entire assembly was thus virtually a congress with a senate (the elders) and a lower house (the arms-bearing men), and the whole has been described as a sort of primitive democracy. This institution was reflected in the belief that the gods reach their decisions in a similar assembly, and this belief in democracy among the gods survived even long after monarchy ensued on earth.[39]

As for law, a Sumerian legal code of Ur-Nammu king of Ur (2112–2095 B.C.),[40] an Akkadian code from the kingdom of Eshnunna (c. 2000),[41] and a Sumerian code of Lipit-Ishtar king of Isin

37. Samuel Noah Kramer, "Death and Nether World According to the Sumerian Literary Texts," *Iraq* 22 (1960): 59–68; Raphael Kutscher, "Utu Prepares for Judgment," in *Kramer Anniversary Volume,* ed. Barry L. Eichler, 305–9. See also H. W. F. Saggs, "Some Ancient Semitic Conceptions of the Afterlife," *Faith and Thought* 90 (1958): 157–82.

38. Kramer, *History Begins at Sumer.*

39. Ibid., 30–35; Jacobsen, *Toward the Image of Tammuz,* 132–70; Henri Frankfort, *Kingship and the Gods,* 215, 236–37.

40. *ANET,* 523–25.

41. *ANET,* 161–63.

(1934–1924)[42] are all predecessors of the famous Code of Hammurabi (1792–1750).[43] Each regulation in these codes deals with a specific case and describes both the offending action and the consequent penalty. There is also reference to the divine source of law: the Eshnunna code acknowledges the authority of Tishpak, god of the city of Eshnunna; in the epilogue of the Lipit-Ishtar code the king says, "Verily, in accordance with the pronouncement of Enlil, I, Lipit-Ishtar, the son of Enlil . . . caused righteousness and truth to exist"; and in the bas-relief on the Hammurabi stele the king stands before the enthroned sun-god Shamash, the patron of law and justice, and the text declares that the gods chose Hammurabi "to make legislation appear in the land, to destroy the evil and the wicked, so that the strong should not harm the weak."

It is evident, therefore, that Mesopotamian religion was fundamentally concerned with relationship to the transcendent power or powers upon which human existence was believed to be dependent, and that the religion was also intimately connected with the ordering of the life of individuals and of society.

## Biblical Relationships

According to Genesis 11:31 and other biblical passages, Abraham came from "Ur of the Chaldeans" (a city usually identified with Ur in Lower Mesopotamia, although possibly to be identified instead with a city of the same name in Upper Mesopotamia). We have seen that there are Mesopotamian antecedents for such items as the biblical manner of speech about the creation, the phrase *the God of your fathers* (Exod. 3:15), and the biblical record of the flood (Gen. 6–8). Likewise the form of Mesopotamian law is characteristic of most law in the Hebrew Scriptures, and not a few of the biblical laws are comparable in phrasing and import with those of Hammurabi.[44]

In the time of the Jewish captivity in Babylon, however, the Hebrew prophets declared their monotheistic belief in unequivocal terms and cast scorn on Bel (Marduk) and Nebo (Nabu) and the idols by which the Babylonian gods were represented (Isa. 46). This repudiation persisted in Christianity and in Islam. Nevertheless, the Mesopotamian influences continued in the Hebrew Scriptures and therewith also in

42. *ANET*, 159–61.
43. *ANET*, 165–80; *ANEP*, fig. 246.
44. William W. Hallo, "Sumerian Literature: Background to the Bible," *BR* 4.3 (June 1988): 28–38.

# 2

# Egyptian Religion

## History

In the valley of the Nile River[1] the Egyptians developed a long, continuous civilization. For the scope of ancient Egyptian history the list of thirty successive dynasties compiled by Manetho (high priest in Heliopolis under Ptolemy II Philadelphus, 285–246 B.C.) provides the basic outline.[2] On this basis and in terms of larger main periods and approximate dates we speak of the Early Period (Dynasties I–II, 3100–2686 B.C.), the Old Kingdom (Dynasties III–VI, 2686–2181), the Middle Kingdom (Dynasties XI–XII, 2133–1786), and the New Kingdom (Dynasties XVIII–XX, 1552–1070), with the First Intermediate Period (Dynasties VII–X) between the Old and Middle Kingdoms and the Second Intermediate Period (Dynasties XIII–XVII) between the Middle and New Kingdoms. The Late Period (Dynasties XXI–XXXI, 1070–332) included rule by foreign dynasties (Libyan, Kushite, Per-

---

1. John Baines and Jaromír Málek, *Atlas of Ancient Egypt.*
2. Manetho, "The History of Egypt" (trans. W. G. Waddell; LCL; 1940). Prior to the mortal kings of the First Dynasty and following, Manetho (as cited in the Armenian version of the *Chronicle* of Eusebius) puts the demigods (also called the spirits of the dead), who ruled for 11,025 years, and prior to them the gods, who reigned for 13,900 years, making a total of 24,925 years (Josef Karst, *Die Chronik aus dem armenischen Übersetzt mit textkritischem Kommentar,* 64). In the fragmentary list of kings in the Turin Papyrus (Museo Egizio, Turin, no. 1874; probably written in the reign of Ramses II, 1290–1224 B.C.) the *Shemsu Hor* or "Followers of Horus" are probably the same as Manetho's demigods/spirits of the dead, and are recorded as reigning for 13,420 plus x years; the "reigns before the Followers of Horus," probably the same as the rule of Manetho's gods, are shown as lasting for 23,200 plus x years, thus making a total of more than 36,620 years (*CAH* 1.250). If the gods and demigods were dimly-remembered early rulers, these records would be putting Egyptian origins back nearly forty thousand years. With reference to these very large figures Eusebius thinks that the Egyptian year was a lunar year consisting of thirty days, and reduces his total round number of twenty-four thousand years to months, making 2,206 solar years, but there is no evidence that the Egyptian year was ever equal to a month; there was a short year of 360 days and a long year of 365 days. For the early dates and for Egyptian civilization as a legacy of "Atlantis," see John Anthony West, *The Serpent in the Sky: The High Wisdom of Ancient Egypt,* 13–14, 229.

sian) as well as by natives until, in the wake of Alexander the Great (332), the Ptolemies ruled, only at last to give over the land to the Romans (30 B.C.).

## Sources

The written records of this long history are set down in hieroglyphics (picture-writing with sound value), demotic (the popular form of the Egyptian language written in cursive script), and Greek—all three conveniently in parallel on the famous Rosetta Stone.[3] The writings of chief relevance to Egyptian religion include the Pyramid Texts (ritual formulas for royal burials, found in the pyramids of the Fifth and Sixth Dynasties but embodying much older materials),[4] the Coffin Texts (in the sarcophagi of private individuals from the Middle Kingdom onward),[5] and the "Book of the Dead," an inclusive name commonly used for "Going Forth by Day" and other works about the beyond (in papyri of the New Kingdom),[6] as well as temple and tomb inscriptions and other papyri.[7]

As in Mesopotamia and elsewhere in the ancient world it is evident that the ancient Egyptians looked upon and dealt with the natural world as such. The Egyptian calendar, for example, was based upon observation of natural events. The year was divided into three seasons related to the Nile: "inundation," when the Nile overflowed and covered the valley; "coming forth," when the fields emerged again from the water and there were the planting and growth of crops; and "deficiency," when there were harvest and again low water levels. The month was determined by the lunar cycle and began when the old crescent of the moon could no longer be seen just before sunrise in the east, which was every twenty-nine or thirty days. Twelve such lunar months made the calendrical year on average eleven days shorter than the natural year, so, from time to time, a thirteenth or intercalary month was added to keep the seasons in place. This calendar (also known in the form of twelve months of thirty days each) was of early origin and was used in temples and religious festivals.

3. H. Kees et al., "Ägyptologie: Ägyptische Schrift und Sprache," in *Handbuch der Orientalistik* 1.1, ed. B. Spuler (Leiden: E. J. Brill, 1959).

4. Samuel A. B. Mercer, *The Pyramid Texts in Translation and Commentary*; R. O. Faulkner, *The Ancient Egyptian Pyramid Texts*.

5. Adriaan de Buck and Alan H. Gardiner, *The Egyptian Coffin Texts*; R. O. Faulkner, *The Ancient Egyptian Coffin Texts*.

6. Thomas George Allen, *The Book of the Dead; or, Going Forth by Day*.

7. Hartwig Altenmüller et al., "Ägyptologie: Literatur," in *Handbuch der Orientalistik* 1.2, ed. B. Spuler (2d ed.; Leiden: E. J. Brill, 1970).

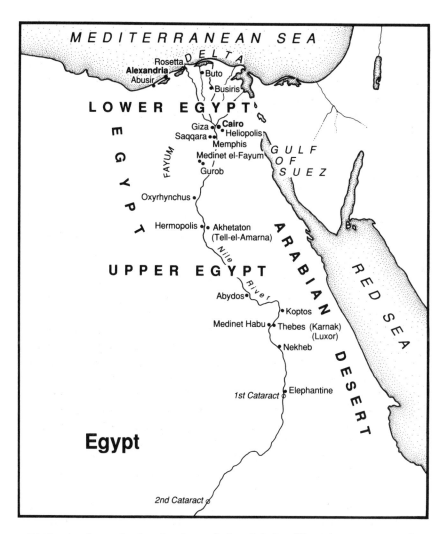

No later than the beginning of the third millennium B.C. another calendar was established. A small ivory tablet that belonged to the second king of the First Dynasty contains the notation: "Sothis, the opener of the year; the inundation." Annually after a period of invisibility the star Sothis (Egyptian, Sopdu; our Sirius) appeared again just before sunrise on the eastern horizon (heliacal rising) at just about the time when the Nile normally began to rise in its annual inundation. The coincidence of these events was striking, and the precision of the astronomical happening probably provided the beginning point for a secular calendar, commonly called the civil calendar. This calendar had three seasons of four thirty-day months each, with five epagomenal days ("five days added to the year," mentioned in the Pyramid Texts §1961) added at the end of the year (the shortage of a quarter of a day in a year produces the so-called Sothic cycle of 1,460 years).[8] The heliacal risings of thirty-six stars or constellations (Orion, etc.), which occurred approximately every ten days, were also noted and used, under the name of *decans,* to mark as many periods of the year.[9]

## Sacred Powers

The Egyptians, like the Mesopotamians and others, also responded to and thought about what they recognized as revelations of divine power or powers in the natural world, and conceptualized the great principles involved as gods and goddesses. Thus the divine essence of the Nile was the god Hapi (depicted as a man with female breasts indicative of fertility; sometimes viewed as two gods, he of the Upper Nile with a cluster of lotus plants on his head, he of the Lower Nile with a cluster of papyrus plants on his head). The divine principle of light was the sun-god Re, the moon was associated with the gods Thoth and Khonsu, the constellation Orion was identified with Osiris, and the star Sirius was equated with the goddess Isis (the Greeks called the star the Dog Star, and Isis-Sothis was then shown riding on a dog, on whose head was the star). Thus here, as also in Mesopotamia, where written records as well as artifacts are available, we find already an extensive number of gods and an elaborate mythology.[10]

As in Mesopotamia, too, we may assume a long development behind what is found in the extant texts, a development that included both nomadic and peasant backgrounds. The former is seen, for example, in the association of the wilderness-god Seth with a strange wild animal, perhaps first a wild ass held in regard by the nomads, and eventually an imaginary animal that cannot be zoologically identified; the latter is seen, for example, in Hapi's depiction as the god of the Nile and of fertility. More plainly evident is the fact that a multiplicity of early territorial units in the Nile valley came together in the kingdoms

8. Richard A. Parker, *The Calendars of Ancient Egypt;* idem, "Ancient Egyptian Astronomy," in *The Place of Astronomy in the Ancient World,* ed. F. R. Hodson, 51–65.

9. Wilhelm Gundel, *Dekane und Dekansternbilder.*

10. E. A. Wallis Budge, *The Gods of the Egyptians;* Adolf Erman, *Die Religion der Ägypter;* Veronica Ions, *Egyptian Mythology;* Siegfried Morenz, *Egyptian Religion;* Manfred Lurker, *The Gods and Symbols of Ancient Egypt;* Erik Hornung, *Conceptions of God in Ancient Egypt: The One and the Many;* and the relevant sections in the *Lexikon der Ägyptologie.*

of Upper Egypt and Lower Egypt and these in turn, at the beginning of historic times, emerged as the constituent parts of a combined Egyptian kingdom. Parallel with this political development, on the side of religion, many gods that belonged originally to local places emerged in new combinations and with significance for larger areas, in not a few cases for all of Egypt and even for the Egyptian Empire.[11]

Historic times in ancient Egypt are themselves long and provide opportunity for many changes and developments subsequent to those surmised for prehistoric times. Particularly notable developments in the existing records are what may be called a multiplicity of approaches (e.g., the several functions attributed to the sun-god) and a multiplicity of answers (e.g., the origination of existence attributed to Atum, Re, Ptah, and others). In general these multiple viewpoints do not appear as contradictions but rest rather upon recognition of the complexity of natural phenomena and reveal therefore a sense of the manifoldness of the divine power.[12]

In Egypt the perception of divine power(s) focused to a considerable degree upon animals—chiefly wild animals, although not to the exclusion of domesticated animals. In the animal—perhaps in its apparent wisdom, its competent action, the continuity of its species—is apparently recognized that which is other and more than human and thus significant in terms of religion.[13] Examples of animals so regarded are the wild animal of Seth and the cow of Hathor, the bulls Mnevis and Apis (manifestations of Atum and Ptah at Heliopolis and Memphis, respectively), the jackal (the god Anubis), the cat (the goddess Bastet), the lion (the goddess Sekhmet), the crocodile (the god Sobek), the baboon (the god Thoth), and the cobra (the goddess Uto). Certain birds were also considered divine symbols: the falcon (associated with Horus, Re, Montu, Hathor, and the *ba*), the vulture (the goddess Nekhbet), the ibis (an incarnation of the god Thoth), and the mythical phoenix (Egyptian *benu,* probably a heron). The latter was considered the *ba* of Re and also a form of Osiris; according to Greek tradition it was a symbol of life renewed through flaming death—a picture of the sun rising out of the red of the morning.[14] In token of their place many animals and birds were mummified, sometimes in great numbers, and were buried in large cemeteries, for example, the Apis at Saqqara, the crocodile of Sobek at Medinet el-Fayum (Greek, Krokodilopolis), and

---

11. Eberhard Otto, "Die Religion der alten Ägypter," in *Handbuch der Orientalistik* 1.8.1.1, ed. B. Spuler (Leiden: E. J. Brill, 1964), 1–6.

12. H. Frankfort, *Ancient Egyptian Religion,* 16–21.

13. Ibid., 12–15.

14. Roelof Van den Broek, *The Myth of the Phoenix According to Classical and Early Christian Traditions.*

the ibis of Thoth (Greek, Hermes) at Tuna el-Gebel near el-Ashmunein (Greek, Hermopolis).

Some plants also had divine connotations. The lotus and the papyrus were the symbols of Upper Egypt and Lower Egypt, respectively, and many goddesses carried the papyrus stalk as a scepter. At Memphis the lotus deity Nefertem sat as a youthful god upon a lotus blossom, while Hathor was the "lady of the southern sycamore." At Heliopolis the Isched tree was the holy willow on which the Phoenix was supposed to dwell (as well as on the Benben stone).

Sacred objects were many. A primeval hill (*Ta-tenen,* "the risen land" or "height") was claimed to exist at a number of places (Heliopolis, Memphis, Thebes), and represented the first land that emerged from the primeval ocean (Nun) in the creation of the world, even as annually the Egyptian land emerged from the receding flood waters of the Nile.[15] Equated with the primeval hill at Heliopolis was the sacred Benben stone. The hieroglyphic sign for the primeval hill looks like a step pyramid, and the sign for the Benben stone shows a tapering, somewhat conical shape; in addition, the pyramidion of an Egyptian obelisk, often covered with copper or gold and reflecting from its shining top the rays of the sun, is called by a name (*bnbnt*) etymologically related to Benben. Therefore it is probable that both the pyramid and the obelisk derive from these antecedents and are intended to glorify the sun-god and to point to his creative power. The Djed pillar, probably originally a column of papyrus stalks, was associated with Busiris (Egyptian, Djedu or Per-Osiris), the home of Osiris, and is a symbol of resurrection and continuing existence and therewith eventually an amulet of good fortune. Similarly the *ankh* cross stands for "life."

Human beings of course had special powers, too, and might be seen as divine; they might also provide appropriate models after which to visualize the gods. In fact the Egyptian deities were pictured from the earliest times in both animal and human forms. By itself the human form was not as readily recognizable in the identification of a particular deity; therefore some theriomorphic mark might be retained in the anthropomorphic form. For example, the goddess Hathor appears both as a cow and as a woman, and on the Narmer Palette she is represented by a human face with cow's horns and ears. Other symbols also served to differentiate the deities; thus Isis, for example, thought of as the mother of the king, wears a throne upon her head as a symbol of the enthronement of the ruler.

Of persons recognized in their present position as divine the chief was god-king of the land: he stood at the apex of the state and guar-

---

15. Hermann Alexander Schlögl, *Der Gott Tatenen.*

anteed the continuance of the social order in harmony with the divine order of the cosmos. The renewal of his office was the object of the royal festival called the Heb-sed.[16] Of individual persons who became gods, an example is the multitalented Imhotep, builder under the Third Dynasty king Djoser of the step pyramid at Saqqara, who became in the Late Period a god of medicine and healing.

As to the nature of a person, Egyptian anthropology does not separate body and soul, but considers a person as a unit; there are, however, different aspects of that unity. The *kha* is the gross, mortal, perishable body (the word can also designate the corpse). The *ba, ka,* and *akh* are subtle, immortal elements, and may belong to deities as well as to human beings. The *ba* (sometimes translated as "soul") may be defined as a personification of the vital force that animates the *kha*; it is also seen as a manifestation of the power of a god or king. At death the *ba* escapes from the body, and is pictured as a human-headed bird that hovers over the mummy or flutters in the vicinity of the grave and may be benefited by water, shade, and offerings. The *ba* is also pictured as a migratory stork ( *jabiru*), accompanied by a pot with a flame burning in it; the suggestion may be of the possibility of return, that is, of reincarnation. The *ka* (sometimes translated as "double") is also in some sense the life force in a person, but here the special picture is of a spirit double born at the same time as the child. Thus, when the ram-headed creator-god Khnum of Elephantine fashions human beings and deities on his potter's wheel (e.g., Amunhotep III in a relief in the "birth house" in the Luxor temple), we see two almost identical child figures, each marked with the child's long lock of hair, one with the child's gesture of finger to mouth, one with the *ka*-sign (a pair of upraised open arms) on the head; these are the infant child and the double that will accompany it throughout life. At the end, to die is to go to one's *ka,* for in death the *ka* leaves its mortal residence and returns to its divine origin. At the same time a narrow "false door" is left in the tomb, through which the *ka* may come and go to partake of the food offered there, either concretely or (no less effectively) in pictures on the tomb walls. Thus the *ka,* like the *ba,* remains to some extent attached to earthly life, and may also have to do with possible reincarnation. The term *akh* (sometimes translated as "spirit") is related to the Egyptian word "to shine, to be resplendent," and thus signifies the transcendent life-form of a person and the correspondingly transfigured existence of the person in the beyond— and presumably beyond reincarnation. The *akh* is pictured as the

16. Claas Jouco Bleeker, *Egyptian Festivals: Enactments of Religious Renewal,* 96–123: Erik Hornung and Elisabeth Staehelin, *Studien zum Sedfest.*

crested ibis (*Ibis comata*), the name of which was also *akh*. This bird
lived on the Arabian side of the Red Sea and migrated to Ethiopia in
the winter; both places were near the sources of sacred incense and
were called the "divine land." Thus the symbolism of the bird figure
was appropriate to the transcendent goal implied in the term. A Pyramid Text (§474) says: "The spirit [*akh*] is bound for heaven, the body
[*kha*] is bound for the earth."[17]

The great cosmic entities—the heaven, the sun and moon, the planets
and stars—were also viewed as sacred. For example, in one conception
the heaven was the god Horus, seen as a falcon with outstretched
wings and with the sun and moon as his eyes. From the beginning of
historical times the heaven falcon was equated with the king, and the
"Horus name" of the king was written within a palace facade (*serekh*)
with a falcon enthroned above. Not only the heaven but also the sun
itself was seen as a falcon; hence there was an equation of king and
sun and heaven, which found expression in the sacred and royal symbol of the winged sun disk. In another representation the heaven is
the goddess Nut seen as a woman bowed over the earth with feet and
hands resting upon the eastern and western horizons. Nut is the mother
of the sun-god, whom she swallows in the evening in the west and to
whom she gives birth again in the morning in the east; she is also the
mother of the stars, and these she bears in the evening in the east and
swallows in the morning in the west. In another picture heaven is a
great cow overarching the earth; the cow was a form of the goddess
Hathor, hence Hathor was also the mother of the sun-god. Again, however, Hathor is the sun-eye and, as such, she is also the daughter of
the sun-god.[18]

The best-known name for the divine principle of light, which penetrates the sun and causes it to shine, is Re (or Ra), and from Redjedef
(builder of the unfinished pyramid at Abu Roash) and Khafre (builder
of the second pyramid at Giza; both Fourth Dynasty) onward the kings
called themselves by the title *son of Re*. The name of Re was also
combined with the names of many other deities, for example, with
Atum at Heliopolis as Atum-Re, with Horus at Heliopolis as Re-Harakhte ("Re-Horus of the horizon"), with the ram-headed potter-creator
Khnum at Elephantine as Khnum-Re, with the crocodile god Sobek in
the Fayum as Sobek-Re, with Amun at Thebes as Amun-Re. Most
characteristically the sun-god travels across the sky in a boat; properly,
indeed, there are two boats, a day boat (Mandet) for the day's journey

---

17. Lucie Lamy, *Egyptian Mysteries: New Light on Ancient Spiritual Knowledge*, 24–26. Herodotus (2.123) and other Greek authors refer to reincarnation as an udoubted belief of the Egyptians
(see W. M. Flinders Petrie, "Transmigration [Egyptian]," in *HERE* 12.431; cf. n. 16 in chap. 5, "Greek
Religion," p. 168).

18. Erik Hornung, *Der ägyptische Mythos von der Himmelskuh*.

on the celestial Nile, and a night boat (Mesektet) for the nocturnal journey on the Nile that is under the earth. On the sun boat other deities travel with Re, including his vizier Thoth and his daughters Hathor and Maat.[19] As the boat comes up over the horizon in the morning Seth stands in the front of the vessel where he contends valiantly and successfully against the serpent-demon Apophis, the embodiment of the powers of darkness (although on occasion Seth is himself equated with Apophis as the enemy of the gods). The dependence of all life and all growth upon the sun made natural the attribution of creative power to Re. The daily rising of the sun out of the darkness of the night was seen as pointing to victory over the darkness of death. The steady course of the sun through the sky exemplifies the dependable order of the world, and it is in this respect that Maat, in particular, the embodiment of order, justice, and truth, journeys with Re.[20]

The moon with its phases is of special importance for the calendar. Thoth, the scribe of the gods, is himself a moon-god and the reckoner of the year. Khonsu, son of Amun and Mut at Thebes, is also a moon-god; his name means "traveler," the reference being to his traverse of the heavens. The phases of the moon are also a natural symbol for life and death, and are taken as pointing to the death and resurrection of Osiris.

The five main planets are associated with gods: Mercury with Seth, Venus with Osiris, and Mars, Jupiter, and Saturn all with Horus as (respectively) Horus the red, Horus who illuminates the two lands, and Horus the bull.

The significance of the star Sothis for the calendar has already been noted (p. 41). The goddess of the star is Isis; in the New Kingdom Isis is closely related to Hathor, who, on occasion, is considered the goddess of Sothis. Of the constellations, Orion (Egyptian, Sah), which appears just before Sirius (the star of Isis), is equated with Osiris. The place of the stars and constellations known as *decans* has been noted above (p. 42), and all are associated with deities. Special regard was paid to "the imperishable ones," that is, the circumpolar stars that never set and are thus demonstrably immortal, hence identifiable with the transfigured dead, including the king and others.

## Mythology

Since religion is not only response in feeling to what is perceived as divine power or powers but also response in thought to the felt need

---

19. Claas Jouco Bleeker, *Hathor and Thoth: Two Key Figures of the Ancient Egyptian Religion.*
20. Siegfried Morenz, *Gott und Mensch im alten Ägypten.*

to comprehend and explain life and the world, it is understandable
that such perceptions of the divine as have been enumerated above
provided the materials for speculative and mythical thinking to construct theological systems and mythologies.

Several factors influenced the form of such constructions, including
the geographical and political duality of the "two lands" combined in
the union of Egypt. Reflecting this situation, the vulture goddess
Nekhbet of Nekheb (el-Kab) representing Upper Egypt and the cobra
goddess Wadjet (Greek, Uto) of Buto representing Lower Egypt are
pictured side by side on the brow of the pharaoh (the cobra on the
king's brow is called the *uraeus*). Likewise Horus and Seth constitute
a divine pair—albeit in opposition to each other—and in this case
there is reflected not only the duality of the upper and lower portions
of the Nile valley but also the duality and the opposition of the fertile
land and the desert.

The dualities just mentioned may be seen further as examples of a
numerical motif that runs through the theological systems. Prominent
here are the numbers three, seen in the frequent triad of father, mother,
and son (e.g., Amun, Mut, and Khonsu); four (two times two) and eight
(two times four), found in the cosmogony developed in the Upper Egyptian city of Hermopolis, in which the origin of everything is traced
back to four pairs of deities, each pair consisting of one masculine and
one feminine being; and nine (three times three), which can designate
nine (or more) individual gods as constituting an ennead (at Abydos
the ennead actually comprises eleven deities; at Karnak it is fifteen).

The myth of Osiris was the most widespread of Egypt.[21] In essential
outline the story tells of a ruler slain by his brother, and of the ensuing
struggle for the sovereignty between the ruler's son and the murderer—a story so conceivable in human life as perhaps to be accounted
basically a legend, that is, to rest upon actual historical reminiscence.
In the elaborated myth the slain ruler is Osiris and his brother, the
murderer, is Seth. By a stratagem Osiris was encased in a coffin and
cast into the Nile; in another view, his body was cut into many pieces
and scattered over the land, and where the pieces fell the land was
fertile and green plants grew. Osiris, it is evident, is a god of vegetation
and agriculture, Seth a god of the wilderness and of destruction.[22]

Isis, in the myth, is the wife of Osiris. In grief and tribulation over
the death of Osiris she searches for and finally recovers the body. (In
the astronomical form of the myth the sorrowing Isis is the star Sirius

21. Eberhard Otto, *Osiris und Amun: Kult und heilige Stätten,* 11–65; John Gwyn Griffiths,
*The Origins of Osiris and His Cult.*
22. H. Te Velde, *Seth: God of Confusion.*

Isis and Horus, on the first pylon of the temple of Isis at Philae in Egypt.

and follows Orion, which is "the glorious soul [*ba*]" of Osiris.) When the body of Osiris is found Isis prepares it for burial with the help of Anubis, the jackal-god of the western desert and the god of embalmment. Together Isis and her sister Nephthys (herself sister and wife of Seth) speak charms over the body of Osiris and he experiences resurrection. In union with him Isis becomes the mother of a son, Horus, while Osiris goes on into the beyond to be the god of the dead. The child Horus (Greek, Harsiese, "Horus, son of Isis"; also Harpokrates, "Horus the child," seen with a child's long lock of hair and the finger in the mouth) is raised in the safety of the papyrus swamps and grows up to avenge his father's death in successful combat with Seth and claims his father's throne. Then—in variant forms of the myth—Horus and Seth rule in the two parts of the land (Horus in Lower Egypt, Seth in Upper Egypt), or Horus rules the whole land while Seth is relegated to the wilderness. Thereafter every king of Egypt rules as Horus (or as both Horus and Seth, a representation that provides some inconsistencies in what follows) and, when he dies, becomes Osiris and rules in the underworld while his son, the new king, rules on earth as the new Horus.

Osiris is thus the dead king, and the myth has to do with the succession in the rulership of Egypt with its promise of stability in the land, but it is plain that the theme of resurrection is also prominently involved. Osiris is revived and becomes immortal. His immortality is also associated with the circumpolar stars that never set, and his resurrection is associated with such other natural events as the annual rising of the Nile and the death and life of vegetation. From this point of view, and when some of the prerogatives of the king gradually spread to his nobles and on to the common people, Osiris became not only the dead king and the ruler of the dead but also the prototype and savior of the common dead.

As such, the myth of Osiris was the basis of the Osirian mysteries, in which the death and life experiences of the god were presumably reenacted in dramatic form and, under the guidance of the priests, became also the experience of the devotee.[23]

Many cities were centers of the Osirian cult, the most important being Busiris in the Delta (supposed birthplace of Osiris and site of the Djed pillar, his symbol) and Abydos in Upper Egypt (supposed place of his tomb; the present Umm el-Qaab). As the cult spread throughout Egypt other deities were incorporated into the framework of the myth—naturally gods of the dead such as Anubis and Khentamentiou (the wild dog-god of the dead in Abydos), the chthonian god Sokaris in Memphis, plus other local deities. At Heliopolis it was necessary to find accommodation with the doctrine of the world rule of Atum-Re, and this was done by establishing a genealogical relationship between the sun-god and the Osirian cycle (see p. 52).

The works known as the Coffin Texts and the "Book of the Dead" (represented both in texts and in tomb paintings) also express in detail the prevalent belief in and hope for life in the beyond. Here Osiris as the god of the dead is associated with strongly ethical ideas. In their resurrection the dead are pictured as standing in the presence of Osiris as their judge; to obtain blessed immortality their soul must be able to affirm moral worthiness by reciting a long list of sins that have not been committed and by reporting good deeds that have been per-

23. For a text on a stele from the tomb or cenotaph of an official in the Osiris temple at Abydos (under Sesostris III, 1878–1843 B.C.), which describes some of the drama enacted at Abydos, see Heinrich Schäfer, *Die Mysterien des Osiris in Abydos unter König Sesostris III.* For the possibility of mystical initiation in ancient Egypt, see Edward F. Wente, "Mysticism in Pharaonic Egypt?" *JNES* 41 (1982): 161–79. See also Édouard Schuré, *The Great Initiates,* 141–56; idem, *The Mysteries of Ancient Egypt* 47–72; Rudolf Steiner, *Christianity as Mystical Fact and the Mysteries of Antiquity,* 130–31; Paul Brunton, *A Search in Secret Egypt,* 184–89; M. Grosso, "Jung, Parapsychology, and the Near-Death Experience: Toward a Transpersonal Paradigm," *Anabiosis* 3 (1983): 3–38 (see also n. 21 in chap. 5, "Greek Religion," p. 170).

formed, for example, "I have given bread to the hungry, water to the thirsty, clothing to the naked, and a ferry-boat to him who was marooned."[24] Other works (originally of New Kingdom date, and also represented both in texts and in tomb paintings), the "Book of What is in the Underworld" (Amduat) and the "Book of the Gates," describe the sun-god Re as journeying in his barge during the twelve hours of the night through all the realms of the netherworld. For the blessed dead the promise is presumably implied of traveling through the night with Re, to then be brought with him out of the darkness into the light of the morning. For those condemned in the judgment, however, the Amduat pictures the most horrifying punishments.[25]

## Theological Systems

In distinction from the Osiris myth with its themes of life renewal and kingly succession, the theological systems associated with Heliopolis, Memphis, and Thebes were cosmogonic in aspect, that is, they were oriented toward an explanation of the origin and character of the cosmos. Heliopolis was a very ancient religious center, Memphis was the capital of united Egypt in the Old Kingdom, and Thebes was the capital in the Middle and New Kingdoms; the prominence of the three theological systems was at least in part due to the prominence of these cities.

### Heliopolis

In the cosmogony of Heliopolis (Egyptian, Onou; biblical On), for which the Pyramid Texts are the main source, Atum ("the complete one") is the primeval god, who stands between the nonexistence prior to creation and the created world. Like the primeval hill that emerged out of the primeval ocean, Atum came into being of himself out of the primeval chaos, and he is equated with both the primeval hill and the scarab beetle (*Scarabaeus sacer*), which was believed to originate of itself out of the dung heap and which, pushing a dung ball in front of itself as the sun is apparently pushed across the sky, symbolized the sun and was a form of the sun-god, called Khepri. Thus Atum is saluted in the Pyramid Texts (§1587):

24. *ANET*, 34–36; *ANEP*, fig. 639.
25. Erik Hornung, *Altägyptische Höllenvorstellungen*; Karol Myśliwiec, *Eighteenth Dynasty before the Amarna Period*, 29–30, plates xxv–xxix.

Hail to you, Atum!
Hail to you, Khepri, the Self-created!
You are high in this your name of "Height,"
You come into being in this your name of Khepri.

Like other primeval deities in Egyptian thought, Atum combined
the masculine and the feminine, and alone brought forth as children
the two deities Shu and Tefnut. Some passages in the Pyramid Texts
(§§1248–49) use sexual terminology and others (§§1652–54) the language of discharge from the throat to describe the creation of Shu and
Tefnut. The latter passage is the opening part of a prayer for the king
and his pyramid, and contains multiple allusions to matters at
Heliopolis:

O Atum-Khepri, you became high on the "Height," you rose up as the
Benben stone in the temple of the Phoenix in On [Heliopolis], you spat
out Shu, you expectorated Tefnut, and you set your arms about them as
the arms of a *ka*[-symbol], that your *ka*[-essence] might be in them. O
Atum, set your arms about the king, about this construction, and about
this pyramid as the arms of a *ka*[-symbol], that the king's *ka*[-essence]
may be in it, enduring for ever.

O Atum, set your protection over this king, over this pyramid of his,
and over this construction of the king, prevent anything from happening
evilly against it for ever, just as your protection was set over Shu and
Tefnut.

In turn Shu and Tefnut became the parents of Geb and Nut. Shu is
air, Tefnut is perhaps moisture, Geb is the earth, and Nut is the heaven.
Together Shu and Tefnut are the atmosphere, and it is they who separated Geb and Nut. In visualization the earth-god (Geb) lies prostrate, while the heaven-goddess (Nut) stretches herself overhead (see
the earlier description of Nut, p. 46).

The deities of the Osirian cycle were also brought into relationship
with the Heliopolitan cosmogony in that Osiris, Isis, Seth, and Nephthys were considered to be the children of Nut. By adding these
names to those of Atum, Shu and Tefnut, Geb and Nut, there was
constituted the Heliopolitan ennead. This also comes into focus as the
preceding prayer for the king and his pyramid continues (§§1655–56):

O you Great Ennead which is in On, [namely,] Atum, Shu, Tefnut, Geb,
Nut, Osiris, Isis, Seth, and Nephthys, O you children of Atum, extend
his heart [i.e., his good will] to his child in your name of Nine Bows
[here a name for the ennead].

Horus was also of course an important figure in the Osirian cycle, and by giving Atum a separate place as the primeval father and adding the name of Horus the Heliopolitan ennead comprised Shu, Tefnut, Geb, Nut, Osiris, Horus, Seth, Isis, and Nephthys. The last five deities (in this order according to Plutarch, *On Isis and Osiris* 12) were supposed to have been born on the five epagomenal days of the calendar year.

There must also have been from an early time a cult center of the sun-god Re in On—the city that the Greeks distinguished above all as the "city of the sun" (*heliopolis*). Atum was not only equated with the self-created sun-god Khepri (as Atum-Khepri) but was also associated with Re in the form of Atum-Re (or Re-Atum). By way of distinction Atum is specifically the god of the setting sun, Re is the god of the midday, and Khepri or Re-Harakhte ("Re-Horus of the horizon") is the god of the rising sun.

As seen in the Pyramid Text (§1652), the primeval hill and the Benben stone were original forms of the appearing of Atum-Khepri. These are no doubt the prototypes of the platform surmounted by a massive obelisk that stood under the open sky in the excavated sun temples of the Fifth Dynasty (one built by Userkaf at Abusir, another by Neuserre at Abu Gurab), these presumably reflecting the configuration of an earlier, now utterly lost sun temple at Heliopolis. Also closely associated with the sun at Heliopolis were the Mnevis bull and the Phoenix bird.

### Memphis

In the cosmogony of Memphis (Egyptian, *Ineb hedj,* "White Wall") the god Ptah, known in anthropomorphic form already in the First Dynasty, has the chief place; and Ptah, the lion-goddess Sekhmet, and the lotus-god Nefertem form a triad of father, mother, and son. Along with them are associated the Apis bull, the tree-goddess Hathor (the "lady of the southern sycamore"), and the chthonic god Sokaris. A text found on the so-called Shabaka Stone (British Museum no. 498), which was copied by order of King Shabaka (716–702 B.C.) of the Twenty-fifth Dynasty from a scroll in the temple of Ptah at Memphis, outlines the Memphite theology. In terms already familiar from the Heliopolitan system, Ptah is the primeval hill and the primeval deity who, combining the masculine and feminine, brought forth Atum. Ptah is therefore himself the creator-god. In the description of his creative work we hear of his "heart," corresponding to his knowledge, and of his "tongue," corresponding to his creative command. Through his knowledge and command he has brought into being all that exists, the entire cosmos, the Egyptian state with its districts and cities, and the "bodies" of the gods, that is, the images into which they enter. Because Horus and Thoth were commonly equated with the powers of thought and speech, it was said that they both became Ptah. Because Ptah is the creator of the order of the world and of the state, he is himself the embodiment of *maat* (cosmic order, that which is right and true). The Shabaka Stone summarizes the creative work of Ptah in the statement: "Indeed, all the divine order [literally, every word of the god] really came into being through what the heart thought and the tongue commanded."[26]

Incorporating both Heliopolitan and Osirian elements, the Memphite ennead consisted of Ptah, Atum-Re, Shu, Geb, Osiris, Seth, Horus, Thoth, and Maat. Especially important for its political consequences was the affirmation that Memphis was the place where the body of Osiris washed up out of the Nile and was recovered by Isis and Nephthys. Here also was the place where the strife of Horus and Seth over the succession came to an end: Geb first gave Upper Egypt to Seth and Lower Egypt to Horus, then regretted the decision and gave all of Egypt to Horus since Horus was the firstborn, the son of Osiris, who was the son of Geb. Memphis is where all of this took place; thus it is appropriately the residence of the living king, for the king is himself Horus. Also here the chthonic god Sokaris becomes Osiris-Sokaris, the god of the dead; and the deified Apis bull and Osiris become Osiris-Apis, introduced into Alexandria by Ptolemy I Soter (323–285 B.C.) as the Hellenistic Sarapis, a god who became widely worshiped in the Roman Empire.[27]

### Thebes

The city of Was (or Waset), which the Greeks called Thebes,[28] was the capital of the Eleventh and Twelfth Dynasties of the Middle Kingdom, and the center of the local princes who arose to expel the Hyksos from Egypt and inaugurate the Eighteenth Dynasty under whose rulers (notably Thutmose III, 1490–1436 B.C.) an Egyptian Empire was established that extended from above the fourth cataract of the Nile to beyond the Euphrates. Concurrent with the rise of the city was the rise of Amun ("the hidden one"), a god known in Thebes at least from the Eleventh Dynasty onward.[29]

26. *ANET*, 5.
27. John E. Stambaugh, *Sarapis under the Early Ptolemies*; Wilhelm Hornbostel, *Sarapis*.
28. Charles F. Nims, *Thebes of the Pharaohs: Pattern for Every City*.
29. Otto, *Osiris und Amun*, 71–127.

Amun appeared in both theriomorphic and anthropomorphic forms. He was represented as a serpent, a bull, and especially a ram (note the avenue of ram-headed sphinxes at the Karnak temple). In human form he wears tall double feathers on his head and holds a flail aloft; sometimes he is ithyphallic, probably borrowing the fertility symbolism from the god Min of nearby Koptos. Evidently also known at Thebes from an early time were a vulture-goddess named Mut and a moon-god named Khonsu, and in human form these together with Amun formed the Theban triad of Amun, Mut, and Khonsu as father, mother, and son. Other deities known in the city and district of Thebes were Sobek, Horus, and Hathor, and the falcon-god Montu and the goddesses Iunit and Tanenet, the latter three all of the city of Hermonthis. With the addition to these six of the Heliopolitan ennead (Atum, Shu, Tefnut, Geb, Nut, Osiris, Isis, Seth, Nephthys) there was constituted the Theban "great ennead" of no less than fifteen members.

Politically Amun was the national god of Egypt at the height of Egyptian power. It was in the name of Amun that the Theban princes had fought successfully against the Hyksos; it was under the aegis of Amun that the Egyptian armies of the Eighteenth Dynasty marched triumphantly throughout Asia. The king was the son of Amun, and during a thousand years successive kings made additions to the temple of Amun at Karnak until it was the largest ever built in the world. The wealth of the temple became great, and its priesthood was extremely powerful.

Theologically Amun was understood to be manifest in the wind, which pervades all things, and in the breath, which is the source of life. As such Amun is often designated as "soul" (ba), with the addition of epithets such as "living soul" and "hidden soul." The sun-god Re was of course also well known at Thebes, and it was natural to conclude that the creative power of the air and the creative power in the sun were one and the same; thus the god became Amun-Re, the king of the gods, considered (much like Atum-Re and Ptah) the primeval deity and creator of all.

As the chief Egyptian god in the days when Egypt ruled the East there was a tendency to think of Amun in universal terms, and in the theological speculations concerning Amun in terms of wind and soul there was something approaching a conception of his essential character as spiritual. A hymn written (on two steles, British Museum no. 826 and Cairo no. 34051) in the name of two brothers, Seth and Horus, who were architects at Thebes under Amunhotep III (1402–1364 B.C.), praises the sun under the names of Amun, Harakhte, Re, Khepri, and Aten (sun disk):

Praising Amun, when he rises as Harakhte, by the Overseer of the
Works of Amun, Seth, and the Overseer of the Works of Amun, Horus.
They say:

Hail to thee, beautiful Re of every day, who rises at dawn without
ceasing, Khepri wearying [himself] with labor! . . .

When thou crossest the sky, all faces behold thee. . . . Steadfast is thy
sailing. . . . A brief day—and thou racest a course of millions and hundred-
thousands of leagues. Every day under thee is an instant, and when it
passes, thou settest. So also thou hast completed the hours of the night:
thou hast regulated it without a pause coming in thy labors. . . .

Hail to thee, sun disk [Aten] of the daytime, creator of all and maker
of their living! . . . The sole lord, who reaches the ends of the lands every
day. . . . He who rises in heaven, [his] form being the sun. . . .[30]

It was Amunhotep IV (1364–1347 B.C.) who introduced the radical
conception of one supreme and universal god who was representable
in neither theriomorphic nor anthropomorphic form, but only in the
form of the Aten, seen in the sun disk and pictured with rays extending
beneficently earthward and terminating in hands holding the *ankh*
sign of life.[31]

The doctrine of Amunhotep IV was of course not without antecedents, for the Heliopolitan theology had long since made the sun-god of
high esteem, and Aten was an old name for the sun disk and (as seen
in the quotation just above) occurs occasionally under Amunhotep III
(1402–1364 B.C.), even with the designation of the Aten as "the god."
Heliopolitan influence is also to be seen in that one of the early titles
of Amunhotep IV was "prophet of Re-Harakhte," and also in that he
early intended to provide a grave at his new capital city for the bull
Mnevis.

At Thebes, however, although Amunhotep IV was crowned in the
traditional way, he did not assume the position of the Horus-king, and
soon built several temples specifically designated for the Aten. Although these were later demolished by Horemheb (1334–1306 B.C.), a
great many broken blocks from them were reused in other buildings
by Horemheb and Ramses II and many thousands of these blocks (originally carved in relief and painted, now known as *talatat*) have been
recovered. Although fragmentary, in many of the scenes the king and
his queen Nefertiti ("a beautiful one comes") are plainly to be recognized, with the sun disk overhead and its rays descending upon them.[32]

30. *ANET*, 367–68.

31. Cyril Aldred, *Akhenaten, Pharaoh of Egypt: A New Study*; idem, *Akhenaten and Nefertiti*;
Donald B. Redford, *Akhenaten: The Heretic King*; Robert Hari, *New Kingdom Amarna Period: The
Great Hymn to Aten*.

32. Ray Winfield Smith and Donald B. Redford, *The Akhenaten Temple Project*, vol. 1, *Initial
Discoveries*.

In the fifth year of his reign the king left Thebes, Amun, and the temple and priesthood of Amun behind, and built an entirely new capital on the right bank of the Nile about halfway down the river between Thebes and Memphis, the site now known as Tell el-Amarna. The new city was called Akhetaten ("horizon of Aten"), and the king changed his own name from Amunhotep ("Amun is content") to Akhenaten ("well-pleasing to Aten"). Like Akhenaten's buildings for the Aten at Thebes so also his city Akhetaten was later almost completely destroyed by Horemheb. Enough remains of foundations and fragments of reliefs to learn that there was a palace with a "window of appearances" where the king would show himself to the people, a "mansion of the sun disk," and a "house of the sun disk" containing several independent temples, each with a court open to the sky so that the sun might shine down upon the rites in which Akhenaten worshiped the power manifest in the heavenly disk.

The tomb of the king and the tombs of many of his nobles were in the cliffs surrounding the plain. Inscribed in the tomb of Ay (Ay was private secretary to the king and later held the throne briefly, 1338–1334 B.C.) is a great hymn, generally believed to have been composed by Akhenaten himself, which is the major written source for knowledge of the king's view of the Aten. Some of the words of the hymn appear to have been echoed centuries later in Psalm 104:

> When thou settest in the western horizon,
> The land is in darkness, in the manner of death [cf. Ps. 104:20].
> They sleep in a room, with heads wrapped up. . . .
> Every lion is come forth from his den [cf. Ps. 104:21]. . . .
>
> At daybreak, when thou arisest on the horizon,
> When thou shinest as the Aten by day,
> Thou drivest away the darkness and givest thy rays. . . .
> All the world, they do their work [cf. Ps. 104:23]. . . .
>
> How manifold it is what thou hast made [cf. Ps. 104:24]. . . .
> O sole god, like whom there is no other!
> Thou didst create the world according to thy desire,
> Whilst thou wert alone. . . .
>
> Thou settest every man in his place,
> Thou suppliest their necessities:
> Everyone has his food, and his time of life is reckoned [cf. Ps.
>     104:27]. . . .
>
> Thou art the Aten of the day. . . .
>
> Thou art in my heart.[33]

33. *ANET*, 370–71.

Along with such an affirmation that the Aten was the only god, unique and supreme over all the universe, Akhenaten also closed many of the temples of the gods previously worshiped, and caused the name of Amun to be chiseled out in many places. After his fifth year the plural word *gods* is not found in his own inscriptions, and in existing inscriptions the offending word is sometimes erased. In modern terms the king's religion is properly described as monotheism.[34]

The religious program of Akhenaten did not, however, endure long after the king's death. Smenkhkare, married to Akhenaten's oldest daughter Meretaten, may have reigned briefly; then Tutankhaten, married to Akhenaten's third daughter Ankhesenpaaten, took the throne (1347–1338 B.C.) and soon left Akhetaten for the old religious centers of Memphis and Thebes. The two changed their names to Tutankhamun and Ankhesenamun, and on a stele at Thebes the king attributed recent woes in Egypt to neglect under Akhenaten of the gods and goddesses formerly worshiped, and announced his own restoration of their sanctuaries.[35]

In the ensuing Nineteenth Dynasty the political center of gravity shifted to the Delta, largely because of the increased significance of Egypt's Asiatic relationships, and the city of Per-Ramses (located at Tell ed-Dab'a/*Khata*'na/Qantir, on the site of ancient Avaris), built by and bearing the name of Ramses II the Great (1290–1224 B.C.), became of much importance and is presumably the store-city of Raamses of Exodus 1:11.[36]

In the Delta the Hyksos had taken Seth (equated with the Semitic Baal) as their chief god, and Seti I (1304–1290 B.C.), father of Ramses II, bore the name *Seth's man*. In Per-Ramses four temples of four gods were symmetrically located in the four quarters of the city, as a passage in Papyri Anastasi II and IV (British Museum nos. 10243 and 10249, the earlier text written under Merneptah, 1224–1204 B.C., son and successor of Ramses II) tells us: "Its western part is the house of Amun, its southern part the house of Seth; Astarte is in its orient, and Uto in its northern part."[37]

Of all the deities it was still Amun-Re of Thebes who was the chief

34. Donald B. Redford, "The Monotheism of the Heretic Pharaoh: Precursor of Mosaic Monotheism or Egyptian Anomaly?" *BAR* 13.3 (May–June 1987): 16–32, esp. 27.

35. *ANET*, 251–52; Christiane Desroches-Noblecourt, *Tutankhamen*.

36. Manfred Bietak, "Ramsesstadt," in *Lexikon der Ägyptologie*, 5.128–46; Christiane Desroches-Noblecourt, *The Great Pharaoh Ramses II and His Time*.

37. Alan H. Gardiner, "The Delta Residence of the Ramessides," *JEA* 5 (1918): 179–200, esp. 187. Astarte is the Middle Eastern Ishtar, goddess of love and war, frequently equated with Hathor and regarded as a consort of Seth.

god for Seti I and Ramses II, and solar and Osirian theology coexisted. The major extant temple built in this time is the one erected by Seti I and completed by Ramses II at Abydos (in Upper Egypt about one hundred miles below Thebes on the Nile). Here in the sanctuary the central chapel is that of Amun, while on either side there are chapels of Re-Harakhte, Ptah, and the deceased and deified Seti I himself on the left, and of Osiris, Isis, and Horus on the right. Also in fine painted reliefs throughout the temple both Seti I and Ramses II are shown in the company not only of Amun-Re and the foregoing deities but also of others as well—Thoth, Anubis, Mut, and many more. In one relief Osiris lies upon his bier, with Isis and Horus and two falcons at his head and feet, while in the form of another falcon Isis hovers over the mummy in the posthumous union from which Horus was to be born.[38]

In fact in the Egypt of this time it is widely felt that in the last analysis there is one personal divine reality in and behind the various names and images of the deities. Much like the hymn of Seth and Horus from the time of Amunhotep II (pp. 55–56), spell 15 of the "Book of Going Forth by Day" (in Papyrus Clot Bey, British Museum no. 9901, from Thebes in the Nineteenth Dynasty) hails the power in the sun under different names as the sole and universal deity:

> Hail to thee, Re at his rising, Atum at his setting. . . . Thou art lord of sky and earth, who made the stars above and humankind below, sole God, who came into being at the beginning of time, who made the lands and created common people, who made the deep and created the inundation, who made the water and gave life to what is in it, who fashioned the mountains and brought into being humankind and beast. . . .
>
> Hail to thee, Amun-Re, who takes pleasure in truth. Thou crossest the sky, everyone seeing thee. . . . O my Lord, living through eternity, thou who shalt exist forever; O thou disk [Aten], lord of rays, when thou risest everyone lives. Let (me) see thee at daybreak every day.[39]

Another text of the Nineteenth Dynasty (Papyrus Leiden 1.350, from Thebes in the reign of Ramses II) is oriented similarly and subsumes the trinity of Amun, Re, and Ptah in a unity. The text is divided into a series of "houses" or chapters, numbered from 1 to 9, then from 10 to 90 numbered in tens, and from 100 to 900 numbered in hundreds only. In chapter 100 (4.9–11) it is stated that at the beginning Amun came into existence of himself, without father or mother, and all the

---

38. Ann Rosalie David, *A Guide to Religious Ritual at Abydos*; Eberhard Otto, *Egyptian Art and the Cults of Osiris and Amon*, 69 and plate 17.

39. Allen, *Book of the Dead*, 18–19.

gods were created after he began to be. In chapter 200 (4.12–21) it is said that his name is "hidden" because he is a mystery: "too mysterious that his glory should be revealed, too great that question should be made of him, too powerful that he should be known." And then in chapter 300 (4.21–26) it is stated that there exist only three gods, namely, Amun, Re, and Ptah, and that they are actually only one:

> Three [gods] are all the gods—Amun, Re, and Ptah—and there is none like them. "Hidden" is his name as Amun, Re belongs to him as his face, and Ptah is his body. Their cities on earth are established for ever; Thebes, Heliopolis, and Memphis until eternity.[40]

## Pyramids, Tombs, Temples, and the Beyond

As to architecture related to and expressive of Egyptian religion, the most impressive monuments are the pyramids and the pyramidion-topped obelisks, both of which doubtless reflect the Heliopolitan primeval hill and Benben stone, and point to the worship of the sun. The pyramid of course also serves as a tomb, with tomb chambers within or underneath it. In the architectural evolution, superimposition of the earlier rectangular flat-topped tombs called *mastabas*, one above the other in decreasing size, may have resulted in the step pyramid of Djoser and Imhotep at Saqqara. The true pyramid that followed had sloping sides and was the center of a complex that all together could include a valley temple, a causeway up from the river, an enclosing wall, subsidiary pyramids, the main pyramid with a mortuary temple on the east side and a chapel on the north side, and boat pits containing actual boats, presumably intended for the use of the deceased in the afterlife.

In all there are more than seventy pyramids in Egypt; the best known are those of the great kings of the Fourth Dynasty (2613–2494 B.C.)—Snefru, Khufu, and Khafre—at Giza. When Khufu's great pyramid was built the North Pole star was Alpha Draconis (Thuban, the first star in the constellation of the Dragon), and the northern so-called air-shaft leading diagonally upward from the king's chamber in the great pyramid was centered on this star, in apparent accordance with the idea that the soul of the king might travel thither to the realm of the imperishable circumpolar stars. Of the king's journey the Pyramid Texts (§§1120–23) say:

---

40. Alan H. Gardiner, "Hymn to Amon from a Leiden Papyrus," *ZÄS* 42 (1905): 12–42. In the Late Period and notably under the Kushite kings of the Twenty-sixth Dynasty there was a line of priestesses at Thebes, mostly royal princesses, who constituted a sort of feminine dynasty, continued through adoption, and who exercised much power in both the political and religious realms. They were known by the title *god's wife of Amun*. See Constantin Emil Sander-Hansen, *Das Gottesweib des Amun.*

The sky thunders, the earth quakes ... when he ascends to the sky, traversing the firmament. . . . He ascends to the sky among the imperishable stars; his sister is Sothis, his guide is the Morning Star.

The southern air-shaft in the pyramid of Khufu was centered on the three stars in the belt of Orion; it has been suggested that the two shafts can point to the possibility of two ways for the individual—one to the north to final liberation and eternal life, one to the south to reincarnation and new experience in a mortal body.[41]

While the pyramid is the typical royal burial place in the Old Kingdom, the rock-hewn tomb is characteristic of the New Kingdom, chief of which are the tombs of the kings, queens, and nobles in western Thebes.

From the material arrangements for the deceased, the associated art, and the literature, it is plain that the Egyptians firmly believed that life would continue beyond death, and also be subject to ethical judgment (e.g., the scene of the weighing of the soul in the papyri of the "Book of the Dead"). In these tombs, fine paintings picture many circumstances of earthly life, presumably hoped to be continued or repeated in the life beyond (e.g., the scene of fowling in the marshes, now in the British Museum, from the no-longer identifiable tomb of Nebamun, a noble of the time of Thutmose IV or Amunhotep III). Astronomical depictions are also prominent, no doubt because the deceased were expected to travel among the stars. Of many astronomical ceilings in the tombs, the earliest presently known is in the tomb of Senmut (no. 71 in the Tombs of the Nobles), the architect and favorite of Queen Hatshepsut (1490–1468 B.C.). It shows both *decans* and planets; for example, Osiris is in a bark, which represents the constellation Orion, and Isis is in a bark, which represents Sothis. The finest and most extensive painted reliefs are in the tomb of Seti I (no. 17 in the Valley of the Kings), with pictures of the journey of the sun during the twelve hours of the night, a list of the decanal stars, and a depiction of the constellations near the North Pole. Ursa Major (the Great Bear) was called the thigh of Seth or the foreleg of a bull, and is shown as the bull Meshketiu on a platform; at the right is a hippopotamus with a crocodile on her back, possibly the constellation Draco (the Dragon). The representation corresponds with the "Book of the Day and of the Night": "As to this thigh of Seth, it is in the northern sky, tied to two mooring posts of flint by a chain of gold. It is entrusted to Isis as a [female] hippopotamus guarding it."[42] At the

---

41. Lamy, *Egyptian Mysteries*, 28.
42. Alexandre Piankoff, *Le livre du jour et de la nuit*, 24.

left along with other figures are the constellation Leo (Lion), shown as a lion with many stars on its head and back, and the goddess Serqet, who is equated with Isis and is a friend of the deceased.

Egyptian temples are of two kinds as far as their purpose is concerned.[43] The mortuary temple is for the remembrance of, and offerings to, the deceased; it may stand over the tomb or at a different site, even far away (e.g., the tomb of Ramses III is in the Valley of the Kings, his mortuary temple at Medinet Habu). The cult temple is the house of the god (or gods) and the place of worship. In either case the characteristic features are a great pylon or gateway, a large open court surrounded by columns, a hypostyle hall with columns supporting a high roof, and the most sacred area at the back with the sanctuary containing the divine image or images and surrounding rooms for temple equipment and the boats in which the gods were transported. Thus Amun, Mut, and Khonsu, for example, sailed up and back on the Nile between Karnak and Luxor for the beautiful Feast of Opet, an annual festival the outward circumstances of which are depicted on the walls of the Luxor temple, although the inner meaning of the ceremony is hardly evident.[44]

## Human Life and Society

With respect to the shaping of life and society in relation to religious belief, already in the Old Kingdom there was thought of a normative order of existence, designated by the term *maat*. This term means truth, justice, and righteousness and was also personified as the goddess Maat, the daughter of the sun-god Re, whose unvarying circuit is the most striking manifestation of cosmic order. The symbol of Maat is the feather of truth. The king is properly under obligation to reign in accordance with *maat*, and all of human life and society should be shaped in accordance with *maat*.

In the same Old Kingdom Period there were wise sages who formulated proverbs for the correspondingly appropriate guidance of life. These included Imhotep, vizier and builder of the step pyramid at Saqqara under King Djoser (Third Dynasty); Kagemni, vizier under King Snefru (Fourth Dynasty); and Hardedef, son of King Khufu (Fourth Dynasty, builder of the great pyramid at Giza); but their written works have perished and they are known only by their lasting

---

43. For the Egyptian belief that the historical temple was a continuation of a mythical temple created by the gods at the beginning of the world, see Eve A. E. Raymond, *The Mythical Origin of the Egyptian Temple.*

44. Myśliwiec, *Eighteenth Dynasty before the Amarna Period,* 19–22, plates ix–x, xiv.

reputation for wisdom. The "Maxims of Ptahhotep," vizier under King Djedkare Isesi (Fifth Dynasty), however, have survived, and have been called "the earliest formulation of right conduct to be found in any literature."[45] In the text of Ptahhotep there is strong emphasis upon righteousness (*maat*), and among other items of interest there is a description of old age, which may be compared with Ecclesiastes 12:1–8, and a maxim on prudent conduct at the table of a superior, which may be compared with Proverbs 23:1–2.[46]

Especially in troubled times in later Egyptian history there were further works of wisdom literature. Prophets spoke against the wrongs in society, and expressed hopes for the future, which are comparable to the messianic hopes of the Bible. Probably composed in the First Intermediate Period (c. 2000 B.C.), the "Admonitions of Ipuwer" constitute an arraignment of the ruling king who should have adhered to *maat*, but instead brought strife and tumult to the land, together with constructive exhortations looking toward the renewal of society and a hoped-for golden age in which an ideal king will reign as the good shepherd of all the people.[47] Probably belonging to the same period, the "Prophecy of Neferyt" (the name has also been read as Neferti and, earlier, as Neferrohu) pictures the same disorganization of society and likewise the restoration under a king who will reign in accordance with *maat*, causing the people of his time to rejoice.[48] In the Late Period, during Egyptian decline (c. 1000 B.C.), the "Wisdom of Amunemope" contains a series of proverbs that teach responsibility to and reliance upon god, and offer advice on honesty, integrity, self-control, and kindliness. A striking picture of two trees contrasts the truly tranquil man and the hot-headed man, a picture comparable to Jeremiah 17:5–8 and Psalm 1; many of the proverbs have close parallels in the biblical Book of Proverbs.[49]

## Biblical Relationships

In the preceding chapter it was noted that some Mesopotamian sources are reflected in some legend and law in the Bible, and that this is understandable since Mesopotamia was the original homeland of Abraham. Likewise in the present chapter it has now been seen that there are reminiscences of Egyptian literature in some of the

45. James Henry Breasted, *The Dawn of Conscience*, 129.
46. *ANET*, 412–14.
47. *ANET*, 441–44.
48. *ANET*, 444–46; Hans Goedicke, *The Protocol of Neferyt (The Prophecy of Neferti)*.
49. *ANET*, 421–24.

psalms, wisdom books, and prophetic works of Israel. Again this is not surprising inasmuch as the children of Israel are said to have dwelt in Egypt for a long time (Exod. 12:40), and afterward continued to maintain diplomatic ties with Egypt (e.g., 1 Kings 3:1).

It has also been suggested (by Sigmund Freud and others) that Moses lived in the time of Akhenaten and that Mosaic monotheism was derived from the monotheism of Akhenaten.[50] The date of Moses, however, is more probably in the time of Ramses II the Great (1290–1224 B.C.), since in the time of Moses the children of Israel were enslaved for the building of the city of this king (Raamses, Exod. 1:11). Furthermore the antecedents to which Moses himself appealed were those of the patriarchal age (Exod. 3:6, "I am the God of your father, the God of Abraham, the God of Isaac, and the God of Jacob"), which makes it probable that, although Moses was instructed in all the wisdom of the Egyptians (Acts 7:22), his theological orientation was primarily in the Israelite tradition rather than the Egyptian.[51]

The influence of Egypt was also particularly strong among the Greeks and Romans, especially through the mysteries of Osiris and of Sarapis (see pp. 177, 196).

Apart from continuing influence abroad, however, Egyptian religion is, like Mesopotamian religion, of no small significance in and of itself. It represents the spiritual and cultural achievements of one of the earliest and most creative civilizations known, emphasizing the ordering of life and society in accordance with a normative dimension of existence, and a vision, not yet then convincingly seen in Mesopotamia, of the continuation under ethical demands of personal life in the beyond. Pervading the whole there is too, as enunciated in the Leiden Papyrus cited above (p. 60), a sense of transcendent mystery, and it may be, as some think, that the Egyptian texts and monuments veil still deeper mysteries.[52]

---

50. Sigmund Freud, *Moses and Monotheism,* 26–40; Tertius Chandler, *Moses and the Golden Age,* 6ff.

51. Redford, "Monotheism of the Heretic Pharaoh," 32.

52. R. A. Schwaller de Lubicz, *Symbol and the Symbolic: Ancient Egypt, Science, and the Evolution of Consciousness*; West, *Serpent in the Sky*; Lamy, *Egyptian Mysteries.*

# 3

# Zoroastrian Religion

The homeland of Zoroastrianism was the ancient Aryan land in Central Asia, larger than Iran proper and extending into present Afghanistan to the east and the Soviet Union to the north; especially important was the basin of the Helmand River, the region later called Sakastan (from the Sakas or Scythians), the modern Sistan, now divided between Iran and Afghanistan.[1]

## Sources

The textual sources for Zoroastrianism include in the first instance the authoritative scriptures called the Avesta, written in the so-called Avestan language, an ancient Iranian language similar to Sanskrit and related to Old Persian, Middle Persian, and New Persian.[2] The chief works extant are (1) the Gathas, seventeen verse compositions in "Gathic Avestan," the oldest form of the language, almost certainly by Zarathushtra himself. The Gathas are contained in (2) the *Yasna,* a large liturgical compilation, (3) the *Yashts,* hymns of praise, (4) the *Vendidad,* laws of purity as a means of combating the forces of evil, (5) the *Visparad,* mainly invocations, and (6) the *Nyaishes,* a collection of short litanies composed of fragments from the *Yasna* and *Yashts.* The texts were repeated in worship, handed down orally, and eventually put into writing, but in conquests by Alexander the Great, Arabs, Turks, and Mongols much was destroyed and lost forever.[3]

In the time of the Sasanians (the last Zoroastrian dynasty to rule Iran, A.D. 226–651) and in their language known as Pahlavi (Middle

---

1. *Historical Atlas of Iran; General Atlas of Afghanistan.*
2. Mary Boyce, *Textual Sources for the Study of Zoroastrianism,* 1–8.
3. For these works, see *Sacred Books of the East,* ed. F. Max Müller, vols. 4, 23, 31. For the Gathas in particular, see p. 78.

Persian), a version of the Avesta was made with much explanatory commentary added. This was known as the Zand ("interpretation"), hence the term *Zand-Avesta*. In the course of time an extensive literature dealing with religious subjects also came into existence in the Pahlavi language. At least fifty-five works are known, of which the most important are (1) the *Bundahish* ("original creation")—cosmogony, mythology, legend, and history, (2) the *Dinkard* ("acts of religion")—doctrines, customs, traditions, (3) the *Dadistan-i Dinik* ("religious opinions") of the high priest Manushkihar, (4) the *Epistles of Manushkihar,* (5) the *Selections of Zadsparam,* by the younger brother of Manushkihar, (6) the *Shayast la-shayast* ("proper and improper")— laws of purity, (7) the *Dinai-i Mainog-i Khirad* ("opinions of the Spirit of Wisdom"), (8) the *Shikand-gumanik Vijar* ("doubt-dispelling explanation") in respect to the problem of evil, and (9) the *Arda Viraf Namak* or *Book of Arda Viraf,* describing a visit by the author to heaven and hell. Manushkihar lived around A.D. 881; most of these works are probably from the ninth century. In addition the *Sad Dar* or treatise on "a hundred subjects," written in Persian, is a sort of appendix to the Pahlavi texts and provides a convenient summary of many of the religious customs handed down by the Pahlavi writers.[4]

The compilation of a large Persian chronicle, the *Book of Kings,* was also begun in the Sasanian period, and was completed in an epic version written in New Persian, the *Shah Namah,* in A.D. 1011 by the Persian poet Abul Kasim Mansur, or Firdausi, active under Mahmud, the Muslim ruler of Ghazni in Afghanistan.[5]

## Zoroastrian View of World History

The *Bundahish* provides an account of world events that, although first written down in about the ninth century A.D., no doubt rests upon oral tradition from remote antiquity.[6] According to this account (1.1ff.), Ahura Mazda (Pahlavi, Ohrmazd), the supremely omniscient and good lord of wisdom, dwelling in the region of endless light, realized the existence of Angra Mainyu (Pahlavi, Ahriman), the evil spirit, dwelling in endless darkness, and foresaw his attack and the ultimate outcome of events in which Ahriman would be utterly defeated. To prepare for the final victory Ahura Mazda created the cosmos with all of its elements in a spiritual state, in which everything remained for three

---

4. For these texts, see *Sacred Books of the East,* vols. 5, 18, 24, 37, 47; and Martin Haug and Edward William West, *The Book of Arda Viraf.*

5. Arthur G. Warner and Edmond Warner, *The Sháhnáma of Firdausi Done into English.*

6. *Sacred Books of the East,* 5.3ff.; *CHI* 3.1.350ff.; John R. Hinnells, *Persian Mythology.*

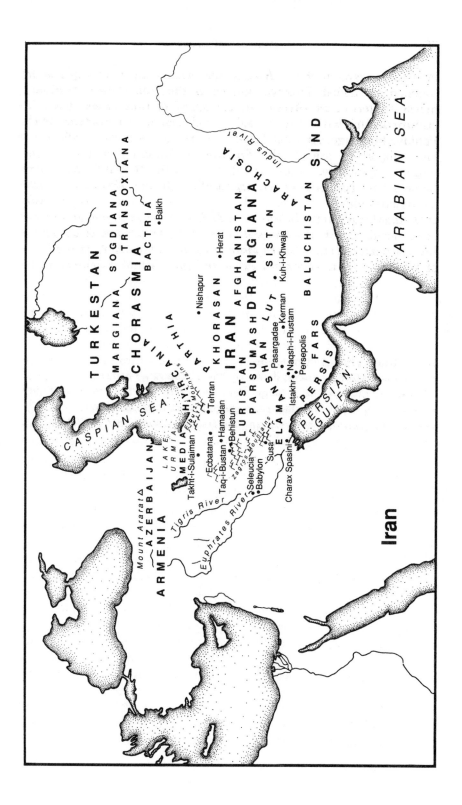

Iran

thousand years (1.8). Beyond that, Ahura Mazda agreed with Ahriman upon a further nine thousand years of conflict between the good and the evil (1.18). Ahura Mazda began by uttering some powerful words, the so-called *Ahuna vairya* prayer (1.21), which has remained the most sacred Zoroastrian prayer (see p. 91).

Confounded by this recital, Ahriman remained in a state of confusion for a second period of three thousand years (1.22), which is also the first three-thousand-year period in the nine thousand years of conflict. During this time Ahura Mazda created beneficent helpers (the Amesha Spentas, see p. 87), and the visible world in the sequence sky, water, earth, plants, animals, and humankind; he also made the stars, the moon, and the sun. But at the end of this period Ahriman and his confederate demons (*daevas, devs*) made their attack upon the world that Ahura Mazda had created (3.10–27). Noxious creatures spread throughout the earth; blight withered vegetation; avarice, want, pain, hunger, disease, lust, and lethargy were spread abroad; smoke and darkness were mingled with fire; and both the primeval ox (Sarsaok) and the primeval man (Gayomard) were injured and passed away. Even though the heavenly angels hurled the demons into hell, the whole creation was disfigured and the world was brought into the duality of a "mixed state."

The next period of three thousand years is divided into three millennia. In the first one thousand years humanity began its course (15.1ff.). Although the primeval man Gayomard was dead, from his seed grew up Mashya and Mashyoi, the first human pair, from whom descended fifteen races of humankind. These were distributed in the seven regions (Avestan, *karshvar*; Pahlavi, *keshvar*) of the world (15.27), namely, Savah on the east, Arzah on the west, Fradadhafshu and Vidadhafshu on the southeast and southwest, Vorubarshti and Vorujarshti on the northeast and northwest, and Khwanirah in the middle (5.9; 11.2–3). Khwanirah, surrounded by the other six regions, was not only the central but also the most favored region. It included Eranshahr, that is, Iran, and here among the descendants of Mashya and Mashyoi lived Hoshyang, from whom arose the Iranians (15.28). The title of Hoshyang was Pishdad, and he became the first world-king and the founder of the Pishdadian dynasty. He was succeeded by Takhmorup (17.4) and by the latter's brother, Yim (17.5; known in the *Shah Namah* as Jamshed). From the time of Hoshyang down to the Sasanians all the legitimate sovereigns of Iran were supposed to be accompanied by divine "glory" (Avestan, *khvarenah*; Pahlavi, *farnah*), a term that carries the connotation of good fortune divinely bestowed, giving rightful kings their victories and approved persons their prosperity and riches.[7] At this time, however, the world was still in a "mixed state," and the Pishdadian kings had to contend continually against the demons.

Although Yim reigned for more than six hundred years, in the end his "glory" departed and, throughout the next and second thousand years, Dahak held sway, the name perhaps referring to a foreign dynasty personified as a single king (31.6; 34.5).

The tyranny of Dahak was so oppressive that at last there was popular rebellion against him. Fredon, a descendant of Yim (Jamshed) and a possessor of the divine "glory," was chosen king and was able to capture Dahak. Confined in Mount Demavend (near Tehran, 17,930 feet—29.9), Dahak will live there until the end of the world, when he will break free to join in the last great battle. The reign of Fredon endured for five hundred years (34.6), the first half of the third one thousand years, but before he died he divided his world empire among his three sons, Salm, Tur, and Eraj. Eraj, the youngest and the favorite son, received the most favored Khwanirah (including Iran), but Salm and Tur, out of jealousy, murdered him and his sons, leaving only his daughter. Eventually Manushkihar, a descendant of the daughter, killed both Tur and Salm in battle and thus avenged the death of Eraj and took the throne himself (31.9–12).[8]

Manushkihar is generally considered to be a member of the Pishdadian dynasty, but at this point the world is no longer ruled by a single king; rather the Iranians and the Turanians to the north are involved in long continued battles. In the struggles the chief protagonists are Franrasyan (31.14–15; called Afrasiyab in the *Shah Namah*), the Turanian king, and Rudhastam (31.41; called Rustam in the *Shah Namah*), the valiant warrior descended from the vassal kings of Sistan and the most famous figure in the Persian national epic (i.e., the *Shah Namah*).

The 120-year reign of Manushkihar begins the second half of this third one thousand years presently under consideration (34.6–7). Manushkihar is followed by Zob (ruled five years; also known as Auzobo), but a genealogy (31.23) identifies Zob as the son of Nodhar the son of Manushkihar, so it is possible that the name of Nodhar has dropped out of the sequential list of *Bundahish* 34. Nodhar was also the father of Tus, who is otherwise known as one of the immortals who will assist in the renovation of the world in the end time (29.6). But Zob

7. Harold Walter Bailey, *Zoroastrian Problems in the Ninth-Century Books*, 1–51.
8. This Manushkihar, a descendant of Eraj and an ancestor of Zarathushtra (*Bundahish* 32.1–2), is not to be confused with the high priest Manushkihar, author of the *Dadistan-i Dinik* and of several epistles.

rather than Tus was evidently considered properly qualified for the succession.

Zob in turn was responsible for the place in the succession of Kai Kavad, for the latter was at the outset only a "trembling child," abandoned on a river and found and adopted by Zob as his own son (31.24). With the fifteen-year reign of Kai Kavad a sequence of sovereigns begins, each of whose names is prefixed with *kai* (Avestan, *kavi*), which here means "king." (The plural is *kayan* ["kings"], and this is therefore called the Kayanian dynasty.) With the shorter reigns of several of the kings, and with other information given about most of them, we have probably at least by now moved from mythological accounts to legendary records concerning historical rulers.[9]

After Kai Kavad the next in the series was his grandson, Kai Kavus. He ruled seventy-five years "till he went to the sky"—a reference to his attempt, narrated in the *Shah Namah*,[10] to fly in a machine lifted by four eagles, each attracted upward by meat set on a spear above its head—and then ruled an additional seventy-five years "after that." In turn Kai Khusrau, a grandson of Kai Kavus (31.25), ruled sixty years; Kai Luhrasp, a more distant descendant of Kai Kavad (31.28), ruled 120 years; and Kai Vishtaspa (also known as Gushtasp), the son of Kai Luhrasp (31.29), ruled thirty years before "the coming of the religion [of Zarathushtra]," the decisive event that marked the end of the preceding nine thousand years and the inauguration of the final three thousand years of world history.

In the final three thousand years the struggle against evil will still go on, but three great helpers of the good, born of the seed of Zarathushtra, will appear, one at the end of each millennium, namely, Ukhshyatereta, Ukhshyatnamah, and Astvatereta. The term *saoshyant* ("helper, benefactor") is applicable to each, but the last, Astvatereta ("he who embodies righteousness"), is generally known simply as Saoshyant. With his work prepared for by his two predecessors and also extended into the six *keshvars* (regions) that surround Khwanirah by six other helpers, Astvatereta will be the great world savior of the end time who, subsequent to a final battle with evil, will conduct the last judgment and the renovation of the universe (*Yasht* 13.128–29; *Bundahish* 30.4–28).

## Zarathushtra

### Date

In the traditional life of Zarathushtra (Pahlavi, Zaratusht; Greek, Zoroaster) the major points are birth (*Dinkard* 7.3.1ff.; *Zadsparam*

---

9. Arthur Emanuel Christensen, *Les Kayanides*.
10. Warner and Warner, *Shāhnāma of Firdausi*, 2.103–4.

14.6ff.); the first "conference" in which he met the spiritual beings, when he was thirty years of age (*Dinkard* 7.3.51–62; *Zadsparam* 21); the winning of his first follower, his cousin Medyomah, after ten years of work (*Zadsparam* 23.1); the acceptance of his religion by Kai Vishtaspa, after two more years, thus when Zarathushtra was forty-two years of age (*Zadsparam* 23.5); and the death of Zarathushtra at the age of seventy-seven years and forty days (*Zadsparam* 23.9).

The decisive event known as "the coming of the religion" could conceivably be interpreted as referring to the birth of Zarathushtra, to his first spiritual "conference," or to the conversion of Kai Vishtaspa. The *Dinkard* (7.8.51), however, states explicitly that the first century of the religion of the Mazda worshipers was reckoned from the time when Zarathushtra came forward to his conference. Since Zarathushtra was himself thirty years of age at this time, and since Kai Vishtaspa had reigned thirty years before the coming of the religion (*Bundahish* 34.7), the traditional chronology dates the birth of Zarathushtra at the time of the accession of Vishtaspa.

After "the coming of the religion" the *Bundahish* (34.7–8) shows Kai Vishtaspa reigning an additional ninety years, to be followed by Vohuman for 112 years, Humai for thirty years, Darai for twelve years, and Darai son of Darai for fourteen years (a total of 258 years), after which is listed Alexander the Ruman for fourteen years. "Darai son of Darai" is presumably Darius III, the last Achaemenid king, whose reign (335–331 B.C.) was ended by Alexander the Great (Macedonian accession 336, death 323 B.C., with fourteen years between; here called "the Ruman" because he came from what was later part of the Roman [Byzantine] Empire). Alexander conquered Persia in 331 B.C. and began his first official regnal year in Babylon on Nisanu 1 (April 3), 330. Counting back 258 years from 330 yields 588 B.C. as the date of "the coming of the religion." If this event were to be taken as the conversion of Vishtaspa when Zarathushtra was forty-two years of age, the resultant dates of Zarathushtra's life would be birth in 630, first "conference" in 600, conversion of Medyomah in 590, conversion of Kai Vishtaspa in 588, and death of Zarathushtra in 553 B.C.[11]

The Muslim scholar al-Biruni, writing in A.D. 1000, gives the same figure of 258 years, but says, "From his [Zoroaster's] appearance till the beginning of the Era of Alexander, they count 258 years."[12] Here "his appearance" may be intended to refer to the birth of Zoroaster, and the "Era of Alexander" is probably a designation common among Islamic authors for the Seleucid era (reckoned from 312/311 B.C.).

11. For these dates, see Walther Hinz, *Zarathustra*, 25; cf. *CHI* 2.415, where Max Mallowan places Zoroaster about one generation before Cyrus the Great (c. 588–529 B.C.), and the conversion of Vishtaspa in about 586 B.C.

12. C. Edward Sachau, *The Chronology of Ancient Nations*, 14 (p. 17 in Lahore reprint).

Assuming these understandings of the statement of al-Biruni, the 258 years lead back from 312 B.C. to 570 for the "appearance" (birth) of Zoroaster, and accordingly the first "conference" is in 540, the conversion of Medyomah in 530, the conversion of Kai Vishtaspa in 528, and the death of Zarathushtra in 493.[13] Although there are yet other ways of dealing with the 258 years, something like the foregoing (either 630–553 or 570–493) has been widely accepted as the traditional date of Zoroaster. The sources that present the figure of 258 years are late, however, and it is not improbable that late and artificial calculations were involved.[14]

The Greeks, on the other hand, assigned an immensely greater antiquity to Zoroaster. Xanthus the Lydian (c. 450 B.C.) was quoted by Diogenes Laertius (c. A.D. 230) as stating that six thousand years elapsed between Zoroaster and the invasion of Xerxes (c. 480 B.C.). Hermodorus, a disciple of Plato (c. 427–347 B.C.), was also quoted by Diogenes as putting Zoroaster five thousand years before the taking of Troy, an event dated by Eratosthenes (c. 276–195 B.C.) to 1194 B.C. Eudoxus (c. 365 B.C.) was said by Pliny the Elder (A.D. 23–79) to have placed the life of Zoroaster six thousand years before the death of Plato, and to have had in this assertion the support of Aristotle (384–322 B.C.). Hermippus (c. 200 B.C.) was also cited by Pliny as dating Zoroaster five thousand years before the Trojan War. Plutarch (c. A.D. 46–120) gave the same date of five thousand years before the Trojan War.[15] A possible basis for such an extremely early date could lie in a misunderstanding of the Zoroastrian belief concerning the preexistence of Zoroaster's spiritual body. According to the *Dinkard* (2.15), the spiritual body of the prophet was framed at the end of the three thousand years of spiritual existence of the elements of the cosmos, that is, six thousand years before Zoroaster was born on earth.[16]

Between these two extremes, the seventh/sixth century B.C. and the seventh/sixth millennium B.C., other evidence points to a date that is more likely and still relatively early. In general the social and cultural milieu reflected in the Gathas is hardly that of the Achaemenid world empire, but rather that of an early seminomadic society. In particular the language of the poems of Zarathushtra in the Gathas is close to that of the hymns in the *Rigveda,* which suggests at least rough contemporaneity. The date of the *Rigveda* is also not precisely established: textual evidence points to 1500 B.C., other internal evidence suggests

---

13. Ernst Herzfeld, "The Traditional Date of Zoroaster," in *Oriental Studies in Honour of Cursetji Erachji Pavry,* ed. Jal Dastur Cursetji Pavry, 132–36.

14. A. Shahbazi, "The 'Traditional Date of Zoroaster' Explained," *BSOAS* 40 (1977): 25–35.

15. Carl Clemen, *Fontes historiae religionis Persicae,* 74, 42, 48.

16. Émile Benveniste, *The Persian Religion According to the Chief Greek Texts,* 15–16.

2500–2000 B.C., and astronomical reckoning is held to put some parts about 4500 B.C. or even earlier.[17] For Zarathushtra a date in the second millennium B.C. appears probable; Zoroastrian scholars suggest around 1700 B.C.[18]

*Geography*

In the first chapter of the *Vendidad* there is a list of sixteen lands that Ahura Mazda created in perfection, into which in a countercreation Ahriman introduced his plagues. The list begins (1.3): "The first of the good lands and countries which I, Ahura Mazda, created, was the *Airyanem Vaejah* [Pahlavi, *Eranvej*] by the good river Daitya." The name *Airyanem Vaejah* is probably a general term, meaning something like the "Aryan expanse." Of the river Daitya (Pahlavi, Daitik) the *Bundahish* says that it "comes out from *Airyanem Vaejah*, and goes out through the hill country" (20.13) and is "the chief of streams" (24.14). It is probably also identical with "the Vanguhi of wide renown" (*Yasht* 8.2), or the Vanguhi Daitya, but it is not otherwise identifiable with a presently known river.[19] There follow, however, the names of specific lands (the second to the sixteenth items in *Vendidad* 1), of which those plainly identifiable are Sughda (Sogdiana), Mouru (Margiana), Bakhdhi (Bactria), Haroyu (Herat), Harauvati (Arachosia), Haetumant (Drangiana, later Sistan, the region of the Haetumant/Helmand River), and Hapta Hindu (Rig Vedic Sapta Sindhu, the Seven Rivers of the Indus valley).

17. Venkatarama Raghavan, "Hinduism," in *Historical Atlas of the Religions of the World,* ed. Isma'il Rāgī al-Fārūqī, 73. For an extremely early date for the Vedas on astronomical grounds, and for a date of 7129–7052 B.C. for the life of Zarathushtra, see Bal Gangadhar Tilak, *The Orion; or, Researches into the Antiquity of the Vedas;* see also Hormusjee Shapoorjee Spencer, *Are the Gathas Pre-Vedic? and, The Age of Zarathushtra.*

18. Maneckji Nusservanji Dhalla, *Zoroastrian Theology,* 11; and idem, *History of Zoroastrianism,* 11, 13 (Gathic period and Zarathushtra at about 1000 B.C.); Gherardo Gnoli, *Zoroaster's Time and Homeland,* 175 (Zoroaster between the end of the second and the beginning of the first millennium B.C.); Mary Boyce, *A History of Zoroastrianism,* 1.3 (the *Rigveda* around 1700 B.C., Zarathushtra not later than about 1000 B.C.); and idem, *Textual Sources for the Study of Zoroastrianism,* 11, 22 (Zarathushtra between 1400 and 1200 B.C.). For skepticism about this early date, see Richard Nelson Frye, *The History of Ancient Iran,* 57–58.

For modern Zoroastrian scholars (Zabih Behrooz, Ali A. Jafarey), see *The Zoroastrian* 3.7 (Aug. 1985): 2 (Zarathushtra around 1700 B.C.); 3.1 (Feb. 1985): 2, and 5.5 (Oct–Nov. 1987): 1 (birth of Zarathushtra in the spring of 1767 B.C.); 5.6 (Nov.–Dec. 1987): 4 (with Zarathushtra's birth in 1767, his conversion of Vishtaspa falls in the year 1725; to commemorate the day on which Vishtaspa chose his religion, Zarathushtra founded an observatory in the Kayanian capital [now Zabol] on an auspicious day when Aries entered the vernal equinox to mark the beginning of the New Year [Zoroastrian Nowruz]; the date calculated, because of the precession of the equinoxes, to have been March 21 in 1725 B.C.).

19. Josef Markwart, *Wehrot und Arang: Untersuchungen zur mythischen und geschichtlichen Landeskunde von Ostiran,* 122.

In *Yasht* 10 (*Mihir Yasht*) there is a series of hymns of praise addressed to Mithra as the god of heavenly light, whose victorious power is manifest in the sun. The hymn in 10.13–16 describes the sun as it rises over the "lofty mountain range" in the east and sweeps on over the seven regions (*keshvars*) of the whole world, the central one of which is "this bright *keshvar* of Khwanirah."[20] The hymn names Mithra and begins:

> Who first of the heavenly gods reaches over the Hara, before the undying, swift-horsed sun; who, foremost in a golden array, takes hold of the beautiful summits, and from thence looks over the abode of the Aryans [*Airyo Shayana*] with a beneficent eye.

Then there follows a description of this "abode of the Aryans":

> Where the valiant chiefs draw up their many troops in array; where the high mountains, rich in pastures and waters, yield plenty to the cattle; where the deep lakes, with salt waters, stand; where wide-flowing rivers swell and hurry toward. . . .

Here several names follow and, of the plainly recognizable ones, we find Mouru, Haroyu, and Sughdha—as in *Vendidad* 1—and also Khwarezm (Chorasmia).

In this text the "abode of the Aryans" (*Airyo Shayana*) is probably synonymous with the "Aryan expanse" (*Airyanem Vaejah*) in the *Vendidad*. The specific lands recognizably named in the two texts are thus in modern eastern Iran (from the southeast to the northeast) and in adjacent regions in Soviet Central Asia, Afghanistan, and the Punjab in Pakistan. The "Aryan expanse" is thus substantially the same as the Ariana described by Strabo (15.2.8; following Eratosthenes, c. 276–195 B.C.) as extending from the Indus on the east to the Arabian Sea on the south, and from the Paropamisus range (Hindu Kush) and the mountains that continue it to the Caspian Gates on the north, to the borders of Media and Persis on the west. Likewise the Hara, over which (in *Yasht* 10.13) Mithra comes to look upon this region, must be the "lofty mountain range" (*hara berezaiti*) named in *Yasht* 19.1 and *Bundahish* 5.3–4, and must be the Hindu Kush Mountains. The *Bundahish* (29.12) states that *Airyanem Vaejah* "is in the direction of Ataropatakan," that is, Azerbaijan in the northwest; the *hara berezaiti* was later likewise thought to be the Elburz Mountains south

20. Ilya Gershevitch, *The Avestan Hymn to Mithra*; F. B. J. Kuiper, "Remarks on 'The Avestan Hymn to Mithra,'" *IIJ* 5 (1961–1962): 36–60; Mary Boyce, "On Mithra's Part in Zoroastrianism," *BSOAS* 32 (1969): 10–34.

of the Caspian Sea. But these are probably only the later opinions of the Zoroastrian Magi, originally a tribe of the Medes (Herodotus 1.101), who settled in the northwest and thus were naturally inclined to relate traditional places to their own region. The older references in the Avesta as just cited, however, plainly describe the region with which the Zoroastrians were first familiar and thus the region that must have been the homeland of Zarathushtra himself (with his birthplace probably in the northeast of Iran, and work at Vishtaspa's court probably in the southeast of Iran).[21]

As to the center of the Kayanian dynasty, with whose king Vishtaspa Zarathushtra was closely associated, the *Bundahish* (21.7) states, "Kayansih is . . . where the home of the Kayan race is." In an earlier passage of the same work (13.6ff.), which reckons that there are twenty-three small salt "seas" or lakes (the same word is used for both), Kayansih is described as follows (13.16–17):

Of the small seas that which was most wholesome was the sea Kayansih . . . in Sakastan; at first, noxious creatures, snakes, and lizards were not in it, and the water was sweeter than in any of the other seas; later it became salt. . . . When the renovation of the universe occurs it will again become sweet.

In Pahlavi the name *Kayansih* corresponds with the Avestan *Kasaoya.* The lake is mentioned under the latter form of the name in the statement that the royal glory (*khvarenah*) accompanies him "who rules there where is the Lake Kasaoya, which receives the Haetumant River; there where stands Mount Ushidhau, surrounded by waters, that run from the mountain" (*Yasht* 19.66).

The name *Haetumant* means "dam-full," referring to a network of irrigation canals, and is also the name of a land (*Vendidad* 1.14). Here it is the name of the major river that gives its name to the land, namely, the modern Helmand, which comes down from the Hindu Kush and flows through Afghanistan to a great basin on the border of Afghanistan and Iran. The Sakas (Scythians), nomadic invaders from Central Asia, settled here in the second century B.C. (and also moved into India), and it is from them that the region became known as Sakastan (modern Sistan). In the Persian Empire the region was the satrapy of Drangiana, from the yet earlier name *Zranka,* which means "sea-land." The lake in question—Kasaoya/Kayansih—which is in Sakastan and receives the Haetumant River, is therefore identifiable

---

21. Gnoli, *Zoroaster's Time and Homeland,* 130–31; Ali A. Jafarey in *The Zoroastrian* 5.3 (June–July 1987): 5–7.

with the lake now called Hamun ("the desert"; also Zarah, "the sea") or Hamun-i Helmand, and is adjacent to the present town of Zabol in the delta of the Helmand in Sistan in southeastern Iran.

Near Lake Hamun and in a shallow depression (which in winter is flooded to become a wide stretch of water), rises an impressive, broad, flat-topped hill of black basalt, known as the Kuh-i Khwaja, the "hill of the lord." The place may have been sacred in very ancient times, and it seems likely that it is the Mount Ushidhau ("surrounded by waters") in *Yasht* 19. Mount Ushidhau is called "the keeper of understanding" (*ushi-darena*—*Yasht* 1.31), and from this phrase comes the Pahlavi name Mount Aushdashtar (*Bundahish* 12.15, where the mount is located in Sistan). The great significance of "the mountain Ushidarena . . . with its sacred brilliance" (*Yasna* 1.14) is that it is the seat of the *khvarenah,* the divine glory of the kings, to which *Yashts* 18 and 19, for example, are largely devoted.

It is therefore most probable that the present Zabol, together with Lake Hamun and the Kuh-i Khwaja, represents the ancient capital of the Kayanian kings. In fact the "Kayani" tribes still found in the region continue to claim descent from the Avestan Kayanians. Archeological excavations are also beginning to invite comparisons between the most ancient civilization in the Helmand valley and its contemporary civilizations in the Indus valley to the east and in Mesopotamia and Egypt to the west. By present reckoning from Greenwich, the longitude of Zabol is sixty-one degrees east, but ancient names of the place were "center-of-the-earth" and "meridian" (*Yasht* 10.140; 12.21; *Vendidad* 10.14.18). When the sun was at high noon over this point it was indeed setting in the far east of Asia and rising in the far west of Europe, an appropriate place for the observatory said to have been founded here by Zarathushtra in 1725 B.C.[22]

It is true that Ammianus Marcellinus (c. A.D. 360) speaks of "the Bactrian Zoroaster" (23.6.32), and that al-Biruni and the *Shah Namah* associate Vishtaspa and Zoroaster with the city of Balkh in Bactria, but the placement of the court of Vishtaspa that far northeast is probably a late tradition reflecting the later time when the dominant power was in that region.

It is likely, therefore, that the court of Kai Vishtaspa was at Zabol and vicinity, and that it was here that Zarathushtra won the allegiance of the king, and from here that Zarathushtra's religion, with royal support, began to spread more widely. In this respect it is significant

---

22. Zabih Behrooz, *Taghvim va Tarikh dar Iran* (Calendar and Chronicle in Iran); and other works summarized in *The Zoroastrian* 2.11 (Dec. 1984): 3–5; Ali A. Jafarey in *The Zoroastrian* 5.6 (Nov.–Dec. 1987): 4–6.

that Saoshyant, the future world savior, is to come from Lake Hamun (Kasaoya/Kayansih), as indicated, for example, in *Yasht* 19.92, which looks forward to the time "when Astvatereta shall rise up from the Kasaoya water, messenger of Mazda Ahura." Saoshyant is to be born of the seed of Zarathushtra, so that the future savior is in effect a reappearance of the prophet himself, and it is probable that belief in the reappearance of a prophet would be connected with the place where the prophet lived. Therefore it is a reasonable surmise that the hill (Kuh-i Khwaja) in the lake was a place of importance in the life of Zarathushtra, perhaps a place of meditation.[23]

## Society

Society at the time of Zarathushtra, reflected in the Avesta, was seminomadic and pastoral, a collectivity of "cattle-[and-]men" (*pasu-vira*) according to a traditional Avestan expression. The chief categories of persons, indicated by Gathic terms, are *nar*, "man," that is, the fighting man or warrior; *vastar*, "pasturer," that is, the herdsman who tends the cattle in their grazing grounds (these two categories often combined in the one person who is both a herdsman and a warrior); and *zaotar*, "priest," either "he who makes the offerings" or "he who invokes."[24] In the Gathas there is also frequent mention of the *karapan* and the *kavi*. The root *karap* of the former term corresponds with the Sanskrit *kalp* (the sound *l* being unknown in Avestan and always represented by *r*), which means "to perform a ceremony"; the *karapan* is therefore probably a ritualistic priest, the performer of the sacrificial rites of the old religion.[25] The word *kavi* means "poet" in Sanskrit, and is used in the Vedas to refer to priests and seers, particularly the seer who pronounces a magically potent spell (a *kavya*).[26] But here *kavi* (Pahlavi, *kai*) can also mean a princely ruler or king, and Vishtaspa, who became the royal patron of Zarathushtra, and Vishtaspa's ancestors bore that title. In the Gathas, however, both the *karapan*s (priests) and the *kavi*s (their princely helpers) appear as the opponents of Zarathushtra, who spoke against them strongly, disputed with them upon occasion at a great assembly, and was cast into prison temporarily because of their hostility.

Zarathushtra calls himself in the Gathas both a priest (*zaotar*,

23. Ernst Herzfeld, *The Persian Empire: Studies in Geography and Ethnography of the Ancient Near East*, 331–32.

24. Boyce, *History of Zoroastrianism*, 1.5–6; and idem, *Textual Sources for the Study of Zoroastrianism*, 9.

25. Martin Haug, *Essays on the Sacred Language, Writings, and Religion of the Parsis*, 289–90.

26. John Brough, "Soma and *Amanita Muscaria*," BSOAS 34 (1971): 22–36, 339.

equivalent to the Vedic *hotar*; *Yasna* 33.6) and a prophet (50.6), and he repeatedly (50.5; etc.) uses in connection with himself the terms *manthran* and *manthra,* the equivalents of the Vedic *mantrin* and *mantra.*[27] The *manthran/mantrin* is one "knowing the *manthras/mantras*," which is an "instrument of thought," an inspired utterance of power. In this respect Zarathushtra is not like his opponents, the *kavis*, with their presumably magical spells, but may be compared rather with the Vedic *rishis*, whose poetic utterances express profound intuitions achieved by mental energy and visionary insight.[28] In fact the poems of Zarathushtra in the Gathas are most often impassioned appeals for understanding, addressed to Ahura Mazda with thankfulness and devotion—for example, "This do I ask thee, tell me truly, O Ahura" (*Yasna* 44.1)—and he describes himself as "one who knows" (*vaedemna*), an initiate who possesses divinely inspired wisdom (*Yasna* 28.5).[29]

## Life

Many of the sources listed at the beginning of this chapter contain traditional biographical information concerning Zarathushtra, while the Gathas in particular are believed to be the utterances of the prophet himself. There are seventeen Gathas, commonly called hymns, arranged in five groups; each group is called a Gatha and, except for the first group, is named for its opening word or words. The five groups are found in the *Yasna* as follows: (1) *Gatha Ahunavaiti* (*Yasna* 28–34), (2) *Gatha Ushtavaiti* (*Yasna* 43–46), (3) *Gatha Spenta Mainyu* (*Yasna* 47–50), (4) *Gatha Vohu Khshathra* (*Yasna* 51), and (5) *Gatha Vahishta Ishti* (*Yasna* 53).[30]

The *Dinkard* (7.2ff.), *Zadsparam* (13ff.), and other sources tell of the life of Zarathushtra; his genealogy (*Dinkard* 7.2.70; *Zadsparam* 13.6; *Bundahish* 32) is traced back to Manushkihar, Hoshyang, and even to Mashya and Gayomard. A nearer ancestor in the list is Spitaman, and it was from this personage that the family designation of Spitama was derived. Zarathushtra's father was Porushasp and his mother, Dughda. In a list and description of rivers in the *Bundahish* it is stated: "The Daraja River is in *Airyanem Vaejah*, on the bank of

27. Mary Boyce, "Zoroaster the Priest," *BSOAS* 33 (1970): 22–36.

28. Jan Gonda, *The Vision of the Vedic Poets.*

29. For Zarathushtra as priest, prophet, and inspired poet, see C. J. Bleeker, "Wer war Zarathustra?" *Persica* 7 (1975–1978): 36–37.

30. For the Gathas, see Jacques Duchesne-Guillemin, *The Hymns of Zarathustra*; S. Insler, *The Gāthās of Zarathustra*; Irach J. S. Taraporewala, *The Divine Songs of Zarathushtra*. The extended quotations of the Gathas that follow in the present book are from the translation by Taraporewala.

which was the dwelling of Porushasp, the father of Zaratusht" (20.32). A little later it is explicitly stated that Zarathushtra was born at this place: "The Daraja River is the chief of exalted rivers, for the dwelling of the father of Zaratusht was on its banks, and Zaratusht was born there" (24.15). Specific identification of the Daraja with a presently known river is lacking, but the river and the birthplace of Zarathushtra are most probably to be located in northeastern Iran.[31] It is true that in *Zadsparam* (16.12) it is stated that "Zaratusht arose from Ragh [the modern city of Ray, just to the south of Tehran]," but like the late location of *Airyanem Vaejah* in the direction of Azerbaijan (*Bundahish* 29.12; see pp. 74–75), this is probably a late localization at a place of importance to the Median Magi, facilitated by the supposition that the city was identifiable with the similarly named eastern region of Ragha (*Vendidad* 1.16). The birthday of Zarathushtra is celebrated by his followers on the day of Hordad (Avestan, Haurvatat) in the month of Farvardin, the sixth day of the first month (Mar.–April) in the Zoroastrian calendar.[32]

At the age of fifteen an Iranian youth was reckoned to have reached maturity and was invested with a sacred girdle, and it was so with Zarathushtra (*Zadsparam* 20.2). At the age of twenty Zarathushtra left home, against the wishes of his parents, and traveled about inquiring about righteousness and compassion (*Zadsparam* 20.7). At the age of thirty he experienced his first spiritual "conference" (*Dinkard* 7.3.51–62; *Zadsparam* 21). The event transpired at a place on the Daitya River (*Vendidad* 1.3), where people came together from many quarters for the midspring festival (*Maidhyoizaremaya*), which took place forty-five days after New Year's Day (the latter is Nowruz, at the spring equinox).[33] Starting out on the day of Anagran in the month of Spendarmad (the last day of the twelfth month, Feb.–Mar.), Zarathushtra was at the river on the day of Daipad-Mihr in the month of Ardvahisht (the fifteenth day of the second month, April–May; *Zadsparam* 21.1–4).

At the appointed time and place on the river Zarathushtra was evidently to function in his capacity as a priest, and in particular with respect to the preparation of the *haoma* (Vedic, *soma*) sacrifice (*Zadsparam* 21.5ff.). This plant has not been positively identified but was probably crushed and mixed with water to produce a drink that gave exhilaration and inspiration. In India the *Śatapatha Brahmana* (5.1.2.10; 5.1.5.28; cf. 12.8.1.4) praises the beneficial gifts of the *soma*

31. Ali A. Jafarey in *The Zoroastrian* 5.5 (Oct.–Nov. 1987): 1.

32. For the months and days of the Zoroastrian calendar, see *Bundahish* 25.20; 27.24; see also Boyce, *Textual Sources for the Study of Zoroastrianism*, 19–20.

33. For the Zoroastrian festivals, see Mary Boyce, "On the Calendar of Zoroastrian Feasts," *BSOAS* 33 (1970): 513–39; and idem, *Textual Sources for the Study of Zoroastrianism*, 18.

juice and contrasts it with the damaging effects of an evidently fermented and intoxicating liquor called *sura*: "The *soma* is truth, prosperity, light, and the *sura* untruth, misery, darkness." In the Zoroastrian literature an entire section of the *Yasna* (9–11) is devoted to the *haoma*. In one passage (10.5), it is described as having stems, branches, and shoots—thus, apparently a tall plant (hardly a mushroom). In another passage (10.8–9) the drink is spoken of much as in the *Śatapatha Brahmana*: not like intoxicants that induce violence, but as revealing light and truth, going hand in hand with friendship, and coming to bring healing. Yet again *haoma* is personified, saluted, and supplicated (*Yasna* 11.10):

> To thee, O holy Haoma . . . I offer this my person . . . to Haoma the effective do I offer it, and to the sacred exhilaration which he bestows; and do thou grant to me . . . O holy Haoma, thou that drivest death afar, the best world of the saints, shining, all brilliant.[34]

In the performance of his priestly task Zarathushtra went accordingly at dawn into the stream to procure the needed water. There were four channels of the Daitya, and he waded through the first three, each deeper than the last, and out into the fourth, the deepest of all, in order to procure the very purest water. Returning to the main bank, he saw a vision. A shining personage, the archangel Vohu Manah, met him and asked, "Who mayest thou be, and from whom of them mayest thou be? Also what is mostly thy desire, and the endeavor in thy existence?" Zarathushtra replied, "I am Zaratusht of the Spitamas; among the existences righteousness is more my desire, and my wish is that I may become aware of the will of the sacred beings, and may practice so much righteousness as they exhibit to me in the pure existence." Upon this reply Vohu Manah led Zarathushtra "to an assembly of the spirits," where Zarathushtra offered homage to Ahura Mazda and the archangels, and "sat down in the seat of the inquirers," whereupon Ahura Mazda instructed him in the doctrines of the pure religion (*Zadsparam* 21.9ff.). This was the first spiritual "conference" of Zarathushtra.

In the Gathas Zarathushtra narrates the same decisive event in his

---

34. See Brough, "Soma and *Amanita Muscaria*," 331–62, for the difference between the divine *soma* and the harmful and presumably fermented *sura*, and against R. Gordon Wasson's identification of the Soma plant as the red, white-spotted mushroom *Amanita muscaria*; also against identification as the Himalayan *Ephedra intermedia*. For another view see Ilya Gershevitch, "An Iranianist's View of the Soma Controversy," in *Mémorial Jean de Menasce*, ed. P. Gignoux and A. Tafazzoli, 45–75.

own words (*Yasna* 43.7–8, 12, 15). The Wise Lord (Ahura Mazda) came to him as Good Mind (Vohu Manah) and asked him who he was and what he desired, and he replied that he was Zarathushtra, dedicated to the Good and, as far as he was able, an inveterate adversary of the follower of Untruth, wishing always to follow the Truth and thus to gain Wisdom. So Good Mind taught him that quiet and silent meditation was the best procedure for the growth of the soul, and it was in this way that Zarathushtra received the message that he was to proclaim.

From this beginning Zarathushtra knew that he had been chosen for his mission by the Wise Lord (44.11), but he knew too that his zeal to carry out what the Lord had told him was the greatest good, would bring him into many difficulties (43.11). In fact Zarathushtra met much opposition and felt himself called upon to contend valiantly against many forms of what to him was wickedness. In the Gathas he speaks in general against the strong who oppress the weak (34.8), and in particular against the false teachers who distort the word of Ahura Mazda and turn people away from the best course of action (32.9–14). Referring to the priests of the old religion (*karapan*s) and their princely helpers (*kavi*s), he says, "Through [their] powers the priests and the princes would yoke mankind to evil acts for destroying Life" (46.11). So he asks (48.10):

> When shall they smite down the rotting mass of this infatuation,
>   through which the priests falsely fascinate [people],
>   as also [do] the wicked rulers of the lands through [their evil]
>     intent?

And he urges his followers to oppose the forces of evil through thought and word and deed, and thus frustrate the wicked designs of the followers of Untruth (33.2).

At one point Zarathushtra felt that he was opposed on every hand, left alone, isolated, and friendless. He did not know where to turn and, in his perplexity and loneliness, he asked (46.1):

> To what land shall I bend [my steps]? Whither shall I turn to go?
> They hold [me] apart from the self-reliant and from the friends;
>   [there is] no satisfaction for me, which [may come] through [my] co-
>     workers,
>   nor yet [from these] rulers of the land, who [are] followers of
>     Untruth;
>   how [then] shall I satisfy thee, O Mazda Ahura?

Although his own possessions and friends were few, he asked that the Wise Lord might give him support as a dear friend (46.2). As he went on his way he prayed for strength to traverse roads, mountains, forests, and rivers, and he prayed for wisdom and health to promote the religion (*Yasht* 16). He also continued to receive revelations. Finally, ten years after his first spiritual conference, when he was forty years of age, he won his first convert—his own cousin Maidhyo-maungha or Medyomah, the son of Arastai (Arastai and Zarathush-tra's father, Porushasp, were brothers). "On the completion of revelation, that is, at the end of ten years, Medyomah, son of Arastai, became faithful to Zaratusht"; but Zarathushtra said despondently, "In ten years only one man has been attracted by me" (*Zadsparam* 23.1–2).

This, however, marked a turning point. By "the advice and command of Ahura Mazda" Zarathushtra took his departure alone to the residence of Kai Vishtaspa (*Dinkard* 7.4.65). By the river Daitya Zarathushtra offered sacrifice and prayed that he might bring both Kai Vishtaspa and his queen Hutaosa "to think according to the religion, to speak according to the religion, to do according to the religion" (*Yasht* 5.104–5; 9.25–26). Before the conversion of the king and queen was accomplished, however, Zarathushtra experienced a "terrible combat with evil," in which he was slandered by the priests of the old religion, suffered imprisonment and almost died, and was involved "in controversy about the religion with the famous learned of the realm" (*Dinkard* 7.4.69–73).

But with the conversion of Kai Vishtaspa, Zarathushtra had a powerful supporter. In the Gathas (*Yasna* 46.14) in answer to the question, "Who is thy friend?" Zarathushtra replies that it is Kai Vishtaspa. Vishtaspa was "the gallant one, who . . . made wide room for the holy religion, who made himself the arm and support of this law of Ahura, of this law of Zarathushtra" (*Yasht* 13.99). As the author of the *Dinkard* says (7.4.63), if Vishtaspa and the people of that time had not accepted the religion announced by Zarathushtra, "it would not have reached unto us."

Other praiseworthy supporters of Zarathushtra, named in the Gathas, are descendants of Fryana the Turanian and two members of the Hvogva family, Frashaoshtra and Jamaspa (*Yasna* 46.12, 16–17; 49.8–9). There is favorable mention, also, of the Spitamas (46.15), so it would appear that after possible earlier hostility (46.1) the family of Zarathushtra also stood with him.

Zarathushtra was married three times but only the third wife's name is preserved, namely, Hvovi. By his first wife he had a son and three daughters, by the second wife two more sons. The sons were Isatvastra a priest, Urvatatnara an agriculturalist, and Hvarechithra a warrior; the daughters were Freni, Thriti, and Pouruchista (*Yasht* 13.98, 139; *Bundahish* 32.5–6). Pouruchista, the youngest, was married to Jamaspa, the prime minister of Kai Vishtaspa, and one of the Gathas tells about the wedding (*Yasna* 53). In further interrelationship Frashaoshtra was the father of Hvovi and gave her in marriage to Zarathushtra. Hvovi was childless, but (in the most developed form of the tradition) from the seed of Zarathushtra, preserved in Lake Kasaoya, in the final three thousand years of world history three holy maids will bear the three future saviors ("helpers of the good"), namely, Srutatfedhri the mother of Ukhshyatereta, Vanghufedhri the mother of Ukhshyatnamah, and Eredatfedhri the mother of Saoshyant (*Yasht* 13.62, 141–42).

The acceptance of the religion of Zarathushtra by Kai Vishtaspa involved the king in many battles with hostile princes, the latter evidently adherents of the old religion. In these struggles Vishtaspa prays that he "may overcome Tathryavant of the bad religion, and Peshana the worshiper of the *daeva*s, and the wicked Arejataspa, in the battles of this world" (*Yasht* 5.109). Those fighting together with Vishtaspa are his prime minister Jamaspa, who prays for victory when he sees "the army of the wicked, of the worshipers of the *daeva*s, coming from afar in battle array" (5.68–69); his brother Zairivairi, who prays that he "may overcome Peshochangha the corpse-burier [referring to the burial custom of the old religion, repudiated in Zoroastrianism], Humayaka the worshiper of the *daeva*s, and the wicked Arejataspa" (5.113); and Vishtaspa's own son, "the holy and gallant Spentodata" (13.103).

The "wicked Arejataspa" (Pahlavi, Arjasp) was the king of Turan (also called the king of the Hyaonas; Pahlavi, Khyons—*Yasht* 9.30) and "the mightiest of the tyrants at that time, and the most hideous of all." It was he who sent envoys to Vishtaspa demanding that Vishtaspa submit to him and abandon the religion of Zarathushtra, which led to an "awful battle," in which Vishtaspa was victorious over Arejataspa and other foreigners (*Dinkard* 7.4.77, 87; 7.5.7). The incursion of the Khyons into the country of Iran took place in the thirtieth year of the Zoroastrian religion (*Zadsparam* 23.8), and the war was remembered as "the war of the religion" (*Bundahish* 12.33).

Spentodata (Pahlavi, Spenddad) is called Isfendiyad or Isfandiyar in sources of the Muslim period (which also reflect the late opinions localizing Zoroastrian events in Azerbaijan and Balkh), and he plays a very important part in the spread of the religion of Zarathushtra and in the wars of the Iranians against the Turanians. Thus al-Biruni writes in his work on India (1.10):

Zarathushtra went forth from Adharbaijan [Azerbaijan] and preached Magism in Balkh. His doctrines came into favor with King Gushtasp [Vishtaspa], and his son Isfendiyad spread the new faith both in east and west, both by force and by treaties. He founded fire temples throughout his whole empire, from the frontiers of China to those of the Greek empire. The succeeding kings made their religion [i.e., Zoroastrianism] the obligatory state religion for Persis and Iraq.[35]

Likewise in the account of the Irano-Turanian wars in the *Shah Namah* we learn of Isfandiyar's heroic part in achieving the victory through which the religion of Zarathushtra was established on a firm foundation, and we are also told that Zarathushtra himself lost his life when the Turanians stormed Balkh and destroyed the Zoroastrian temple of Nush Azar:

> The host reached Balkh, the world was wrecked with sack
> And slaughter. Making for the Fane of Fire [Nush Azar],
> For hall and palace decked with gold, they gave
> Them and the Zandavasta to the flames.
> The fane had eighty priests, God's worshipers,
> And all before the Fire the Turkmans slew,
> And swept that cult away. The Fire, that erst
> Zarduhsht had litten, of their blood did die;
> Who slew that priest himself I know not I.

The same story is repeated a little later, and it is also told how a messenger carried to the absent Vishtaspa the news of the fall of the city, of the death of Luhrasp, the father of Vishtaspa, and of the slaying of Zarathushtra:

>                     The Turkmans
> Have slain at Balkh Luhrasp, the king of kings,
> And turned our days to gloom and bitterness,
> Proceeded thence to Nush Azar and there
> Beheaded both Zarduhsht and all the archmages,
> Quenched in whose blood the radiant Fire expired.[36]

In Zoroastrian tradition the killing of Zarathushtra is ascribed to Bradro-resh the Tur (*Dinkard* 5.3.2) or Tur-i Bradar-vakhsh "by whom the best of men [i.e., Zarathushtra] was put to death" (*Dadistan-i Dinik* 72.8). The date is also given (*Zadsparam* 23.9): "In the forty-seventh year Zarathusht passes away, who attains 77 years and 40

---

35. C. Edward Sachau, *Alberuni's India*, 1.21.
36. Warner and Warner, *Shāhnāma of Firdausi*, 5.92–93.

days in the month Ardavahisto on the day Khur [the eleventh day of the second month, April–May]."

### Message

In his references to the realm of the divine in the Gathas, Zarathushtra uses terms from a common Aryan heritage, but in his own distinctive way. The Gathic term *ahura* is the Aryan word for "lord" (cognate with the Vedic *asura*), which in the oldest parts of the *Rigveda* denotes a god or spirit, although it later comes to have the reverse sense of an evil spirit or demon. Also the *daevas* in the Gathas (the Vedic *devas*, "shining ones") are to Zarathushtra false gods (i.e., the deities of the old religion) to be rejected as maleficent supernatural beings. For Zarathushtra the supreme lord (*ahura*) is characterized above all by supreme intellect and wisdom (*mazda*; corresponding to Vedic *medha*). With emphasis upon this characteristic, the supreme being is named the Wise One (Mazda occurs alone 116 times in the Gathas); with emphasis upon his sovereignty he is called Lord (Ahura used alone sixty-four times); and together he is the Wise Lord (Mazda Ahura twenty-eight times) or the Lord Wise (Ahura Mazda six times); while in Pahlavi Ahura Mazda becomes Ohrmazd.

From the Gathas we gather that it is by way of his own wondering and thoughtful questioning that Zarathushtra comes to his belief in the Wise Lord and to the elements of his own teachings. In *Yasna* 44, for example, each of twenty stanzas (except the last) begins with the question, "This do I ask thee, tell me truly, O Ahura. . . ." The questions look to the cosmos, for example (44.3–5):

> What Being laid down the path of the sun and of the stars?
> Who [is it] through whom the moon waxes [and] wanes alternately?
> · · · · · · · · · · · · · · · · · · · · · · · · ·
> What Being holds [apart] the earth and even the heavens also?
> Who [holds] apart the waters and the plants?
> Who imparts swiftness to the wind and to the dark clouds?
> · · · · · · · · · · · · · · · · · · · · · · · ·
> What Great Architect fashioned the realms of light and also the
> realms of darkness?

Turning to the order of things in its bearing on human life, the questions continue (44.5, 7):

> What Great Architect fashioned sleep and also activity?
> Who [is it] through whom [have arisen] dawn, day, and night,
> that admonish the wise about the purpose [of life]?
> · · · · · · · · · · · · · · · · · · · · · · ·
> Who made the son dutiful to the father [even] with [his] living breath?

The answer to such questions is not difficult to find. In the very asking of them Zarathushtra is striving to recognize the Wise One as the creator of all things (44.7). Even as through the mind Zarathushtra has come to know the Wise One, so it must be through the mind—indeed, through a Good Mind—that the Wise One has done everything (31.8, 11):

> So that I might realize thee, [as] the Most Ancient,
>     [and] ever, O Mazda, [as] the Youngest in [my] mind,
>     [as] the Father of Good Mind [Vohu Manah].
> . . . . . . . . . . . . . . . . . .
> Since for us, O Mazda, from the beginning
>     thou didst create bodies and also souls,
>     and [mental] powers through thine own thought.

But questions are to be asked not only about things as they are but also about the outcome of things (44.13, 15–16, 19):

> How shall we keep away Untruth from us?
> . . . . . . . . . . . . . . . .
> When both the hosts came together . . .
>     [then] in accordance with these laws which thou, O Mazda, hast laid down,
>     where, [and] to which of the two, wouldst thou grant the victory?
> . . . . . . . . . . . . . . . . . . . . . . . .
> Who [shall be] the victor protecting through thy teaching [all those]
>     that exist?
> . . . . . . . . . . . . . . . . . . . . . . . .
> [He] who gives not the due reward to the deserving,
> when, indeed, [the latter] goes up to him with Truth,
>     to such what punishment for this shall come here now?
>     [I am] sure of that which shall come to him at last.

In respect to questions such as these Zarathushtra perceives that the supreme being is not only the Wise One (Mazda) who has made all things, but also the Lord (Ahura) who is responsible for all that is right and good (31.7):

> Who through that [holy word] first decreed
>     [that his] Light shall stream forth through heavenly lights,
> He himself in his wisdom [is] the creator of Eternal Law [asha].

The word asha is the equivalent of the Sanskrit rita or "cosmic order," so here also the meaning is the principle that governs the world, hence order, truth, righteousness, and the like. It seems plainly evident that for Zarathushtra the Wise Lord is the one god, the good creator and ruler of all. Herein is the ground of assurance that the whole human world can and will be transformed into the shape of what is right and

good and, when it is, Zarathushtra's praise and worship will be un-
restrained (34.6):

> Since ye are such in very truth,
>   O Mazda, [and] Asha, [and] Vohu Manah,
> therefore, grant unto me such guidance,
>   through all changes of this [earthly] life,
> so that [as] your worshiper
>   [and as your] praiser I may be free from the fetters of the soul.

Not only is Ahura Mazda associated with Good Mind (*vohu manah*)
and Eternal Law or Righteousness (*asha*), but there are several other
terms that are similarly associated with the supreme being, namely,
Dominion (*khshathra*), Devotion (*aramaiti*), Perfection (*haurvatat*), and
Immortality (*ameretat*). These appear to be aspects or qualities of
Ahura Mazda, through which he orders his creation for good. But they
can also be personified to the extent that in *Yasna* 33.11, for example,
Zarathushtra appeals in the imperative plural to the Wise Lord, Devotion, Righteousness, Good Mind, and Dominion to hear him and be
merciful to him. Yet even here they are not separate beings for, in the
very next stanza (33.12), the Wise Lord is himself spoken of as acting
through Devotion, Righteousness, and Good Mind. Then in the *Yasna
Haptanghaiti* or Yasna of the Seven Chapters (*Yasnas* 35–41), considered to rank next in antiquity after the Gathas, the same aspects are
for the first time called *Amesha Spentas* ("Bountiful Immortals") and
there is some suggestion of their worship individually and separately:
"And now we worship the Bountiful Immortals, the good, both male
and female, ever living, and ever helpful" (39.3). The Amesha Spentas
are also called by the term *yazata,* which means "one worthy of worship." The same term designates other lesser aspects of the divine as
well, for example, the *yazata* Sraosha or Obedience, who is saluted in
the Gathas ("let Sraosha come unto him with Vohu Manah, unto any
one so ever whom thou dost love, O Mazda"; *Yasna* 44.16) and is hon-
ored in two later Avestan hymns (*Yasnas* 56, 57).

In the Gathas we also learn of the Holy Spirit (*spenta mainyu*) who
is equated with the Wise Lord (33.12); in *Yasna* 47 he is mentioned in
close association with the Wise Lord at the beginning of each stanza.
Over against Spenta Mainyu we hear too of an opposing spirit, to
whom the epithet *hostile* or *enemy* (*angra*) is applied in *Yasna* 45.2,
later known as Angra Mainyu (Hostile Spirit). Likewise, over against
*asha* (Eternal Law or Righteousness—closely associated with Ahura
Mazda) is *druj* (Untruth or Lie—closely associated with Angra Mainyu;
e.g., *Yasna* 48.2).

In *Yasnas* 30 and 45 the two spirits are called twins, and we learn that their opposition originated at the very beginning of existence, when the holier said to the other that their thoughts, words, and deeds were not in agreement (45.2):

> And I will explain about the Twin Spirits of creation in the beginning,
> of whom the holier spoke to the other—the Evil One—thus:
> "Between us two neither thoughts, nor teachings, nor wills,
> nor yet beliefs, nor words, nor yet deeds,
> neither selves, nor souls conform."

At this point it would appear that not only is Spenta Mainyu closely associated with Ahura Mazda but Angra Mainyu is also in some wise under the authority of the Wise Lord (e.g., *Yasna* 44.15). Thus the one good god remains supreme and the dualism of the two spirits is subsumed under the monotheism, being also destined to ultimate elimination in the final renovation of the universe in which evil will be destroyed.[37]

In the course of time, however, the antagonism of the two spirits was turned into a simple opposition of Ahura Mazda versus Angra Mainyu (Ohrmazd and Ahriman in the Sasanian period). But this apparent simplification is actually a transformation of the dualistic formula in the Gathas into something quite different. Some thinkers even went further and deduced from the word *twins* that Ahura Mazda and Angra Mainyu had a common father, whom they found in Time (*zurvan*), but this theory was eventually repudiated as heresy.[38]

As told in the Gathas, in their initial opposition the two contrary spirits established, respectively, life and not-life (30.4). Between the two the wise choose rightly, but not so the unwise (30.3); even the *daeva*s did not choose aright, and thus contributed to the pollution of human life (30.6). But those who choose aright contribute to the renewal of the world (30.9).

Finally there will be a decisive division of the sinners and the righteous. In the Gathas there are two pictures as to how this will come about, one picture relating to the time of the death of the individual, the other to the end time of the world.

At the death of the individual there will be a bridge to cross, called Cinvat (46.10–11; 51.13). The name *Cinvat* has the etymological connotation of sorting out or separating, and indicates the separating of the righteous and the unrighteous, so this is "the Bridge of the Separator" or "the Bridge of the Judge." In the Gathas it is always Ahura

---

37. James W. Boyd and Donald A. Crosby, "Is Zoroastrianism Dualistic or Monotheistic?" *JAAR* 47 (1979): 557–88.

38. Robert Charles Zaehner, *Zurvan: A Zoroastrian Dilemma*; and idem, *The Dawn and Twilight of Zoroastrianism*, 175–247.

Mazda himself who discriminates between the wise and the unwise (46.17), and later in *Yasna* 19.6 it is Ahura Mazda who will lead the believer across the Bridge "to the lights of heaven." In the *Book of Arda Viraf* (3–5), however, the future savior Saoshyant is at the Bridge, together with angels and Rashnu "the most just" (cf. *Yasna* 1.7, etc.). The latter weighs the pious and the wicked in his balance. It is also said that at the Bridge the soul meets a maid, who is either of great beauty or of fiendish ugliness according as the person was good or bad, and the maid leads the way into heaven or hell. The maid is the person's own conscience (*Vendidad* 19.30; *Yasht* 22.9; *Arda Viraf Namak* 4.18ff.; 17.12ff.).

At the end of the world there will be a "fiery test" by "molten metal" (*Yasna* 30.7; 32.7; 51.9). This is elaborated in the *Bundahish* (30.19–20) to the effect that a stream of molten metal will flow over the earth like a river, through which the righteous will pass as if walking through "warm milk," whereas the wicked will feel the full heat.

In the respective lots of the evil and the righteous, the Gathic representation is that Zarathushtra himself will cross the Bridge, and those who have accepted his message will be with him (*Yasna* 46.10) and will be rewarded with immortality (45.7). But the doers of evil will miss their path and fall from the Bridge, and their habitation will be in the abode of the Lie forever (46.11).

Another Gathic passage (31.20) expects for the follower of Untruth a long lifetime in a place of darkness, foul food, and woeful crying. This may possibly imply a promise of salvation ultimately even to the sinner, when once the sinner returns to the path of righteousness.[39] The *Dadistan-i Dinik* also speaks of the possibility that ablution in the molten metal of the end time will purify from guilt and infamy and lead to purity and pardon (32.12–13; 37.109–111). It describes an intermediate place called "ever-stationary" (*hamestagan*) where those not good enough for heaven yet not bad enough for hell will remain until the resurrection (20.3; 24.6; 33.2; see also *Arda Viraf Namak* 6).

At that "mighty day of resurrection" (*Vendidad* 18.51), the souls of the righteous dead will go to "the best world of the saints, shining, all glorious" (*Yasna* 16.7). The Amesha Spentas will show the way "to long glory in the spiritual world, to long happiness of the soul in paradise; to bliss and paradise, to the Garonmana of Ahura Mazda [the supreme heaven, the abode of the Wise Lord], beautifully made and fully adorned." Thus it will be for the righteous, "when his soul goes out of his body ... when I, Ahura Mazda, gently show him his way as he asks for it" (*Yasht* 24.32–33; see also *Vendidad* 19.32 and

---

39. Taraporewala, *Divine Songs of Zarathushtra*, 170.

*Arda Viraf Namak* 12ff. and 19ff. for detailed descriptions of heaven and hell).

A summary of Zoroastrian belief is found in *Yasna* 12, which is in the Gathic dialect and considered to be of antiquity next after the *Yasna Haptanghaiti*. The follower of the teachings of Zarathushtra makes confession in part as follows (12.1, 8–9):

> I confess as a Mazda worshiper of the order of Zarathushtra, estranged from the *daevas*, devoted to the lore of the Lord, a praiser of the Bountiful Immortals; and to Ahura Mazda, the good and endowed with good possessions, I attribute all things good, to the Holy One, the resplendent, to the glorious, whose are all things whatsoever which are good. . . .
>
> A Mazda worshiper I am, of Zarathushtra's order; [so] do I confess, as a praiser and confessor, and I therefore praise aloud the well-thought thought, the word well spoken, and the deed well done.
>
> Yes, I praise at once the faith of Mazda, the faith which throws off attacks, which causes weapons to be laid down, which upholds *khvastvadatha* [next-of-kin marriage, an early Zoroastrian custom], which is righteous, which is the most imposing, best and most beautiful of all religions which exist, and of all that shall in future come to knowledge, Ahura's faith, the Zarathushtrian creed. Yea, to Ahura Mazda do I ascribe all good, and such shall be the worship of the Mazdayasnian belief!

### Practices

It is not unlikely that Zarathushtra himself established the custom of five times of daily prayer (*Vendidad* 18.16; etc.), a custom later adopted from Zoroastrianism by Islam. Likewise the distinctive badge of the follower of Zarathushtra may well have been instituted by the prophet himself, namely, the sacred girdle (Avestan, *yah*; Persian, *kusti*), a woven cord wound around the waist three times, knotted at the back and the front, and repeatedly untied and retied when praying (*Dadistan-i Dinik* 39.19–32; compare the cord worn over one shoulder by the *brahmanas* of India).[40]

Associated with the Gathas are four especially sacred prayers (actually declaratory formulas), all, except for the first, named from their opening words, *Ahuna vairya*, *Ashem Vohu*, *Yenhe hatam*, and *Airyema ishyo*.[41] In liturgical usage they are arranged to frame the five Gathas, the first three preceding the first *Gatha Ahunavaiti* (which takes its name from the *Ahuna vairya*), and the fourth (forming *Yasna* 54) following the last, *Gatha Vahishta Ishti*.

---

40. Mary Boyce, *Zoroastrians: Their Religious Beliefs and Practices*, 31–33; idem, *History of Zoroastrianism*, 1.257–59 and n. 36.

41. Taraporewala, *Divine Songs of Zarathushtra*, 17, 23, 26, 821, 858.

The *Ahuna vairya* was uttered originally by Ahura Mazda (it is said), who taught it to Zarathushtra, and the prophet taught it to his followers (*Yasna* 9.14; 19.1–8). The prayer is, in fact, in the Gathic dialect and may well come from Zarathushtra himself. Referring to the first three of the Amesha Spentas (Vohu Manah, Good Mind; Asha, Righteousness; Khshathra, Dominion), as well as to Ahura Mazda, the text says:

> Just as the sovereign Lord [is] all-powerful,
>> so [is] the spiritual teacher by reason of the store of his
>> Righteousness;
> the gifts of Good Mind
> [are] for deeds [done] for the Lord of creation,
> and the Dominion of Ahura [descends], indeed,
>> upon [him], who becomes a shepherd to the meek.

The *Ashem Vohu* is a recital in praise of Righteousness (Asha), and the delivery of the words is appropriate on many occasions; for example, going to sleep at night, and departing this life at its end (*Yasna* 20; *Yasht* [fragment] 21):

> Righteousness is the highest good, is the
> illumination [of life];
> [this] illumination [comes] to that [life], which
> is righteous for the sake of the highest Righteousness.

The *Yenhe hatam* is said, in a commentary on the prayer (*Yasna* 21.1), to be "a word . . . by Zarathushtra." Actually it appears to be a later paraphrase of the Gathic verse *Yasna* 51.22, which reads:

> [Him] I think whom by reason of [his] Righteousness
> in every act of worship [as] the best
> Mazda Ahura doth regard;
> both [among those] who have been and [who] are;
> these will I revere in their own names,
> and will devotedly reach unto [them].

The *Yenhe hatam* reads:

> [Him], indeed, of those that are, of whom in every act of worship
> Mazda Ahura knows [to be] of higher worth
> by reason of [his] Righteousness, [also] the woman of whom [he
> knows] likewise—
> [all such] both these men and these women do we revere.

The *Airyema ishyo* (*Yasna* 54) is not traditionally attributed to Zarathushtra but uses Gathic terminology and may perhaps be by a very early disciple. Airyaman, whose name the prayer bears, is recognizably the Aryaman of *Rigveda* 2.27, one of a group of a half-dozen *aditya*s along with Mitra and Varuna. Here he is a *yazata* whose name, like Mitra's, means "the friend," and, like Mitra, he is associated with the heavenly light and is kind and helpful to people. In particular he is "the much-desired Airyaman," who, in view of the fact that Angra Mainyu has created 99,999 diseases, is called upon to "smite all manner of diseases and deaths" (*Vendidad* 22), and, in fact, shows "diligence . . . in the medical treatment of the world" (*Dinkard* 8.44.80). Airyaman is also expected to participate in the ultimate renovation of the universe, and he is invoked for help in the present prayer, looking forward to the "precious reward" that Ahura Mazda will at last bestow. The prayer reads:

> May the much-desired Airyaman come hither for [our] rejoicing,
> for the men and for the women of Zarathushtra—
> for the fulfilment of Good Mind;
>> whosoever's inner self earns the precious reward,
>> I will pray to Righteousness for the blessing,
>> which, greatly to be desired, Ahura Mazda has meant [for us].

As for the practice of sacrifice, at least in later texts, Zarathushtra is described as offering up sacrifice with both meat and *haoma* (e.g., *Yasht* 5.104; 9.25), and in the chief Zoroastrian liturgy found in the *Yasna* (the word itself means worship including sacrifice) both meat and *haoma* are offered (e.g., *Yasna* 3.20–21; 4.1–3; 7.1–2). Along with meat and *haoma* in these passages we also hear of the *baresman* (Pahlavi, *barsom*)—the term for grasses strewn for the sacrifice, and for a bundle of consecrated twigs or rods held in the hand of the priest or the worshiper.

In prayer and sacrifice there is reference not only to Ahura Mazda and the various aspects of the divine character, but also to the sun, moon, and stars (e.g., *Yasna* 2.11), to fire, earth, and water, all good creations of Ahura Mazda.

In its bright intensity, fire is a suitable symbol of the righteousness of the Wise Lord. In the Gathas Zarathushtra declares: "Unto thy fire the offering of [my] homage [I will pay], [and] I will esteem Righteousness above all, as long as I am able" (43.9). And before the sacred fire Zarathushtra prays (34.4):

And for thy fire, O Ahura,
  mighty through Righteousness, do we yearn
earnestly to be desired, possessing power,
  giving clear help to the faithful constantly;
but, O Mazda, as regards the unfaithful
  [He] sees through the evil at the merest glance.

In the later literature fire (*atash*) is personified as the *yazata* Atar (Adar) and is called the son of Ahura Mazda (2.4; 6.1; etc.). Recalling that Ahura Mazda made six visible creations—sky, water, earth, plants, animals, humankind—it is explained that there was also a seventh creation, which, although visible in itself, was "diffused originally" through the other six creations, and this was fire (*Zadsparam* 1.20–21). According to its place of origin and manifestation, fire is of five kinds (*Yasna* 17.1–11; *Bundahish* 17), namely, the lofty fire that is in the presence of Ahura Mazda, the good and friendly fire in the bodies of persons and animals, the beneficial fire in plants, the fire in the clouds in the form of lightning, and the bountiful fire in use in the world. Likewise there is the Bahram (Vahram) fire, which is the sacred fire at places of worship.

The earth (personified as the *yazata* Yam) is sacred, and the object of reverence (e.g., *Yasht* 13.153). *Yasht* 19 (the *Zamyad Yasht*) is inscribed to the divinity of the earth and devotes its first sections (19.108) to a description of the mountains, said in all to number 2,244.

Water is sacred in all its forms (wells, rivers, lakes, etc.). The action of Zarathushtra in obtaining the purest river water for the *haoma* sacrifice has been noted above (p. 80) and upon occasion he is pictured as offering up prayers "to the good waters of the good Daitya [River]" (*Vendidad* 19.2). The Avestan word for the waters is *apas* (Pahlavi, *aban*) and, in personified form, the Apas are goddesses who are the wives of Ahura Mazda.

In the *Yasna Haptanghaiti* expressions of reverence are directed to all three—the fire, the earth, and the waters (*Yasna*s 36, 38):

As the most friendly do thou give us zeal, O fire of the Lord, and approach us with the loving blessing of the most friendly. . . . And now we worship this earth which bears us, together with thy wives, O Ahura Mazda. . . . O ye waters, that are showered down and that stand in pools, ye who are productive and ye maternal ones, we will now address you as the best and the most beautiful.

Likewise in the *Nyaish*es there are prayers and ascriptions of praise addressed to the sun, moon, water, and fire.[42]

Because of their sacred character it is important that fire, earth, and water all be treated with due respect and kept from contamination. With regard to the earth, for example, "he who rejoices the earth with greatest joy is he who cultivates most corn, grass, and fruit." But on the other hand to bury a corpse in the earth is to defile the earth, and likewise to bring a corpse into the waters or the fire is to make these unclean (*Vendidad* 3.23, 36; 7.25). Hence arises the custom that when a person dies "they shall look for a *dakhma,* they shall look for a *dakhma* all around," and the dead shall lie on the *dakhma,* with eyes toward the sun, "until the birds have eaten up the corpse" (*Vendidad* 5.14; 8.2). Originally the *dakhma* was probably a place, not necessarily a structure, where the corpse was exposed; eventually the Parsi communities in Bombay and Calcutta erected structural *dakhma*s in the form of the so-called towers of silence.

For the part of a living being that is other than the perishable body, there are two hardly distinguishable terms, *urvan* (usually translated "soul"), and *fravashi* (the eternal part, the divine essence in a human being, therefore also translatable as "soul," but usually left untranslated). Both occur already in the *Yasna Haptanghaiti,* where we read of the souls (*urvan*) of domestic animals (39.1) and of the *fravashi*s of the saints (37.3). In the plural the *fravashi*s are the subject of *Yasht* 13, or the *Farvardin Yasht* (the name is the Middle Persian plural of the Avestan *fravashi*). Here the *fravashi* is not only the everlasting and deified soul of the deceased; but also the gods and even physical objects such as the sky and the earth each have their own *fravashi*. Thus in the first part of the *Farvardin Yasht* (13.1–84) the powers and attributes of the *fravashi*s in general are praised; in the latter part (13.85–158) the *fravashi*s of the most celebrated heroes, from the first man (Gaya Maretan, or Gayomard) down to the last (Saoshyant), are praised. So, in sacrifice and praise to the *fravashi*s, *Yasna* 26 says in part:

We worship here the *fravashi* of Ahura Mazda, which is the greatest and best. . . . And we worship the good, heroic, bountiful *fravashi*s of the Bountiful Immortals. . . . And we worship the *fravashi*s of those holy men and women who early loved and strove after Righteousness. . . . And we worship the *fravashi* of Gaya Maretan the holy, and the sanctity and *fravashi* of Zarathushtra Spitama the saint; and we worship the *fravashi* of Kavi Vishtaspa the holy. . . . And we worship the *fravashi*s

42. Maneckji Nusservanji Dhalla, *The Nyaishes; or, Zoroastrian Litanies.*

of the saints male and female who have striven after the truth, which
are those of the dead and living saints, and which are those also of
people as yet unborn, of the future prophets who will help on the renovation, and complete the human progress. . . . And we worship the *fravashi*s of all the next of kin who have passed away in this house. . . .
And we worship the *fravashi*s of the saints from Gaya Maretan to Saoshyant the victorious. Yea, we worship the souls of the dead which are the
*fravashi*s of the saints!

## Zoroastrianism after Zarathushtra

### Under the Achaemenians (549–331 B.C.)

It was several centuries after the time of Zarathushtra that the
religion he inaugurated comes again into view in historical relationships, and that in Persia under the Achaemenian rulers. In their records Zoroaster himself is not named, but there is evidence of adherence
to his teachings.

In 549 B.C. Cyrus II the Great, a descendant of the Persian Achae-
menes, united the Medes and the Persians under his own rule and
founded the Persian Empire, with his capital at Pasargadae. The evidence of probable Zoroastrian belief on the part of Cyrus is chiefly
archeological. At Pasargadae, in the so-called sacred precinct, there
are two massive limestone plinths, aligned from north to south and
twenty-five feet apart. In each case a monolithic cube stands upon deep
foundations; at the southern plinth a monumental staircase block rises
to the top of the central cube; at the northern plinth there were no
such steps. Remembering the devotion of Zarathushtra and his followers to fire, the suggested interpretation is that it was the custom
of Cyrus—and later of his successors—to ascend the southern plinth
to worship before a portable fire altar installed on top of the adjacent
monument. Fragments of several stepped stone altars have been found
at Pasargadae, presumably fire altars. In another area some distance
away from the two plinths is one remaining tall wall of what was once
a square stone tower, known locally as the Zendan-i Sulaiman "prison
of Solomon"), which was evidently almost identical with the still well-
preserved tower known as the Ka'bah-i Zardusht ("cube of Zoroaster")
in front of the tomb of Darius I the Great at Naqsh-i Rustam. In each
case the architecture provided for a square or rectangular room at the
top of the tower, reached by a tall, monumental staircase. Near the

tower at Naqsh-i Rustam there are also two large open-air rock-hewn altars, close together and aligned in a north-south direction.[43]

The use of such open-air fire altars accords with the statement of Herodotus (1.131) that the Persians worshiped under the open heaven. Likewise it is required in Zoroastrian texts that the sacred fire not be extinguished or contaminated in any way (*Sad Dar* 11, 39, 92).[44] In the light of this requirement the upper room in the towers at Pasargadae and Naqsh-i Rustam may be understood as a "place of fire" (*atashgah*) in which the sacred fire was kept always burning, protected from the weather, guarded, and kept pure and unharmed, and from which fire was from time to time brought out to the open-air altars for worship under the open sky.[45] So interpreted (not without debate), the archeological materials at both Pasargadae and Naqsh-i Rustam indicate the Zoroastrian orientation of both Cyrus the Great and Darius the Great, and in the case of the latter there are also his own inscriptions and reliefs. In the case of Cyrus there is also one other item of possible relevance in the fact that he named one of his daughters Atossa (Herodotus 3.68–69, 88), which is probably the rendering in Greek of Hutaosa, the name of the queen of Kai Vishtaspa.

When Cyrus took Babylon (539 B.C.) he said in his own Cylinder Inscription that it was the god Marduk who sent him.[46] In his first regnal year in Babylon (538/537) he allowed the Jewish exiles to return to Jerusalem to rebuild their temple, saying that this was done at the instruction of the Lord worshiped by the Jews (2 Chron. 36:23; Ezra 1:2–4). But these are doubtless simply examples of appropriate recognition of the religious beliefs of those with whom he was dealing rather than indication of his own religious allegiance. In fact Aeschylus (*Persae* 772) describes Cyrus as a gracious man (εὔφρων) and says that "the gods hated him not," and the tolerant and generally enlightened rule of Cyrus (appreciated in Isa. 44:28–45:1) may well be understood as expressions of his desire to rule well in accordance with Zoroastrian righteousness (*asha*).

Beginning with Cyrus, the bodies of the Achaemenian kings were at death embalmed and laid in tombs built of stone or hewn in the rock, which might appear to be in disregard of the usual Zoroastrian practice of exposure. The stone tomb of Cyrus at Pasargadae[47] and

43. David Stronach, *Pasargadae: A Report on the Excavations Conducted by the British Institute of Persian Studies from 1961 to 1963*, 117–18, 135ff., plates 95–107; Erich F. Schmidt, *Persepolis*, 3.11–12, 34ff., plates 3–13.

44. *Sacred Books of the East*, 24.270ff., 301, 355–56.

45. Schmidt, *Persepolis*, 3.48–49; Kurt Erdmann, *Das iranische Feuerheiligtum*, 17–22, plates i–iii; Klaus Schippmann, *Die iranischen Feuerheiligtümer*, 208; Hinz, *Zarathushtra*, 17, 147–48.

46. *ANET*, 315–16.

47. Stronach, *Pasargadae*, 24–43, plates 19–39.

the rock-hewn tombs of the later kings at Naqsh-i Rustam and Persepolis, however, did prevent contamination of earth or water or fire, and perhaps were thus entirely acceptable.[48]

Cyrus was followed on the throne by his son Cambyses II (529–522 B.C.), who took Egypt in 525, but in his absence and shortly before his own death in 522 his younger brother Bardiya, also called Smerdis, took the rule in Persia. The latter was murdered at the instigation of Cambyses, after which a Magian impersonated Smerdis and seized the throne. Thereafter an Achaemenian prince of a younger line, Darius I the Great (521–486 B.C.), son of Hystaspes, came forward to avert the threatened breakup of the empire and in fact to enlarge it to its furthest extent: "So Darius son of Hystaspes was made king, and the whole of Asia, which Cyrus first and Cambyses after him had subdued, was made subject to him" (Herodotus 3.88; see also 3.30–31, 61ff., 73ff.).

Like the name of Cyrus's daughter Atossa/Hutaosa (who became in succession the wife of Cambyses, the Magian impersonator, and Darius I), the name of Darius's father Hystaspes (Herodotus 1.209) probably reflects Zoroastrian influence, for it is recognizably a Greek rendering of Vishtaspa, the name of the royal patron of Zoroaster. That Darius was himself an adherent of the Zoroastrian religion is quite evident in his own monuments, beginning with his inscriptions and sculptures on the Rock of Behistun.[49] Here in the first long inscription (DB 1.11 —17, 26 —61) he declares that it is by the favor of Ahuramazda (the name in Old Persian combining in one word the Avestan Ahura Mazda) that he is king and ruling over the then twenty-three provinces of the Persian Empire. Describing the revolts that threatened the empire at the beginning of his reign, he says that the Lie (using the Old Persian word *drauga,* the equivalent of the Avestan *druj,* the name of the demon of Untruth, the enemy of *asha*) multiplied in the land. Telling of his suppression of the rebellions, he says that he besought the help of Ahuramazda and with a few men slew Gaumata the Magus (as he names the Magian who impersonated Bardiya/Smerdis) and his foremost followers.[50]

In the accompanying sculptured relief panel[51] Darius is pictured with a foot upon the prostrate form of Gaumata, the latter followed

48. Boyce, *History of Zoroastrianism,* 2.54–57.

49. L. W. King and R. C. Thompson, *The Sculptures and Inscription of Darius the Great on the Rock of Behistûn in Persia.*

50. Roland G. Kent, *Old Persian: Grammar, Texts, Lexicon,* 119–20. The abbreviation DB stands for the inscription of Darius the Great at Behistun. For the meaning of similar abbreviations on the next few pages, see Kent, p. 4.

51. George G. Cameron, "A Photograph of Darius' Sculptures at Behistun," *JNES* 2 (1943): 115–16, plate ii.

by a row of nine captive rebel leaders, roped together. Hovering in the air above Darius and his captives is a winged disk out of which rises the upper part of a bearded man, wearing Persian dress and a cylindrical crown adorned with horns and a small eight-rayed solar disk, while the lower part of his body ends in feathers spread out beneath the large winged disk, with scrolls hanging down on either side. One hand is extended as if in blessing, while the other holds forth a circular ring. As an iconographical symbol the winged disk comes originally from Egypt where it belonged to Horus as the sky- and sun-god, and appears as early as the Middle Kingdom and is frequent in the New Kingdom. In Assyria, where the symbol probably stands for the national god Ashur, it appears on monuments of kings in the early first millennium B.C., and assumes the form of a human figure, the lower part of the body spreading out into the tail of a bird. The horns, solar disk, and ring are ancient symbols of divinity and authority. Where it appears on this and other monuments of Darius and also of other Achaemenian kings, and where accompanying texts speak so much of Ahuramazda, the representation must surely be intended to be the symbol of the Wise Lord of Zoroaster, now the national god of the Achaemenian Empire.[52]

At the rock-hewn tomb of Darius I at Naqsh-i Rustam (near his capital of Persepolis)[53] the king also speaks in terms of Zoroastrian devotion even as at Behistun, saying in part (DNb 1–12, 32–33, 41–49):[54]

A great god is Ahuramazda, who created this excellent work which is seen, who created happiness for man, who bestowed wisdom and activity upon Darius the king.

Says Darius the king: By the favor of Ahuramazda I am of such a sort that I am a friend to right, I am not a friend to wrong; it is not my desire that the weak man should have wrong done to him by the mighty; nor is that my desire, that the mighty man should have wrong done to him by the weak.

What is right, that is my desire. I am not a friend to the man who is a Lie-follower. . . .

This indeed is my activity: as far as my body has the strength, as a

52. Alternate proposed interpretations are that this symbol represents the Avestan *fravashi* (Pahlavi, *fravahar*), the divine essence that motivates the ascent of the soul (Mobed Bahram Shahzadi, *Message of Zarathushtra*, vol. 1, *Religious Instruction*, 51–52); or that it is the *khvarenah* (*farnah*), the kingly "glory," hypostatized as a heavenly being with a place in the dwelling of Ahuramazda (A. S. Shahbazi, "An Achaemenid Symbol. I. A Farewell to 'Fravahr' and 'Ahuramazda'; II. Farnah '(God Given) Fortune' Symbolized," *AMI* 2.7 (1974): 135–44; 13 (1980): 119–47.

53. Schmidt, *Persepolis*, 3.80–90.

54. Roland G. Kent, "Darius' Naqš-i-Rustam B Inscription," *JNES* 4 (1945): 41–42; and idem, *Old Persian*, 140.

battle-fighter I am a good battle-fighter. . . . As a horseman I am a good horseman. As a bowman I am a good bowman both afoot and on horseback. As a spearman I am a good spearman both afoot and on horseback.

And the (physical) skillfulnesses which Ahuramazda has bestowed upon me and I have had the strength to use them—by the favor of Ahuramazda, what has been done by me I have done with those skillfulnesses which Ahuramazda has bestowed upon me.

Here also in the panel of relief sculptures[55] is the winged disk with the anthropomorphic figure—doubtless the symbol of Ahuramazda—while the king himself stands with a bow in his left hand and with his right hand uplifted toward an altar on which a fire is burning. This altar appears to be of exactly the same type as that represented by the fragments of the fire-altars at Pasargadae.[56]

Xerxes I (485–465 B.C.), son and successor of Darius I, who did much of the construction at Persepolis, completed works begun by his father or built or began works of his own. Quite regularly in his building inscriptions he refers to the favor of Ahuramazda, for example, on the Gate of Xerxes (XPa 11–12, 17–20): "Says Xerxes the king: 'By the favor of Ahuramazda I built this gateway called All Lands. . . . May Ahuramazda protect me, and my kingdom, and what was built by me, and what was built by my father, that also may Ahuramazda protect.' "
In a long Persepolis inscription (XPh) he enumerates the many countries under his rule, now around thirty in number, refers to one in which there was rebellion that he put down, and then goes on (XPh 35–41):

And among these countries there was (a place) where previously *daivas* were worshiped. Afterwards, by the favor of Ahuramazda, I destroyed that sanctuary of the *daivas* [*daivadana*], and I made proclamation, "The *daivas* shall not be worshiped." Where previously the *daivas* were worshiped, there I worshiped Ahuramazda and *arta* reverently.[57]

Here the Old Persian *daiva* is the equivalent of the Avestan *daeva* and, even as Zoroaster contended against the *daevas* as the gods of the old religion in his time, so also Xerxes evidently wished to eliminate the still-continuing worship of such deities in his own time, and to further the worship of Ahuramazda and *arta* (the Old Persian equivalent of Avestan *asha* and Sanskrit *rita,* "cosmic order, right, righteousness"). The tomb of Xerxes at Naqsh-i Rustam is adjacent to that

55. Schmidt, *Persepolis,* 3, plates 18–39.
56. David Stronach, "Urartian and Achaemenian Tower Temples," *JNES* 26 (1967): 287.
57. Kent, *Old Persian,* 148, 151.

of Darius I, and adorned with exactly the same sort of sculptures as those of his father.[58]

Quite certainly, therefore, both Darius the Great and Xerxes his son were fully devoted to the Zoroastrian religion, to which in all probability Cyrus the Great himself had already adhered.[59] The same is true also of Artaxerxes I (464–424 B.C.) and Darius II (423–405). They too were buried at Naqsh-i Rustam in tombs similar to those of Darius I and Xerxes and with similar sculptured panels,[60] and they also refer in their few extant inscriptions (A$^1$Pa; D$^2$Sb) to the favor of Ahuramazda.[61]

It was in about 460 B.C. and thus in the time of Artaxerxes I that Herodotus visited Babylon and subsequently wrote his *History*. Although Herodotus probably never visited Iran, he tells about Persian religion as he learned of it no doubt in Babylonia and also in Asia Minor. Concerning "the usages of the Persians," he reports (1.131):

> It is not their custom to make and set up statues and temples and altars, but those who make such they deem foolish, as I suppose, because they never believed the gods, as do the Greeks, to be in the likeness of men; but they call the whole circle of heaven Zeus, and to him they offer sacrifice on the highest peaks of the mountains; they sacrifice also to the sun and moon and earth and fire and water and winds. These are the only gods to whom they have ever sacrificed from the beginning.

Continuing, Herodotus (1.132) tells how a Persian makes a sacrifice and, when the flesh of the sacrifice has been seethed,

> spreads the softest grass . . . and places all of it on this. When he has so disposed it a Magus comes near and chants over it the song of the birth of the gods, as the Persian tradition relates it; for no sacrifice can be offered without a Magus. Then after a little while the sacrificer carries away the flesh and uses it as he pleases.

The Magi, one of the six Median tribes (Herodotus 1.101), were evidently a priestly tribe from the beginning. In the time of Darius I they were probably still the representatives of the old religion, for in the Behistun inscription Darius says that the leader of rebellion when "the Lie" was spreading in the land was a Magian. Now, however, in the time of Artaxerxes I, the sacrifice that Herodotus describes is

---

58. Schmidt, *Persepolis*, 3.90–93, plates 40–47.

59. Ilya Gershevitch, "Zoroaster's Own Contribution," *JNES* 23 (1964): 16–17; Stronach, *Pasargadae*, 145.

60. Schmidt, *Persepolis*, 3.93–99, plates 48–62.

61. Kent, *Old Persian*, 153–54.

evidently Zoroastrian (note the spread-out grass, corresponding to the Zoroastrian *baresman*; see p. 92), and the services of a Magian priest are said to be indispensable for any such sacrifice. It must be, therefore, that in this time the Magi were themselves becoming Zoroastrians and the Zoroastrian priestly tribe. Confirming the emergence of the Magi as Zoroastrian priests, in his time Strabo (c. 63 B.C.–A.D. 24) describes the customs of the Magi in Cappadocia (15.3.14–15), where they were known as Pyraethi ("fire-kindlers") and kept an altar fire ever burning, making incantations before it, holding in their hands a bundle of slender myrtle wands (again the *baresman,* in this form).[62]

Herodotus also speaks (1.138–40) of the reverence of the Persians for rivers (corresponding with Zoroastrian reverence for water), of the disposition by the Magi of dead bodies, which "are not buried before they have been mangled by bird or dog" (corresponding with Zoroastrian exposure of the dead), and of the Magi killing ants, snakes, and creeping and flying things (corresponding with Zoroastrian conception that these are evil creatures that Angra Mainyu brought into existence to harm the good creation of Ahura Mazda).

Artaxerxes II (404–359 B.C.) and Artaxerxes III (358–338) were not entombed at Naqsh-i Rustam, where the great cliff was substantially occupied by the earlier tombs, but rather in the "royal hill" east of the main palace terrace at Persepolis. Their rock-hewn tombs are like those of their predecessors with similar sculptured panels.[63] Their inscriptions, however, contain new elements, in particular the naming of Anahita and Mithra along with Ahuramazda. Concerning his reconstruction of the Apadana (hall of columns) built by Darius I at Susa, Artaxerxes II states (A²Sa 3–5):

> This palace Darius my great-great-grandfather built; later under Artaxerxes my grandfather it was burned; by the favor of Ahuramazda, Anahita, and Mithra, I built this palace. May Ahuramazda, Anahita, and Mithra protect me from all evil, and that which I have built may they not shatter nor harm.

Likewise in a building inscription at Persepolis Artaxerxes III writes (A³Pa 24–26): "May Ahuramazda and the god Mithra protect me and this country and what was built by me."[64]

The importance of water as a sacred element in Zoroastrian religion is significant for the understanding of Anahita, probably an early Indo-Iranian river-goddess who was accepted into developing

---

62. Gershevitch, *Avestan Hymn to Mithra,* 16–22.
63. Schmidt, *Persepolis,* 3.99–107, plates 63–75.
64. Kent, *Old Persian,* 154, 156.

Zoroastrianism. In *Yasht* 5 (the *Aban Yasht* or "Yasht of the Waters") there is a long hymn of praise in honor of Anahita. Here she is called Ardvi Sura Anahita, the first of these three names being otherwise unknown, the second meaning "strong, mighty," and Anahita meaning "undefiled, immaculate." At the opening of the *Yasht* she is a spring-fed river itself, which pours down from a lofty mountain to the sea (5.1, 3):

> Ahura Mazda spake unto Spitama Zarathushtra, saying: "Offer up a sacrifice, O Spitama Zarathushtra, unto this spring of mine, Ardvi Sura Anahita, the wide-expanding and health-giving, who hates the *daevas* and obeys the laws of Ahura, who is worthy of sacrifice in the material world, worthy of prayer in the material world; the life-increasing and holy, the herd-increasing and holy, the fold-increasing and holy, the wealth-increasing and holy, the country-increasing and holy.... The large river known afar, that is as large as the whole of the waters that run along the earth; that runs powerfully from the height Hukairya down to the sea Vourukasha."

At the end of the same *Yasht* the mythical river is fully personified, and Anahita appears (5.64, 78, 126) "in the shape of a maid, fair of body, most strong, tall-formed, high-girded, pure, nobly born of a glorious race." As life-giving water Anahita is a goddess of fertility; as a hater of the *daevas* she is also a goddess of war and, upon occasion, she rides in a chariot drawn by four white horses, which are wind, rain, cloud, and sleet. Many heroes of the past offered sacrifice to her, including Zarathushtra himself and his convert Kai Vishtaspa (5.104, 108).

Herodotus (1.131) says that the Persians "learned to sacrifice to the heavenly Aphrodite from the Assyrians and Arabians," and that the Persians call this deity Mitra. Since Mitra was a masculine deity, the name is probably a mistake for Anahita (who was closely associated with Mithra). Among the Assyrians (and Babylonians) the "heavenly Aphrodite" would probably be Ishtar (and earlier the Sumerian Inanna), the goddess of both love and war, so there was probably assimilation between Ishtar and Anahita. Elsewhere in the Middle East Anahita was also assimilated with Artemis, Cybele, and the Magna Mater.[65]

In another case there is probably also assimilation with a foreign deity, namely, with the Babylonian Nabu, god of the planet Mercury and god of wisdom and writing. The Persian deity Tiri (identified with the Avestan Tishtrya, *yazata* of the star Sirius—*Bundahish* 2.7) was

---

65. Franz Cumont, "Anāhita," in *HERE* 1.414–15.

also associated with the art of writing, and this name, in the form of Tir, is the Persian name of the Planet Mercury until now.[66]

Mithra is the same as Mitra, the Vedic sky-god (*Rigveda* 1.139.2; 4.13.2; 5.63.1; 7.60–66; etc.),[67] and we have already seen him in the *Mihir Yasht* where, closely connected but not yet identical with the sun, he sweeps over the eastern mountains to look down upon the abode of the Aryans (p. 74). In the same *Yasht* Mithra is also the great protagonist of the good, going forth in his chariot to smite the forces of evil (10.124–25, 130, 133–35):

> With his arms lifted up toward the abode of the immortals, Mithra, the lord of wide pastures, drives forward from the shining Garonmana [paradise] in a beautiful chariot that drives on, ever swift, adorned with all sorts of ornaments, and made of gold. Four stallions draw that chariot, all of the same white color, living on heavenly food and undying. The hoofs of their forefeet are shod with gold, the hoofs of their hindfeet are shod with silver, all are yoked to the same pole. . . . On a side of the chariot of Mithra, the lord of wide pastures, stand a thousand spears well made and sharp piercing. They go through the heavenly space, they fall through the heavenly space upon the skulls of the *daevas*. . . . After he has smitten the *daevas*, after he has smitten down the men who lied unto Mithra, Mithra, the lord of wide pastures, drives forward. . . . Angra Mainyu, who is all death, flees away in fear. . . . Oh, may we never fall across the rush of Mithra, the lord of wide pastures, when in anger! May Mithra, the lord of wide pastures, never smite us in his anger; he who stands up upon this earth as the strongest of all gods, the most valiant of all gods, the most energetic of all gods, the swiftest of all gods, the most fiend-smiting of all gods, he Mithra, the lord of wide pastures.

Later Mithra was identified with the Semitic sun-god, Shamash, and his worship spread into the west, where as *Deus Sol Invictus Mithras* he was prominently known throughout the Roman Empire in the early centuries A.D.

With the naming of Anahita and Mithra along with Ahuramazda by Artaxerxes II we seem to have, therefore, at this time the emergence of a somewhat mixed form of Zoroastrianism in which early Indo-Iranian elements other than those found in the teachings of Zarathushtra himself were included. We are also told by Berossos (priest at Babylon under Antiochus I, 281–261 B.C.; quoted by Clement of Alexandria, *Protreptikos* 5) that Artaxerxes II was the first to make cult statues of Anahita (here called Aphrodite Anaitis), which he put

66. Boyce, *History of Zoroastrianism*, 2.31–33, 204–6.
67. Jan Gonda, *The Vedic God Mitra*.

in temples in various parts of the empire. At Persepolis among the ruins of the streets of the city (one thousand feet northwest of the main palace terrace) a large complex of halls and rooms has been found. One square room appears to have been a temple sanctuary (the so-called Fratadara temple), and has a large stone block with traces of a heavy metal dowel that might have been used to hold a statue in place. Column bases in the complex are of a style belonging to the late Achaemenian period, and the possibility is that the temple was one of the temples of Anahita founded by Artaxerxes II.[68] Along with the establishment of temples in honor of Anahita it is a plausible hypothesis that in the same time (fourth century B.C.) Zoroastrian fire temples—actual buildings in which to conduct the worship of fire, in distinction from the earlier veneration of fire in the open air—came into existence.[69]

### Alexander the Great, the Seleucids, and the Arsacids (331 B.C.–A.D. 226)

Alexander the Great defeated Darius III, the last Achaemenian king, in battle in 331 B.C., captured the capital cities of Susa, Ecbatana (Hamadan), and Persepolis, and burned the palaces of Persepolis to the ground. From the Zoroastrian point of view, he and his armies wrought such devastation in Iran and inflicted such damage upon the religion that Alexander was remembered as the "accursed" and his invasion as the "calamity." The *Book of Arda Viraf* summarizes the matter (1.1–11):[70]

They say that once upon a time the pious Zaratusht made the religion which he had received current in the world; and . . . the religion was in purity and men were without doubts. But afterward the accursed evil spirit, the wicked one, in order to make men doubtful of this religion, instigated the accursed Alexander the Ruman, who was dwelling in Egypt, so that he came to the country of Iran with severe cruelty and war and devastation; he also slew the ruler of Iran, and destroyed the metropolis and empire, and made them desolate.

And this religion, namely, all the Avesta and Zand, written upon prepared cowskins, and with gold ink . . . he burnt up. And he killed several dasturs and judges and herbads and mobads and upholders of the religion [various grades of the Zoroastrian priesthood], and the competent and wise of the country of Iran. And he cast hatred and strife,

---

68. Boyce, *History of Zoroastrianism,* 2.226.
69. Ibid., 221.
70. Haug and West, *Arda Viraf,* 141–43.

one with the other, amongst the nobles and householders of the country of Iran; and self-destroyed he fled to hell.

The *Dinkard* (8.1.21) and later Persian texts (e.g., the *Rivayat* of the Dastur Barzu Qavamu-d-din, c. A.D. 1614–1646) also tell how in the "calamity" much of the scriptures was destroyed, but how some at least was preserved in the memory of the priests and again written down.[71]

After Alexander, his general Seleucus I (312–281 B.C.), ruling from Seleucia on the Tigris, held most of the former Achaemenian Empire, including all of Iran. But succeeding members of the Seleucid dynasty turned their interests more and more to the west, and their possessions in the east soon fell into the hands of the Greco-Bactrians, the Scythians (Sakas), and finally the Parthians. The last-named were nomadic Iranians in what had been the Achaemenian satrapy of Parthava (Parthia) in northeastern Iran, from where under Arsaces (c. 250–248 B.C.), Tiridates (c. 248–211), and notably through the successful campaigns of Mithradates I (c. 171–138/137) and Mithradates II (c. 123–88/87), they established an Arsacid rule that endured until A.D. 226. It extended from the borders of India (in India the Parthians ruled for a time as the Pahlavas) to the western frontiers of Mesopotamia (where for some three hundred years they were engaged in intermittent warfare with the Romans).

The names *Tiridates* ("given by Tiri") and *Mithradates* ("given by Mithra") are recurrent among the Arsacid rulers and, with their references to the Zoroastrian divinities Tiri and Mithra, indicate the Zoroastrian affiliation of the dynasty. Of the later members of the dynasty, Vologases I (A.D. 51/52–79/80) is probably the king called Valkhash the Arsacid in the *Dinkard* (4.24), where he is credited with collecting and preserving as much as possible of the Zoroastrian texts scattered and destroyed by Alexander, whether they had remained in writing or been retained in memory. In A.D. 62 Vologases I put his younger brother Tiridates (not to be confused with the Parthian ruler mentioned just above) on the throne of Armenia, whom Tacitus (*Annals* 15.24) says was a priest and Pliny (*Natural History* 30.6) calls a Magian. Pliny also relates that when Tiridates journeyed to Rome to see Nero he was so scrupulous in the observance of the regulations of his faith that he went all the way by land in order to avoid defiling the sea.

Isidore of Charax, a Greek author who probably lived in Charax Spasini at the head of the Persian Gulf around the end of the first century B.C., says that Arsaces, probably meaning the first ruler of

71. *Sacred Books of the East,* 37.9–10, 437.

that name, was proclaimed king in the city of Asaak, and that "an everlasting fire is guarded there" (presumably in a temple). Isidore likewise mentions "a temple, sacred to Anaitis [the Greek form of the name of Anahita]" at Ecbatana, thus attesting the probable existence of fire temples as well as Anahita temples under the Parthians.[72]

In fact, the oldest remains identifiable as an actual fire temple belong to the Arsacid period and are found at the already-mentioned Kuh-i Khwaja, the "hill of the lord" near Lake Hamun in Sistan. On the southern slope of the hill are the ruins of a palace and a temple, probably dating in their original form from the first century A.D. and then restored in the third century. The palace was built around a large court, while the temple stood upon a higher platform. The temple had an inner room with a cupola over it supported on four corner-piers, and around this inner room ran a narrow closed passageway. There was also a monumental entrance. In the room under the cupola the foundation of a stone altar is still preserved, and not far away is a stone fire altar with pillar shaft and three-stepped base and top, like the fire altars at Pasargadae.

The walls of many of the palace rooms were originally painted. In addition to ornamental compositions, there is a scene on the back wall of the gallery showing a king and queen standing under something like a canopy, and there is a representation on the window wall of the gallery of a series of deities. The gods are portrayed in Greek style and with Greek garments, but their emblems and attributes are half-Greek and half-Oriental. One god, probably Verethraghna, wears a three-winged helmet (in purely Greek art a helmet with two wings would be the emblem of Hermes). Verethraghna (in the Hellenistic world equated with Herakles) is the Zoroastrian *yazata* of victory, made by Ahura and the conqueror of foes, especially of men who have lied to Mithra (*Yasht* 10.70–72; 23.7), and manifest in ten forms (*Yasht* 14). In particular Verethraghna (also called Vahram and Bahram) is the *yazata* of the sacred fire, although fire also has its own name, Atar or Adar. When the *Bundahish* (17.4–9), for example, tells of the three most sacred fires, Adar Farnbag, Adar Gushnasp, and Adar Burzen-mihr, it adds, "All those fires are the whole body of the fire of Vahram" (17.9). Likewise the *Dadistan-i Dinik* (31.7) speaks of when, by the power of the creator, normally invisible spirits put on worldly appearances; it is "as when they see bodies in which is a soul, or when they see a fire in which is Vahram, or see water in which is its own spirit [i.e., Ardvi Sura Anahita]."

In the paintings at Kuh-i Khwaja there is also a god with a trident.

---

72. Wilfred H. Schoff, *Parthian Stations, by Isidore of Charax*, 7, 9 (§§6, 11).

In Greek symbolism this would normally be the mark of Poseidon; here it is more probably the sign of Śiva, the god of India. Thus a far-reaching syncretism prevailed at this place and time, in which Zoroastrianism was mingled with elements from both Greece and India.[73]

## The Sasanians (A.D. 226–651)

It was in Pars (the modern province of Fars; Greek, Persis, hence Persia) and in a family descended from a priest in the fire temple of Anahita at Istakhr (the later capital, about three miles away, which replaced Persepolis) that revolt arose against the Arsacids. The name of the priest was Sasan, and his grandson Ardashir (son of Papak) defeated the last Arsacid king, Artaban V, and became the first king of the Sasanian dynasty.[74]

Crowned perhaps at Istakhr, Ardashir I (A.D. 226–241) took the title "King of the kings of the Iranians." The rise of his dynasty represented a revival of national Iranian or Persian feeling. Consequently the Sasanian Empire is also known as neo-Persian, with the kings consciously and vigorously continuing the traditions of their Achaemenian predecessors. The Sasanians also inherited from the Arsacids a tradition of war with the West, and were involved in intermittent struggles with Rome and then with Byzantium. Ardashir I called himself a "Mazdayasnian," and evidently thought of himself as a reformer of the Zoroastrian faith, which had, of course, continued throughout the Arsacid period, although, as we have seen, with syncretism and the use of images.

The chief priest under Ardashir I was a Zoroastrian *herbad* named Tansar (or Tosar), known directly from a letter that he wrote to Gushnasp, a former vassal of the Arsacids, who ruled in Tabaristan in northern Iran.[75] Gushnasp had written a letter charging Ardashir with arbitrary and improper behavior, and Tansar replies to the charges in detail in his own letter. Gushnasp, himself obviously a Zoroastrian, had written that "although the king seeks the truth of the ancients, yet he may be accused of forsaking tradition; and right though this may be for the world, it is not good for the Faith." In defense of Ardashir, and with obvious exaggeration of the deplorable state of preceding affairs in order to emphasize the magnitude of the king's task, Tansar writes:[76]

---

73. Ernst Herzfeld, *Iran in the Ancient East,* 291–97; and idem, *Archaeological History of Iran,* 58–74.

74. Arthur Emanuel Christensen, *L'Iran sous les Sassanides.*

75. Mary Boyce, *The Letter of Tansar.*

76. Ibid., 36–37.

If your concern is for religious matters . . . know that Alexander burnt the book of our religion—1200 ox-hides—at Istaxr [Istakhr]. One third of it was known by heart and survived, but even that was all legends and traditions, and men knew not the laws and ordinances; until, through the corruption of the people of the day and the decay of royal power and the craving for what was new and counterfeit and the desire for vainglory, even those legends and traditions dropped out of common recollection, so that not an iota of the truth of that book remained. Therefore the faith must needs be restored by a man of true and upright judgment. Yet have you heard tell of, or seen, any monarch save the King of kings [i.e., Ardashir I], who has taken this task upon him?

After telling about the work of Valkhash the Arsacid (probably Vologases I) in re-collecting the Zoroastrian scriptures, the *Dinkard* (4.25) goes on to speak of Artakhshatar son of Papak (i.e., Ardashir I) and says that he

summoned Tosar [Tansar], and also all that scattered instruction, as true authority, to the capital; Tosar having arrived, him alone he approved, and, dismissing the rest of the high priests, he also gave this command, namely: "For us every other exposition of the Mazda-worshiping religion becomes removed, because even now there is no information or knowledge of it below."

Again the *Dinkard* (7.7.3, 17–18) speaks of the devastation caused by Alexander and of the efforts of subsequent rulers to restore the sacred writings from their scattered state. It then names the same Artakhshatar and Tansar, and declares (in the form of a prophecy by Zarathushtra) that evil demon worship and evil strife will not be ended in the country until approval is given to Tansar: "And it is when they grant approval to the spiritual leader, the truthful speaker of eloquence, the righteous Tansar, that those of the country obtain redress when they seek it, and no deviation from the religion of Zaratusht."

In particular the reformation of Zoroastrianism instituted by Ardashir I and continued by his successors involved the repudiation of images and emphasis upon the fire cult. While the temple at Istakhr in which Sasan served is called a fire temple of Anahita, it is possible that even then the Sasanian family was devoted to fire alone as opposed to images, for the Muslim historian al-Mas'udi (d. c. A.D. 956) states that this temple was once an "idol temple," but already in the ancient past the idols were removed and fire installed in their place.[77] Also, already in his initial campaigns against the Arsacids Ardashir I

---

77. Al-Mas'ūdī, *Les Prairies d'Or*, 2.541, par. 1403.

Ardashir I and Ohrmazd in a rock-carved investiture scene at Naqsh-i Rustam in Iran

appears to have begun the destruction of images and their replacement by fire, for in his *History of Armenia* Moses of Khoran (fifth–sixth century A.D.) says that in his conquest of Armenia Ardashir shattered statues of the dead and put a sacred fire (presumably in place of an image) in the temple of Ohrmazd at Pakaran.[78] In a rock-carved investiture scene at Naqsh-i Rustam Ardashir I and the god Ohrmazd face each other on horseback, with Artaban and Ahriman prostrate beneath their horses; Ohrmazd is shown as a crowned, bearded figure in Persian dress.[79] But such an anthropomorphic representation of the god (like the anthropomorphic figure rising out of the sun disk at Behistun and elsewhere) was apparently not considered objectionable as were free-standing cult images.

The son and successor of Ardashir I was Shapur I (A.D. 241–273). In the ongoing conflicts with Rome Shapur I won a great victory with the defeat and capture (A.D. 260) of the Roman emperor Valerian (253–260), an event memorialized in a rock carving at Naqsh-i Rustam.[80] Opposite, on the Ka'bah-i Zardusht, Shapur also left a long inscription (Shahpuhr KZ) in three languages (Parthian, Middle Persian, Greek)

78. Max Lauer, *Des Moses von Chorene Geschichte Gross-Armeniens,* 136.
79. Schmidt, *Persepolis,* 3.122–23, figs. 81–82.
80. Ibid., 127, plates 83–84.

in which he tells of the extent of his empire, the wars in which he has been successful, the Zoroastrian fires that he has founded, and the important persons in his retinue. Among these are two persons by the name of Kartir, but of separate identity: the first is identified as a priest (Parthian, *ayhrpat,* later *herbad*; Greek, *magus*), the second is identified as Kartir son of Ardawan. Kartir the priest served not only under Shapur I but also under several succeeding kings, including Shapur's two sons Hormizd I (273/274) and Bahram I (274–277) and the latter's son Bahram II (277–293). Kartir himself left a later inscription of his own on the Ka'bah-i Zardusht (Kartir KZ), in which he calls himself the *magupati* ("master of *magi,*" later *magbad, mobad*). It is evident that he has become the chief priest in the realm (after Tansar the second such great figure) and that he is a very strong Zoroastrian. In the inscription Kartir speaks of the destruction of images and of the founding of many sacred fires.[81]

The *Dinkard,* the *Bundahish,* and other Pahlavi texts of the Sasanian or later periods likewise contain many passages criticizing idolatry and commending the sacred fire. "Fire," says the *Dinkard,* "represents goodness, and images are its adversary"; "when the worship of images is ended, little departs with it of belief in the spiritual beings."[82]

## Fire and Fire Temples

It was noted above (p. 93) that along with Ahura Mazda's six visible creations—sky, water, earth, plants, animals, humankind—there was also a seventh, namely, fire (*atash, adar*), found in heaven, in human beings and animals, in plants, in lightning, in use in the world, and as the altar fire in the place of worship. Three of the altar fires on earth are the most sacred and ancient: Adar Farnbag, the fire of the priest; Adar Gushnasp, the fire of the warrior; and Adar Burzen-mihr, the fire of the husbandman (*Zadsparam* 11.1–8).

The story of these three great fires is related in *Bundahish* 17.4–9 and *Zadsparam* 11.9–10. In the long distant past in the reign of either Hoshyang or Takhmorup, the first and second Pishdadian monarchs, when people were continually going forth from Khwanirah to the other regions (*keshvars*), riding on the back of the mythical ox Sarsaok, the

81. Martin Sprengling, "Kartîr, Founder of Sasanian Zoroastrianism," *AJSL* 57 (1940): 197–228, exp. 202–3, 215; idem, "From Kartîr to Shahpuhr I," *AJSL* 57 (1940): 330–40; idem, "Shahpuhr I, The Great, On the Kaabah of Zoroaster (KZ)," *AJSL* 57 (1940): 341–420, esp. 414–15, nos. 50 and 60; and idem, *Third Century Iran; Sapor and Kartir,* 34, 39–41.

82. Mary Boyce, "Iconoclasm among the Zoroastrians," in *Christianity, Judaism and Other Greco-Roman Cults: Studies for Morton Smith at Sixty,* ed. Jacob Neusner, 4.107–8.

fire that they were carrying was blown into the sea, but shot up again as three fires on the back of the ox. Yim, the third Pishdadian monarch, established the first fire, Adar Farnbag, on the Gadman-homand ("glorious") mountain in Khwarezm (Chorasmia); later, the Kayanian king Kai Vishtaspa established the same fire at the Roshan ("shining") mountain in the country of Kavul (Kabul), "just as it remains there even now." Kai Khusrau demolished an idol temple on the shore of Lake Chechast (Lake Urumiah) and established the second fire, Adar Gushnasp, on the Asnavand mountain in Azerbaijan (*Bundahish* 12.26). The third fire, Adar Burzen-mihr, was established by Kai Vishtaspa on the Revand mountain in Khorasan (12.18).

Adar Farnbag, described in the foregoing as originally in Chorasmia but then moving to and remaining at Kabul, is placed by a number of Islamic sources at Kariyan, a small town and district in the modern province of Fars,[83] and it may be that the famous fire was moved once again from Kabul to this place.[84] In this case, with Adar Farnbag in Persia, Adar Gushnasp in Azerbaijan (i.e., Media), and Adar Burzen-mihr in Khorasan (i.e., Parthia), the three most famous fires were established one in each of the homelands of the three most important peoples of ancient Iran.

The only remains at the site of Kariyan in Fars to substantiate that this was indeed the location of Adar Farnbag are a ruined wall and tower (probably of Sasanian date) crowning a hill. They are locally called the "fort of the Fire-well," so named from a naphtha spring nearby. Such springs often provide the focus of a cult place; the localization is, however, hardly certain.[85]

The site of Adar Gushnasp and its fire temple on the Asnavand mountain in Azerbaijan was almost certainly at the place now called Takht-i Sulaiman ("throne of Solomon"), about one hundred miles southeast of Lake Urumiah in a wide valley more than 6,560 feet above sea level and surrounded by higher mountains. Here there is a lake on the top of a rocky hill, the hill itself (about 180 feet high and more than 0.6 miles in circumference) built up by the mineral deposits of the spring that feeds the lake. The site is recognizably that described by the Arab geographer Yaqut (A.D. 1179–1229) under the name of the city of Shiz, with citations from the poet Mis'ar ibn Muhalhal (c. A.D. 940) and another unnamed author:[86]

83. A. V. Williams Jackson, "The Location of the Farnbāg Fire, the Most Ancient of the Zoroastrian Fires," *JAOS* 41 (1921): 81–106.

84. Gnoli, *Zoroaster's Time and Homeland*, 36 n. 120.

85. Schippmann, *Die iranischen Feuerheiligtümer*, 86–94; see also Mary Boyce, "On the Zoroastrian Temple Cult of Fire," *JAOS* 95 (1975): 454–65.

86. C. Barbier de Meynard, *Dictionnaire géographique, historique et littéraire de la Perse et des contrées adjacentes, extrait du Mo'djem el-Bouldan de Yaqout*, 132–33.

Here is what Mis'ar ibn Muhalhal says about Shiz: "The town is situated . . . in the midst of mountains containing mines of gold, quicksilver, lead, silver, orpiment, and amethysts. . . . Walls enclose the city, and at the center of it is a lake whose depth is not known. . . . I sounded it to a depth of more than 14,000 cubits, without the plumb line coming to a rest. . . . There is also at Shiz a fire temple, which is for the inhabitants the object of great veneration. From it are lighted all the sacred fires of the Gabars [the name then used for the Zoroastrians remaining in Iran after the Muslim conquest] from the East to the West. The dome is surmounted by a silver crescent, which is considered a talisman, and which many rulers have tried in vain to remove from its foundation. One of the remarkable things in regard to the temple is that the fire has been kept burning in it for 700 years, and has not left any ashes and has not gone out once." . . . Another author states that at Shiz there is the fire temple of Adharakhsh which is highly celebrated among the Magians, and that it was customary for the kings of Persia, when they ascended the throne, to make a pilgrimage thither on foot.

In the foregoing description the name *Adharakhsh* for the fire temple at Shiz can well be a transcription of the name *Adar Gushnasp,* and thus points to this as the site of that famous fire temple. In 1959 and following, excavations were conducted at Takht-i Sulaiman by the German Archaeological Institute, and the ancient city was established as certainly of Sasanian date, with possibly even earlier settlement in Parthian and Achaemenian times. In the time of the city the whole top of the hill was enclosed by a massive mud-brick wall with gateways on the north and south. From the northern gate a processional way led to a temple precinct adjacent to the lake. This precinct was surrounded by walls on three sides, but left open to the lake on the south. The temple complex, built of limestone and baked brick, contained a series of chambers and pillared halls, with a domed square room and an adjacent cross-shaped room in the center; there was a place for fire in the form of a square basin in the latter room. In an entrance room were found many impressions of Sasanian seals, and a number of these contained the term *mobad,* the title of the high priest of a fire temple: "Mobad of the sanctuary of the fire Atur-i Gushnasp." Thus the identification of Takht-i Sulaiman as the site of Adar Gushnasp is almost certain.[87]

Notices in Arab geographers suggest that the district of Revand in Khorasan, on which mountain Adar Burzen-mihr was located, was equivalent to the present province of Nishapur (the city of Nishapur is on the road from Tehran to Mashad, eighty-eight miles before

87. Schippmann, *Die iranischen Feuerheiligtümer,* 309–57.

Mashad). Therefore the mountain named Revand and the fire temple on it would have been somewhere in the mountains northwest of Nishapur, but the exact location remains uncertain.[88]

In addition to the three most sacred and famous fires just described, there were in the Sasanian period many more fires and fire temples, known from both literary references and archeological materials. Some fifty temple ruins have been identified, the majority in Fars, the homeland of the Sasanians.[89] In the inscription of the Sasanian priest Kartir on the Ka'bah-i Zardusht at Naqsh-i Rustam two general categories of fires are recognized, namely, the Atash Vahram or great fire dedicated to Verethraghna, and the Atash Adaran ("fire of fires"), which was a general name for all the other fires.[90] Later there were three categories: the Atash Vahram, the "cathedral fire" of Zoroastrianism, consecrated in an elaborate ceremony and kept ever burning brightly in its domed sanctuary; the Atash Adaran, the "parish fire," installed and maintained more simply; and the Dadgah, the "little fire in an appointed place" (as its full name means), kept in any duly consecrated building or private chapel. Whatever the rank of the fire, once consecrated, it was a distinct entity, and was to be maintained if possible forever, although it could be moved if necessary to another site.[91] Wherever it was, the fire was the symbol of righteousness. Even the hearth fire in the home had its sacred character and was effective for good and against evil. Thus the "Litany to the Fire" (*Atash Nyaish* 9, 17) says:[92]

> Be burning in this house. Be ever burning in this house. Be brilliant in this house. Be increasing in this house . . . until the making of the good Renovation. . . .
> O Ahura! we wish thy mighty powerful Fire . . . to be a manifest help unto the ally, but a visible harm at thy beck, O Mazda! unto the foe.

As such, the fire is the sign of Zoroastrianism, which is far from being either meek or gloomy, but which contends with affirmative vigor for right thoughts, words, and actions.

The last relatively long and splendid reign of a Sasanian monarch was that of Khusrau II (A.D. 590–628), and the sculptured scene at Taq-i Bustan (near Hamadan/Ecbatana) of his investiture is the last such Sasanian carving. Here Khusrau stands between Ohrmazd at the

---

88. Ibid., 23–31.
89. Ibid., 505.
90. Ibid., 511.
91. Mary Boyce, "On the Sacred Fires of the Zoroastrians," *BSOAS* 31 (1968): 52–68.
92. Dhalla, *The Nyaishes*, 161–63, 185.

viewer's right and receives from the god the ring of sovereignty, while Anahita, still the patron *yazata* of the dynasty, stands at the left and also extends the symbol of authority.[93] Khusrau was also known for his activity in founding fire temples and appointing priests to serve the fires; on one occasion when he was at Shiz an Islamic source tells us that he remained constantly at prayer in the great fire temple (Adar Gushnasp).[94]

In the course of his reign Khusrau II engaged in a series of wars with the Byzantine Empire, during which Palestine was invaded and, with the exception of the Church of the Nativity at Bethlehem, Christian churches were destroyed and the "true cross" taken (614). The reciprocal attack by the Byzantine emperor Heraclius (610–642), begun in 622, resulted in the defeat of the Persians and the dethronement and death of Khusrau in 628, as well as the recovery of Palestine and the "true cross" by the Byzantines. In the course of Heraclius's campaign in Iran, Istakhr and its fire temple were destroyed and thereafter left deserted.[95] At Shiz, or Ganzaca as the Byzantines called it, the fire temple (Adar Gushnasp) was burned,[96] but the priests evidently managed to carry the sacred fire to safety, and afterward the temple was restored.

With the death of Khusrau II virtual anarchy ensued and various kings and pretenders followed in succession until Yazdegerd III, grandson of Khusrau, took the throne to reign from 632 to 651. In the year of Yazdegerd's coronation the first Arab forces entered Iran, and in 651 Yazdegerd was assassinated and the entire land fell to the Muslims.

## Later History

The official Muslim policy was that of toleration of Zoroastrianism, but the *Dinkard* speaks of "the ruin and devastation that came from the Arabs."[97] It was therefore an ever-decreasing remnant of Zoroastrians that remained in Iran. Continuing centers were at Yazd and Kerman, two oasis cities in the center of the land, and the two most sacred "cathedral" fires were brought to humble shrines in the secluded village of Sharifabad. These fires were Adar Farnbag and the most important Atash Bahram, perhaps the ancient sacred fire of Istakhr.

93. Ernst Herzfeld, *Am Tor von Asien: Felsdenkmale aus Irans Heldenzeit*, 71–103.

94. Schippmann, *Die iranischen Feuerheiligtümer*, 319.

95. Al-Mas'udi, *Les Prairies d'Or*, 2.541, par. 1403.

96. Georgius Cedrenus, *Historiarum Compendium*, 1.721–22, in J. P. Migne, ed., *Patrologiae cursus completus . . . Series Graeca* 121 (1894), 789–90.

97. *Sacred Books of the East*, 37.xxxi.

Early in the twentieth century, because of the difficulty of maintaining both in the proper manner, the two were united as one in the temple of the greater, Atash Bahram.[98]

From the tenth century onward groups of Zoroastrians made their way to India where, as the survivors and descendants of the ancient Persians, they are called Parsis. Their communities exist chiefly in Bombay and Calcutta; in both places their fires burn and their "towers of silence" receive the bodies of the deceased.[99] Small communities of Zoroastrians are found on almost every continent, and among them the symbols and values of the religion are maintained.[100] In the Western Hemisphere, the Fifth North American Congress of Zoroastrians met in Los Angeles in 1985, and the California Zoroastrian Center continues the work of Zoroastrian scholarship and publication, as well as worship.[101]

## Biblical Relationships

With the prominence of Zoroastrianism in Achaemenian times and later in Iran (probably from Cyrus the Great on), with the presence of the Jewish exiles in Babylonia when Cyrus took Babylon (539 B.C.), with the existence of the returned exiles' small state of Yehud (Judah) within the Persian Empire,[102] and with the continued residence of many Jews in Babylonia on into Parthian and Sasanian times,[103] the way seems open for possible relationships between Zoroastrianism and Jewish thought in the later Old Testament and intertestamental periods and following, and therewith also with the New Testament and early Christianity. In fact, although specific details are often debatable, there are agreements and probably reciprocal influences as well as distinctive differences.[104]

98. Mary Boyce, *A Persian Stronghold of Zoroastrianism*.

99. Jacques Duchesne-Guillemin, *Symbolik des Parsismus*; Sven S. Hartman, *Parsism: The Religion of Zoroaster*; John R. Hinnells, "The Parsis: A Bibliographical Survey," in *JMS* 3.1–2 (1980): 100–49. For current information, see *Parsiana* (published by Jahangir R. Patel, c/o H. L. Rechat, Navsari Chambers, 39 A. K. Nyak Marg, Bombay 400 001).

100. Jacques Duchesne-Guillemin, *Symbols and Values in Zoroastrianism*; Cyrus R. Pangborn, *Zoroastrianism: A Beleaguered Faith*.

101. For current information, see *The Zoroastrian* (published by the California Zoroastrian Center, 8952 Hazard Avenue, Westminster, Calif., 92683).

102. E. L. Sukenik, "Paralipomena Palaestinensia," *JPOS* 14 (1934): 178–84.

103. Jacob Neusner, *A History of the Jews in Babylonia*, vol. 1, *The Parthian Period*; and idem, *Judaism, Christianity, and Zoroastrianism in Talmudic Babylonia*.

104. Isidor Scheftelowitz, *Die altpersische Religion und das Judentum*; Richard N. Frye, "Iran und Israel," in *Festschrift für Wilhelm Eilers*, ed. Gernot Wiessner, 78. For references to other materials in similar sources, see Willard Gurdon Oxtoby, *Ancient Iran and Zoroastrianism in Festschriften*.

It has been thought possible to detect similarities between Cyrus's proclamation concerning his conquest of Babylon[105] and what the biblical prophet Isaiah says about Cyrus (45:1), and between some of the Gathic sayings of Zarathushtra and what Isaiah says about the Lord. For example, Zarathushtra asks Ahura Mazda who the creator of good thought is (*Yasna* 44.4) while Isaiah 40:13–14 asks "Who has directed the Spirit of the LORD . . . and taught him knowledge?"[106] Except for this very general similarity of belief in the Wise Creator, however, the evidence is hardly sufficient to demonstrate actual dependence of the biblical text upon Persian and Zoroastrian sources.[107]

Going beyond the general similarity of ideas to that of specific individual concepts, there is the development of biblical thought about Satan in comparison with Zoroastrian beliefs. In Job 1:6–12 and Zechariah 3:1–2 "the Satan" is the accuser of Job and of Joshua the high priest, and in 1 Chronicles 21:1 Satan is the one who incites David to number Israel (cf. 2 Sam. 24:1). Thus the earlier concept of Satan shows him playing essentially an adversarial role. In the New Testament he is called both Satan and the devil (ὁ διάβολος, the LXX translation of Satan), and is not only the "accuser" (Rev. 12:10) and the "tempter" (Matt. 4:1–3), but a distinctive personality who embodies the power of darkness. He is the enemy of light and of God (Acts 26:18), being "the prince of demons" (Matt. 9:34; etc.), "the ruler of this world" (John 12:31; etc.), the one who has the power of death (Heb. 2:14), and "a murderer from the beginning . . . a liar and the father of lies" (John 8:44); yet in the end he will be defeated forever (Rev. 12:9; 20:10).

In many respects the Zoroastrian Angra Mainyu/Ahriman, who is the hostile spirit, the enemy of Ahura Mazda's holy spirit, Spenta Mainyu, appears like a prototype of the biblical Satan. Angra Mainyu brought death into the world (*Yasna* 30.4); he has the *daeva*s or evil spirits under his control (30.6); likewise the *druj,* the demon of the Lie, the personification of deceit, is on his side against *asha,* the principle of Truth and Righteousness on the side of Ahura Mazda (30.8). But in the final outcome Deceit will be delivered into the hands of Truth (30.8), both "the most wicked *druj,* born of darkness," and "the evil-doing Angra Mainyu" will be overcome (*Yasht* 19.95–96), and with a fiery purge of evil the universe will experience renovation (*Bundahish* 30.29–32). Thus Zoroastrian influence may well be recognizable in the shaping of the biblical concept of Satan.[108]

105. *ANET,* 315–16.

106. Morton Smith, "II Isaiah and the Persians," *JAOS* 83 (1963): 415–21.

107. Jacques Duchesne-Guillemin, "Religion et politique, de Cyrus à Xerxés," *Persica* 3 (1967–1968): 1–9.

108. T. H. Gaster, "Satan," in *IDB,* 4.226.

There appears to be even closer parallelism between the form of Zoroastrianism known as Zurvanism and the doctrine of the Two Spirits in the *Manual of Discipline* (1QS) from Qumran. As noted briefly above (p. 88), in Zurvanism the opposition of the Twin Spirits of the Gathas (*Yasnas* 30 and 45) is turned into the opposition of Ahura Mazda and Angra Mainyu themselves, the two being held to have had a common father in Time (*zurvan*); they are called brothers and described as dwelling the one in Endless Light and the other in Endless Darkness.[109] Much in the same way in the *Manual of Discipline* (1QS 3.13–4.26) it is explained in terms of Jewish monotheism that when God created humans he established two spirits, "the spirits of truth and perversion" or "the spirits of light and darkness." The prince of light rules over the sons of righteousness and they walk in the ways of light; the angel of darkness rules over the sons of perversion and they walk in the ways of darkness. But God "has appointed an end to the existence of perversity," and "at the season of visitation, he will destroy it for ever" (1QS 4.18–19). Although most sources on Zurvanism are from Sasanian and later times, the doctrine probably developed already in the late Achaemenian period,[110] and thus was probably prior to and influential upon the closely similar doctrine at Qumran.[111]

There is also probable Zoroastrian influence in the development of biblical thought about the end of the world and the afterlife. In the earlier concept the abode of the dead, called Sheol (Gen. 37:35; etc.), is in the earth (Job 7:21) in a subterranean region of shadowy darkness (Job 7:9; 10:21–22). Later in Daniel 12:1–3 it is said that after the appearing of Michael, the great angel in charge of Israel, "many of those who sleep in the dust of the earth shall awake, some to everlasting life, and some to shame and everlasting contempt. And those who are wise shall shine like the brightness of the firmament." In the New Testament (Luke 16:23; etc.) the abode of the dead is called Hades (the usual translation of Sheol in the LXX), while there is fiery punishment in hell (γέεννα, Matt. 5:22; etc.; see also Rev. 20:13–15) and blessedness in paradise (Luke 23:43; etc.) and heaven (Rev. 19:1; etc.).

Not a few of these concepts may be compared with similar items in Zoroastrianism. The angel Michael in the passage about the resurrection in Daniel 12:1–3 is similar to Saoshyant, the future "helper of the good," who is described as the one "who makes the evil spirit impotent, and causes the resurrection [and] future existence" (*Bundahish* 11.6). The lake of fire into which Death and Hades will be thrown

---

109. *Dinkard* 9.30.4–5; *Zadsparam* 1.1–2; Zaehner, *Zurvan: A Zoroastrian Dilemma,* 312, 412.

110. Boyce, *Zoroastrians: Their Religious Beliefs and Practices,* 67–70.

111. Jacques Duchesne-Guillemin, *The Western Response to Zoroaster* 92–94; Robert G. Jones, "The Manual of Discipline (1QS), Persian Religion, and the Old Testament," in *The Teacher's Yoke: Studies in Memory of Henry Trantham,* ed. E. Jerry Vardaman and James Leo Garrett, Jr., 94–108.

(Rev. 20:14) is reminiscent of the torrent of molten metal that will destroy the deceitful (and also save the truthful—*Yasna* 51.9).[112] In both traditions there is expectation of an individual last judgment, and in both there is perfect confidence in the complete justice of the Judge (Rev. 16:5; see also *Yasna* 43.5: "Thou didst establish evil for the evil, and happy blessings for the good, by thy [great] virtue [to be adjudged to each] in the creation's final change"). Likewise in both traditions there are to some extent comparable descriptions of hell, paradise (a Persian word), and heaven. Ultimate fellowship with God is a common hope (Rev. 21:3; see also *Yasna* 41.1–2, as follows):

> And now in these thy dispensations, O Ahura Mazda, do thou wisely act for us, and with abundance with thy bounty and thy tenderness as touching us; and grant that reward which thou hast appointed to our souls, O Ahura Mazda! Of this do thou thyself bestow upon us for this world and the spiritual; and now as part thereof [do thou grant] that we may attain to fellowship with thee, and thy righteousness for all duration.

There are also elements in Jewish rabbinical literature that appear to derive from Zoroastrianism. For example, in a midrash to Isaiah 60 the Bridge, which in Zoroastrian representation the individual must cross at the time of death, is brought into relation to the messianic time when God will gather all the nations. It is said that at that time all the nations will have to pass over a long bridge, which extends over hell and leads to paradise. For the godless who set foot thereon the Bridge will become as small as a thin thread and they will fall into the depth of hell, while God himself will lead the pious Israelites across.[113] Also the Zoroastrian conception of an intermediate place between heaven and hell for souls neither good enough for the one nor bad enough for the other (*Dadistan-i Dinik* and *Arda Viraf Namak*; see p. 89) may be reflected in the Babylonian Talmud (*Rosh Hashanah* 16b; see also *Shabbath* 152b): "Three books are opened [in heaven] on New Year, one for the thoroughly wicked, one for the thoroughly righteous, and one for the intermediate."[114]

Beyond Israel and the Bible, Zoroastrianism was also influential in the Greek and Roman world,[115] and especially in Mithraism and Manichaeism.[116]

112. Rudolf Mayer, *Die biblische Vorstellung vom Weltenbrand: Eine Untersuchung über die Beziehungen zwischen Parsismus und Judentum.*

113. Scheftelowitz, *Die altpersische Religion und das Judentum,* 180.

114. Ibid., 186; *The Babylonian Talmud,* ed. I. Epstein, part 2: *Seder Mo'ed,* 4.63; 1.779.

115. Duchesne-Guillemin, *Western Response to Zoroaster,* 70ff.; Ruhi Muhsen Afnán, *Zoroaster's Influence on Greek Thought.*

116. Boyce, *Zoroastrians: Their Religious Beliefs and Practices,* 99, 111–12.

# 4

# Canaanite Religion

## Name and Area

In one manner of speech Canaan is called the land west of the Jordan River (Num. 33:51), but in a larger sense Canaanite territory is also described as extending from Sidon in the north to Gaza in the south and across to beyond Sodom and Gomorrah (southeast of the Dead Sea; Gen. 10:19). Sidon was one of the most ancient cities on the coast of Phoenicia, but in the same context (Gen. 10:15–18) there is also mention of the Arvadites and the Hamathites; the cities of Arvad and Hamath were yet farther north than Sidon, Arvad on an island off the Phoenician coast and Hamath on the Orontes River in north-western Syria. In other words the whole territory here described corresponds with present-day Israel, the so-called Gaza Strip and West Bank, Lebanon, and northwest Syria.[1]

The name *Canaan* is probably related to Akkadian *kinahhu,* which has the meaning of purple in the Amarna Letters and the Nuzi texts. Therefore the country was the Land of the Purple, the reference probably being to the manufacture of purple dye—a color very highly regarded in the ancient world—from the murex shellfish found on the Mediterranean coast. In Greek the word φοῖνιξ means "purple," and from this came the Greek name *Phoenicia* (φοινίκη) as the equivalent of Canaan. Later Phoenicia was the northern coastal region from the Eleutherus River (now Nahr al-Kebir, nineteen miles north of Tripolis) down to Mount Carmel, thus corresponding to modern Lebanon and parts of modern Syria and Israel.

Linguistically there were various dialects in the whole area (Ugaritic, Amorite, Eblaite, Hebrew, Phoenician; see table 1, p. 21), all

1. *Harper Atlas of the Bible,* ed. James B. Pritchard.

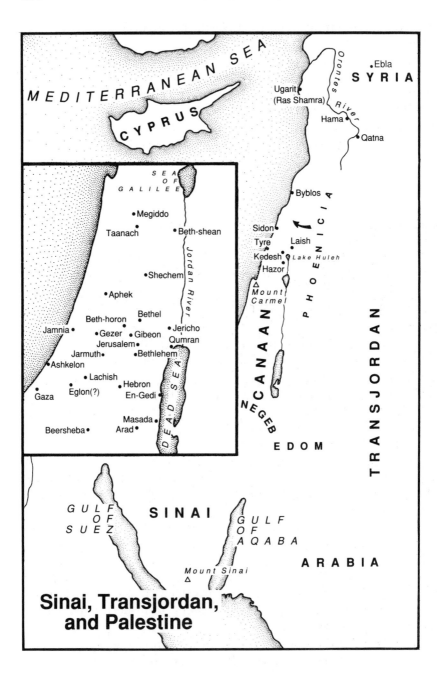

Sinai, Transjordan, and Palestine

included in the family known as Northwest Semitic and collectively called Canaanite.

Biblically the Canaanites are seen as descendants of Canaan (the son of Ham, Noah's second son) and include Sidon, Heth, Jebusites, Amorites, Girgashites, Hivites, Arkites, Sinites, Arvadites, Zemarites, and Hamathites (Gen. 10:15–18; 1 Chron. 1:13–16). Heth or the Hittites are best known as an Indo-European people who settled in Anatolia in the twentieth to eighteenth centuries B.C., and in the eighteenth and seventeenth centuries moved into northern Syria as well. Their Old Kingdom was founded around 1650, and their empire flourished from 1400 to 1200. According to Genesis 23 there were Hittites in Canaan when Abraham arrived there (probably around 1900), and there is no reason why they could not have been there in the nineteenth and eighteenth centuries.[2]

Otherwise all of the tribes listed, although perhaps diverse ethnically, presumably spoke a Northwest Semitic language. The Semitic Amorites are the best known: in Mesopotamian sources they are the *mar-tu* (Sumerian) and *amurru* (Akkadian), both of which words mean "west," and they are referred to as desert people who "know not grain."[3] In the third millennium B.C. the conquests of Sargon of Akkad (2371–2316) extended to "the upper sea,"[4] meaning that he must have marched west to the Mediterranean. In the second millennium the Amorites established their First Dynasty in Babylon in which Hammurabi (1792–1750) was the most famous king; contemporary with that dynasty there were Amorite kings in Mari on the Middle Euphrates. At Jericho and other sites in Canaan cultural changes toward the end of the third millennium suggest the influx of new nomadic tribal people, probably Amorites.[5] According to Ezekiel 16:3 Jerusalem was founded by a combination of Amorites and Hittites. Under Moses the Israelites found the Amorites in the hill country around Kadesh-barnea (Deut. 1:19–20), then conquered two Amorite kings, Sihon and Og, in Transjordan (Deut. 4:46–47). Joshua in turn overcame the Amorite kings of the five cities of Jerusalem, Hebron, Jarmuth, Lachish, and Eglon (Josh. 10:5). In time Amorites and Canaanites were no doubt so mingled as to be indistinguishable, and the name *Amorite* was used as a general term for the inhabitants of the land, which

2. James G. Macqueen, *The Hittites and Their Contemporaries in Asia Minor*; Aharon Kempinski, "Hittites in the Bible: What Does Archaeology Say?" *BAR* 5.5 (Sept.–Oct. 1979): 20–45; Kenneth A. Kitchen, *Ancient Orient and Old Testament*, 52.
3. *ANET*, 648.
4. George A. Barton, *The Royal Inscriptions of Sumer and Akkad*, 113, 115.
5. Kathleen M. Kenyon, *Digging Up Jericho*, 208–9; idem, *Amorites and Canaanites*, 34–35.

could equally well be called the land of the Amorites (Josh. 24:15) or the land of the Canaanites.

Of the remaining lesser tribes the Jebusites are relatively prominent because they were still in control of Jerusalem (sometimes called Jebus after them—Josh. 18:28; Judg. 19:10–11; 1 Chron. 11:4–5) when David captured the city and made it his capital (2 Sam. 5:6–10; 1 Chron. 11:4–9); he also purchased the threshing floor of Araunah the Jebusite and built an altar to the Lord on it (2 Sam. 24:15–25).

## Archeological Information

In the area described above and with reference to the archeological periods in the region (see table 2), the early presence of the Canaanites is attested by the names of cities such as Jericho, Megiddo, Beth-yerah, Arad, and others. All are shown by excavation to date from before 3000 B.C., and in some cases even back into the Chalcolithic and Neolithic periods. Since all the names are certainly Semitic, this provides evidence that most, if not all, of the inhabitants even in these early periods were Canaanites.[6]

Jericho (probably named for the Semitic moon-god, *yerah*)[7] was the oldest city, and already in the prepottery Neolithic Age (c. 7000 B.C.) occupied an area of ten acres and was surrounded by a defensive stone wall and tower (twenty-five feet in diameter and still standing to a height of nearly that much). There was also a building believed to have been a temple, a structure with a porch, hall, and inner shrine— a threefold division that was the usual rule in later Canaanite and

TABLE 2
## Archeological Periods in the Holy Land

| | |
|---|---|
| Neolithic Age | 7000–4500 |
| Chalcolithic Age | 4500–3100 |
| Early Bronze Age | 3100–2100 |
| Middle Bronze Age | 2100–1500 |
| Late Bronze Age | 1500–1200 |
| Early Iron Age | 1200–900 |
| Middle Iron Age | 900–586 |
| Late Iron Age | 586–332 |

6. William F. Albright, *Yahweh and the Gods of Canaan*, 97; *AEHL*, 71.
7. T. H. Gaster, "Moon," in *IDB* 3.436.

Israelite temples. In the late Chalcolithic Period (c. 3300–3200 B.C.) there was a temple at Megiddo with a long, oblong hall and a base of mud-brick construction for the image of a deity and for offerings. On a high hill overlooking the oasis of En-Gedi and the western shore of the Dead Sea in the same period there was a large, walled rectangle with a shrine containing an object tentatively identified as an altar, an identification supported by the finding of animal bones, pottery, and ashes.[8]

## The Third Millennium

In the Early Bronze Age (mostly corresponding with the third millennium B.C.) there were many Canaanite cities and villages besides those already mentioned. In general preferred locations were on hills near a supply of water, usually a spring. Jerusalem, where the earliest settlement was on the slope of the southeastern hill above the Gihon Spring, is an example; but the remains of the Early Bronze settlement are minimal, chiefly fragments of pottery and part of the foundation of a rectangular structure, probably a house.[9]

Particularly where cities commanded routes of trade or passes used in war, they were fortified with walls of large, unhewn stones or bricks. At Megiddo (commanding the pass from the Mediterranean coastal plain) the first wall belongs to the Early Bronze Age and was about fifteen feet thick built of brick on a stone foundation. At Beth-yerah ("the house of the moon," Khirbet el-Kerak, at the southeastern end of the Sea of Galilee where the Jordan River flows out) the city wall of the same period was twenty-five feet thick, with a vertical section in the center and sloping walls on both sides. At Arad (in the Negev on the main road to Edom) in the Early Bronze Age the wall was of stone, about eight feet thick, and strengthened by projecting semicircular towers.

Houses were usually rectangular and built at first of unbaked mud brick, later of stone. Crops were cultivated on plains adjacent to the town; grain was stored in clay-lined pits. Burial was commonly in shaft graves, with a deep shaft leading to the burial chamber; the burial places were outside the inhabited area. Pottery, found in the houses and in the tombs, was made on the wheel, burnished, and painted.

## The Second Millennium

In the Middle and Late Bronze ages (corresponding approximately to the second millennium B.C.) Canaanite cities were larger and more

8. *AEHL*, 103, 165, 310–11.
9. Yigal Shiloh, *Excavations at the City of David*, vol. 1, *1978–1982*, 25.

Canaanite altar on the summit of the excavated mound of ancient Megiddo

prosperous. Jerusalem was now a formidably fortified city as shown by the archeological excavation of two segments of a solid, massive city wall midway down the slope of the hill above the Gihon Spring, a wall dated by its excavators to about 1800 B.C.[10] On the slope of the hill above the wall an entrance (twenty-six feet deep) cut in the rock gives access to a tunnel (118 feet long), first stepped, then horizontal, which leads to a point outside the wall but still underground. There a vertical shaft (forty feet deep) descends to another tunnel, which brings water from the Gihon Spring (seventy-two feet to the east); thus protected access was provided the inhabitants to the only natural water supply of the city. Other remarkable water shafts are at Hazor, Gezer, and Gibeon. Most such systems are thought to have been constructed in the Iron Age (tenth century B.C.), but the Jerusalem system has been dated as early as the Late Bronze Age and was probably the system of the Jebusites prior to the coming of David (assuming that the word צִנּוֹר [ṣinnôr] in 2 Samuel 5:8 is correctly translated as "water shaft," RSV).[11]

Houses were built in the usual oriental style, with rooms arranged

10. Kathleen M. Kenyon, *Digging Up Jerusalem,* 83; Shiloh, *City of David,* 26.
11. Kenyon, *Digging Up Jerusalem,* 88–89; Shiloh, *City of David,* 23, 27.

around a central court, and usually in two stories. Large houses are often thought to have been palaces, and such identification may be considered very likely at least in cases where a hoard of ivory or gold, or inscribed material, is found. At Megiddo, for example, there is a Middle Bronze Age building quite near the city gate, similar to the private houses in plan, but more carefully built; in the Late Bronze Age it was extended to 150 feet in length and surrounded by a wall six feet thick. A washroom is a new feature, and under the floor of one of the rooms more than two hundred carved and incised ivories were found, dated by the excavators to 1350–1150 B.C.[12] One of these is an ivory pen case that belonged to an Egyptian who bore the title, "Royal Envoy to Every Foreign Country"; it is to be dated just after 1200 B.C. since it carries the cartouche of Ramses III (1184–1153). Another is an ivory plaque that apparently shows the prince of Megiddo in the celebration of a victory: at the right he drives naked captives before his chariot; at the left he sits upon a sphinx-sided throne and drinks from a bowl while a musician plays upon a harp; at the extreme left is a large jar decorated with animal heads. At Taanach (five miles southeast of Megiddo) forty clay tablets written in Akkadian in about the fifteenth century B.C. were found in the palace of the local ruler. Some of these mention Amunhotep, possibly the second of this name, who served as governor of Canaan before he became the king of Egypt (1438–1412). One letter refers to divination practiced in the name of Asherah, doubtless the goddess also known from Ras Shamra (see p. 141): "If there is a wizard of Asherah, let him tell our fortunes, and let me hear [quickly]; and the [oracular] sign and interpretation send to me."[13]

In the archeological sites of the Middle and Late Bronze ages many Canaanite temples have also been found. In general they have the threefold architectural division already noted in the very early temple at Jericho (porch, hall, and inner shrine), and their sacred character is further confirmed by various cult objects, altars, votive statues, remains of offerings, and the like. Orientation in the Middle Bronze Age was mostly east-west, in the Late Bronze Age north-south.[14]

At Hazor, for example, four temples have been found. In the Lower City in Area H the so-called Orthostat (meaning stones "standing upright") Temple was begun in the seventeenth or sixteenth century and rebuilt several times until the destruction of the city in the thirteenth century. In the ruins were incense altars and libation tables, as well

---

12. Gordon Loud, *The Megiddo Ivories.*

13. Ernst Sellin, *Tell Ta'annek,* 108, 113–14; William F. Albright, "A Prince of Taanach in the Fifteenth Century B.C.," *BASOR* 94 (April 1944): 12–27; *AEHL,* 303.

14. *AEHL,* 311.

as the seated statue possibly of a king and the broken statue of a deity standing on a bull. On the breast of the deity and also on an incense altar is a four-pointed star enclosed in a circle. Both the circle-and-rays emblem and the bull were otherwise associated with the Semitic weather- and storm-god Hadad, so the temple was probably a sanctuary of this deity.

The basic plan of this and many other Canaanite temples seems prototypical of the later temple of Solomon in Jerusalem as described in 1 Kings and 2 Chronicles, with porch (vestibule—1 Kings 6:3), main hall (nave, Holy Place—1 Kings 6:3; 8:8), and inner shrine (inner sanctuary, Most Holy Place, Holy of Holies—1 Kings 6:5; 6:16; Heb. 9:3). In the Orthostat Temple there are also two pillar bases at the entrance from the porch into the main hall, and these may resemble the pillars Jachin and Boaz in Solomon's temple (1 Kings 7:21).

The small Stelae Temple in Area C in the Lower City featured upright slabs, perhaps like the מַצֵּבָה (maṣṣēbâ, cultic pillars) frequently mentioned and condemned in the Old Testament (Exod. 23:24; etc.). On one stele a relief depicts two hands stretched upward toward an emblem composed of a crescent and a disk within the crescent, presumably the crescent and the full moon. The crescent emblem is also on the breast of a seated male statue, the head of which had been knocked off. Presumably this was a sanctuary of the moon-god, and the statue a representation of the moon-god himself.

The third temple in the Lower City (in Area F) began as a double temple in the Middle Bronze Age and was made into a square temple in the Late Bronze Age. One theory as to the original form is that the double temple was for two deities, like another double temple of about the same period found in Ashur, Assyria, which was dedicated to the sun-god Shamash and the moon-god Sin. The fourth excavated temple at Hazor is in the Upper City (in Area A), and consisted of a single room, long and rectangular, with a platform in front of its entrance on which were votive offerings, pottery, and the remains of animals. This sanctuary was in use in the Middle Bronze Age in the eighteenth–sixteenth centuries B.C.[15]

Cult objects found in the Canaanite temples have been mentioned in the foregoing. Particularly numerous in Canaanite sites, both in private houses and in cult places, are female figurines of clay or metal. Many of these are believed to be representations of the mother goddess, associated with fertility, love, and war, known to the Israelites through the Canaanites and called Ashtoreth (plural, Ashtaroth—Judg.

15. Yigael Yadin, *Hazor: The Rediscovery of a Great Citadel of the Bible*; Yohanan Aharoni, "Temples, Semitic," in *IDBS*, 874.

2:13; 1 Kings 11:5; Astarte in Greek). A study based primarily on metal figurines from datable contexts in excavated sites places their time range from the late third millennium to the early first millennium B.C. but mainly in the second millennium, and both the chronological and geographical evidence justify their attribution chiefly to the Canaanites.[16]

## Mesopotamian and Egyptian Relationships

In the Middle and Late Bronze ages (corresponding approximately to the second millennium B.C.) there are external sources, both Mesopotamian and Egyptian, for the knowledge of Canaan and the Canaanites. The city of Mari (Tell Hariri on the Middle Euphrates in Syria), a prosperous city already in the first half of the third millennium B.C., was at its height in the first quarter of the second millennium under a dynasty of Amorite kings who were contemporary with the First Dynasty of Babylon. The names of three of the Mari kings in direct line of descent are known: Iagitlim, Iakhdunlim, and Zimrilim. Zimrilim lost the kingdom to Hammurabi of Babylon, who destroyed Mari in 1761 and 1759 B.C. In the palace of the Mari kings, in levels dated around 1800–1760, some twenty thousand cuneiform documents were found, almost all written in the Akkadian language, most belonging to the reign of Zimrilim, and most being administrative and economic texts and political and diplomatic communications.[17]

In the texts and especially in an inventory of incoming and outgoing shipments of tin (valued because bronze was an alloy made of copper and tin), there is mention of several places on trade routes in the Syrian/Palestinian area. These include Aleppo, capital of Yamkhad in northern Syria; Ugarit, on the northern Syrian coast; Qatna (Tell el-Mishrife), east of the Orontes River in middle Syria; Laish, at the southern foot of Mount Hermon (this Canaanite city was later renamed Dan and in the phrase *from Dan to Beersheba* was considered the northernmost point of Israelite territory (Judg. 18:29; 20:1; now Tel Dan); and Hazor, some twenty miles south of Laish.[18]

That cuneiform documents—including literary materials—circulated in Canaan itself is shown by the discovery at Megiddo, probably

16. James B. Pritchard, *Palestinian Figurines in Relation to Certain Goddesses Known Through Literature*; Ora Negbi, *Canaanite Gods in Metal: An Archaeological Study of Ancient Syro-Palestinian Figurines*.
17. Stephanie Dalley, *Mari and Karana: Two Old Babylonian Cities*, 10ff.
18. A. Malamat, "Syro-Palestinian Destinations in a Mari Tin Inventory," *IEJ* 21 (1971): 31–38.

from the palace archives, of a cuneiform tablet containing some forty lines of the "Epic of Gilgamesh."[19]

At the accession of Sesostris I (1971–1928 B.C., the second king in the Twelfth Dynasty of the Egyptian Middle Kingdom) an Egyptian noble named Sinuhe fled the country for political reasons and the story of his adventures (in texts from the Twelfth to the Twenty-first Dynasty) tells how he passed through Qedem, meaning the East generally, and arrived in Upper Retenu, Retenu being the usual Egyptian name for Palestine and Syria. Here Sinuhe settled in "a good land, named Yaa," which is described in language similar to that later applied to Palestine in the Old Testament (Exod. 3:8; Deut. 8:8; etc.):

> Figs were in it, and grapes. It had more wine than water. Plentiful was its honey, abundant its olives. Every (kind of) fruit was on its trees. Barley was there, and emmer. There was no limit to any (kind of) cattle.[20]

From the time of Sesostris III (1878–1843) and on into the Second Intermediate Period in Egypt, the so-called Execration Texts (on pottery bowls from Thebes, now in the Berlin Museum, and on clay figurines of bound captives, now in the Cairo and Brussels museums) name among enemies of Egypt a number of rulers and places in Palestine and south Syria. These include Ashkelon in the southern coastal plain of Palestine, Beth-shemesh southwest of Jerusalem, Shechem in the hills in the interior of Palestine, Hazor southwest of Lake Huleh, Acco (Acre) and Byblos on the Phoenician coast, and Jerusalem listed with two different rulers, Yaqar-Ammu and Setj-Anu.[21]

In spite of such efforts by magical execrations to ward off enemies, a dynasty of foreign rulers known as the Hyksos established themselves in control not only of Syria and Palestine but also of Egypt itself during approximately the years 1650–1542 B.C. Their name corresponds to the Egyptian "rulers of foreign lands," but was also understood to mean "shepherd kings." They were probably preponderantly Semitic Amorites/Canaanites.[22]

After the Hyksos were expelled by native Egyptian princes at the beginning of the Egyptian Eighteenth Dynasty and New Kingdom, Thutmose III (1490–1436) marched repeatedly across Syria-Palestine (called Djahi in his inscriptions) in campaigns that reached as far as

---

19. G. Ernest Wright in *BA* 18 (1955): 44; A. Goetze and S. Levy, "Fragment of the Gilgamesh Epic from Megiddo," *'Atiqot*, English series 2 (1959): 121–28; Yohanan Aharoni, *The Archaeology of the Land of Israel*, 142–43, photo 24.

20. *ANET*, 19.

21. *ANET*, 329.

22. Robert Martin Engberg, *The Hyksos Reconsidered*; John Van Seters, *The Hyksos: A New Investigation*, 190; Raphael Giveon, in *Lexikon der Ägyptologie* 1:464; *AEHL*, 150.

the Euphrates. He fought a notable and successful battle at Megiddo against a coalition of foreign country princes and thus, as he says, overthrew the wretched Retenu and extended the frontiers of Egypt.[23] Likewise his successor, Amunhotep II (1438–1412), campaigned several times in Retenu, and he records the bringing back of booty and captives, including 640 Canaanites.[24] These pharaohs and later ones, especially Ramses II (1290–1224) and Sheshonq I (945–924), give in their inscriptions long lists of conquered places in Palestine/Syria, many of them well-known biblical sites.[25]

The Amarna Letters, found at Tell el-Amarna in 1887, are some 350 cuneiform documents, written in Akkadian (the main language of international communication). They are originals and copies of correspondence between Babylonian, Hittite, and Mitannian rulers; vassal princes and governors in Syria, Phoenicia, and Palestine; and Amunhotep III (1402–1364) and Amunhotep IV (Akhenaten, 1364–1347) in Egypt. In Canaan it is evident that the cities and city-states were by no means united, were often in rivalry, and besides were under attack from without, especially from the invaders called Habiru (probably meaning "those who have crossed a boundary"). Egyptian sovereignty was not effectively manifested in Canaan, although Egyptian help was often urgently requested, and that with extravagant protestations of loyalty to the Egyptian throne.[26]

With the Egyptian presence in Canaan came also Egyptian writing (hieroglyphic/hieratic). Such inscriptions have been found, for example, at Tell Shera and Tel Lachish; likewise in Aphek the dedication plaque of a temple that Ramses II erected to the goddess Isis; and in Lachish a bronze cartouche of Ramses III (1184–1153), as well as the cartouche of the same pharaoh at Megiddo already mentioned (p. 125).[27]

## The Alphabet

Situated as they were between Mesopotamia with its cuneiform and Egypt with its hieroglyphic and presumably with some knowledge of both systems of writing, it is the Canaanites themselves who are credited with the invention of the alphabet, an invention that may be dated around 1700 B.C. as the following evidence will show.[28]

---

23. *ANET*, 234–38.
24. *ANET*, 245–47.
25. *ANET*, 242–43.
26. *ANET*, 483–90.
27. Moshe Kochavi, "At That Time the Canaanites Were in the Land . . .," in *Recent Archaeology in the Land of Israel*, ed. Hershel Shanks and Benjamin Mazar, 34.
28. Godfrey Rolles Driver, *Semitic Writing from Pictograph to Alphabet*, ed. S. A. Hopkins, 98–99; Joseph Naveh, *Early History of the Alphabet*, 23–42, 53–54, 65–66, 175–86.

The so-called Proto-Canaanite alphabetic script is known from early inscribed objects, a potsherd from Gezer (c. 1800–1650 B.C.), a plaque from Shechem of approximately the same period, a dagger from Lachish (c. 1700–1550), and others; while the so-called Proto-Sinaitic texts (found at Serabit el-Khadem on the Sinai Peninsula, dating c. 1500) are of much the same type. The signs used were pictographic at first, most with acrophonic values (i.e., the picture symbolizes the initial sound of the depicted word). These evolved into linear letters, initially twenty-seven in number and by the thirteenth century reduced to twenty-two. A cuneiform alphabetic script of thirty letters has also been found on clay tablets recovered from ancient Ugarit (fourteenth–thirteenth centuries B.C.), evidently an adaptation of the cuneiform to the alphabetic system. The writing of the alphabetic script was in any direction: right-to-left, left-to-right, vertical, or horizontal.

By the mid-eleventh century the twenty-two letters of the later Proto-Canaanite became the standardized Phoenician script, written in right-to-left horizontal lines. Presumably in the twelfth or eleventh century the incoming Israelites took over from their Canaanite/Phoenician neighbors the same script in which to write the Hebrew language. The earliest extant Hebrew inscription is the Gezer Calendar (c. 925 B.C.). From Phoenicia the alphabet also passed on to Greece (archaic Greek script, c. 1100 B.C.), brought according to Greek mythology by Kadmos, son of Agenor king of Phoenicia, and from there in completed form it came to all the nations of the Western Hemisphere. The invention of the alphabet was indeed "an act of stunning innovation, a simplification of writing which must be called one of the great intellectual achievements of the ancient world."[29]

## The Israelites

Israelite tradition concerning the migration of Abraham, the exodus, and the settlement in Palestine puts these events most probably in the main Canaanite period of the second millennium B.C. (approximately the Middle and Late Bronze ages). Biblical chronology puts Abraham most probably around 1900 B.C., and the statement of Exodus 1:11 that the children of Israel in Egypt were constrained to labor in the building of the city Raamses, which must be the city of Ramses

29. Frank Moore Cross, "Early Alphabetic Scripts," in *Symposia Celebrating the Seventy-fifth Anniversary of the Founding of the American Schools of Oriental Research (1900–1975)*, ed. Frank Moore Cross, 101.

II (1290–1224)—now located at Tell ed-Dab'a/Khata'na/Qantir in the Egyptian Delta—suggests a date around 1290 for the exodus.[30]

When Abraham came from Haran, "the Canaanites were in the land" (Gen. 12:6). His first stopping place was at Shechem and the oak of Moreh. Shechem must have been already an important place because it is mentioned not only in the Execration Texts, but also in an inscription of Khu-sebek who took part in a military campaign to Shechem under Sesostris III. The excavation of Shechem (Tell Balatah near Nablus) revealed an older stone wall nearly eight feet thick, and although the date of the wall is not certain, Shechem was surely already fortified at the time of the Egyptian campaign in the first half of the nineteenth century. Later Abraham planted a tamarisk tree at Beersheba "and called there on the name of the LORD" (Gen. 21:33), but at Shechem he built only an altar. Nothing is said of his having planted the oak of Moreh, so this tree must already have marked an older place of Canaanite worship.[31] Going on (Gen. 12:8), Abraham pitched his tent and built an altar on the ridge east of Bethel (Beitin, eleven miles north of Jerusalem), "and called on the name of the LORD." Here excavation indicates foundation of the city around 2000 B.C., at least a century before Abraham's time, and tombs in the neighborhood of the ridge suggest holy ground.[32]

When Joshua led the Israelites into Palestine he confronted Canaanites, Hittites, Hivites, Perizzites (the Perizzites presumably among the branches of the Canaanites, although not mentioned in the lists in Gen. 10:15–19 and 1 Chron. 1:13–16), Girgashites, Amorites, and Jebusites (Josh. 3:10). A city prominently mentioned as conquered, utterly destroyed, and burned was Hazor (Josh. 11:10–12). The excavation of the site shows that the city was completely destroyed by fire in the second half of the thirteenth century (which the excavator attributes to Joshua as in the biblical record), with seminomadic settlement thereafter in the twelfth century (which the excavator attributes to the incoming Israelites). As a generalized statement of the outcome of the Israelite invasion, it is said that "Joshua took the whole land . . . and . . . gave it for an inheritance to Israel" (Josh. 11:23). But it is also explained that "much land [yet remained] to be possessed" (Josh. 13:1), and at many places the Canaanites "persisted in dwelling" in the land, although "when Israel grew strong, they put the Canaanites to forced labor, but did not utterly drive them out" (Judg. 1:27–35). Among

30. William F. Albright, *From the Stone Age to Christianity*, 150, 195.
31. W. L. Reed, "Moreh," in *IDB* 3.438; Aharoni, *Archaeology of the Land of Israel*, 94, 99.
32. J. L. Kelso, "Bethel (Sanctuary)," in *IDB* 1.391.

these were the inhabitants of Jerusalem, the Jebusites (Josh. 15:63), from whom the city was finally taken by David (2 Sam. 5:6–9).[33]

After the relative eclipse of their civilization in Palestine the Canaanites emerged again in the first millennium B.C. in their famous maritime kingdom centered in Tyre and Sidon in Phoenicia. Hiram king of Tyre was a contemporary of David and Solomon and furnished materials and craftsmen for the building of David's palace (2 Sam. 5:11; 1 Chron. 14:1) and the temple of Solomon (1 Kings 5:10, 18; 2 Chron. 2:3, 7–8, 13–16; 4:11–16). From Phoenicia came also Jezebel, daughter of the priest-king of Tyre and Sidon, Ithobaal (887–856 B.C.— whom the Bible calls Ethbaal king of the Sidonians), to marry Ahab king of Israel (874–853), and to be condemned by the prophet Elijah and murdered at the command of Jehu (841–814; 1 Kings 16:31; 21:23; 2 Kings 9:33). Later the district of Tyre and Sidon was visited by Jesus (Matt. 15:21; Mark 7:24). Christians fleeing from the persecution that followed the martyrdom of Stephen came to Phoenicia (Acts 11:19), Paul and Barnabas passed that way (Acts 15:3), and Paul landed at both Tyre and Ptolemais (Acco/Acre; Acts 21:3, 7).[34]

## Biblical Information
## about Canaanite Religion

Specific references to the religion of the Canaanites in the Old Testament generally represent it very unfavorably. There are many references to the god Baal (בַּעַל [ba'al] means "master, owner, lord"),

33. Yadin, *Hazor*, 145, 253; idem, "Hazor," in *IDBS*, 389; idem, "The Transition from a Semi-nomadic to a Sedentary Society in the Twelfth Century B.C.E.," in *Symposia*, ed. Cross, 57–68; and idem, "Is the Biblical Account of the Israelite Conquest of Canaan Historically Reliable?" *BAR* 8.2 (Mar.–April 1982): 16–23, esp. p. 23: "Archaeology broadly confirms that at the end of the Late Bronze Age, semi-nomadic Israelites destroyed a number of major Canaanite cities; then, gradually and slowly, they built their own sedentary settlements on the ruins, and occupied the remainder of the country." See also Abraham Malamat, "Israelite Conduct of War in the Conquest of Canaan," in *Symposia*, ed. Cross, 35–55; and idem, "How Inferior Israelite Forces Conquered Fortified Canaanite Cities," *BAR* 8.2 (Mar.–April 1982): 24–35.

Rather than such a military conquest some now hold that the Israelite occupation of Canaan was accomplished by a primarily peaceful infiltration and subsequent expansion of settlement— Yohanan Aharoni, "The Israelite Occupation of Canaan: An Account of the Archaeological Evidence," *BAR* 8.3 (May–June 1982): 14–23; Manfred Weippert, *The Settlement of the Israelite Tribes in Palestine*; idem, "Canaan, Conquest and Settlement of," in *IDBS*, 125–30. Others maintain that what really transpired was an indigenous social movement in the form of a peasant revolt against the powerful classes—Norman K. Gottwald, "Were the Early Israelites Pastoral Nomads?" *BAR* 4.2 (June 1978): 2–7; idem, "John Bright's New Revision of *A History of Israel*," *BAR* 8.4 (July–Aug. 1982): 56–61; and idem, *The Tribes of Israel*. These theories, however, require radical reinterpretation of the plain meaning of the biblical accounts.

34. For the Phoenicians, see Sabatino Moscati, *The World of the Phoenicians*; Gerhard Herm, *The Phoenicians: The Purple Empire of the Ancient World*.

and also to a plurality of Baals, and references to the altar (Judg. 6:25), the house (1 Kings 16:32), the prophets (1 Kings 18:19), and the high place (בָּמָה [bāmâ], Jer. 19:5) of Baal. Worship of Baal was practiced with the burning of incense (2 Kings 23:5), upon occasion by the prophets' outcry and the cutting of themselves with swords and lances (1 Kings 18:26), and by the burning of children in fire as burnt offerings to Baal (Jer. 19:5).

The word *Asherah* (masculine plural, Asherim; feminine plural, Asheroth) is both the name of a goddess and also the term for a cult object by which the goddess was represented. As a cult object the Asherah was normally made of wood and accordingly could be cut down and burned (Judg. 6:25–26). A tree could be planted as an Asherah (Deut. 16:21), or a graven image of Asherah could be made (2 Kings 21:7). Mention can therefore be made of both Asherah (plainly meaning the goddess) and "her image" (2 Chron. 15:16). As a cult object the Asherah could well stand beside the altar of Baal (Judg. 6:25). Like Baal, Asherah also had prophets and upon occasion they appear in almost as great numbers (four hundred) as the prophets of Baal (450, 1 Kings 18:19). Cult prostitutes—both male and female (1 Kings 14:23–24; Deut. 23:17)—were also associated with Asherah (2 Kings 23:7), and their practices were presumably considered efficacious in the promotion of fertility in family, herds, and fields.

The Hebrew name *Ashtoreth* (plural, Ashtaroth) is rendered as Astarte ('Ἀστάρτη) in the Greek translation of the Old Testament (e.g., 1 Kings 11:5), and the goddess so named appears to be the same as the Akkadian Ishtar and the Sumerian Inanna and like them to have aspects of fertility, love, and war (see p. 26). The form of the name in Hebrew embodies the vowels of the word *bosheth* (shame), and she is called both "the goddess of the Sidonians" (1 Kings 11:5, 33) and "the abomination of the Sidonians" (2 Kings 23:13). She did in fact have a great temple in Sidon, which is mentioned by the second-century A.D. Greek author Lucian.[35] In Canaan there was a temple of Ashtaroth at Beth-shan (1 Sam. 31:10); in the excavation of the site many of the so-called Astarte figures were found in Layers IX–V of the Late Bronze Age and the beginning of the Iron Age, and the "northern temple" in Level V was possibly the temple of Ashtaroth just mentioned.[36] The similarity of names and character suggests the possibility that Asherah and Ashtoreth were one and the same; yet they are mentioned separately and may have been distinct goddesses.

35. *The Syrian Goddess (De Dea Syria); Attributed to Lucian*, ed. Harold W. Attridge and Robert A. Oden, 13, §4.
36. T. C. Mitchell, "Ashtaroth, Ashtoreth," in *NBD*, 96; idem, "Beth-shean, Beth-shan," in *NBD*, 146, fig. 36; *AEHL*, 51–52.

That the incoming Israelites were often attracted by the Canaanite religion, and upon occasion served the Baals and the Ashtaroth and made their own Asherim, is attested in many biblical passages (e.g., Judg. 2:11, 13; 1 Kings 14:15); equally plain is the biblical denunciation of such practice as the forsaking of the Lord, the God of their fathers (Judg. 2:12).

## Canaanite Literature and Biblical Relationships

Canaanite literature itself, to some extent, has now become available and provides firsthand information about Canaanite culture and religion. The reference is to written documents found at Ebla and Ugarit.

### Ebla

Like his grandfather, Sargon of Akkad, Naram-Sin (2291–2255 B.C.) marched far to the west, and in an inscription at Ur that records the expedition and its conquests there is the name of Ebla.[37]

The ancient city is identified with Tell Mardikh in north Syria (halfway between Hamath and Aleppo), and was excavated in 1964 and following by an Italian mission under the direction of Paolo Matthiae, with Giovanni Pettinato as epigrapher.[38] The most important find was that of nearly twenty thousand cuneiform tablets and fragments of tablets in the ruins of the royal palace. Most of these are written in the Sumerian script in a language now called Eblaite, which is a dialect of Northwest Semitic and related to biblical Hebrew (see table 1, p. 21). A number of syllabaries provide bilingual vocabularies in Sumerian and Eblaite. The majority of the texts are essentially state archives, including economic and administrative records; they reveal Ebla as a city of 260,000 inhabitants and the center of a kingdom that controlled much of Syria and Palestine and flourished around 2400–2250 B.C., that is, until Ebla was destroyed by Naram-Sin on his

37. *Ur Excavations: Texts,* part 1, *Royal Inscriptions,* ed. C. J. Gadd and L. Legrain, 1.74–75, no. 275; 2, plate 56.

38. Paolo Matthiae, *Ebla: An Empire Rediscovered;* Giovanni Pettinato, *The Archives of Ebla: An Empire Inscribed in Clay;* Chaim Bermant and Michael Weitzman, *Ebla: A Revelation in Archaeology; Eblaitica: Essays on the Ebla Archives and Eblaite Language,* ed. Cyrus H. Gordon, Gary A. Rendsburg, and Nathan H. Winter, vol. 1.

campaign in the west. There is also said to be a relatively small number of literary compositions, containing some twenty myths.[39]

As named in the texts, the Eblaite pantheon numbered about five hundred divinities, but only a relatively few are important.[40] In the highest position is Dagan, a West Semitic vegetation- and fertility-god, especially connected with grain (which takes over his name in Hebrew). Dagan is recognized also in the Code of Hammurabi,[41] and credited by both Sargon of Akkad and Naram-Sin for their conquests in the west.[42] In the Old Testament this is Dagon, the national god of the Philistines (Judg. 16:23; etc.). In Ebla a whole city quarter and one of the city gates bear the name of Dagan, and the first month of the calendar year was dedicated to him under the appellation of "lord." Among other deities, mostly known elsewhere in the Semitic tradition, are Hadad, the storm-god; Sipish, the sun-god; Rashap, the god of pestilence; Ashtar, the male god of war and love; and Baal, the storm-god. The otherwise unknown "Dabir, the god of Ebla," appears as the tutelary divinity of the city and of its dynasty. Female deities are Belatu ("lady"), the companion of Dagan; Ashtarte, the counterpart of the male Ashtar; and Ishatu, a fire-goddess. Whether *il* and *ya,* which appear as components of personal names, are also divine names or only mean "god" generally, is debated.[43]

Although there are many gods, the use of *il* and *ya* in personal names (if these are indeed divine names) and the special application of the term *lord* to Dagan, suggest the special worship of one god. And one literary text, preserved in three fragmentary copies, is something like a litany that salutes one god, not otherwise named, as simply the "Lord of heaven and earth":

> Lord of heaven and earth:
> the earth was not, you created it,
> the light of day was not, you created it,
> the morning light you had not [yet] made exist.
> Lord: effective word
> Lord: prosperity
> Lord: heroism
> Lord: . . .
> Lord: untiring
> Lord: divinity
> Lord: who saves
> Lord: happy life.[44]

39. Pettinato, *Archives of Ebla*, 238.
40. Ibid., 245ff.; Bermant and Weitzman, *Ebla*, 154, 164–66.
41. *ANET*, 165.
42. *ANET*, 268.
43. Bermant and Weitzman, *Ebla*, 178–82.
44. Pettinato, *Archives of Ebla*, 249, 259–60.

The Ebla tablets are thus of unquestioned importance for knowledge of Northwest Semitic language, culture, and religion. Unfortunately controversy arose between the expedition leader, Matthiae, and the original epigrapher, Pettinato, and in 1980 Pettinato was replaced by Alfonso Archi.[45] The controversy focused especially on the question of the relevance of the Ebla texts to biblical research. At one point the Syrian Department of Antiquities obtained from Pettinato an official "Declaration" in which he repudiated various reports of "pretended links with the biblical text."[46] As to points at issue, for example, it has been both affirmed (by Pettinato)[47] and denied (by Archi and his associates)[48] that the tablets contain the names of Ur (in the territory of Haran), the biblical Sodom and Gomorrah, and Jerusalem. Other reported items of possible but debated relevance to the Old Testament are a flood story said to have some similarities to the flood story in Genesis, and the litany quoted just above with its statements about creation, which have been said to echo the first chapter of Genesis.[49] Obviously much further publication and unprejudiced study of the Ebla texts are needed,[50] and it is certainly necessary, as Pettinato has said, "to be willing to study again and above all the Old Testament in the light of Ebla."[51]

## Ugarit

The ancient city of Ugarit is named already in the second millennium B.C. in Egyptian inscriptions of Amunhotep III (1402–1364) and Horemhab (1334–1306)[52] and in Hittite texts,[53] and is identified with the site named Ras Shamra not far north of Latakia on the coast of Syria, opposite the island of Cyprus. Together with the nearby necropolis of the city at Minet el-Beida ("white harbor"), Ugarit has been

45. "New Ebla Epigrapher Attacks Conclusion of Ousted Ebla Scholar," *BAR* 6.3 (May–June 1980): 55–56.

46. "The Official 'Declaration' Submitted by Chief Ebla Epigrapher," *BAR* 5.2 (Mar.–April 1979): 38; cf. "The Known, the Unknown and the Debatable," *BAR* 6.3 (May–June 1980): 48–50; "Ebla Scholarship à la Syrienne," *BAR* 8.1 (Jan.–Feb. 1982): 54.

47. "BAR Interviews Giovanni Pettinato," *BAR* 6.5 (Sept.–Oct. 1980): 47–48, 51.

48. Alfonso Archi, "Are 'The Cities of the Plain' Mentioned in the Ebla Tablets?" *BAR* 7.6 (Nov.–Dec. 1981): 54–55; James D. Muhly, "Ur and Jerusalem Not Mentioned in Ebla Tablets, Say Ebla Expedition Scholars," *BAR* 9.6 (Nov.–Dec. 1983): 74–75.

49. Giovanni Pettinato, "Ebla and the Bible—Observations on the New Epigrapher's Analysis," *BAR* 6.6 (Nov.–Dec. 1980): 38–41; "Archi Responds to Pettinato," *BAR* 6.6 (Nov.–Dec. 1980): 42–43.

50. Paul C. Maloney, "The Raw Material," *BAR* 6.3 (May–June 1980): 57–59.

51. "The Official 'Declaration,'" 38. For further possible biblical connections, see Mitchell Dahood, "Are the Ebla Tablets Relevant to Biblical Research?" *BAR* 6.5 (Sept.–Oct. 1980): 54–60; and idem, "Ebla, Ugarit, and the Bible," in Pettinato, *Archives of Ebla*, 271–321.

52. *ANET*, 243.

53. *ANET*, 352.

under excavation by the French Mission Archéologique de Ras Shamra
ever since 1929, when the site was first investigated by Claude F.-A.
Schaeffer, the first and long-time director of the mission.[54]

The excavations have uncovered stratification levels from the Neolithic and Chalcolithic ages through the Early, Middle, and Late Bronze
ages. Ugarit flourished in the Late Bronze Age (1500–1200 B.C.). The
destruction of the city in about 1200 B.C. resulted, it appears, from a
combination of natural disaster, drought, famine, earthquakes, and
ultimately fire, with resumption of settlement only in the Late Iron
Age and on a much less extensive scale.[55] At its height in the fifteenth
to thirteenth centuries the city occupied an area of fifty acres, with
both narrow lanes and tight-packed buildings, but also wide thorough-
fares and large houses, some with their own libraries. In the western
section of the city was the royal palace, with some ninety rooms, five
large courtyards, and collections of royal archives. On slightly higher
ground in the north were two great temples, one for Baal and one for
Dagan, and between the two temples was the large house of the high
priest, which contained a library and probably also served as a scribal
school.

The written clay tablets that have been recovered from the libraries
and archives now number in the thousands. Those from the palace
archives are largely economic, legal, and administrative and contain
important historical material;[56] those from the priest's house are largely
legend, myth, and ritual; and there are also religious and other texts
from private houses. The texts are in a variety of languages and scripts;
most are in Akkadian cuneiform, the international language of the
time; others are in Sumerian, Hurrian, Hittite, and Cypro-Minoan,
with some Egyptian hieroglyphic inscriptions; while about fourteen
hundred are in the Northwest Semitic language now known as Ugaritic, written in the alphabetic cuneiform mentioned above (p. 130).
The latter are of the most importance for the religion and biblical
relationships of Ugarit.[57] The literary texts are almost all in the form

54. See reports in *Syria* 10 (1929): 285–97, and subsequent issues; in the series Mission de Ras
Shamra (vol. 1 in 1931), which included the subseries of volumes entitled *Ugaritica* (vol. 1 in 1939);
and in Claude F.-A. Schaeffer, *The Cuneiform Texts of Ras Shamra–Ugarit.*

55. Claude F.-A. Schaeffer, "Les causes de la disparition d'Ugarit," in *Ugaritica*, 5, 760–68; idem,
"The Last Days of Ugarit," *BAR* 9.5 (Sept.–Oct. 1983): 74–75.

56. For the kings of Ugarit, see Kenneth A. Kitchen, "The King List of Ugarit," *UF* 9 (1977):
131–42.

57. Centers of study are at Münster (*Ugarit-Forschungen: Internationales Jahrbuch für die
Altertumskunde Syrien-Palästinas* [Neukirchen-Vluyn: Neukirchener Verlag, 1969– ]) and Clare-
mont, Calif. (*Ras Shamra Parallels* 1– [Analecta Orientalia 49–; Rome: Pontificium Institutum
Biblicum, 1972– ]); see also Peter C. Craigie, "Ugarit and the Bible: Progress and Regress in 50
Years of Literary Study," *Ugarit in Retrospect*, ed. Gordon Douglas Young, 103–4.

of poetry, and exhibit the same distinctive feature of parallelism as does Hebrew poetry.[58]

Among the religious texts found at Ugarit there is a "Pantheon of Ugarit" (found in three texts, two Ugaritic and one Akkadian) in which the chief gods of Ugarit are listed.[59] The first item in the Akkadian version (lines 1–2) is DINGIR (the determinative for god), followed by *a-bi ilum*; the fragmentary Ugaritic probably reads *il ib*. The word *il*, *ilu(m)*, or *el* is common to all the Semitic languages; in the broadest sense it can have the general appellative meaning of "god," but it can also be the proper name of a specific deity.[60] The word *ib* or *ab* means "father." Here the text can be read as a reference to "the god of the [or, my] father" and be reminiscent of the concept of "the god of the fathers" noted in chapter 1 (p. 30); or the reading can be, "god the father," referring to the god El, one of whose titles is Father, or to a god so designated but distinct from El.

At any rate, as known throughout the religious texts of Ugarit, El is the first of the major gods and the head of the pantheon.[61] In the epithets that are applied to him, he is seen as the father of the gods and human beings, and as the creator of heaven and earth. The totality of the gods constitutes his family, and he presides over the assembly of the gods.[62] The title "Bull" is frequently given to him, presumably to signify his power and/or procreative ability, and he is called king, wise, holy, and everlasting or eternal (*olam*).[63]

> Indeed our creator is eternal,
> Indeed ageless is he who formed us.
>
> Your decree, O El, is wise,
> Your wisdom is eternal.[64]

The abode of El and the place where he presides over the assembly of the gods is described as on a mountain located at the source of two rivers; he dwells there in a tabernacle or tent-shrine. The place envisioned is apparently a cosmic mount somewhere in the north.[65]

58. Peter C. Craigie, *Ugarit and the Old Testament,* 53–55.

59. Jean Nougayrol, "Panthéon d'Ugarit (RS 20.24)," in *Ugaritica,* 5.42–64; Frank Moore Cross, *Canaanite Myth and Hebrew Epic,* 14ff.

60. J. J. M. Roberts, *The Earliest Semitic Pantheon,* 21, 31–32.

61. Marvin H. Pope, *El in the Ugaritic Texts.*

62. E. Theodore Mullen, Jr., *The Divine Council in Canaanite and Early Hebrew Literature.*

63. Pope, *El in the Ugaritic Texts,* 27, 35, 42–43.

64. Mullen, *Divine Council,* 17, 145.

65. Ibid., 130–33; Cross, *Canaanite Myth and Hebrew Epic,* 36–39. For El as possibly earlier located on Mount Sapan/Zaphon and displaced there by Baal, see Ulf Oldenburg, *The Conflict Between El and Ba'al in Canaanite Religion.*

In the Old Testament El (and also Elohim, plural but usually used in a singular intensive sense) is of course a very frequent word and has the generic Semitic appellative connotation of God, alongside the personal name of YHWH (written with the vowels of Adonai or Lord, resulting in "Jehovah," but in the RSV, "the LORD"; e.g., Exod. 3:15). While the biblical El is thus a general term and does not refer to the personal name of the Ugaritic god El, there are linguistic reminiscences of Ras Shamra. For example, at Ugarit El was characterized as everlasting or eternal (*olam*), and likewise (e.g., Gen. 21:33) the Lord is the Everlasting God (YHWH *el olam*). Also the location of the Ugaritic El and the assembly of the gods over which he presides on a cosmic mountain in the north appears to be reflected in the vaunt of the Day Star, who says in Isaiah 14:13, "I will sit on the mount of assembly in the far north." Also the representation that El dwelt in a tent-shrine on a mountain calls to mind the presence of the Lord on Mount Sinai (Exod. 19:20), the making of the tabernacle by Moses according to the plan shown to him on the mountain (Exod. 26:30), and the fact that the earthly "tent of meeting" was the chief sign of the presence of the Lord among his people (Exod. 29:42–45).[66]

Although the object is uninscribed, a stele found at Ras Shamra and dated to the thirteenth century is most probably a representation of El. The personage is seated on a lion-footed throne and rests his feet on a footstool. Mature in age and paternal and majestic in appearance, he wears a long robe and a high crown with horns coming up from its base, and raises his right hand as if in benediction. A lesser figure stands in front, holding a vase and an animal-headed scepter, perhaps the king of Ugarit making an offering or a supplication. Overhead is a winged disk with an eight-pointed star in the middle.[67]

Next in order in the "Pantheon of Ugarit" lists (lines 3–4) are Dagan (the Semitic vegetation-god, see p. 135) and Baal Sapan. Baal, frequently spoken against in the Old Testament, is in fact the most prominent deity in the Ras Shamra texts, and many designations apply to him.[68] He is not only the Lord of Sapan, but also is called the son of Dagan, is identified with the Semitic storm-god Hadad, and is named Aliyan Baal (meaning "the one who prevails: Baal"), Lord of Ugarit, Lord of Earth, and Zebul Baal (meaning "Prince Baal"). In 2 Kings 1:6, 16, the god of the Philistine city of Ekron is called Baal-zebub (זְבוּב) [*zĕbûb*] means "fly," rendered βααλ μυῖαν, "Baal Fly," by

66. Richard J. Clifford, *The Cosmic Mountain in Canaan and the Old Testament*; and idem, "The Tent of El and the Israelite Tent of Meeting," *CBQ* 33 (1971): 221–27.

67. *Syria* 18 (1937): 128–34 and plate facing p. 128; *ANEP*, fig. 493; Schaeffer, *Cuneiform Texts of Ras Shamra–Ugarit*, 60.

68. Arvid S. Kapelrud, *Baal in the Ras Shamra Texts*.

the Septuagint; see also Josephus, *Antiquities* 9.19). This may be an intentional and disparaging distortion of the name. In Matthew 12:24 and elsewhere in the New Testament Beel-zebul is presumably the same god, and is identified as the prince of demons.[69]

The name *Baal Sapan* identifies Baal as the god of the mountain Sapan (also spelled Zaphon). This mountain is almost certainly to be identified with Jebel Aqra, anciently called Mons Casius (in Hellenistic-Roman times the seat of Zeus Kasios), a lofty mountain that can be seen to the north of Ras Shamra (about half-way to the mouth of the Orontes River) and is frequently covered with heavy clouds from the storms that come in from the Mediterranean.[70] While the mountain is in the north, its name (*sapan*) does not occur in Ugaritic with the meaning of north, but in the Hebrew Old Testament the same word (*zaphon*), presumably derived originally from the mountain, is of frequent occurrence and always means simply "north." In Psalm 48 Mount Zion is "in the far north, the city of the great King."

### The Baal Cycle

The mythology concerning Baal is found in some eight large tablets and a number of fragments. Because of damage there are gaps in the narrative, and the sequence of events is not beyond question. Nevertheless three major episodes are recognizable: the conflict of Baal with the god Yamm (Sea); the building of a palace for Baal; and the conflict of Baal with the god Mot (Death).[71]

In the first episode,[72] Yamm, son of El, whose name, like the related word in Hebrew, means Sea, and who is called by the parallel titles "Prince Sea" and "Judge River," demands of the assembly of the gods that Baal and his powers be delivered over to him, and El agrees that Baal shall be the servant of Yamm. Kothar wa-Khasis, however, the craftsman of the gods, whose name means something like "skillful and clever," provides Baal with two clubs and promises that Baal will be able to smite his enemy and take his own "eternal kingdom" and "everlasting dominion." Thereupon Baal does battle with Yamm and is victorious. Henceforward Yamm is evidently confined to his proper realm, the seas, while Baal is indeed the lord of the earth. In other words the forces of chaos typified by the ocean have been brought under control

---

69. T. H. Gaster, "Baal-zebub," in *IDB* 1.332; idem, "Beelzebul," in *IDB* 1.374.

70. Otto Eissfeldt, *Baal Zaphon: Zeus Kasios und der Durchzug der Israeliten durchs Meer*, 3–7, 30–35; Stan Rummel, "Narrative Structures in the Ugaritic Texts," in *Ras Shamra Parallels*, 2.318–24.

71. Helmer Ringgren, *Religions of the Ancient Near East*, 144ff.

72. *ANET*, 130–31; J. C. L. Gibson, *Canaanite Myths and Legends*, 37–45; Michael David Coogan, *Stories from Ancient Canaan* 86–89.

and order established in the world. The goddess Ashtoreth is mentioned in the account, but the text is so fragmentary that it is not possible to know what role she played. Although named frequently in Old Testament references to Canaanite religion, Ashtoreth appears only a few times in the Ugaritic texts, in contrast with the numerous appearances of Asherah, which gives some support to the theory that Ashtoreth and Asherah are one and the same.

On one hand, the victory of Baal over Yamm is reminiscent of the victory of Marduk over Tiamat as the unruly primeval ocean in Mesopotamian myth (see pp. 33–34). On the other hand there is something of the same theme of the restriction of the might of the sea in biblical language: the Lord "by his power . . . stilled the sea" (Job 26:12); he prescribed bounds for the sea, saying, "Thus far shall you come, and no farther, and here shall your proud waves be stayed" (Job 38:10–11).

The episode of the building of a palace for Baal is recounted in two texts.[73] In the story, as elsewhere in much of the Ugaritic mythology, two female deities are prominent, namely, Anath (or Anat) and Asherah (or Athirat) (see the "Pantheon of Ugarit," lines 20, 24). Both have largely the same characteristics as warlike goddesses of love and fertility and both are sometimes called daughters of El. Lady Asherah of the Sea, as she is named in full, however, is also called the "creatress of the gods." From this point of view she must be the wife of El, the father of the gods. Asherah, it will be remembered, is also named frequently in Old Testament references to Canaanite religion. Anath, often called the Virgin Anath, is the consort of Baal and also called his sister; she is regularly at his side and is his helper in many circumstances.[74]

In the first of the two texts concerning the palace for Baal, Anath is the central character.[75] For some unexplained reason she engages in a fierce battle in a plain where she wades in the blood of her enemies up to her knees and thighs. After the battle Baal, evidently weary of war, sends messengers to ask Anath to

> withdraw war from the earth,
> set upon the land love,
> pour forth peace in the midst of the earth,
> increase love in the midst of the fields.

73. *ANET,* 131–35; Gibson, *Canaanite Myths and Legends,* 46–67; Coogan, *Stories from Ancient Canaan,* 89–106.

74. Kapelrud, *Baal in the Ras Shamra Texts,* 66–78; and idem, *The Violent Goddess: Anat in the Ras Shamra Texts;* U. Cassuto, *The Goddess Anath*—see the frontispiece for a stele with a relief of Anath seated and holding a weapon in each hand.

75. Cassuto, *Goddess Anath,* 82–105 (the quotations from the first text about the palace are from this translation).

Anath agrees to the proposal for peace, but in the same context also recalls the earlier victory over Yamm, otherwise attributed to Baal, and seems to claim it for herself:

> Behold, I smote El's Beloved, Sea,
>   I destroyed the Great Rivers of El,
> I muzzled Tannin [the Sea Dragon], yea, I muzzled him,
>   I smote the Crooked Serpent,
>   the monster of seven heads.[76]

In another text the same crooked or twisting serpent is named Lotan.[77] Lotan is probably a contracted form of the name *Leviathan* in the Bible, and the Ugaritic *tannin* is the same as the regular Hebrew word for "dragon"; thus we can understand that it is these very mythical figures that are used in the Old Testament as symbols of wicked powers overcome by the Lord in the past or to be overcome in the end time:

> Thou didst divide the sea by thy might;
>   thou didst break the heads of the dragons on the waters.
> Thou didst crush the heads of Leviathan. [Ps. 74:13–14]

> In that day the LORD . . . will punish Leviathan the fleeing serpent, Leviathan the twisting serpent, and he will slay the dragon that is in the sea. [Isa. 27:1]

After another gap in the text we come to the specific matter of the palace for Baal. The problem is that Baal has no "house" like the other gods and, at Baal's request, Anath goes off to ask El for permission to build such a palace. Displaying her violent character again, Anath says that if El refuses she will even bring down the hoary head of the deity to the grave. El evidently agrees, however, and the text breaks off with the sending of a message to the craftsman of the gods, Kothar wa-Khasis, who is evidently to build the house.[78]

The second text about the palace begins with Baal's lament that he has no house like the gods. He and Anath then go together to ask Asherah, El's wife, to help them. Asherah agrees and she and Anath go to El, while Baal leaves for his own mountain, Sapan. El is

76. The Ugaritic text is not without ambiguity and it is possible that it should be translated in such a way that Anath claims only to have taken some part in the battle along with Baal: "O Baal . . . did you not crush Sea and destroy River? Did I not muzzle Tannin? You crushed the Crooked Serpent. . . ." (Kapelrud, *Violent Goddess*, 54–62).

77. *ANET*, 138; Cassuto, *Goddess Anath*, 50.

78. Cassuto, *Goddess Anath*, 98, 105; *ANET*, 137–38.

persuaded and decrees that such a house be built, while Lady Asherah of the Sea is pleased and compliments El upon the wisdom of his decision and remarks that Baal will thereby be able to exercise his proper functions as god of storm and rain:

> You are great, El, you are truly wise;
> your gray beard truly instructs you. . . .
> Now Baal will begin the rainy season,
> the season of wadis in flood;
> and he will sound his voice in the clouds,
> flash his lightning to the earth.[79]

So Anath returns to Baal with the good news, and Baal summons Kothar wa-Khasis and commissions him to build the palace among the peaks of Sapan. It was "a house of silver and gold, a house of purest lapis lazuli." For Baal as a king the house was his palace and proof of his royal status; for him as a god it was his temple, like the "houses" of the other gods. To celebrate, Baal gave the gods a great feast, and then sent off a message to his enemy, Mot (Death), to tell him that the house was built. This further sequence of events in which, after the conquest of Yamm, the palace is built and the gods eat the banquet, is also reminiscent of the Mesopotamian story in which, after Marduk's victory over Tiamat, the gods built Esagila, the temple tower of Marduk at Babylon, and then gathered in festive banquet (see p. 34).

In another text Baal appears enthroned on his mountain and in the exercise of his functions as god of the storm, as Asherah said he would do when once he had his "house." Therefore in the sequence of events this item presumably follows upon the completion of the palace. The broken text is translated in part as follows:[80]

> Baal sits as a mountain sits, Hadd . . . as the ocean;
> In the midst of his mount, Divine Sapan, in . . . the mount of his
>     dominion.
> Seven lightning bolts, . . . eight storehouses of thunder; a shaft of
>     lightning. . . .
> On his head. . . .
> His feet stamp on the wicked, [his] horn(s) [ris]e above him.

79. Coogan, *Stories from Ancient Canaan*, 101; see also *ANET*, 133; Gibson, *Canaanite Myths and Legends*, 60–61.

80. Charles Virolleaud, "RS 24.245 (Ba'al assis sur sa montagne)," in *Ugaritica*, 5.557–59; Loren R. Fisher and F. Brent Knutson, "An Enthronement Ritual at Ugarit," *JNES* 28 (1969): 157–67; Marvin H. Pope and Jeffrey H. Tigay, "A Description of Baal," *UF* 3 (1971): 117–30 (with the translation given here).

Insofar as this text is a description of Baal it may be compared with a stele from Ras Shamra that is surely depicting Baal. The god wears a belted kilt and a horned cap or helmet, stands upon a mountain, raises a club in his right hand, and in his left hand holds a long pointed shaft, the upper part of which looks something like a tree but is probably stylized lightning.[81] This text, with Baal enthroned on his mountain after his victory over Yamm (the sea), has been compared with Old Testament passages that speak of the Lord as "enthroned" (e.g., Ps. 29:3, 7–8, 10):[82]

> The voice of the LORD is upon the waters;
>   the God of glory thunders,
>   the LORD, upon many waters.
> . . . . . . . . . .
> The voice of the LORD flashes forth flames of fire.
> The voice of the LORD shakes the wilderness.
> . . . . . . . . . . . . . . .
> The LORD sits enthroned over the flood;
>   the LORD sits enthroned as king for ever.

The third episode in the Baal cycle is that of the conflict of Baal with Mot, a text found on two tablets, these also with many gaps.[83] Like the related word in Hebrew, the name of Mot means Death, and he is here called "divine" and "the beloved of El," so Mot is the god of the underworld. His city is called " 'Miry,' where a pit [cf. Ps. 88:6; etc.] is the throne on which (he) sits, filth the land of his heritage."

At the end of the palace episode Baal sent a message to Mot to tell him that his own house had been built, a message that seems to be in the nature of an assertion of his own new status and a challenge therewith to Mot. As the present text begins, Mot appears to be responding to Baal with a statement in which he says (if rightly translated) that even if Baal has done great things, still he must die:

> For all that you smote [Leviathan the slippery serpent]
> (and) made an end of [the wriggling serpent],
> the tyrant [with seven heads]. . . .
> [I myself will crush] you [in pieces]. . . .
> [Indeed you must come down into the throat of divine Mot.]

---

81. *Syria* 14 (1933): plate facing p. 122; Schaeffer, "La grande stèle du Baal au foudre de Ras Shamra," in *Ugaritica,* 2.121–30, plates xxiii–xxiv; *ANEP,* fig. 490; Schaeffer, *Cuneiform Texts of Ras Shamra–Ugarit,* 64.

82. Cross, *Canaanite Myth and Hebrew Epic,* 151–56.

83. *ANET,* 138–41; Gibson, *Canaanite Myths and Legends,* 68–81 (the quotations are from this translation); Coogan, *Stories from Ancient Canaan,* 106–15; Baruch Margalit, *A Matter of "Life" and "Death": A Study of the Baal-Mot Epic (CTA 4-5-6).*

Baal accepts the inevitable, says that he is the servant of Mot, and evidently goes down into the underworld. When the fate of Baal becomes known both El and Anath lament and perform rites of mourning, crying "Baal is dead," and asking what will become of all Baal's people. El then suggests that Athirat of the sea (Asherah) give one of her sons to be king in place of Baal, and she proposes her son Athtar the terrible. Athtar, accordingly, attempts to occupy the throne of Baal on Mount Sapan, but is inadequate and comes back down to a more limited sovereignty on earth.

> Thereupon Athtar the terrible
> went up into the recesses of Zaphon;
> he sat on the seat of mightiest Baal,
> (but) his feet did not reach the foot-stool,
> his head did not reach its top.
> And Athtar the terrible spoke:
> "I cannot be king in the recesses of Zaphon."
> Athtar the terrible came down,
> he came down from the seat of mightiest Baal,
> and became king over the whole broad earth.

Astronomically Athtar was the planet Venus, which rises before dawn as the harbinger of the new day, and was the son of Shachar (Dawn; see p. 152) and the morning star or the Day Star (Hebrew, הֵילֵל [hêlēl], "bright one"). It is the mythological event just described that is reflected in the taunt against the king of Babylon in Isaiah 14:12–15:

> How you are fallen from heaven,
>   O Day Star, son of Dawn!
> How you are cut down to the ground,
>   you who laid the nations low!
> You said in your heart,
>   "I will ascend to heaven;
> above the stars of God
>   I will set my throne on high;
> I will sit on the mount of assembly
>   in the far north;
> I will ascend above the heights of the clouds,
>   I will make myself like the Most High."
> But you are brought down to Sheol,
>   to the depths of the Pit.

On the other hand the morning star (Greek, φωσφόρος, lit. "bringing light," "light-bringer") has an entirely good connotation in the

exhortation in 2 Peter 1:19 to pay attention to scriptural prophecy
"until the day dawns and the morning star rises in your hearts."

Meanwhile, as the episode continues, with Baal dead and the rains
no longer coming that he would otherwise send, the sun blazes and
the fields dry up. Anath, however, demands that Mot give up her brother.
She then cleaves Mot with a sword, winnows him with a sieve, burns
him (i.e., the chaff and straw from the winnowing) with fire, grinds
him with millstones, and sows him in the field (i.e., to fertilize the
fields for the next crop). Mot is therefore associated not only with the
summer and its drought, but also with ripening fruits and grain. El
then saw in a prophetic vision that "the heavens rained oil, the ravines
ran with honey." In that way he knew that Baal was alive again. So
El was glad, and

> he lifted up his voice and cried:
> "Even I may sit down and be at ease,
> and (my) soul within me may take its ease;
> for mightiest Baal is alive,
> for the prince lord of earth exists."

It is plainly the succession of the seasons that is represented by Baal
and Mot, and that succession is the symbol of death and resurrection.

Tied together by the palace episode, the two conflicts of Baal—the
one with Yamm and the other with Mot—are a structural pair.[84] They
differ, however, in that the first, in which Baal brought under control
the chaotic forces of the universe represented by the sea, presumably
occurred only once, whereas the second, in which Baal goes down into
the mouth of Death but comes up again, plainly occurs over and over
in every year's alternation of dry season with the death of plants, and
rainy season with the revival of vegetation. With this, however, is
expressed the hope of life again after death.

### The Legend of Keret

The Ugaritic texts also contain two legends, those of Keret and of
Aqhat. The legend of Keret is contained on three broken tablets.[85]
Keret is a king, and at the outset he has lost no less than seven wives
through various disasters. One wife was carried off by Resheph (the
god of pestilence, equated with the Mesopotamian Nergal ["Pantheon

84. David L. Petersen and Mark Woodward, "Northwest Semitic Religion: A Study of Relational Structures," *UF* 9 (1977): 233–48, esp. 237–43.

85. *ANET*, 142–49; Gibson, *Canaanite Myths and Legends,* 82–102 (the quotations are from this translation); Coogan, *Stories from Ancient Canaan,* 58–74; John Gray, *The Krt Text in the Literature of Ras Shamra: A Social Myth of Ancient Canaan.*

of Ugarit," line 26]; in Hebrew the word means "flame," as in Job 5:7 where the sparks that fly upward are literally "sons of the flame"); another was lost to "the pages of Yamm" (i.e., in the waves of the sea). As a result Keret has no heir to the throne. The king is himself called the page and the servant of El (in the sense of "favorite" and "intimate") and El is called his father (cf. Ps. 2:7). El appears to Keret in a dream and tells him to offer sacrifices and prepare for war. He is to campaign against the state of Udm, a seven-day march away, and demand of King Pabil his daughter in marriage. She is named Huray, and is as beautiful as Anath and Astarte. This is accomplished and, in due time, Keret and Huray have many sons and daughters. Keret is later so seriously ill that he is expected to die. El, however, sends a female spirit named Shataqat, who heals Keret's fever. Yet more trouble follows, when one of the king's sons, Yassib, demands the throne on the grounds that Keret is still too ill to rule properly.

> You have been brought down by your failing power.
> You do not judge the cause of the widow,
> you do not try the case of the importunate. . . .
> Because you have become brother to a bed of sickness,
> companion to a bed of plague,
> come down from the (throne of your) kingdom (that) I may be king.

Keret, however, is strong again and will not yield; he instead utters a curse on his presumptuous son in the names of Horon (evidently a deity with power over life and death, probably also worshiped at two towns in Palestine named Beth-horon, "house of Horon," Josh. 16:3, 5) and of Astarte-name-of-Baal (i.e., hypostasis of Baal).

So the legend ends, a story something like that of the biblical Job in the succession of disasters for the king, and a story that emphasizes the importance of proper kingly succession and of kingly strength and will (in biblical language) to execute justice for the fatherless and the widow and to deliver the poor who cry and the fatherless who have none to help (Deut. 10:18; Job 29:12).

### The Legend of Aqhat

Like the legend of Keret the legend of Aqhat is also contained on three incomplete tablets.[86] At the outset of the story a man named Danel (not Daniel), known as He-of-Harnam (presumably the name of

---

86. *ANET*, 149–55; Gibson, *Canaanite Myths and Legends*, 103–22 (quotations are from this translation); Coogan, *Stories from Ancient Canaan*, 32–47.

his city), has no son but desires one to care for him in his old age[87] and to continue his line after his death. To bring his desire before the gods Danel sleeps in a temple and, on the seventh day, Baal intercedes on his behalf with El, who promises a son. Danel returns home and holds a seven-day feast in his house for the Kotharat. (These are goddesses associated with childbirth, whose name means "skillful" and who are described as "the swallow-like daughters of the crescent moon" [lit. "the swallows," these birds being commonly associated with happiness in the home]). When Danel's son is born he is named Aqhat, and it is for him that the legend is named.

When Aqhat is older, Kothar wa-Khasis, the "skillful and clever" craftsman of the gods, brings a bow for him so that he may be a great hunter. The bow is evidently of marvelous character, and the goddess Anath asks for it, promising silver and gold and even the gift of immortality in exchange. Aqhat refuses, for immortality is something that even Anath cannot give.

> Do not lie, O Virgin;
> for to a hero your lying is unseemly.
> As (his) ultimate fate what does a man get?
> What does a man get as (his) final lot?
> Glaze will be poured [on] (my) head,
> quicklime on to my crown;
> [and] the death of all men I shall die,
> even I indeed shall die.

Beyond that, Aqhat adds that a bow is a proper weapon for warriors, not for women. Anath is greatly offended and, exhibiting her violent character, she asks her own warrior, named Yatpan, to murder Aqhat. Both Anath and Yatpan assume the form of birds (variously translated as eagles, hawks, or vultures) and, while Aqhat is eating, Yatpan plunges down upon him and strikes him twice on the crown and three times on the ear. Although Aqhat is dead, Anath does not obtain the desired bow; for some reason, which the fragmentary text does not allow us to discern, the bow is broken and falls into the sea. Also, because of the death of Aqhat, the rains fail and the crops wither.

Eventually Danel learns that his son is dead; he finds Aqhat's remains inside a bird, and inters them. For seven years Danel mourns;

87. In this connection note the discovery under residential houses at Ugarit of family vaults with installations for supplying the needs of the dead (Marvin H. Pope, "The Cult of the Dead at Ugarit," in *Ugarit in Retrospect,* ed. Young, 159). For prophetic repudiation of ancestor worship in Israel, see Bernhard Lang, "Afterlife: Ancient Israel's Changing Vision of the World Beyond," *BR* 4.1 (Feb. 1988): 17.

then he dismisses the weeping women (i.e., professional mourners, familiar in the ancient Middle East—see Jer. 9:17–18) and makes sacrifice to the gods. After that, Pughat, daughter of Danel, goes forth to find and slay the murderer of her brother. She washes herself in the sea, then "rouge[s] herself with rouge from the shell of the [sea], whose source is a thousand tracts away in the sea" (i.e., the red-purple color derived from the murex shellfish of the Mediterranean coast), puts on the garb of a warrior with a dagger in her girdle and a sword in her belt, "and on top she put[s] the garments of a woman." Pughat has thus disguised herself as the goddess Anath, who in an Egyptian papyrus in a passage probably translated from Canaanite myth (Chester Beatty Papyrus 7.1.5ff.) is described as "a woman who is like a man, dressed like a man and girded like a woman."[88]

So Pughat, in the guise of Anath, sets out "at the rising of the gods' torch Shapash" (the Ugaritic sun goddess ["Pantheon of Ugarit," line 21], the equivalent of the Hebrew Shamash, who is most often masculine but sometimes feminine, e.g., Exod. 22:3; etc.),[89] and at the setting of Shapash she arrives at the encampment of Yatpan. Being taken, as she intended, for Anath, the goddess of Yatpan, she is invited in to share wine with him. When Yatpan has drunk, his tongue is loosened and he boasts of what he has done and will further do for his goddess, and thus unwittingly confesses his guilt: "The hand that smote the hero Aqhat shall smite thousands of (my) Lady's foes."

Here the available text breaks off, but it is not unlikely that in the lost sequel Yatpan fell asleep from the wine and was killed by Pughat (much as Sisera was killed in his sleep by Jael—Judg. 4:18–21). Since with the death of Aqhat the crops failed, it is possible that when the crops grew again Aqhat also revived, as in the myth of Baal and Mot, but this is only a surmise. At any rate, with the appearance of the divine figures along with the human in the story, the narrative certainly contains mythic as well as legendary elements.

As to the locale of the legendary events in the story of Aqhat, there are some indications in the text of places that are identifiable with considerable probability.[90] At the point where Danel recovers the remains of his son from within the bird and buries them, the text is broken, but the crucial final word is plausibly restored as *bknrt* and read as referring to the Sea of Galilee (יָם־כִּנֶּרֶת, *yām kinneret*, the

---

88. Wolfgang Helck, *Die Beziehungen Ägyptens zu Vorderasien im 3. und 2. Jahrtausend v. Chr.,* 494–95.

89. For the translation, see *ANET*, 155; for the sun-god/goddess see T. H. Gaster, "Sun," in *IDB* 4.463.

90. Baruch Margalit, "The Geographical Setting of the *Aqht* Story and Its Ramifications," in *Ugarit in Retrospect,* ed. Young, 131–58.

Sea of Chinnereth; Num. 34:11; etc.).[91] Thus the disposition was in the waters of the lake. This is confirmed by the following translation of the succeeding lines about Danel:

> He raised his voice and cried:
> "The wings of eagles Baal will break,
>      Baal will break their pinions;
> If they fly over the grave of my son,
>      If they disturb him from his sleep (midst) the pool-of-water."[92]

Danel then goes to the place where his son was killed (named already in the narrative of the murder, and apparently the actual home of the murderer as well), and utters a curse upon it, calling down blindness and banishment upon the inhabitants for their share in the guilt (a custom of cursing places near the scene of a crime seen also in Deut. 21:1–9; 2 Sam. 1:21):

> He proceeded to Qart-Abilim,
> Abilim city of prince Yarikh,
> he lifted up his voice and cried:
> "Woe to you, Qart-Abilim,
> near whom the hero Aqhat was struck down!
> May Baal this instant render you blind!
> [Be a fugitive now] and evermore,
> now and to all generations;
> let every last one make ready a staff for his hand."

Here the city (*qrt*) named Abilim (*ablm*) is identified as the city of prince Yarikh. Yarikh (Yerah) is the name common to all the Semitic languages for the moon and the moon-god (equivalent to the Akkadian Sin; "Pantheon of Ugarit," line 13), whose worship was widely familiar in the Canaanite area, for example, in a temple at Hazor (see p. 126; in Deut. 4:19 and other Old Testament passages the worship of sun, moon, stars, and all the host of heaven is forbidden). The city in question here may therefore most probably be recognized as Beth-yerah ("the house of [the moon-god] Yerah"; Arabic, Khirbet el-Kerak), an archeological site about fifty acres in area on the southwestern shore of the Sea of Galilee (see p. 123).

From Abilim Danel "proceeded" (as in the preceding quotation the expression suggests a short distance)[93] to his own house, presumably

---

91. George A. Barton, "Danel, A Pre-Israelite Hero of Galilee," *JBL* 60 (1941): 217 and n. 19; Baruch Margalit, "Studies in Krt and Aqht," *UF* 8 (1976): 174.

92. Margalit, "Geographical Setting," 133.

93. Ibid., 135 n. 22.

in a place called Harnam since Danel was He-of-Harnam. It was also from this home in Harnam that Danel's daughter, Pughat, went to the "sea" to wash, and then went on between sunrise and sunset to Yatpan's camp, which was apparently at Abilim. Since Pughat would assuredly not have gone to the Mediterranean, the sea in question would again appear to be the Sea of Galilee. A place for Harnam and the home of Danel and Pughat, which would fulfil the implications of the whole account, could be somewhere in the region of Tell Mashrafawi, which is in the Golan Heights less than two miles from the east shore of the Sea of Galilee (twelve to fifteen miles from Khirbet el-Kerak), and which gives evidence of settlement beginning in the Middle Bronze Age (c. 1900–1550). This time period is considered the likely period for the composition of the story of Aqhat as it is now known.[94]

Danel is probably the personage of the same name mentioned in Ezekiel 14:14, 20; 28:3 (where the four consonants of the Hebrew name should probably also be read as Danel, not Daniel). Named between Noah and Job, this Danel is apparently thought of as relatively far back in time, perhaps in the patriarchal period; and he is also remembered for his wisdom. In these traits there is broad agreement with the character of the Ugaritic Danel. Like the biblical elders who determine cases "at the gate" of their city (Deut. 21:19; Amos 5:10, 12, 15), Danel

> sat at the entrance of the gate
> beneath the trees which were by the threshing-floor;
> he judged the cause of the widow,
> tried the case of the orphan.

Likewise in the manner of the hospitality evidenced particularly in the time of the biblical patriarchs (Gen. 18:1–8; 19:1–3; 24:31–33; see also Judg. 19:20–21; Heb. 13:2), in which one might even entertain angels, Danel upon seeing the approach of Kothar wa-Khasis, the craftsman of the gods, cried to his wife:

> Hear, maiden Danatay,
> make ready a lamb from the youngling(s) . . .
> feed, give drink to the gods,
> wait upon (and) do them honor.

### Shachar and Shalim

Among the religious texts from Ras Shamra, two single tablets, each inscribed on both sides, contain yet somewhat more of the mythology

94. Ibid., 149–50.

and give additional information about the pantheon. The myth of
Shachar and Shalim and the gracious gods[95] begins with an invocation to "the gracious gods and fair," then tells briefly of the destruction of the god of death. The latter is called Mot waShar (variously
explained as meaning Death and Prince, or Death and Dissolution).
Although he has "in his one hand the scepter of bereavement, in his
other hand the scepter of widowhood," the vinedressers cut him down.

In a longer episode the god El sees two women on the seashore,
seduces them, and they become his wives and the mothers of Shachar
and Shalim. The name of Shachar means Dawn. Shachar appears in
Isaiah 14:12, where the Day Star (Athtar) is his son. The name of
Shalim (who is also listed in the "Pantheon of Ugarit," line 33) probably has the connotation of "ending" the day, and is Dusk or Sunset.
In the Amarna Letters (fourteenth century B.C.)[96] the name of Jerusalem is written as Urusalim, and as the name of the Canaanite city
the meaning can be "foundation of Shalim," referring to the Canaanite
god.[97]

In the continuation of the mythological text and of El's marital
activity, El becomes the father of "the gracious gods." Assuming that
the mothers are the same two women and wives of El, it may be
supposed that the gracious gods are identical with Shachar and
Shalim.[98] Alternatively, if Dawn and Dusk were born first and the
gracious gods are the gods of Ugarit in general, born later, then a
similarity could be suggested with Genesis 1:3–4, where at the outset
there is the creation of light and the division of day and night.[99]

### Nikkal and the Kotharat

A single tablet from Ras Shamra contains the myth of Nikkal and
the Kotharat.[100] Here the essential story is that of the marriage of
Yarikh the moon-god (equivalent to the Akkadian Sin) and Nikkal
(the equivalent of the Akkadian Ningal, "great lady," the consort of
Sin), who is also known in a composite name as Nikkal-and-Ib. The
story involves an intermediary, "Khirkhib king of summer," and the
payment of a large "bride-price" (mahar, the same as the marriage
present in Gen. 34:12).

95. Gibson, *Canaanite Myths and Legends*, 123–27; Theodor H. Gaster, "A Canaanite Ritual
Drama: The Spring Festival at Ugarit," *JAOS* 66 (1946): 49–76.

96. *ANET*, 488–89.

97. M. Burrows, "Jerusalem," in *IDB* 2.843.

98. Gaster, "Canaanite Ritual Drama," 67–70.

99. Gibson, *Canaanite Myths and Legends*, 30 and n. 2.

100. Ibid., 128–29.

Yarikh lamp of heaven sent (word)
to Khirkhib king of summer, (saying):
"Give Nikkal (that) Yarikh may marry (her),
(give) Ib (that) she may enter his mansion;
and I will give as her bride-price to her father
a thousand (pieces) of silver and ten thousand (pieces) of gold,
I will send brilliant (stones of) lapis-lazuli,
I will give vineyards (to be) fields for him,
. . . (to be) fields for him to delight in."

In addition to the gods and goddesses already named there were certainly many others worshiped by the Canaanites. Some are seen in representations in art, without their names being known. For example, a small ivory from a tomb at Minet el-Beida, attributed to the four-teenth century B.C., shows a seated goddess, wearing only a full skirt, a necklace, and a diadem. She raises her hands to hold stalks of grain and on either side a goat rears up as if to reach for the grain. In the absence of any name, she has been called a queen of wild beasts.[101] Likewise a bronze figurine from a house at Minet el-Beida, dated to the fifteenth–fourteenth century, shows a standing, kilt-clad god. He wears a headdress much like the White Crown of Upper Egypt; both head and headdress are still covered with gold and the body with silver. A gold ring is around his right arm, which is raised as if to wield a weapon; his left arm is extended forward as if to hold a spear or staff. Again lacking positive identification the figure has been variously thought to be Baal or Resheph or Hadad.[102]

## Canaanite Contributions

Canaanite religion was not only polytheistic but also characterized by much that was sanguinary and sensual, features presumably re-flecting various aspects of daily life and to that extent justifying the strictures of the biblical prophets.[103] Nevertheless, as also seen above, Israel derived from the Canaanites the alphabet as well as tradition and help in architecture, shared with Canaan many linguistic usages and customs, and even utilized many themes of Canaanite mythology in transmuted form in their Scriptures. In fact the main gods of the

101. Schaeffer in *Ugaritica,* 1.32 frontispiece, plate 11; *ANEP,* fig. 464.
102. Schaeffer in *Ugaritica,* 1.113, plate 25; *ANEP,* fig. 481; Marie-Henriette Gates, "From Ebla to Damascus: The Archaeology of Ancient Syria," *BAR* 12.3 (May–June 1986): 64.
103. Emmanuel Anati, *Palestine before the Hebrews,* 427.

Canaanite pantheon were by no means minor spirits of limited localities. Although appearing in local manifestations and with different
titles and hypostases,[104] they were great cosmic deities, representing
the great powers upon which the existence of all things depends, and
thus not of small significance in the history of human response to the
transcendent.

104. Cross, *Canaanite Myth and Hebrew Epic,* 49.

# 5

# Greek Religion

## History

In the Mediterranean area that became the Greek world,[1] the Minoan civilization, centered in Crete, came to an end in about 1450 B.C. (perhaps in part due to the catastrophic volcanic eruption of Thera/Santorini). Meanwhile the first Greek-speaking people had entered the area and, by around 1600 B.C. had a chief center at Mycenae (in the Peloponnesos twenty-five miles southwest of Corinth). Their culture also extended to Attica on the Greek mainland and southward as well to Crete (where the Linear B script shows that, unlike the Minoans, they spoke the Greek language), and their trading ventures reached at least to Cyprus, Rhodes, and parts of Syria and Asia Minor (as evidenced by the distinctive Mycenaean pottery).[2] According to the *Iliad* it was from Mycenae that King Agamemnon led an army of these people—whom Homer calls Achaians—in the war against Troy (also known as Ilion), which fell, according to the Greek scientist Eratosthenes of Alexandria (c. 276–192 B.C.) in 1194 B.C. Subsequent to the Achaians, in about 1100 B.C., a second wave of Greek-speaking people, the Dorians, came into the region and brought the Achaian-Mycenaean civilization to an end. There followed in mainland Greece a three-century dark age.

Around 1000 B.C., Ionians, probably descendants of the Achaians and refugees from the Dorians, crossed the Aegean Sea and settled on the coast of Asia Minor in the region that became known as Ionia. Here they built an essentially Greek civilization, and adopted the Phoenician alphabet. Greek mariners also carried Greek colonists as far afield as the Black Sea in the north, Cyprus in the east, Libya in

1. *Atlas of the Classical World,* ed. A. A. M. van der Heyden and H. H. Scullard.
2. Leonard R. Palmer, *Mycenaeans and Minoans.*

the south, and Sicily and southern Italy in the west. In all these places, the Greek people, although individualistic lovers of independence, came to feel as one, sharing a common language, political practices, religion, and outlook on life. Their homeland they called Hellas, themselves Hellenes, and their civilization Hellenic.

In the fifth century B.C., after the defeat of the Persians at Marathon (490) and Salamis (480), Athens, on the rocky peninsula of Attica, emerged as the leader of Greece. Under the administration of Pericles (c. 495–429) the golden age ensued, and Athens was adorned with the buildings and sculptures of Phidias (c. 490–432). By the time the Parthenon was completed (built between 447 and 432) Socrates (469–399) was engaged in his work of inquiry into the right conduct of life; his disciple was Plato (c. 429–347), the teacher of Aristotle (384–322), who in turn was the tutor of Alexander the Great (356–323).

## Sources

The oldest surviving works of Greek literature, from which we may gather information concerning Hellenic religion, are the epic poems, the *Iliad* and the *Odyssey*. These epics about the war against Troy and the return journey of Odysseus are usually attributed to Homer, an Ionian Greek of about the ninth century B.C. After Homer, Hesiod, a farmer and poet living in Boeotia probably around 800 B.C., provides in his *Theogony* a systematized account of the origin of the world and the deities. A later compendium of Greek mythology called the *Library* is extant under the name of Apollodoros of Athens (c. 140 B.C.), but the authorship is questioned. A guidebook to Greece by Pausanias (c. A.D. 170) includes many myths and ceremonies associated with the sites he describes.

## Sacred Powers and Mythology

Like the peoples of Mesopotamia and Egypt the ancient Greeks also had a sense of the divine and a belief in power or powers beyond the human but best conceivable as beings resembling humankind except for their immortality and superior abilities. As in Mesopotamia and Egypt, by the time the Greek pantheon and mythology come into view in written sources the deities were numerous and clearly

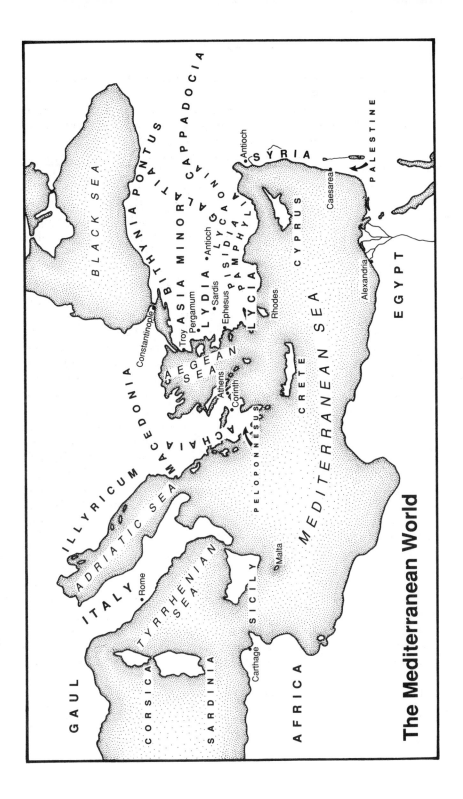

The Mediterranean World

characterized, and the stories associated with the deities and various heroes were elaborate.[3]

As to earlier origins and antecedents, the Greeks are identified as an Indo-European people by their language, which is related to other languages of the same family, from Sanskrit in the east to Latin and many European languages in the west. It may be presumed that the Greek religion preserves an Indo-European heritage. This is certainly the case with the chief deity in the Greek pantheon, Zeus, whose name is an Indo-European word akin to the Sanskrit *Dyaus* and probably means "sky-god." Other similarities with materials in Mesopotamia leave no doubt of derivations from that area, no matter through what intermediaries. For example, in the Mesopotamian legend of the flood the god Ea warns the hero Utnapishtim of what is to come and advises him to build a ship. Utnapishtim does so and goes on board with family and kin and wild creatures of the field. The flood rages for six days and six nights, and on the seventh day the ship grounds on Mount Nisir; afterward Utnapishtim offers sacrifice to the gods. In the Greek legend when Zeus undertakes to destroy the human race by a flood Prometheus advises his son Deukalion, who makes an ark and goes on board with his wife Pyrrha. They float on the waters for nine days and nine nights and finally land on Mount Parnassos, whereupon Deukalion disembarks and makes sacrifice to Zeus. For another example, in Sumerian mythology Dumuzi, who descended to the underworld and returned again, was an embodiment of dying and reviving vegetation, and was the consort of Inanna, the goddess of love. The two became in the Semitic world Tammuz and Ishtar, with cultic weeping for the dying Tammuz still practiced in Jerusalem in the sixth century B.C. (Ezek. 8:14). In the west Adonis was the lover of Aphrodite (Venus), the goddess of love. Every year Adonis experienced death and was carried off to spend part of the year with Persephone in the underworld, returning for part of the year with Aphrodite. At the death of Adonis, Aphrodite mourned; every year in annual ceremonies the grief of the goddess was reenacted in the weeping of devotees, a tradition that was continued in the Roman Empire as well as in Greece. In the second century A.D. the emperor Hadrian, putting Roman shrines on sacred sites of Jews, Samaritans, and Christians, installed a grove of Tammuz/Adonis in Bethlehem, and Jerome, who lived there in the fourth century, says: "My own Bethlehem . . . was overshadowed by a

---

3. *Ausführliches Lexikon der griechischen und römischen Mythologie*, ed. Wilhelm Heinrich Roscher; Pierre Devambez et al., *The Praeger Encyclopedia of Ancient Greek Civilization*; John Pinsent, *Greek Mythology*; Edward E. Barthell, Jr., *Gods and Goddesses of Ancient Greece*; Karl Kerényi, *The Gods of the Greeks*; idem, *The Heroes of the Greeks*; Michael Stapleton, *A Dictionary of Greek and Roman Mythology*; and relevant articles in *PWRE*.

grove of Tammuz, that is of Adonis; and . . . lamentation was made for the paramour of Venus" (Letter 58 to Paulinus of Nola; see also Paulinus of Nola, Letter 31.3).[4]

Admittedly, then, Hellenic religion owed not a little to earlier and foreign sources. Nevertheless in its indigenous development and total configuration it is distinctive. In the cosmogony outlined by Hesiod we learn that at the beginning there was Chaos (the Greek word can mean emptiness or infinite space). From Chaos emerged Gaia (Earth), who became both the mother and the wife of Ouranos (Heaven); they, in turn, became the parents of the Titans, the one-eyed Kyklopes, and the Hekatoncheires (hundred-handed giants).

Among the Titans was Iapetos, the father of several sons including Atlas and Prometheus. Atlas stands at the edge of the earth and supports the sky upon his shoulders, or holds the pillars that keep earth and sky asunder. Prometheus, in one form of tradition, is the creator who fashions humankind out of a lump of clay. In another form of myth humankind is already in existence. At any rate it is Prometheus who steals fire from heaven and brings it to earth, where he also teaches humankind how to build, to use tools and metal, to understand the positions of the stars, and to use herbs for healing.

Among the Titans were also Okeanos (Ocean, the water enclosing the earth), Tethys (sister and wife of Okeanos), Kronos (Time), and Rhea (sister and wife of Kronos). When Ouranos confined the Kyklopes and the Hekatoncheires in Tartaros, the gloomiest part of the underworld, the Titans divided the world among themselves under the leadership of Kronos. Kronos and Rhea in turn became the parents of Hestia, Demeter, Hera, Hades, Poseidon, and Zeus. Hestia was the goddess of the hearth fire. Demeter was the goddess of the fruitful earth. Diodorus [1.12.4] explains that the name was originally *Ge Meter,* i.e., Earth Mother), whose daughter (originally referred to as Kore, the maiden, and later known as Persephone) was carried to the netherworld by Hades to be his queen, but, in a compromise, was allowed to return to earth for part of each year. Hera was the chief wife of her brother Zeus, and was the patroness of marriage. When Zeus reached manhood he overthrew his father Kronos, and Zeus, Hades, and Poseidon drew lots to divide the universe among themselves. Zeus received the heavens, Poseidon the sea, and Hades the realm of the dead, while the earth was the possession of all the gods, under the general sovereignty of Zeus.

In the *Iliad* Zeus is called the "cloud gatherer" (νεφεληγερέτης, 1.511)

---

4. Bernard C. Dietrich, *The Origins of Greek Religion,* 29, 241; G. S. Kirk, *The Nature of Greek Myths,* 262–63.

and the one "who hurls the thunderbolt" (τερπικέραυνος, 1.419), which accords with the supposition of his original character as a sky- and weather-god. He is also named the "father" (saluted as Ζεῦ πατήρ, 1.503, etc., from which comes the Latin Jupiter) of men and gods (5.426). In relation to the gods the main connotation of his description as father is to indicate his supreme place in the pantheon, but in conjunction with various wives he was said (with some variations in the different myths) to be the literal father of a number of deities (see table 3).

In relation to humankind Zeus was the father not in the sense of the creator but in the sense that he was the protector and ruler of the human family. Some individual persons were, however, his offspring. In the form of a white bull Zeus joined himself with the beautiful Europa (daughter of Agenor king of Tyre and sister of Kadmos founder of Thebes in Boeotia). Their son was Minos, the great king of Crete. In the form of a swan Zeus joined himself with Leda (daughter of Thestios king of Aetolia and wife of Tyndareos king of Lacedaemon). Their daughter was the beautiful Helen (wife of Menelaos king of Sparta), whose abduction by Prince Paris of Troy was the cause of the Trojan War. In the assumed guise of Amphitryon king of Thebes Zeus joined himself with the king's wife Alkmene. Their son was Herakles, the hero who performed twelve famous "labors," and was eventually considered a god. In the form of a golden shower Zeus joined himself with the imprisoned Danaë (daughter of Akrisios king of Argos). Their son was the hero Perseus, also eventually considered a god.

Poseidon, who received the realm of the sea, has the epithets of "earthshaker" and "holder of the earth," thus evidently having an early connection with earthquakes and with the earth in general. It was presumably this general connection that brought him into his best-known association with the waters—with rain and rivers, and especially with the seas (as in both the *Iliad* and the *Odyssey*). Another sea god was Nereus, who was the father of the Nereids or sea nymphs. One of the Nereids was Thetis, the mother of Achilles, the principal warrior among the Achaians in the Trojan War.

Hades, who received the realm of the dead, was regarded with dread and was often called Pluto ("wealthy one"). As among many ancient people, so also among the Greeks the realm of the dead was at first thought of as in the west (the place of the setting sun), but later in the underworld. Here the river Styx (the name is associated with the verb "to hate"; the nymph of the river is a daughter of Okeanos and Tethys) nine times encircles the region. The deceased must be rowed across by Charon, whose fee is one obol. The other rivers in the underworld are the Kokytos ("wailing for the dead"), Acheron ("pain"),

TABLE **3**

# Children of Zeus

By Hera (daughter of Kronos; sister and chief wife of Zeus)

 Ares (god of war)

 Hephaistos (god of fire)

By Metis (daughter of Okeanos and Tethys)

 Athena (goddess of everything artistic and intellectual; patroness of the city of Athens where, as a virgin goddess, her famous temple was the Parthenon [from Greek παρθένος "virgin"])

By Dione (a nymph, daughter of Nereus)

 Aphrodite (goddess of beauty and love; also said to have come up out of the sea foam at Paphos on the south coast of Cyprus, the site of her most famous center of worship, another center being the city of Aphrodisias in Asia Minor)

By Leto (daughter of the Titan Koios)

 Apollo (god of medicine, music, and prophecy; in the last respect he killed the serpent Python and supplanted him as the oracular god at Delphi and also at other sanctuaries; Apollo was the father of Asklepios, god of health, who had Hygieia, goddess of health, as his daughter or as his wife [according to variant traditions])

 Artemis (goddess of wild animals and the hunt; Artemis of Ephesus was of different character as a goddess of fertility, and it was her temple at Ephesus [Acts 19:27] that became known as one of the seven wonders of the world)

By Leda (daughter of Thestios king of Aetolia; wife of Tyndareos king of Lacedaemon)

 Pollux (one of the Dioscuri, the heavenly twins, the other, Castor, being the son of Leda and Tyndareos)

By Maia (daughter of Atlas)

 Hermes (messenger of the gods and guide of souls [ψυχοηομπός, ψυχαγαγός] to Hades)

By Semele (daughter of Kadmos; founder of Thebes in Boeotia)

 Dionysos (Latin, Bacchus; god of wine, worshiped in the frenzied exercises of the Maenads ["mad women"; Latin, Bacchae])

By Mnemosyne (daughter of Ouranos and Gaia; goddess of "memory")

 the Nine Muses (patronesses of the arts, all led by Apollo):

 Kleio (history)

 Euterpe (music)

 Thaleia (comedy)

 Melpomene (tragedy)

 Terpsichore (light poetry and dancing)

 Erato (amorous poetry)

 Polyhymnia (singing and rhetoric)

 Ourania (astronomy)

 Kalliope (epic poetry; the son of Kalliope was Orpheus, who charmed even the wild beasts with his poetry and lyre, presented to him by Apollo; Orpheus loved the nymph Eurydike, and when she died from the bite of a serpent he went with his lyre to Hades and charmed Persephone into letting her go, but on the condition that while leading her to safety he not look back at her; when Orpheus failed to keep the condition Hermes Psychopompos carried Eurydike back to Hades, and Orpheus thereafter rejected all other women and wandered with a band of Thracian men, preaching his mysteries, until he was set upon and killed by Thracian women)

Pyriphlegethon ("burning like fire"), and Lethe ("forgetfulness"). In the underworld the majority of the dead go to the Plain of Asphodel (a wild flower) to continue a shadowy existence. The most fortunate who have earned the gods' favor go to Elysion, the Elysian fields, also called the Isles of the Blest, to enjoy a happy life. Those who have offended the gods go to Tartaros, the prison and place of punishment of the wicked. Three judges, just men of former times—Minos king of Crete, Rhadamanthys brother of Minos and lawgiver in Crete, and Aiakos king of Aegina, all three sons of Zeus—allot the appropriate place to each who comes. When the dead drink from the river Lethe they lose the memories of their former lives—in the case of rebirth (a doctrine held by Pythagoras and Plato)[5] this accounts for the non-remembrance of former existences.

The residence of the chief gods is on Mount Olympos (the highest peak in Greece, 9,600 feet), the place chosen by Zeus. Here the gods live in much the fashion of human beings, with the same virtues and vices (as some of the foregoing references well illustrated), but they are superior in power, and immortal, due to their divine food and their divine drink of ambrosia and nectar. As to exactly which deities dwell on Olympos there are some different reckonings; one relief, said to be of the early fifth century B.C. and to come from Tarentum in south Italy, shows twelve Olympians, each with distinguishing attributes, in the order: Apollo with lyre, Artemis with bow, Zeus with thunderbolt, Athena with her favorite bird the owl, Poseidon with trident, Hera with scepter (topped by pomegranate, symbol of fecundity), Hades with staff, Persephone with ears of corn, Ares wearing a helmet, Aphrodite holding a flower, Hermes in a cap and with his herald's staff (*caduceus*), and (probably) Demeter with a basket.[6] Thus of the highest twelve, there are five children and one grandchild of Kronos and Rhea (Zeus, Poseidon, Hera, Hades, Persephone, Demeter), and six offspring of Zeus and several different wives (Apollo, Artemis, Athena, Ares, Aphrodite, Hermes).

Powerful as the Olympian deities are, they are not always able to accomplish their will, nor are they exempt from inevitable results that come from their actions. In fact they themselves, as well as human beings, are in the last analysis subject to Fate (μοῖρα), the ultimate determiner of destiny. Here too, however, this concept was expressed mythologically. Fate is a goddess bearing the several names of Ananke (necessity), Tyche (fortune), Heimarmene (allotted portion), Dike (justice), and Nemesis (retribution). Again there are three Fates, and they

5. A. C. Pearson, "Transmigration (Greek and Roman)," in *HERE* 12.432–34.
6. Pinsent, *Greek Mythology*, 30–31.

Hygieia, Greek goddess of health, daughter of Asklepios, god of medicine. The serpent is associated with both and here the goddess holds one in her hand. At her feet is a small Eros-Hypnos. The statue is in the museum on the Greek island of Kos.

are pictured as weavers: Lachesis (the measurer), Clotho (the spinner), and Atropos (the cutter of the thread of life).

As for human history, on earth humankind degenerated and Zeus resolved to destroy all people in a flood but, as related above, Deukalion and his wife Pyrrha survived. Afterward, being so instructed, Deukalion cast stones that turned into men, and Pyrrha cast stones that turned into women; thus humanity was reconstituted. The eldest son of Deukalion and Pyrrha was Hellen, the ancestor of the race of the Hellenes (the name by which by around the seventh century B.C. the Greeks as a whole were named).[7]

The pantheon and mythology outlined above still provided the framework of popular Greek religion when Hellas reached its height

7. The name *Greek* derives from the Latin *Graecia*, the country from which the Doric settlers known as the *Graii* came to live in Italy (in Magna Graecia), and it was the local Italians who first called them "Greeks."

in the late fifth and fourth centuries B.C. The historian Xenophon (c. 434–355 B.C.) makes many references to beliefs and practices related to the Olympian deities. When he considered going with the younger Cyrus on the Persian expedition (401 B.C.) that he made famous in his *Anabasis,* Xenophon first went, upon the advice of Socrates, to Delphi to consult Apollo, the god of the oracle, in regard to the journey (*Anabasis* 3.1.4–8). Later from money that came to him from the sale of booty Xenophon made votive offerings for Apollo and for Artemis of the Ephesians (*Anabasis* 5.3.5–6). From the same pantheon and mythology the sculptor Phidias (c. 490–432) and his pupils drew their themes as they decorated Athens with the buildings (e.g., the Parthenon, built between 447 and 432) and the statuary that were its chief material glory at the height of its ancient splendor. Likewise many dedicatory inscriptions from steles, votive columns, statue bases, and other objects from the Acropolis show private men and women of many occupations expressing their personal devotion to Athena, with gratitude for past favors and hope for future benefits.[8] In their declamations in the law courts of Athens, orators addressed large cross-sections of Athenian society in the juries and no doubt undertook to speak in terms appropriate to the sensibilities of their hearers. Therefore their religious references may be assumed to be such as were familiar and acceptable to the majority of Athenian citizens of the time. For example, Antiphon (c. 480–411 B.C.), the author of the earliest extant legal speeches and a member of the council (βουλή) in Athens, delivered a speech in about 419 in defense of a person alleged to have been responsible for the death of a chorister who had been given a drug to improve his voice. In it he tells of how in the council chamber (βουλευτήριον) there stands a shrine of Zeus Boulaios (the councilor) and Athena Boulaia (the councilor), "where members offer prayers as they enter," and says that he himself, as a member, "did as they did" (*On the Choreutes* 45). The statesman Lykurgos (c. 390–324 B.C.), in his prosecution of a certain Leokrates for treason, delivered in the year 330 what is now his only surviving speech, and began with a prayer that "Athena and those other gods and heroes whose statues are erected in our city and the country around" might make him a worthy prosecutor (*Against Leokrates* 1–2). In the same year Demosthenes (c. 384–322) opened a major speech in defense of his public career with a prayer to "all the gods and goddesses" that he might receive a fair hearing from his jury (*De Corona* 1–2).[9] It was undoubtedly the many images of the same

8. For a collection of these inscriptions, see David G. Rice and John E. Stambaugh, *Sources for the Study of Greek Religion,* 150–51.

9. Jon D. Mikalson, *Athenian Popular Religion,* 7–17.

classical deities, as well as an altar inscribed "To an unknown god," which in the first century A.D. led the apostle Paul to say of the Athenians that they were in every way very religious (Acts 17:16, 22–23).

The same pantheon was also carried by the Greeks as they settled in other lands. In the Hellenistic and Roman periods there were many Greeks living in Egypt in particular, along with the Italians, Syrians, Libyans, Cilicians, Ethiopians, Arabs, Bactrians, Scythians, Persians, and even Indians, whom Dio Chrysostom (c. A.D. 100) mentions as present in Alexandria in Discourse 32 to the People of Alexandria (§40). In the resultant amalgam of religions Asian deities were accepted (e.g., Astarte was identified with the Greek Aphrodite and made the daughter of the Egyptian Ptah), and many Greek and Egyptian deities were recognized as equivalent (see table 4).[10]

## Science and Philosophy

In Greece, however, unlike in ancient Mesopotamia and Egypt, the mythology and its deities and heroes came under sharp criticism, and the religious response to the world was replaced by the attempt to understand the world using reason. The new trends are in evidence from the sixth century B.C. onward. Xenophanes (c. 570–488 B.C.) voiced both the negative criticism and also the positive affirmation that people acquire knowledge through their own striving and, even if they never attain complete enlightenment, they always have it in their power to seek out better things:

### TABLE 4
### Equivalences of Greek and Egyptian Deities

| | |
|---|---|
| Apollo | Horus |
| Aphrodite | Hathor |
| Athena | Isis |
| Dionysos | Osiris |
| Hephaistos | Ptah |
| Herakles | Herishef |
| Hermes | Thoth |
| Kronos | Anubis |
| Typhon | Seth |
| Zeus | Amun |

---

10. Thomas Allan Brady, *The Reception of the Egyptian Cults by the Greeks (330–30 B.C.)*.

Both Homer and Hesiod have attributed to the gods all things that are shameful and a reproach among mankind: theft, adultery, and mutual deception. . . . Mortals believe the gods to be created by birth, and to have their own [mortals'] raiment, voice, and body. But if oxen [and horses] and lions had hands or could draw with hands and create works of art like those made by men, horses would draw pictures of gods like horses, and oxen of gods like oxen, and they would make the bodies [of their gods] in accordance with the form that each species itself possesses. . . .

Truly the gods have not revealed to mortals all things from the beginning, but mortals by long seeking discover what is better.

Likewise Protagoras (c. 490–415 B.C.) wrote in *On the Gods*: "About the gods, I am not able to know whether they exist or do not exist, nor what they are like in form; for the factors preventing knowledge are many: the obscurity of the subject, and the shortness of human life." And in his book entitled Truth he declared that "man is the measure of all things."[11]

Thus negatively the classical mythology was accounted fictitious and fallacious, and positively the attempt was inaugurated to find the meaning of things in other than supernatural terms. Notable personages who engaged in that positive attempt included Thales (c. 640–546 B.C.), Anaximander (sixth century B.C.), and Anaximenes (sixth century B.C.), who sought to reduce the material world to some common element; Hecataeus of Miletus (sixth–fifth century B.C.), who was the first to use *historia* in the sense of "research"; Socrates (469–399 B.C.) and Plato (429–347 B.C.), who endeavored to make philosophy (lit. "the love of wisdom") the guide of life; Aristotle (384–322 B.C.), who based his work upon the observation of natural phenomena and created sciences ranging from botany to meteorology; and Aeschylus (525–456 B.C.), Euripides (480–406 B.C.), and Sophocles (c. 496–406 B.C.), who used drama as the vehicle for such an understanding of human nature as amounts to penetrating psychology. Thus it was the Greeks who first established the ideal of rational thinking, which proceeds by observation, analysis, and reason, as the way to truth, and who contributed this ideal to the modern mind of the West, where it is now widely accepted as the sole way.[12]

## Symbolic Thought

At the same time the ancient ideal of insight (seen in the countries already dealt with in previous chapters), which consists not in the ability to comprehend the laws of nature but in the wisdom that

11. Kathleen Freeman, *Ancilla to the Pre-Socratic Philosophers*, 22, nos. 11, 14–15, 18; 125–26, nos. 1, 4.
12. Bruno Snell, *The Discovery of the Mind: The Greek Origins of European Thought*.

recognizes the divine order of things and, for the welfare of the individual and of society, endeavors to bring life into conformity therewith, was not entirely lost. Symbolic thought—which gives priority to contemplation, intuition, and vision, and finds expression in myth—continued, as we shall shortly see, in aspects of the thought of Socrates and especially of Plato, and in the "mysteries."[13]

In this respect the external contacts of Greece with other lands and especially with Egypt may be recalled. In his work *On Isis and Osiris* Plutarch (c. A.D. 46–120) names a number of earlier Greeks who went to Egypt and were in touch with Egyptian priests; these include Solon, Pythagoras, and Plato. We will note other evidence as well for visits to Egypt by these three, and also by Herodotus and by Plutarch himself.

Solon (c. 639–559 B.C.), one of the Seven Wise Men of Greece, visited Amasis (570–526 B.C.) in Egypt (Herodotus 1.30), and says in a fragment of a poem that he lived "where Nile pours forth his floods, near the Canobic shore." The poem is quoted by Plutarch (*Life of Solon* 26.1), who states that Solon studied with very learned Egyptian priests, Psenophis of Heliopolis and Sonchis of Sais, and heard from them the tory of the lost Atlantis, as Plato also says (*Timaeus* 20–25; *Critias* 113–121).

Pythagoras (c. 589–490 B.C.) is identified by Herodotus (4.95) as a son of a Samian named Mnesarchos, and is called "one of the greatest Greek teachers." Isocrates (436–338 B.C.) states briefly that Pythagoras visited Egypt, became a student of the religion of the people, and was the first to bring their philosophy to the Greeks (*Busiris* 28–29). Iamblichus (c. A.D. 250–325) relates in more detail in his *Life of Pythagoras* (11–19, 25, 265)[14] that Pythagoras left his home in Samos at the age of eighteen, and studied under Thales, Anaximander, and Pherecydes. After four years Pythagoras went to Egypt where he lived for twenty-two years. He was admitted to the innermost sanctuaries of the temples, studied astronomy and geometry, and received initiation in the mysteries of the gods. He was taken by Cambyses as prisoner of war to Babylon where he studied with the Magi. After twelve years Pythagoras returned to Samos, later settled in Croton for twenty years, and retired to Metapontum for another nineteen years until his death (these latter being towns in southern Italy).[15]

---

13. C. J. Bleeker, *Egyptian Festivals: Enactments of Religious Renewal,* 13; Édouard Schuré, *From Sphinx to Christ: An Occult History,* 273–74; Rudolf Steiner, *Between Death and Rebirth,* 82–83; R. A. Schwaller de Lubicz, *Symbol and the Symbolic: Ancient Egypt, Science, and the Evolution of Consciousness,* 9–10, 82–83.

14. Thomas Taylor, *Iamblichus' Life of Pythagoras.* For Thomas Taylor and his writings, see Kathleen Raine and George Mills Harper, *Thomas Taylor, the Platonist: Selected Writings.*

15. If Pythagoras settled in Croton in about the year 529, as it is supposed in the dates of his life given above, the reference to Cambyses must be in error, for Cambyses ruled in Egypt from 525

Herodotus (484–425 B.C.) is not mentioned by Plutarch among those who went to Egypt (in *On the Malice of Herodotus* 857, Plutarch criticizes him as a "pro-barbarian" who is too favorable to Egypt). Herodotus was in Egypt (2.3ff.) in about 450 B.C., however, as well as in Babylon (1.178–83) in about 460. In Egypt he visited priests in Memphis, Heliopolis, and Thebes, and went as far as Elephantine (2.3, 29). He reports the outcome of his own observation, judgment, and inquiry (2.99), to the effect that most of the names of the gods came to Hellas from Egypt (2.50), and that the Egyptians were the first to teach that the human soul is immortal and that it goes through a series of rebirths (2.123).[16]

The visit of Plato to Egypt (probably around 390) is mentioned by Plutarch not only in *On Isis and Osiris* but also in his *Life of Solon* (2.4) where Plutarch explains that Plato defrayed the expenses of his sojourn in Egypt by the sale of oil (evidently brought from Greece as a valuable commodity). Plato himself praises the example of Egypt for the continuity of its art and music and says, "If you look there, you will find that the things depicted or graven there ten thousand years ago . . . are no whit better or worse than the productions of today, but wrought with the same art" (*Laws* 656d–e). This suggests that he is speaking on the basis of his own travel observations, and it is therefore probable that he did in fact visit Egypt.[17]

Plutarch's travel in Egypt is attested by his own reference to his "return from Alexandria" (*Table-Talk* 5.5.1) and by his citation of what "the priests [in Egypt] say" (*On Isis and Osiris* 21). He was himself a priest at Delphi, not far from his home at Chaeronea, and he addresses *On Isis and Osiris* to Clea, "a leader of the Thyiades [Bacchae] at Delphi . . . and consecrated in the Osirian rites" (§35). That Plutarch was himself probably initiated in the mysteries of Isis and Osiris is suggested by his major work on the subject and by language therein, such as when he says, "if we approach the sanctuaries of the goddess with reason and reverence" (§2) and "as the initiates know" (§28).

Turning now to Socrates and Plato and then to the mysteries, we may note first the religious dimension in the predominantly philosophical

---

to 522. For doubt that Pythagoras went to Egypt, see J. A. Philip, *Pythagoras and Early Pythagoreanism*; for an affirmative view, see Cornelia J. de Vogel, *Pythagoras and Early Pythagoreanism*.

16. The proper Greek term for the doctrine of rebirth is *palingenesia*; *metempsychosis* is also used. For doubt that Herodotus is correct in what he says about Egyptian belief in rebirth, see Louis V. Žabkar, "Herodotus and the Egyptian Idea of Immortality," *JNES* 22 (1963): 57–63; and John A. Wilson, *Herodotus in Egypt*, 8–12; but on the other hand, see Walter Federn, "The 'Transformations' in the Coffin Texts: A New Approach," *JNES* 19 (1960): 241–57.

17. H. Leisegang, "Platon," in *PWRE* 20.2350, doubts that Plato went to Egypt; but for the above view, see Ulrich von Wilamowitz-Moellendorff, *Platon: Sein Leben und seine Werke*, 186–88; and Paul Friedländer, *Plato*, 1.101.

thought of Socrates. It was mentioned above that Socrates once advised Xenophon to consult the oracle at Delphi, and Xenophon says that Socrates himself offered sacrifices, made use of divination, and received signs from the deity (δαιμόνιον) who, upon occasion, gave him guidance (*Memorabilia* 1.1.2–4). Xenophon also pictures Socrates as holding that the order of the world points to a divine intelligence (νοῦς) behind the material universe (*Memorabilia* 1.4.4–9), and Plato confirms Xenophon to the extent of representing Socrates as persuaded that the entire cosmos is ordered to an end that is good (*Phaedo* 97c). However, Socrates declares that he has no knowledge of the gods of whom the myths profess to tell (*Euthyphro* 6a–b), thus enunciating an agnosticism much like that of his contemporary Protagoras. As to what comes after death he does not know, being only convinced that "no evil can come to a good man either in life or after death" (*Apology* 29a–b, 40c, 41d). Granted that ultimate realities are beyond human knowing, there is no question but that the beautiful and the good (καλός τε καὶ ἀγαθός, *Lysis* 216d) are true virtues or excellences (ἀρεταί—"virtue . . . a kind of health and beauty and good condition of the soul," *Republic* 445a), and it is with virtue/excellence, moral and intellectual, that the philosophical way is concerned ("virtue is either wholly or partly wisdom," *Meno* 89a). For Socrates the philosophy that pursues such virtue/excellence is religion, and to the jury at his trial he declared that his conduct of philosophy was his service of the deity (*Apology* 30a).[18]

Plato (who puts his own thoughts into dialogues between Socrates and others) appears to allow for the existence of the deities as previously conceived in the Greek world when he speaks of "all the gods who share, each in his own sphere, the rule of the Supreme Spirit" (*Politicus* 272e). But he also has Timaeus express to Socrates an agnosticism with which Socrates would presumably have been in agreement: "Now to discover the Maker and Father of this universe were a task indeed; and having discovered him, to declare him unto all men were a thing impossible" (*Timaeus* 28c). Plato's own essential conviction is of the independent reality of transcendent, universal Ideas (Greek, ἰδέα), which are the Forms (Greek, εἶδος) or archetypes of all concrete things (*Republic* 476a); in the ideal realm the supreme place is held by the beautiful and the good, the two terms being virtually synonymous (*Republic* 505b; Phaedo 65d). The soul belongs by nature (*Phaedo* 80d) to the realm of Ideas/Forms (although it is different because it is a particular and not a universal), and hence is immortal

18. James Beckman, *The Religious Dimension of Socrates' Thought,* 41, 74, 78, 96–97, 178–81, 247, 250.

(*Phaedo* 76c–77d). It has been born many times, and wisdom is in part recollection of what was known before (*Meno* 81b–c). After earthly death the soul will live on and will experience successive rebirths on the way to ultimate deliverance (in which there will be retention of individual existence, not reabsorption into a world-soul—*Phaedo* 114c; *Republic* 611a; *Menexenus* 248c; etc.).[19]

In his investigation of the beautiful and the good (*Republic* 531c) Plato proceeds by logical thinking (which he calls dialectic, e.g., *Republic* 533a; *Phaedrus* 276e–277c), but also by symbolic thinking (which we have defined as involving contemplation, intuition, and vision; often expressed in myth). Thus in the *Republic* (527d–e) Plato declares that there is an eye of the soul (literally an "organ") that is more valuable than ten thousand bodily eyes, "for by it alone is truth seen." And in the *Phaedo* (79d) he says:

> When the soul inquires alone by itself, it departs into the realm of the pure, the everlasting, the immortal, and the changeless, and being akin to these it dwells always with them whenever it is by itself and is not hindered, and it has rest from its wanderings and remains always the same and unchanging with the changeless, since it is in communion therewith. And this state of the soul is called wisdom. Is it not so?

As an illustration, in the conclusion of the *Republic* (614bff.), Plato has Socrates tell the tale (μῦθος, 621b)[20] of the Pamphylian soldier, Er son of Armenios, who was apparently killed in battle but, on his funeral pyre, revived and told of his experience in the time that his soul was out of his body.[21] Er journeyed into the world beyond, witnessed scenes of judgment of the deceased and of their selection for the next existence (under the supervision of the Fates: "Lachesis singing the things that were, Clotho the things that are, and Atropos the things that are to be"; 617c), and was charged to return as a messenger (ἄγγελος) to humankind to tell them of that other world. Er did not know in what way he returned to his body, but suddenly recovering his sight he saw himself at dawn lying upon the funeral pyre. Socrates concludes:

19. Robert Leet Patterson, *Plato on Immortality*, 16–17, 32–34, 59, 115, 126–27.

20. In the sense of a "tale" a μῦθος is not necessarily false; it may be true.

21. For modern study of the "near-death" and "out-of-the-body" experiences, see Raymond A. Moody, Jr., *Life after Life: The Investigation of a Phenomenon—Survival of Bodily Death*; Michael Grosso, "Plato and Out-of-the-Body Experiences," *JASPR* 72 (1978): 61–74; Kenneth Ring, *Life at Death*; and *Anabiosis: The Journal for Near-Death Studies* (The International Association for Near-Death Studies, University of Connecticut, Storrs, Conn. 06268).

And so . . . the tale was saved. . . . And it will save us if we believe it, and we shall safely cross the River of Lethe, and keep our soul unspotted from the world. . . . We shall believe that the soul is immortal and capable of enduring all extremes of good and evil, and so we shall hold ever to the upward way and pursue righteousness with wisdom always and ever, that we may be dear to ourselves and to the gods both during our sojourn here and when we receive our reward, as the victors in the games go about to gather in theirs. And thus both here and in that journey of a thousand years, whereof I have told you, we shall fare well. [621b–d]

Again in Plato's *Symposium* (210a–212c) a wise woman named Diotima from the town of Mantinea in Arcadia speaks to Socrates about the steps by which one may ascend from the contemplation of a particular object of beauty to the love of all beautiful objects, then to the beautiful in daily pursuits and in the branches of knowledge, and finally to the ocean of the Beautiful itself.

"Beginning from obvious beauties he must for the sake of that highest beauty be ever climbing aloft, as on the rungs of a ladder, from one to two, and from two to all beautiful bodies; from personal beauty he proceeds to beautiful observances, from observance to beautiful learning, and from learning at last to that particular study which is concerned with the beautiful itself and that alone; so that in the end he comes to know the very essence of beauty. In that state of life above all others, my dear Socrates," said the Mantinean woman, "a man finds it truly worth while to live, as he contemplates essential beauty." [211c–d]

As to the discipline necessarily involved in this ascent Diotima uses the language of the mysteries and says that into these matters "even you, Socrates, might haply be initiated; but I doubt if you could approach the rites and revelations to which these, for the properly instructed, are merely the avenue" (210a). Plato makes Socrates speak about the mysteries in the *Phaedo* (69c–d):

I fancy that those men who established the mysteries were not unenlightened, but in reality had a hidden meaning when they said long ago that whoever goes uninitiated and unsanctified to the other world will lie in the mire, but he who arrives there initiated and purified will dwell with the gods. For as they say in the mysteries, "many are those who carry the staff, but the mystics are few";[22] and these mystics are, I

---

22. The ναρθηκοφόρος is the one who carries a staff of reed (νάρθηξ), commonly the θύρσος (Latin, *thyrsus*), a staff twined around with ivy and vine-leaves, with a pine cone at the top, carried by Bacchus and his devotees, the Bacchae or Bacchantes (*Bakxoi*, here translated as "mystics").

believe, those who have been true philosophers. And I in my life have, so far as I could, left nothing undone, and have striven in every way to make myself one of them.

## The Mysteries

The mysteries (mostly in the plural, μυστήρια) were societies with secret rites and doctrines, admission to which was through instruction, discipline, and initiation (τελετή literally "a making perfect"), the celebrant being called a hierophant (one who discloses the holy), and the one initiated or being initiated a mystic (μύστης).[23] The chief Greek mysteries were the Orphic (associated with Orpheus, Dionysos, and Pythagoras) and the Eleusinian; the chief non-Greek mysteries were those of Isis and Osiris from Egypt.

Orpheus was the legendary singer said to have been a native of Thrace, and to have lived in the time of the Argonauts before the Trojan War.[24] He was said to have endeavored unsuccessfully to bring back his beloved Eurydike from Hades, and to have perished at the hands of Thracian women. According to a fragment of Aeschylus (525–456 B.C.),[25] the Thracian women were urged on by Dionysos, who was jealous of Orpheus's devotion to the rival god Apollo and sent his Maenads to make the attack. Writing about Mount Pieria in Macedonia, the supposed burial place of Orpheus, Pausanias (c. A.D. 170) reports (9.30.4–7) several other traditions about Orpheus's death and says that Orpheus was believed to have discovered divine initiations (τελεταί) and to have taught things in the mysteries (μυστήρια) that had not been heard before.

At least by the fourth and third centuries B.C. there were centers of Orphic teachings in Magna Graecia in southern Italy, for in tombs of that date at the towns of Petelia and Thurii gold plates have been found that constitute a sort of guide for the deceased in the afterlife, and are almost certainly Orphic in character. In one, for example, an evidently long-wandering and thirsty soul comes to a spring on the left of the halls of Hades from which it must not drink, and to another at which it is given cold water and the promise of divinity.[26]

In spite of the tradition that Dionysos instigated the death of Orpheus there was also believed to be a connection between the mysteries of Orpheus and the rites of Dionysos, and the names came to be used

---

23. Joscelyn Godwin, *Mystery Religions in the Ancient World.*
24. W. K. C. Guthrie, *Orpheus and Greek Religion.*
25. Otto Kern, *Orphicorum Fragmenta,* no. 113.
26. Freeman, *Ancilla to the Pre-Socratic Philosophers,* 5–6, nos. 17–21.

interchangeably. Apollodorus says that Orpheus invented the mysteries of Dionysos (*Library* 1.3.2), and a fragment in pseudo-Eratosthenes states that Orpheus composed hymns to Dionysos, and Musaeus (Orpheus's son, according to Diodorus 4.25.1) corrected and copied them.[27] According to Diodorus (1.23.2; 1.96.2, 4–5) Orpheus and Musaeus visited Egypt where Orpheus participated in Egyptian initiations and mysteries and brought back from there the idea of a future state of rewards and punishments, and most of his own mystic ceremonies—the rite of Osiris being the same as that of Dionysos and the rite of Isis being very similar to that of Demeter.[28] This reference also indicates a connection between the Dionysiac/Orphic mysteries and the Eleusinian, and the experience of Orpheus in attempting to recover Eurydike from the underworld was indeed somewhat similar to the story of Demeter and Persephone (which was basic to the Eleusinian mysteries). Dionysos was eventually confused with Iacchos (Latin, Iacchus), a divine personification of the enthusiastic shouting that accompanied the procession from Athens to Eleusis in the Eleusinian mysteries (Herodotus 8.65).[29]

The *Hymns of Orpheus* may well themselves have been used in the Eleusinian mysteries, for the extant texts include not only one (no. 30) to Dionysos (Bacchus) but also one (no. 29) to Persephone (Proserpina) and one (no. 40) to Demeter (Ceres), and there are also many references to the "mystics" and the "mystic suppliants."[30] Demeter is saluted as the "universal mother" (see Diodorus 1.12.4), who dwells "in Eleusina's holy vales," and there is supplication to Persephone in these words:

> Hear, blessed Goddess, send a rich increase
> Of various fruits from earth, with lovely Peace;
> Send Health with gentle hand, and crown my life
> With blest abundance, free from noisy strife;
> Lest in extreme old age the prey of Death,
> Dismiss me willing to the realms beneath,
> To thy fair palace and the blissful plains
> Where happy spirits dwell, and Hades reigns.

At the end of the same body of hymns one (no. 87) is addressed directly to Death:

27. Ibid., 9, no. 19a.
28. For the mysteries of Dionysos as based on those of Osiris, see Paul Foucart, *Les mystères d'Éleusis*, 445ff.
29. For the experience of the Bacchae, see Michael Grosso, "The Cult of Dionysos and the Origins of Belief in Life after Death," *PR* 12.3 (May–June 1981): 5–8.
30. Thomas Taylor, *The Mystical Hymns of Orpheus*; see also M. L. West *The Orphic Poems*.

Hear me, O Death, whose empire unconfined
Extends to mortal tribes of every kind.
On thee the portion of our time depends,
Whose absence lengthens life, whose presence ends.
Thy sleep perpetual bursts the vivid folds
By which the soul, attracting body holds. . . .
O blessed power, regard my ardent prayer,
And human life to age abundant spare.

There was also a connection between the Orphics and the Pythagoreans. In fragments of Philolaus of Tarentum (latter half of the fifth century B.C.), who is said to have written the first published account of Pythagoreanism called *On the Universe,*[31] and was probably a Pythagorean, and in Aristotle (*Metaphysics* 5), who also wrote a now lost work *On the Pythagoreans,* we learn that Pythagorean doctrine saw the universe as a cosmos characterized by number and harmony, by the understanding of which human life can be properly ordered. Pythagoras taught that the soul is immortal and passes through a series of rebirths. His teaching on immortality is reflected, for example, in the report by Herodotus (4.95) that a certain Salmoxis, later considered a god by the Thracians, was once a slave of Pythagoras and learned from him the doctrine of immortality, which he then taught to the Thracians. As to the doctrine of rebirth, Pythagoras was said to have claimed that he was formerly Aethalides (a son of Mercury and herald of the Argonauts), Euphorbos (a Trojan hero, *Iliad* 17.60), and other early personages. As proof of such assertions, he attests that he went into the temple at Delphi where the shield of Euphorbos was hanging, recognized it, and claimed it as his own (Tatian [second century A.D.], *Discourse to the Greeks* 25; Tertullian [c. A.D. 155–220], *On the Soul* 28). Apparently Pythagoras also believed that souls could pass into animal bodies for, in a fragment of Xenophanes that almost certainly refers to Pythagoras, his contemporary, it is said that the latter once saw a dog being beaten and said: "Stop! . . . This is really the soul of a man who was my friend; I recognized it as I heard it cry aloud."[32]

Pythagoras's teaching on immortality and the rebirths of the soul comes most probably from doctrines already enunciated by Pherecydes of Syros (an island in the Aegean); Pythagoras was said to have loved this teacher like a father (Diodorus 10.3.4), and Pherecydes was said to be the first, as far as literature tells, who declared souls to be eternal (Cicero [106–43 B.C.], *Tusculan Disputations* 1.16.38; see also Lactantius

31. Freeman, *Ancilla to the Pre-Socratic Philosophers,* 73–76, nos. 1–19.
32. Ibid. 21–22, no. 7.

[c. A.D. 240–320], *Divine Institutes* 7.7.12). The influence of Egypt, said to have been visited by Orpheus and Pythagoras, is also probable in view of the statement by Herodotus (who was in Egypt around 450 B.C.) that the Egyptians were the first to teach that the human soul is immortal and that it goes through a series of rebirths. India is a yet more distant but probable source, where the theory of reincarnation is fully developed in the *Upanishads* (900–600 B.C.), for example, *Chandogya Upanishad* 5.10.7: "Those whose conduct has been good will quickly attain some good birth. . . . But those whose conduct has been evil will quickly attain an evil birth, the birth of a dog." Similarly in the *Laws of Manu* (500–300 B.C.), for example, 12.40: "Those endowed with Goodness reach the state of gods, those endowed with Activity the state of men, and those endowed with Darkness ever sink to the condition of beasts; that is the threefold course of transmigrations."[33]

Evidences of relationship between the Pythagoreans and the Orphics is seen in the reference by Ion of Chios (active between 452 and 421 B.C.) to Pythagoras's teaching on immortality, and in Pythagoras's ascription of some of his writings to Orpheus.[34] The universal insistence on vegetarianism in the Orphic rule of life (Plato, *Laws* 782c) may well be related to Pythagoras's teaching about souls in animals. The conception expressed by Orphic poets that the body (σῶμα) is the tomb (σῆμα) in which the soul is imprisoned (Plato, *Cratylos* 400c) meshes well with Pythagoras's doctrine of rebirth. In fact, making such relationship probable, in Magna Graecia, for example, the communities of Orpheus and of the Pythagoreans were close together (at Petelia and Thurii, and at Croton and Metapontum).

For the Eleusinian mysteries (centered at Eleusis, near Athens) the chief literary source is the so-called *Homeric Hymn to Demeter* (sixth century B.C.).[35] This text tells the story of how, after the recovery of Persephone from the underworld, Demeter went to Keleos the king of Eleusis, to Triptolemos his son (whom she commissioned to teach humankind how to use corn), and to "mighty Eumolpos" (who became the first hierophant to celebrate the mysteries), and "showed [them] the conduct of her rites and taught them all her mysteries . . . awful mysteries which no one may in any way transgress or pry into or utter, for deep awe of the gods checks the voice" (473–79).

The complete reticence thus enjoined upon and observed by those who had knowledge of the mysteries means that little is known of the

33. M. L. West, *Early Greek Philosophy and the Orient*, 60ff.

34. Freeman, *Ancilla to the Pre-Socratic Philosophers*, 70, no. 2.

35. George E. Mylonas, *The Hymn to Demeter and Her Sanctuary at Eleusis*; and idem, *Eleusis and the Eleusinian Mysteries*, 6, 224.

content of the proceedings at Eleusis. Clement of Alexandria (writing between A.D. 190 and 210) attributes this saying to the Eleusinian initiate: "I have fasted, I have drunk the draught; I have taken out of the chest and placed what I have taken out into the basket, and out of the basket into the chest" (*Protreptikos* 2.18). While it has been held that the "draught" (κυκεών, literally "mixed drink") was psychotropic in effect,[36] Arnobius (writing probably in A.D. 304–310) explains (5.24–26) that the term means wine thickened with barley-meal and was the same as the refreshing drink offered to Demeter when, exhausted by the long search for her daughter, she first came to Eleusis. The chest (κίστη; Latin, *cista*) and the basket (κάλαθος) presumably contained some sort of symbols of the mysteries. Lactantius, giving a brief summary of the mysteries, suggests that in some manner there was a reenactment of the recovery of Persephone from the underworld: "[In] the mysteries of Ceres [Demeter] . . . torches are lighted and Proserpina [Persephone] is sought for through the night; and when she has been found, the whole rite is finished with expressions of joy and brandishing of torches" (*Epitome of the Divine Institutes* 23.7).

Concerning the effect of the experience that came to the initiate in the mysteries, Pindar (522–448 B.C.), quoted by Clement of Alexandria (*Stromata* 3.3), says: "Happy is he who has seen these rites before he descends under the hollow earth; for he knows the end of life and he knows the beginning promised by Zeus." Likewise Cicero lets a speaker in his *Laws* (2.14.35) refer to the "impressive mysteries" of Iacchus (see p. 173) and the Eumolpidae (the family that continued to hold the chief priesthood at Eleusis), and say that among the many excellent and divine institutions that Athens contributed to human life none is better than these mysteries, from which "we have gained the power not only to live happily, but also to die with a better hope" (2.14.36).

A fuller description, which may have applied to either the Orphic or the Eleusinian mysteries, is provided in an essay by Themistios (c. A.D. 317–390) entitled *On the Soul* and preserved in the *Florilegium* of Stobaios, a fifth-century compiler of extracts from Greek authors.[37] Themistios says that the soul that is at the point of death

> has the same experience as those who are being initiated into great mysteries. . . . At first one wanders and wearily hurries to and fro, and journeys with suspicion through the dark as one uninitiated; then come all the terrors before the final initiation, shuddering, trembling, sweating,

36. R. Gordon Wasson, Albert Hofmann, and Carl A. P. Ruck, *The Road to Eleusis*; but see n. 34 in chap. 3, "Zoroastrian Religion," p. 80.

37. August Meineke, *Ioannis Stobaei Florilegium*, 4.107–8.

amazement; then one is struck with a marvelous light, one is received into pure regions and meadows, with voices and dances and the majesty of holy sounds and shapes; among these he who has fulfilled initiation wanders free, and released and bearing his crown joins in the divine communion, and consorts with pure and holy men, beholding those who live here uninitiated, an uncleansed horde, trodden under foot of him and huddled together in mud and fog, abiding in their miseries through fear of death and mistrust of the blessings there.

Brief and allusive as are the foregoing descriptions, they may be understood as at least suggesting that at its highest level the initiation of the mysteries in some way induced an experience perceived as beyond the limits of earthly life, by virtue of which the initiated was thereafter fully persuaded of the continuation of life at death.

As for the mysteries of Isis and Osiris/Sarapis, an inscription found at Piraeus dated 333/332 B.C. records that permission had at some prior time been granted for certain Egyptians to establish a temple of Isis.[38] An Athenian named Timetheos, of the family of the Eumolpidae (who superintended the mysteries at Eleusis), and the Egyptian historian Manetho were involved together in the development of the cult of Sarapis in Egypt under Ptolemy I Soter (323–285 B.C.) (Tacitus, *Histories* 4.83–84; Plutarch, *On Isis and Osiris* 28). Therefore the Egyptian deities were known at Athens at least already in the fourth century B.C.[39] Further details about the mysteries of Isis and Osiris/Sarapis will wait for the chapter on Roman religion, because the chief literary descriptions are by authors writing in the Roman period (e.g., Plutarch, Apuleius).

In the light of this survey of the mysteries in Greece and returning now to Plato, it is plain that Plato has not a little in common with the mysteries, presumably in the first instance with the Eleusinian, whose processions between Athens and Eleusis passed Plato's academy on the outskirts of Athens, but also with the Pythagorean/Dionysiac/Orphic to which he makes specific reference. Since Plato is said to have visited Egypt in person he probably had contact also with the mysteries of Isis and Osiris.

In specific reference to the Orphics, Plato does not hesitate to censure what he considers amiss in them, for example, in the *Republic* (364e–365a) he speaks of the "hubbub" (ὅμαδος) of the books of Orpheus and Musaeus and of unseemly promotion of the Orphic rites of initiation. But he also introduces the language of the mysteries not only when he quotes the saying, "many carry the staff, but the mystics

38. Ladislav Vidman, *Sylloge inscriptionum religionis Isiacae et Sarapiacae*, 3–4, no. 1.
39. Sterling Dow, "The Egyptian Cults in Athens," *HTR* 30 (1937): 183–232.

are few," but also when he speaks of those who in the other world "will lie in the mire" (*Phaedo* 69c). This latter expression is similar to the description by Themistios of those who, in the other world, are "huddled together in mud and fog." That the soul is immortal and born many times was taught by Pythagoras, and in Plato's *Meno* (81a–c) this doctrine is set forth by "certain priests and priestesses," who may well be Pythagoreans.[40] And in *Phaedo* (61d) the doctrine of the immortality of the soul is discussed by Cebes and Simmias, who are identified as pupils of Philolaus (of Tarentum), the author of the first published account of Pythagoreanism. That the universe is characterized by number and harmony, the understanding of which can properly determine human life, was taught by Pythagoras; in Plato's *Gorgias* (506e–508a) order and harmony are principles for moral and social life. In the *Timaeus* (47a–e) contemplation of number and harmony in the universe is seen as the basis of philosophy, a view expounded by Timaeus of Locri (a town in Magna Graecia), who was probably a Pythagorean.[41]

In the setting forth of some of the transcendent matters, with which the mysteries also often deal, Plato frequently uses myth. In some cases the myth serves as illustration of truth arrived at by dialectic; in some cases it serves to express truths perceived but beyond the powers of human reason to demonstrate scientifically; in both cases the language is to be taken as symbolic, not literal.[42] In this respect, there is an extended description in *Phaedo* (113aff.) of the regions to which the souls of the dead go, and then it is said in conclusion (114d):

> Now it would not be fitting for a man of sense to maintain that all this is just as I have described it, but that this or something like it is true concerning our souls and their abode, since the soul is shown to be immortal, I think he may properly and worthily venture to believe; for the venture is well worth while.

On the whole, then, we may recognize that for Plato the experience of the philosopher and the experience of the mystic are analogous. Both must undergo long and strenuous preparation in thought and life, both may hope at last to come to an illumination that is like the torches lighted at Eleusis or, as Plato puts it (Letter 7, 341c–d), "like a blaze kindled by a leaping spark." The mystic who experiences death in initiation wins thereby the assurance that there is the beyond; the thinker who glimpses the realm of transcendent being wins the

---

40. R. S. Buck, *Plato's Meno*, 274–76.
41. For further details on the influence of Pythagoras on Plato, see Friedländer, *Plato*, 1.26–29.
42. Guthrie, *Orpheus and Greek Religion*, 239–43.

assurance of a part in it. In both cases there is a conviction that spiritual existence endures beyond death.[43]

## Neoplatonism

The last school of Greek philosophy/religion was Platonism, now usually called Neoplatonism. In it, in general, as in Plato, (1) it is held that there are levels of reality beyond what is immediately visible and sensible; (2) symbolic thinking is continued with priority given to intuition as compared with empirical forms of knowing; (3) the immortality of the soul is affirmed and usually the doctrine of the rebirths of the soul as well; and (4) the true, the good, and the beautiful are usually identified as one and the same.[44]

The founder of Neoplatonism is considered to be Ammonius Saccas (c. A.D. 175–250), who was a teacher of philosophy at Alexandria. In the *Life of Plotinus* by Porphyry,[45] we learn that as a young man of twenty-seven years with a deep interest in philosophy Plotinus was going to the most highly reputed professors to be found at Alexandria and, when he heard a lecture by Ammonius Saccas, he exclaimed, "This was the man I was looking for." Along with Plotinus a Neoplatonist named Origen and the Christian writer Origen (Eusebius, *Church History* 6.19.6) were also hearers of Ammonius Saccas. Their teacher required of them that they should not disclose his revelations, and Ammonius Saccas left no writings of his own, so little is directly known of him and his doctrines. It is evident, however, that he was of great influence upon Plotinus, who became the first major writer of Neoplatonic doctrine.

Plotinus (A.D. 204–270) probably came originally from Upper Egypt. Porphyry tells us that Plotinus continued with Ammonius Saccas in Alexandria for eleven years. Then, desiring to investigate Persian and Indian teachings, he joined the expeditionary force of Gordian III (238–244) in his campaign against Persia in the year 244. The emperor was killed in Mesopotamia in the same year and Plotinus escaped to Antioch. Then at the age of forty, under the emperor Philip the Arab (244–249), he settled in Rome and taught there until his death at the age of sixty-six.

The great work of Plotinus, and the chief document of Neoplatonism, is known as the *Enneads,* consisting of fifty-four essays arranged

---

43. Heinrich Dörrie, "Mysterien (in Kult und Religion) und Philosophie," in *Die orientalischen Religionen im Römerreich,* ed. Maarten J. Vermaseren, 343–44.
44. *The Significance of Neoplatonism,* ed. R. Baine Harris.
45. Stephen MacKenna, *Plotinus: The Enneads,* 1–20.

in six divisions of nine each, each division called an "ennead." Like
Plato, Plotinus affirms the reality and the immortality of the soul and,
like Plato, considering the beautiful, the good, and the true to be one
and the same, he writes "On Beauty" (*Enneads* 1.6.2, 3, 8):

> We hold that all the loveliness of this world comes by communion in
> Ideal-Form.... And the soul includes a faculty peculiarly addressed to
> Beauty.... But ... how [may we] come to vision of the inaccessible
> Beauty, dwelling as if in consecrated precincts ...? He that has the
> strength, let him arise and withdraw into himself.... You must close
> the eyes and call instead upon another vision which is to be waked within
> you, a vision, the birthright of all, which few turn to use.

Then in conclusion he uses the language of the mysteries to tell of the
vision of which he speaks (*Enneads* 6.9.11):

> This is the purport of that rule of our mysteries: "Nothing divulged to
> the uninitiate"; the Supreme is not to be made a common story, the holy
> things may not be uncovered to the stranger, to any that has not himself
> attained to see.... The man formed by this mingling with the Su-
> preme ... has risen beyond beauty; ... he is like one who, having pen-
> etrated the inner sanctuary, leaves the temple images behind him....
> When the soul begins to mount, it comes not to something alien but to
> its very self.[46]

Porphyry (A.D. 232–305), born in Syria and disciple of Plotinus in
Rome, was the editor and biographer of Plotinus, and the author of a
polemic *Against the Christians* (condemned to be burned by the emperor Theodosius II in A.D. 435) and of other works, including an introduction (*Isagoge*) to and commentary on Aristotle's *Categories*. Due
to the influence of this last work Aristotle became the accepted logi-
cian of Neoplatonism as Plato was the accepted theologian.[47] Another
work by Porphyry is cited by Augustine under the title *Philosophy
from Oracles* (perhaps the same work as *On the Return of the Soul*).
Augustine feels that Porphyry improves upon both Plato and Plotinus
in that Porphyry holds that human souls return only into human bodies (not those of animals) and that at last "the purified soul returns
to the Father, that it may never more be entangled in the polluting
contact with evil" (*City of God* 10.30; 12.20).

In *Auxiliaries to the Perception of Intelligibles,* Porphyry writes about

---

46. Ibid., 57–58, 62–63, 624–25.
47. Edward W. Warren, *Isagogue: Porphyry the Phoenician.*

soul and body in a way reminiscent of the words of the Orphic hymn to Death about "the vivid folds by which the soul, attracting body holds" (p. 174):

> That which nature binds, nature also dissolves; and that which the soul binds, the soul likewise dissolves. Nature, indeed, bound the body to the soul, but the soul binds herself to the body. Nature, therefore liberates the body from the soul; but the soul liberates herself from the body. Hence there is a twofold death: the one, indeed, universally known, in which the body is liberated from the soul; but the other peculiar to philosophers, in which the soul is liberated from the body; nor does the one always attend the other.[48]

Iamblichus (c. A.D. 250–325) was born at one of the towns named Chalcis in Syria, studied under Porphyry, and afterward returned to Syria to establish his own school (at either Apamea or Daphne, both near Antioch). He was the author of commentaries on Aristotle and Plato,[49] and of many other books, some extant, some known only in fragments or from references. Of his work it has been said that "he began the attempt to build upon a Neoplatonic basis a complete and coherent theology encompassing all the rites, myths and divinities of later syncretistic paganism."[50] In his book *On the Mysteries* Iamblichus writes:

> The consciousness of our own nothingness, when we compare ourselves with the gods, causes us to betake ourselves spontaneously to suppliant prayer. But from supplication we are led to the object of supplication, from intimate converse therewith we acquire a similarity to it, and from imperfection we quietly receive the divine perfection.[51]

And in his *Life of Pythagoras* Iamblichus says that Pythagoras

> divinely healed and purified the soul, resuscitated and saved its divine part, and conducted to the intelligible its divine eye, which, as Plato says [*Republic* 527d–e], is better worth saving than ten thousand corporeal eyes; for by looking through this alone, when it is strengthened and clarified by appropriate aids, the truth pertaining to all beings is perceived.[52]

48. Taylor, *Mystical Hymns of Orpheus,* 162 n. 117.
49. John M. Dillon, *Iamblichi Chalcidensis in Platonis dialogos commentariorum fragmenta.*
50. Arthur Hilary Armstrong, "Iamblichus," in *EB* 11.1006.
51. Thomas Taylor, *Iamblichus on the Mysteries of the Egyptians, Chaldeans, and Assyrians,* 62.
52. Taylor, *Iamblichus' Life of Pythagoras,* 37.

Proclus (A.D. 410–485) was the most important figure in the later Neoplatonism that began with Iamblichus.[53] Proclus was a Greek born in Constantinople (Byzantium), studied in Alexandria and with Plutarch and Syrianos in Athens, and became the head for the rest of his life of the Platonic academy at Athens (as the heir to this position and to distinguish him from others of the same name he is known as Proclus Diadochus, the "successor"). Proclus wrote commentaries and an exegetical work (*Platonic Theology*) on Plato, essays (*On Providence and Fate*, and others), hymns (of which only a few survive), and major systematic texts (*Elements of Physics*; *Elements of Theology*).[54] The pupil and immediate successor of Proclus in the academy at Athens was Marinus, who came from Neapolis (Shechem) in Palestine, and was a convert to Neoplatonism from Samaritan Judaism. Marinus wrote a biography of Proclus, in which we are told that Proclus once said that if he could, out of all ancient books, he would leave current only the *Timaeus* of Plato and the *Chaldean Oracles*. We are also given a description of the religious life of Proclus who, in addition to his heavy schedule of lecturing and writing, worshiped the sun three times a day, observed all the Egyptian holy days, and spent part of the night in prayer and praise.[55]

In his *Commentary on Plato's Cratylus* Proclus quotes the *Chaldean Oracles* as stating: "Things divine cannot be obtained by those whose intellectual eye is directed to body; but those only can arrive at the possession of them who stripped of their garments hasten to the summit."[56] In an essay "On the Hieratic Art of the Greeks" (Latin version, *De sacrificio et magia*) Proclus reflects Plato's thought about beginning from obvious beauties and ascending to the highest (*Symposium* 211c):[57]

> In the same manner as lovers gradually advance from that beauty which is apparent in sensible forms to that which is divine, so the ancient priests, when they considered that there is a certain alliance and sympathy in natural things to each other, and of things manifest to occult powers, and discovered that all things subsist in all, they fabricated a sacred science from this mutual sympathy and similarity. Thus they recognized things supreme in such as are subordinate, and the subordinate in the supreme.

Proclus goes on to illustrate his point by reference to the wonderful sympathetic powers of animals, plants, and stones. The lotus, for example,

53. Laurence Jay Rosán, *The Philosophy of Proclus: The Final Phase of Ancient Thought.*
54. Eric R. Dodds, *Proclus: The Elements of Theology.*
55. Rosán, *Philosophy of Proclus*, 13–35.
56. Taylor, *Mystical Hymns of Orpheus*, 193.
57. Taylor, *Iamblichus' Life of Pythagoras*, 213–14.

before the rising of the sun, folds its leaves into itself, but gradually expands them on its rising; unfolding them in proportion to the sun's ascent to the zenith, but as gradually contracting them as that luminary descends to the west. Hence this plant, by the expansion and contraction of its leaves, appears no less to honor the sun than men by the gesture of their eyelids and the motion of their lips.

In a *Hymn to the Sun* Proclus salutes the sun and prays:

> Image of nature's all-producing god,
> And the soul's leader to the realms of light—
> Hear! and refine me from the stains of guilt;
> The supplication of my tears receive . . .
> The punishments incurred by sin remit. . . .
> By thy pure law, dread evil's constant foe,
> Direct my steps, and pour thy sacred light
> In rich abundance on my clouded soul.[58]

The Neoplatonism enunciated at the height of the movement by Proclus in Athens was influential in the system of Christian thought set forth in a series of writings composed in the late fifth century and circulated under the name of Dionysios the Areopagite (Acts 17:34). In these the unknown author, often considered the father of Christian mysticism, outlines the *Celestial Hierarchy* and the *Ecclesiastical Hierarchy,* treats the *Divine Names* that contain the mystery of the divine being, and in *Mystical Theology* describes the ascent of the soul to the vision of God.[59]

In spite of this positive relationship with some Christian thought, in A.D. 529 the academy at Athens was shut down by decree of Justinian I, and Athenian Neoplatonism came to an end. Some of its leaders, however, established themselves thereafter in Byzantium (Constantinople), where later Psellus (A.D. 1018–1079) was notable for his continuation of the ideas of Proclus.

The school of Neoplatonism founded by Iamblichus in Syria was later moved to Pergamum, and one of its leaders, Maximus of Smyrna, was the chosen master of the emperor Julian (A.D. 361–363; see p. 210), who was converted from Christianity to Neoplatonism and thus, from the Christian point of view, called the "apostate." Probably also to be identified with the Pergamene school was Sallust, whose *On the Gods and the World* may have been prepared for Julian.[60] In this

---

58. Thomas Taylor, *Sallust: On the Gods and the World,* 128.
59. Dionysios Areopagita, *Mystische Theologie und andere Schriften.*
60. Taylor, *Sallust: On the Gods and the World.*

work Sallust distinguishes four kinds of myth in which symbolic thought is embodied (theological, psychological, natural, and mixed), and makes it plain that it is only to speak after common custom if "we call the orb of the sun and its rays the Sun itself." After the death of Julian, and with the restoration of Christianity as the state religion, the Pergamene school came to an end.

In Rome, Victorinus (d. c. A.D. 370), an African by birth and a teacher of rhetoric, translated some of the works of the earlier Neoplatonists into Latin, then at last moved from Neoplatonism into Christianity (Jerome, *Illustrious Men* 101). Augustine (A.D. 354–430) read the translations of Victorinus and was deeply influenced by Neoplatonism as he likewise moved on (baptized in 387) into the Christian faith (*Confessions* 8.2). He later declared that of all other philosophers "none come nearer to us than the Platonists" (*City of God* 8.5). Likewise the Roman Christian theologian Boethius (c. A.D. 470–525), who wrote commentaries on works of Porphyry and translated Porphyry's *Isagoge*, reflects Neoplatonism in his own major work *On the Consolation of Philosophy*. Together Augustine and Boethius were mainly responsible for the introduction of Neoplatonic ideas into Latin Christianity. Nevertheless Roman Neoplatonism as a school was at an end by the latter part of the sixth century.

In Egypt, Origen (c. A.D. 185–254), who became the head of the Christian catechetical school at Alexandria, was, according to Porphyry (quoted by Eusebius, *Church History* 6.19.1–14), at one time a hearer of Ammonius Saccas, and was continually studying Plato and busying himself with the writings of Numenius (a Syrian philosopher who also influenced Plotinus) and other Greek philosophers. While Origen (to be distinguished from a contemporary Neoplatonist of the same name)[61] was not officially a Neoplatonist, he entertained many similar views—due to the influence of which Greek Christianity was always more Neoplatonic than Latin Christianity. Nevertheless in A.D. 415 and under Cyril archbishop of Alexandria (d. A.D. 444) Hypatia, the head of the Neoplatonic school at Alexandria and a lady of high attainment in literature and philosophy, was dragged from her carriage by a mob of fanatical Christians and murdered at the church called Caesareum (Socrates, *Church History* 7.15). Finally, with the capture of the city by the Arabs in A.D. 642 the school was shut down.

The long line of thought from Orpheus to Pythagoras to Plato and

---

61. Karl-Otto Weber, *Origenes der Neuplatoniker.*

on to Plato's followers would, however, not end, and of Platonism's lasting contribution it has been said that it is "an emphatic witness to the unseen, the transcendental . . . the beauty . . . which is not for the bodily eye."[62]

62. Walter Pater, *Plato and Platonism*, 126.

# 6

# Roman Religion

## History and Sources

The traditional account of the founding of the city that became the capital of the far-flung Roman Empire[1] is told by the Latin writers, among others, Quintus Ennius (239–169 B.C.) in his *Annals* (of which only extensive fragments remain),[2] Virgil (70–19 B.C.) in the *Aeneid,* and Livy (59 B.C.–A.D. 17) in his *History of Rome* (called *Ab Urbe Condita,* "From the Founding of the City"). The story draws upon Greek mythology and legend, and goes on to Roman traditions.

As the account opens, Aeneas, well-known in the *Iliad* as the son of the goddess Aphrodite and the Trojan ruler Anchises and a participant on the Trojan side in the Trojan War, is making his way to the west. It is seven years after he and his companions escaped from the burning city of Troy, and the long journey is filled with many adventures in which gods and people take part. In Carthage Aeneas is loved by Dido, daughter of the king of Tyre and founder of Carthage; when Aeneas goes on his way, Dido takes her own life. Having arrived at long last at Cumae in Italy, Aeneas consults the Sibyl, the oracular priestess of Apollo, and together they descend into the netherworld, where Aeneas sees both Dido and Anchises his father. Dido will not speak to him, but Anchises shows Aeneas the line of his descendants as yet unborn: the son who will be born after his death; Romulus who will found a great new city, Rome; Numa, Tullus, and other early rulers of that city; and also Augustus who will be a powerful emperor. Then Aeneas and the Sibyl return to the upper world (*Aeneid* 6.752–898).

As adumbrated by Anchises in the underworld in Virgil's story, and

---

1. Tim Cornell and John Matthews, *Atlas of the Roman World.*
2. E. H. Warmington, *Remains of Old Latin,* 1.3ff.

as also recounted by Livy and others in the further unfolding of events, Aeneas and the Trojans resume their journey and land in Latium at the mouth of the Tiber. Latinus, the ruler of the region (and the eponymous hero of the Latin race), receives them well, although the Trojans must fight against some of the Latins and also against some of the Etruscans. In due time Aeneas marries Lavinia, the daughter of Latinus, and founds Lavinium (sixteen miles southeast of the site of Rome). Later Aeneas's son Ascanius moves inland to begin a new city, Alba Longa (probably where Castel Gandolfo now stands), and both Lavinium and Alba Longa become parent cities of Rome. In due time the more distant descendants of Aeneas, the twins Romulus and Remus, are born as the sons of the Latin princess Rhea Silvia (Ilia), a vestal virgin and daughter of Numitor king of Alba Longa; she claims that Mars was their father. Cast adrift in a floating basket upon the Tiber, the twins come ashore at the site of the future Rome, where they are rescued and suckled by a she-wolf (Latin, *lupa*; remembered later in the annual festival called the Lupercalia), and Romulus becomes the founder and first ruler of Rome, named after him (Livy 1.7.3).

The most widely accepted date (established by Varro [116–27 B.C.]; see also Plutarch [c. A.D. 46–120], *Life of Romulus* 12) of the founding of Rome is 753 B.C., which was more than four hundred years after the Trojan War (1194 B.C.) with which Aeneas was associated. For more than two hundred further years (753–510 B.C.) Rome was ruled by kings—Numa, Tullus, and others and, in a final sequence, several Etruscans, Lucius Tarquinius Priscus (616–578 B.C.), Servius Tullius (578–534), and Lucius Tarquinius Superbus (534–510).[3] In 510 the Latin nobles of Rome, the patricians, overthrew the Etruscan dynasty and instituted a republican government based upon the authority of the senate and the people (*senatus populusque Romanus,* often abbreviated S.P.Q.R.) and presided over by two consuls elected annually— a republic that endured for nearly five hundred years (510–30 B.C.). Within that period in successive wars Rome mastered all of Italy (including the Greek colonies of Magna Graecia in the south) and overcame its major rival, Carthage in North Africa (in the Punic [Latin for Phoenician] Wars, between 264 and 146), but in the last two centuries of the period civil wars ensued among the Roman generals. In 48 B.C. Julius Caesar defeated Pompey; in 31 B.C. Octavian defeated Mark Antony, with whose death in 30 B.C. Octavian emerged as the real master and first emperor of the Roman Empire (given the title Au-

3. For the Etruscans, see Emeline Richardson, *The Etruscans: Their Art and Civilization*; Rick Gore, "The Eternal Etruscans," *NG* 173.6 (June 1988): 696–743.

gustus by the senate in 27 B.C.). This empire came to extend from Britain in the west to Mesopotamia in the east, and endured until A.D. 476 when the last emperor, Romulus Augustulus, was deposed by Teutonic invaders and replaced by Odoacer, the first barbarian ruler of Italy.

## Sacred Powers

While the earliest works of Latin writers are relatively late (Roman historiography in Latin begins with the fragmentary *Annals* of Quintus Ennius and the also fragmentary *Origines* of Marcus Porcius Cato the Censor [234–149 B.C.]),[4] they provide many references to items of religion not only in the time of the republic but also in the earlier time of the kings.[5]

From the outset the fundamental belief seems to have been in power or powers, to which the term *numen* (plural, *numina*) was applied. Varro (*On the Latin Language* 7.85) cites a sentence of Lucius Accius (170–c. 85 B.C.), "By invoking your name and your *numen* with many a prayer," and explains:

> *Numen* "divine will or sway," they say, is *imperium* "power," and is derived from *nutus* "nod," because he at whose *nutus* "nod" everything is, seems to have the greatest *imperium* "power"; therefore Homer uses this word in application to Jupiter [e.g., *Iliad* 1.528].

Thus the *numen* is most characteristically the *numen dei*, the will and power of a particular deity, as in the *Aeneid*, which speaks, for example, of the queen of heaven (Juno) as "thwarted in will" (1.8–9, *numine laeso*), of honoring with prayer "mighty Juno's power" (3.437, *Iunonis magnae . . . numen*), and of praying to "the holy power of Pallas [Athena]" (3.543–44, *numina sancta . . . Palladis*).

As for the individual and personal deity (Latin, *deus*; plural, *dei* and *di*) Augustine (*City of God* 4.8–11, 16–25, 34; 7.1–4) cites Varro as his authority on the gods worshiped by the Romans and names a group of "select and chief gods" and another group of lesser deities thought to have "the charge of minute and trifling things," all from Augustine's point of view of course to be criticized as not the one true God. Varro's list of the "select" gods contains twenty names: Janus, Jupiter, Saturn, Genius, Mercury, Apollo, Mars, Vulcan, Neptune, Sol,

4. Hermann Peter, *Historicorum Romanorum Reliquiae*, 1.51–94.
5. Georges Dumézil, *Archaic Roman Religion*.

Orcus, father Liber, Tellus, Ceres, Juno, Luna, Diana, Minerva, Venus, and Vesta; the first twelve are masculine, the last eight feminine.

Of the foregoing major deities Jupiter (properly in Latin, *Juppiter,* akin to the Greek vocative, Ζεῦ πατήρ; also *Jovis,* "Jove") was the foremost. Romulus is said to have consecrated to Jupiter the first temple built in Rome (Livy 1.10.6–7), and Romulus's successor Numa (Numa Pompilius, traditionally 715–672 B.C.) appointed a *flamen* (a priest of one particular deity) for Jupiter as his perpetual priest (Livy 1.20.2). Jupiter was the god of light and the sky, and became the great protector of Rome and the Roman state, being worshiped as Jupiter Optimus Maximus, the Best and Greatest (in inscriptions often abbreviated as D.O.M., *Deo Optimo Maximo*).

Numa also appointed *flamens* for Mars and Quirinius (Livy 1.20.2). The lance was the symbol of Mars, the god of war. Varro (cited by Clement of Alexandria, *Protreptikos* 4) says that in ancient times the cultic image of Mars was a lance, because the artists had not yet begun to make images in human form, and Plutarch says that there was a lance called Mars in the Regia (a building in the Forum, originally the dwelling of the kings of Rome). Quirinius may also have been originally a war god; at least later he was identified with Romulus deified after death (Plutarch, *Life of Romulus* 29.1–2).

The major temple of Jupiter was on the Capitoline Hill, the most prominent of the seven hills of Rome. The temple was said to have been constructed originally by the last Etruscan king, Lucius Tarquinius Superbus, in fulfilment of a vow made by his father, Lucius Tarquinius Priscus (Livy 1.55.1ff.). Here Jupiter was associated with the two goddesses Juno and Minerva. Juno is the queen of heaven and sister and wife of Jupiter; she was especially the protectress of women and associated with childbirth. Minerva is the goddess of arts and trades and of those who practice them.

There were many lesser deities named by Augustine and they were associated with the major deities in somewhat the same way as lesser servants were associated with the head of a household or lesser officials were associated with the high magistrate under whom they served. Thus Juno, the goddess of women and children, is assisted by many lesser goddesses: Lucina (also Juno Lucina) makes the baby see the light (*lux*) for the first time, Cunina protects the child in the cradle (*cunae*), Edusa (from *edo,* "to eat") and Potina (from *poto,* "to drink") supply food and drink, Juventas presides over the age of youth (*juventa*), and so on. Janus (from *eo, ire,* "a going through") is the god of gates and represented with two faces; but if the beginnings of things pertain to him there is another god for the ends of things, namely, Terminus, the deity who presides over boundaries. At the entrance of a house there are three deities: Forculus the god who presides over the door (foris), Cardea the goddess who presides over the hinge (cardo), and Limentinus the god who presides over the threshold (limen).

In the household the Penates are guardians of the storeroom (penus), and the Lares (singular, Lar) are protectors of the home in general and also of other places. A play by Plautus (c. 254–184 B.C.), the Aulularia, for example, begins with a prologue in which the speaker says: "I am the household god [Lar . . . familiaris] of that family from whose house you saw me come. For many years now I have possessed this dwelling, and preserved it for the sire and grandsire of its present occupant." And in Plautus's Mercator (5.2.24) a traveler prays: "I call upon you, gods of the roadsides [Lares viales], to keep me under your kindly care."

The focus of the household is the hearth (the Latin word focus means hearth), and the goddess of the hearth was Vesta, who was worshiped along with the Penates and the Lares. Likewise the shrine of Vesta in the Forum was the symbolic public hearth, where the fire was kept perpetually burning by the vestal virgins; thus Vesta became one of the major deities. Cicero explains that Vesta is the same goddess whom the Greeks call Hestia; she has power over altars and hearths, and has taken the city hearth (focum urbis) under her protection, with virgins to have charge of her worship. Since she is the guardian of the innermost things, all prayers and sacrifices end with this goddess (De Natura Deorum 2.67; Laws 2.29). Many virtues and benefits were also personified as divinities, for example, Hope, Faith, and Fortune (Spes, Fides, Fortuna) on a wall erected at Capua in 110 B.C.[6]

With the contact of the Romans with the Greeks (in Magna Graecia in south Italy, and in Greece proper, conquered by the Romans in 146 B.C.) some Greek gods such as Apollo and Asklepios were adopted, and many equivalences between Roman and Greek deities were established, for example, that of Vesta and Hestia mentioned just above by Cicero (see table 5).

It was also largely from Greece that the mythology of the deities, as far as it is known, was taken over and adapted,[7] although earlier Roman myths may have been lost, and both Greece and Rome no doubt derived much from a common Indo-European heritage. An example of the last point is seen in the Roman Aurora, the goddess of the dawn, who is plainly the same as the Greek Eos and the Vedic Ushas (Rigveda 7.77, etc.). In Rome she was also known as Matuta or Mater Matuta (e.g., Lucretius [c. 98–55 B.C.], De Rerum Natura 5.656–57: "At a fixed

6. Warmington, Remains of Old Latin, 4.103, no. 118.
7. Stewart Perowne, Roman Mythology, 58.

## TABLE 5
## Twelve Chief Deities
## in the Roman Pantheon
## and Their Greek Equivalents

| Roman | Greek |
|---|---|
| **Masculine** | |
| Jupiter | Zeus |
| Neptune | Poseidon |
| Mars | Ares |
| Apollo | Apollo |
| Vulcan | Hephaistos |
| Mercury | Hermes |
| **Feminine** | |
| Juno | Hera |
| Minerva | Athena |
| Diana | Artemis |
| Venus | Aphrodite |
| Vesta | Hestia |
| Ceres | Demeter |

time Matuta diffuses the rosy dawn [*aurora*].”), and her annual festival was called the Matralia (Plutarch, *Roman Questions* 16–17; *On Brotherly Love* 21).[8]

With respect to human beings, it was believed that the individual person has a Genius, a sort of double personality formed at birth and eventually seen as a separate spirit that is the protector of the person. Horace (65–8 B.C.) defines the Genius as “that companion who rules our star of birth, the god of human nature, though mortal for each single life” (Epistle 2.2.187–89), and makes it plain that the Genius may be appealed to along with the household gods, the Penates (1.7.94).

The description by Horace of the Genius as “mortal for each single life” suggests that the Genius dies with the person; Ovid (43 B.C.–A.D. 17), however, speaks of Aeneas as making offerings to the Genius of his deceased father Anchises (*Fasti* 2.545). As to the continuation of life beyond death, it may be remembered that in the *Aeneid* Aeneas visited his father in the underworld, and there he saw places of both punishment (6.574ff.) and joy (6.637ff.), and was told by Anchises that many who were there would drink of the water of oblivion (i.e., the Lethe River) and then return to new bodies (6.713ff.). In this connection we hear in the *Aeneid* of the soul (*anima*) of the deceased (6.758),

8. Dumézil, *Archaic Roman Religion*, 1.47–59.

and also find the word *manes* as the designation of the departed spirit (6.743). The latter term is also used in the plural as the name of the gods of the underworld (Lucretius, *De Rerum Natura* 6.759, 764), and is familiar in inscriptions with a dedication to the *Dis Manibus* (abbreviated D. M.).

## Eastern Cults and Mysteries

With Rome's contact in the Hellenistic period and under the empire with Greece, Egypt, and the East came also contact with eastern cults and mysteries (for the mysteries in general see pp. 172ff.). The emperor Augustus himself went to Athens and was initiated into the Eleusinian mysteries, and so respected the requirement of silence about the mysteries that when he judged a case at Rome involving priests of Ceres (Demeter) and matters of secrecy he heard the disputants in private (Suetonius [c. A.D. 100], *Augustus* 93). Long before this, however, eastern deities were brought to Rome. Asklepios was introduced in 293 B.C. by order of the Sibylline Books in order to avert a pestilence. A delegation going to Epidauros to obtain an image of Asklepios came back instead with a snake that was supposed to represent him, and the snake was given a temple on an island in the Tiber (Livy 10.47). The usual attribute of Asklepios always remained a clublike staff with a serpent coiled around it.

### Magna Mater/Cybele

It was also because of the Sibylline Books that Cybele, known as the Great Mother (*Magna Mater*), came to Rome.[9] In the Punic Wars in the year 205 B.C., when the Carthaginian invader Hannibal was still in Italy, an oracle was found in the Sibylline Books that declared that "if ever a foreign foe should invade the land of Italy, he could be driven out of Italy and defeated if the Mother of Mount Ida should be brought from Pessinus to Rome"; this suggestion was confirmed by the oracle at Delphi as well. Since her original home, Mount Ida, was near Troy in Asia Minor and since it was from Troy that Aeneas came, the proposed action provided a connection with the earliest history of Rome. Pessinus, whence the Mother was to be brought, was 240 miles inland from Pergamon, and it was to King Attalus of Pergamon that a Roman delegation went with a request that the Mother might come to Rome. This was arranged, and a black stone (probably a meteorite) repre-

9. Maarten J. Vermaseren, *Cybele and Attis: The Myth and the Cult.*

senting the Great Mother was transported by sea to Rome to receive a festive welcome in the spring of the year 204 B.C., and in the next year Hannibal did in fact leave Italy. In the year of the Great Mother's arrival her temple (*aedes Matris Magnae Idaeae*) was begun on the Palatine Hill, and was finally dedicated in 191 B.C. (Livy 29.10–14; 36.36.3; Ovid, *Fasti* 4.247–348; Appian [second century A.D.] 7.56).

In the many traditions concerning her the personal name of the Great Mother is Cybele, and she is associated with Attis. In one form of the many stories about Attis, he was the son of Croesus king of Lydia (561–546 B.C.), and was accidentally slain on the chase by an iron spear (Herodotus 1.34–45). In another version Attis was a Phrygian shepherd youth who was loved by Cybele, to whom he promised lasting obedience. When he fell in love instead with a nymph, the goddess took vengeance: the nymph was killed and Attis went mad and emasculated and destroyed himself (Ovid, *Fasti* 4.223–44). In yet another story Cybele herself was born in Phrygia, the daughter of a king who, having wished for a son and heir instead of this girl, abandoned the baby on Mount Kybelon, from which she derived her name (*Kybele*). As a young woman Cybele secretly loved the native shepherd youth Attis and was about to bear his child when the king found her and brought her back to the palace. Enraged to learn that she, a king's daughter, had consorted with a mere shepherd, he ordered Attis killed and his body cast out unburied. In a frenzy of grief Cybele rushed out of the palace into the countryside where she roamed alone, crying aloud and beating upon a drum, while pestilence fell upon human beings and the land itself ceased to bear fruit (an event something like that associated with Demeter). An oracle advised the burial of Attis and honoring Cybele as a goddess. Since Attis's body had disappeared in the course of time, an image of Attis was made before which the people sang dirges. They made altars and performed sacrifices, and later erected a costly temple for Cybele in Pessinus—whence, as we have seen, the goddess came to Rome (Diodorus 3.58–59).

In Rome the annual festival in honor of Cybele was the Megalensia (from *megale*, "great" goddess; Livy 36.36.5), and it is understandable from the foregoing that the ceremonies would involve the use of musical instruments and the utterance of cries of grief. Ovid's *Fasti* is a calendar of Roman religious festivals, and he speaks at length of the cult of Cybele (4.179ff.):

The festival of the Idaean Mother will have come. Eunuchs [known as Galli] will march and thump their hollow drums, and cymbals clashed on cymbals will give out their tinkling notes . . . the goddess herself will be borne with violent crying through the streets in the city's midst.

That the cult had the nature of the mysteries is indicated by Pausanias (7.17.9), who tells of the temple of Cybele and Attis at Dyme in Achaia and says that he could not learn who Attis really is, for this is a religious secret (ἀπόρρητον, "not to be spoken").

In many inscriptions found mainly in Rome and in the western provinces of the empire, having in the majority of cases to do with the cult of Cybele and less frequently with that of Mithras, there is mention of a ceremony called the *taurobolium*, meaning the sacrifice of a bull (sometimes a *criobolium*, meaning the sacrifice of a ram). In the inscriptions of earlier date the phrase is usually *taurobolium facere*, and the meaning is evidently to "perform" the sacrifice of a bull in honor of Cybele. In later inscriptions the phrase is *taurobolium percipere*, which can mean to "receive" the benefits of the sacrifice, probably implying a sprinkling with the purifying blood of the sacrifice. In the form in which Prudentius (c. A.D. 405; *Peristephanon* 10.1006–50) describes the rite in connection with the Mother Goddess in his time

The altar of Mithras in the Mithraic chapel under the Church of San Clemente in Rome

a priest stood in a trench and was washed by the blood of the bull slain on a platform overhead.[10]

### Isis and Osiris/Sarapis

The Egyptian deities Isis and Osiris were known already in Greece at least in the fourth century B.C. (see p. 177) and came to Italy and Rome at a relatively early date.[11] A temple of the god in the form of Sarapis is attested in Puteoli (the port city to which the grain ships from Egypt came; see Acts 28:13) in 105 B.C.; the first Isis temple in nearby Pompeii was built before 80 B.C.; in Rome a college of priests of Isis (*pastophori*) was founded in the time of the dictator Sulla (d. 78 B.C.; Apuleius, *Metamorphoses* 11.30); and in 43 B.C. the so-called second triumvirate (Antony, Lepidus, Octavian) voted a temple to Sarapis and Isis (Dio 47.15.4). Except, however, for the Great Mother brought by Roman invitation, there was still some resistance at this time to foreign deities and, in particular, because of the war against Antony and Cleopatra (who died in 30 B.C.), there was resistance to things Egyptian. In 28 B.C. Octavian forbade Egyptian rites to be celebrated inside the *pomerium,* the city boundary of Rome within which only Roman gods might be worshiped (Dio 53.2.4). Tiberius (A.D. 14–37) also abolished foreign cults, especially Egyptian as well as Jewish, forcing all who were followers of such "superstitions" to burn their vestments and paraphernalia (Suetonius, *Tiberius* 36.1), and destroying a temple of Isis on account of a scandal that occurred there (Josephus [c. A.D. 37–95], *Antiquities* 18.65–80).

Gaius Caligula (A.D. 37–41), however, was very much attracted by everything Egyptian and, under him, the Isis cult received official recognition.[12] It was probably Caligula who instituted the annual festivals of the goddess known as the *Isia* and the *Heuresis* (the "finding" of Osiris),[13] and who built a temple of Isis (probably a rebuilding of the temple destroyed by Tiberius, the principal Isis temple at Rome) in the Campus Martius (outside the *pomerium*).[14] That Caligula was himself initiated in the cult seems likely from the facts that on the day he was assassinated he was celebrating mysteries (Josephus, *Antiquities* 19.104) and in an all-night vigil Egyptians and Ethiopians

---

10. Robert Duthoy, *The Taurobolium: Its Evolution and Terminology.*

11. Reginald E. Witt, *Isis in the Graeco-Roman World*; France Le Corsu, *Isis: Mythe et Mystères*; Ladislav Vidman, *Isis und Sarapis bei den Griechen und Römern*; and idem, "Isis und Sarapis," in *Die orientalischen Religionen im Römerreich,* ed. Maarten J. Vermaseren, 121–56.

12. Ernst Köberlein, *Caligula und die ägyptischen Kulte.*

13. Michel Malaise, *Les conditions de pénétration et de diffusion des cultes égyptiens en Italie,* 221–28, 396–401.

14. Michel Malaise, *Inventaire préliminaire des documents égyptiens découverts en Italie,* 210–14.

were to represent scenes from the lower world (*argumenta inferorum*; Suetonius, *Caligula* 54.2; 57.4).

Under Claudius (A.D. 41–54) an inscription, dated in the year when Claudius and Orfitus were consuls (i.e., A.D. 51), contains a dedication to the invincible Isis and Sarapis (*Isidi invictai et Serap[i]*).[15] Under Servius Sulpicius Galba (A.D. 68–69) a freedman of the emperor named Alcimus (*Ser. Sulpicio Aug[usti] l[iberto] Alcimo*) is named in an inscription as a temple-keeper of the Pelagian Isis (*aedituo ab Isem Pelagian*),[16] that is, Isis as the goddess of the sea, for whom there was an annual festival called the *navigium Isidis* at the opening of the sailing season in the spring (c. Pausanias 2.4.6).[17] Otho (A.D. 69) was himself a priest of Isis, who "used to celebrate the rites of Isis publicly in the linen garment prescribed by the cult" (Suetonius, *Otho* 12.1).

Vespasian (A.D. 69–79) was proclaimed emperor by his soldiers in Alexandria and later went alone into the temple of Sarapis, where he saw a vision and soon thereafter received word of the death of his enemy Vitellius (A.D. 69; Suetonius, *Vespasian* 6–7; see also Tacitus [c. A.D. 55–117], *Histories* 4.81–82). During the Roman victory in the war with the Jews Vespasian and Titus (A.D. 79–81) spent the night before their triumph (in A.D. 71) in the Isis temple in the Campus Martius (Josephus, *War* 7.123).

In the year A.D. 80 the same principal Isis temple in Rome and the adjacent temple of Sarapis (*Iseum et Serapeum*) were burned (Dio 66.24.2). Domitian (A.D. 81–96), probably early in his reign, rebuilt the temples,[18] and adorned the site with an obelisk; scenes on the pyramidion of the obelisk show Isis crowning Domitian, and hieroglyphic texts give him some of the titles of Ptolemy II Philadelphus (285–246 B.C.) and call him the "beloved of Isis." Ruins of the temples remain under and near the Church of San Stefano del Cacco; the obelisk was erected in 1657 in the Piazza Navona.[19]

Of later emperors Hadrian (A.D. 117–138), Commodus (180–192), Septimius Severus (193–211), and Caracalla (211–217) are especially known for their devotion to the Egyptian religion. It was probably Caracalla who first officially introduced the Egyptian deities within the *pomerium,* and he built on the Quirinal Hill a temple of Sarapis, which is attested by a dedicatory inscription on a large block of marble found in the pavement of the Church of Santa Agatha.[20]

---

15. Ibid., 115, no. 13. See pp. 384–87 for concordance between Malaise's inventory and Ladislav Vidman, *Sylloge inscriptionum religionis Isiacae et Sarapiacae.*

16. Malaise, *Inventaire préliminaire,* 126, no. 45.

17. Malaise, *Les conditions de pénétration,* 217–21.

18. Rudolf Helm, *Die Chronik des Hieronymus,* 191.

19. Malaise, *Inventaire préliminaire,* 203–7, no. 387.

20. Ibid., 119–20, no. 23; 180–82.

In his major work *On Isis and Osiris*[21] Plutarch (c. A.D. 46–120),
who probably visited Egypt and was personally initiated in the mysteries (see p. 198), relates the basic myth of Isis and Osiris quite fully
(mainly in §§ 12–20) as something that "all can freely hear told"
(§ 25), and he calls the goddess the "myriad-named" (§ 53). But of the
"mystic rites" observed in the cult he says that they "are not divulged
by initiates or seen by people at large" (§ 25), therefore he tells little
(see his *Obsolescence of Oracles* 417b–c: "Regarding the rites of the
mysteries, in which it is possible to gain the clearest reflections and
adumbrations of the truth . . .'let my lips be piously sealed,' as Herodotus [2.17] says"). Only in general terms does Plutarch speak (§ 2) of
undertaking

> austere and difficult services in sacred rites, of which the end is knowl-
> edge of the First and the Lord, whom only the mind can understand and
> whom the goddess summons one to seek as a being who is near and with
> her and united to her. The name of her sanctuary also clearly offers
> recognition and knowledge of what really exists; for it is called the Iseion
> to indicate that we shall know what really exists if we approach the
> sanctuaries of the goddess with reason and reverence.

Apuleius (born in North Africa c. A.D. 125 and writing in Latin
c. A.D. 170) is evidently reflecting his own personal experience as he
describes in *Metamorphoses* 11[22] the initiations of his fictional character, Lucius, in the mysteries of Isis at Cenchreae and the mysteries
of Osiris at Rome. Although his report is mostly in the guarded gen-
erality of the initiate pledged to silence, he does allow Lucius to give
a very brief description of the first initiation, but with an adjuration
not to divulge it further (11.23):

> I approached the boundary of death and treading on the threshold of
> Proserpina [the Latin form of the name Persephone, therefore what is
> meant is the realm of the dead], I was carried through all the elements,
> after which I returned. At dead of night I saw the sun flashing with
> bright effulgence. I approached close to the gods above and the gods
> below and worshiped them face to face. Behold, I have related things
> about which you must remain in ignorance, though you have heard them.

With this description may be compared the words of Clement of
Alexandria who, although from the point of view of early Christianity

---

21. J. Gwyn Griffiths, *Plutarch's De Iside et Osiride*.
22. J. Gwyn Griffiths, *Apuleius of Madauros: The Isis-Book (Metamorphoses, Book XI)*.

he opposes the mysteries, nevertheless uses the language of the mysteries to express his own faith (*Protreptikos* 12.1ff.):

> O truly sacred mysteries! O stainless light! I am led by the torchbearer to be initiated into heaven and God. Through initiation I become holy. The Lord is the hierophant, and seals while illuminating him who is initiated, and presents to the Father him who believes, to be kept safe for ever. Such are the reveries of my mysteries.

## Hermetic Literature

The Hermetic literature, attributed to Hermes Trismegistos, is probably to be dated to the second century A.D. or later.[23] With an Egyptian background, the writings also exhibit relationship to Plato, Gnosticism,[24] and other then-current elements of thought.

In Egypt the Greek Hermes (Latin, Mercury) was identified with Thoth, the scribe of the gods and the inventor of writing, medicine, and astronomy. A late hieroglyphic epithet of Thoth, *as as* ("great, great," i.e., "greatest"), shows the meaning of the name of Hermes Trismegistos ("thrice-greatest Hermes"). The identification of Hermes and Thoth is attested by Cicero (*De Natura Deorum* 3.56), who reports the tradition that Mercury went to Egypt where he gave the Egyptians their laws and letters and was known by the name Theuth (Egyptian, Thoth), his name being also the name of the first month (August–September) of the Egyptian year. Lactantius (*Divine Institutes* 1.6) cites this statement by Cicero, adds that Hermes/Thoth built the town called Hermopolis in Greek (the present el-Ashmunein in central Egypt), and goes on to say of him:

> Although he was a man, yet he was of great antiquity, and most fully imbued with every kind of learning, so that the knowledge of many subjects and arts acquired for him the name of Trismegistus. He wrote books, and those in great numbers, relating to the knowledge of divine things, in which he asserts the majesty of the supreme and only God, and makes mention of him by the same names which we use—God and Father.

As to the "great antiquity" of Hermes Trismegistos, Lactantius (*On the Anger of God* 11) avers that Hermes was far more ancient than

23. G. R. S. Mead, *Thrice-Greatest Hermes: Studies in Hellenistic Theosophy and Gnosis*; John D. Chambers, *The Divine Pymander, and Other Writings of Hermes Trismegistus*; Edwin M. Yamauchi, *Pre-Christian Gnosticism: A Survey of the Proposed Evidences*, 71–72.

24. Three Hermetic tractates were found among the Coptic Gnostic texts from Nag Hammadi (Codex VI, nos. 6, 7, 8); see Douglas M. Parrott et al., *Nag Hammadi Codices V, 2–5 and VI, with Papyrus Berolinensis 8502,1 and 4*, 341–451.

Plato, Pythagoras, and the Seven Wise Men of Greece (Thales, Solon, and others). He also praises him, for "Trismegistus . . . by some means or other searched into almost all truth" (*Divine Institutes* 4.9).

Iamblichus (*On the Mysteries* 1.1; 8.1, 4) calls Hermes "the god who presides over language," and says that Manetho attributed to him the writing of 36,525 books, and that the books that circulated under the name of Hermes were translated (into Greek) from the Egyptian "by men who were not unskilled in philosophy." Clement of Alexandria (*Stromata* 6.4) describes an Egyptian religious procession, in which the leading participants know, evidently by heart, many of the books of Hermes on such subjects as astronomy, philosophy, and medicine, forty-two of these books said to be indispensable.

The books of Hermes Trismegistos on "divine things," to which Lactantius refers, are presumably theological works, and it is works of this sort that are extant in the collection of texts known as the *Corpus Hermeticum*.[25] The collection comprises seventeen tractates, of which the most important is the *Poimandres*; next in importance is the *Asclepius,* preserved only in a Latin translation. There are also many quotations of Hermes in Stobaios, Lactantius, and other early Christian writers.

The title of *Poimandres* means either "shepherd man" or "shepherd of men," and it designates a great Being, the representative of Mind (*nous*), who appears to the writer (in chaps. 1 and 11) and becomes his instructor and guide. The writer expresses the desire to learn the things that are, and to know God (1.3), and is granted a vision of the cosmos (1.4ff.) and of the way above (ἄνοδος), that is, of the ascent of the soul out of the body at death (1.24ff.). In most of the fourteen chapters of the book Hermes Trismegistos himself is the instructor, and talks with three other persons, namely, Tat (Thoth) who is identified as his son, Asclepius who is his disciple and grandson, and Ammon who is probably Ammonius Saccas (c. A.D. 175–250), the teacher of Plotinus and usually considered the founder of Neoplatonism (see p. 200).

In the teachings of Hermes Trismegistos it is set forth that God is the source of all things (3.1) and is ever at work (11.14), but is not the author of evil (14.7); even disorder is subject to the master, but he has not yet imposed order on it (5.4). Thus God manifests himself through all the universe (5.2), and it is for this very purpose that he has made all things, that through all things he may be seen (11.22).

So Hermes says to Tat (4.2, 11):

---

25. Walter Scott, *Hermetica: The Ancient Greek and Latin Writings . . . Ascribed to Hermes Trismegistus;* A. D. Nock and A. -J. Festugière, *Corpus Hermeticum;* Chambers, *Divine Pymander.*

It is man's function to contemplate the works of God; and for this purpose was he made, that he might view the universe with wondering awe, and come to know its Maker. . . . In these outlines, my son, I have drawn a likeness of God for you, so far as that is possible; and if you gaze upon this likeness with the eyes of your heart, then, my son, believe me, you will find the upward path; or rather, the sight itself will guide you on your way.

And to Asclepius, Hermes declares (6.4–5):

The very being of God, if "being" can be ascribed to God, is the Beautiful and the Good. . . . All things which the eye can see are mere phantoms, and unsubstantial outlines; but the things which the eye cannot see are the realities, and above all, the ideal form of the Beautiful and the Good. . . . If you are able to apprehend God, then you will apprehend the Beautiful and the Good. . . . If you seek knowledge of God, you are also seeking knowledge of the Beautiful. For there is one road alone that leads to the Beautiful, and that is devotion joined with knowledge [gnosis].

There are then two possibilities (11.21). On the one hand, if you shut up your soul in your body and debase it, and say that you are ignorant and unable and afraid, then you cannot understand anything beautiful and good. On the other hand,

To be capable of knowing God, and to wish and hope to know him, is the road which leads straight to the Good; and it is an easy road to travel. Everywhere God will come to meet you, everywhere he will appear to you, at places and times at which you look not for it, in your waking hours and in your sleep, when you are journeying by water and by land, in the nighttime and in the daytime, when you are speaking and when you are silent; for there is nothing which is not God.

In the book known as the *Asclepius* Hermes declares to Asclepius that God is so great that his being cannot be accurately described by any of the names applied to him (3.20). And with God to will is to accomplish, for when he wills the doing is completed in the same moment as the willing (1.8). As for human beings, in whom are commingled a less pure cosmic part and a divine part, if one understands the design of God one will despise material things and one's vices will be healed, but if folly and ignorance continue the vices will grow in strength and damage the soul (3.22). As to the outcome in the end, Hermes says to his "devoted ones" (1.11–12):

When our term of service is ended, when we are divested of our guardianship of the material world, and freed from the bonds of mortality,

[God] will restore us, cleansed and sanctified, to the primal condition of that higher part of us which is divine. . . . But those who have lived evil and impious lives are not permitted to return to heaven. For such is ordained a migration into other bodies [*in corpora . . . migratio*], bodies unworthy to be the abode of holy mind.

Having taught in this fashion, Hermes Trismegistos requires of his companions that they keep such profound matters to themselves (3.32): "And you, Tat, and Asclepius, and Ammon, I bid you keep these divine mysteries hidden in your hearts, and cover them with the veil of silence."

Finally (Epilogue 41), emerging from the holy place where these teachings have been communicated, the four turn their faces to the west, the place of the setting sun, to pray (as in the morning they will turn to the east, the place of the rising sun). Asclepius suggests the use of incense and unguents, but Hermes says that to offer incense and the rest would be like profanation of their sacred rites, for there is nothing of which God has need, since he is all things or all things are in him. The best incense in God's sight is when thanks are given to him (a passage substantially quoted by Lactantius, *Divine Institutes* 6.25). So they pray thus:

We are glad because thou hast revealed thyself to us in all thy being; we are glad because, while we are yet in the body, thou hast deigned to make us gods by the gift of thine own eternal life. . . .

We have learned to know thee, O thou eternal constancy of that which stands unmoved, yet makes the universe revolve.

With such words of praise do we adore thee, who alone art good; and let us crave from thy goodness no boon save this: be it thy will that we be kept still knowing and loving thee, and that we may never fall away from this blest way of life.

### Chaldaean Oracles

In the time of Antoninus Pius (A.D. 138–161) and Marcus Aurelius (161–180) Julian the Chaldaean (from his Mesopotamian homeland) and his son Julian the Theurgist (θεουργός, meaning "worker of divine things") taught in Rome. Their doctrines are set forth in the so-called *Chaldaean Oracles,* which are known in many fragments quoted by Proclus (A.D. 410–485) and others, chiefly of the Neoplatonic school, no doubt because of recognized affinities in thought.[26]

26. Hans Lewy, *Chaldaean Oracles and Theurgy: Mysticism, Magic, and Platonism in the Later Roman Empire.*

In the *Chaldaean Oracles* there is much about the sun, the planetary spheres, and the like, which probably reflects Persian, Babylonian, and Syrian backgrounds. There is agreement with Plato in such
items as Father (ηάτεϱ) for the name of the Supreme Being (e.g., Plato,
*Timaeus* 28c), the supreme place of intuitive knowledge (see Plato,
*Republic* 508d: "When [the soul] is firmly fixed on the domain where
truth and reality shine resplendent it apprehends and knows them"),
and the conception of the "leading up" (ἀναγωγή) of the soul through
the heavens (see *Republic* 515e, 517b, 521c, where Plato uses the same
and related terms for the soul's ascent to the contemplation of pure
being).

In connection with the "leading up" of the soul there were evidently
also rites of initiation in the Chaldaean mysteries. In his *Commentary
on Plato's Republic* Proclus states that his teacher Syrianos said that
the rites of sacrifice offered by Achilles at the funeral pyre of Patroclos
(in the *Iliad* 23.192–225) "imitate" (μιμεῖται) the "immortali-
zation of the soul" (ἀπαθανατισμὸς ψυχῆς) performed by the Chaldaean
theurgists.[27]

## Mithras

The cult of Mithras also came to the West from the East. Originally
an Indo-Iranian sun-god, the deity was known in India as Mitra, the
son of Aditi, the goddess of infinity. Mitra was outstanding for his
friendliness and seen as mounting a chariot in the highest heaven, the
sun being his eye (*Rigveda* 1.156.1; 5.63.1, 67.1; 10.37.1).[28] Another
of the sons of Aditi was Aryaman (*Rigveda* 2.27), the eponymous
ancestor of the Aryans. In Iran Mitra is Mithra and Aryaman becomes
Angra Mainyu or Ahriman, and in a long Zoroastrian hymn of praise
(*Mihir Yasht*, see p. 103)[29] Mithra drives across the sky in a chariot
of gold, while Angra Mainyu, "who is all death," flees away in fear.

In the Arsacid dynasty of Parthian kings in Iran several of the
rulers bear the name of Mithradates ("given by Mithra"), as do several
kings of Commagene and Pontus. At the colossal tomb of Antiochus I
of Commagene (69–34 B.C.) at Nimrud Dagh in Syria (now eastern
Turkey), the king and the syncretistic deities who are his patron-gods
are represented as enthroned colossi, Apollo-Mithras, the Fortune of
Commagene, Antiochus himself, Zeus-Oromasdes, and Herakles-As-

27. Ibid., 184–85 n. 32.
28. Jan Gonda, *The Vedic God Mitra.*
29. *Sacred Books of the East,* ed. F. Max Müller, 23.119–58.

tagnes, while in a relief panel Antiochus stands before Mithra, the latter's head adorned with his typical Phrygian cap and solar rays.[30]

In 67 B.C. Pompey came east and cleared the Mediterranean of pirates; in 66 he defeated Mithradates VI of Pontus (d. 63 B.C.), Rome's greatest enemy in Asia Minor, and also concluded a treaty with Antiochus I of Commagene. Plutarch (*Pompey* 24) says that Pompey found that the pirates offered strange sacrifices at Olympus (a town in Lycia in southern Asia Minor and one of the pirates' strongholds), "and celebrated there certain sacred rites, among which those of Mithras continued to the present time, having been first instituted by them." Plutarch (*Pompey* 28) adds that of Pompey's more than twenty thousand prisoners, some received citizenship in small cities of Cilicia, many were settled in the city of Soli (on the coast of Cilicia near Tarsus), and most were given a place to live at Dyme in Achaia.

In the region and time where and when Pompey found the pirates celebrating the sacred rites of Mithras, Mithras was certainly well known, for in his long reign (c. 121–63 B.C.) Mithradates VI of Pontus extended the sway of his kingdom over most of Asia Minor and had the pirates (to whom Plutarch refers) on his side in his wars against Rome. And according to his name ("given by Mithra") he himself was an adherent of Mithra(s).

As the Mithraic mysteries come into view in the Roman Empire, their iconography is of cosmic aspect (the bull-slaying scene); in particular Mithras was assimilated with Perseus, the legendary Greek hero. Son of Zeus and Danaë, Perseus was slayer of the Gorgon Medusa and rescuer and husband of Andromeda; their son was Perses, from whom the Persians took their name (Herodotus 7.61).[31]

In this respect it is significant that Perseus was accounted the founder of the city of Tarsus (Ammianus Marcellinus [c. A.D. 330–after 391] 14.8.3), was worshiped there as a god (Dio Chrysostom [c. A.D. 40–after 112], Discourse 33.45), and is frequently depicted on the coins of Tarsus. The representation of a lion attacking a bull was the emblem of Tarsus and also appears frequently on the coins of Tarsus.[32] The latter motif was probably derived from Achaemenid Persepolis, where a lion-bull combat appears at the side of the tribute processions in the sculp-

30. Theresa Goell, "Nimrud Dagh: The Tomb of Antiochus I, King of Commagene," *Archaeology* 5 (1952): 136–44; İlhan Akşit, *Ancient Civilisations of Anatolia and Historical Treasures of Turkey*, 209–10, 212–14.

31. For the relation of the Persian Mithras and the Greek Perseus, see Georg Friedrich Creuzer, *Symbolik und Mythologie der alten Völker, besonders der Griechen*, 4.67–68; and idem, *Das Mithreum von Neuenheim bei Heidelberg*, 21; see also Marc-Mathieu Münch, *La "Symbolique" de Friedrich Creuzer*, 83–84.

32. William M. Ramsay, *The Cities of St. Paul: Their Influence on His Life and Thought*, 129, 150–53; figs. 4, 14–16.

tures of the Apadana stairway. Since lion (Leo) and bull (Taurus) are
figures of the zodiac, and since the tribute processions were for the
annual New Year festival at Persepolis, in the Iranian calendar at the
spring equinox, the scene must be of astronomical significance.[33] Even
farther back, there is probably also Babylonian background, for on a
small group of early Babylonian cylinders there is a representation of
Gilgamesh slaying a bull, and that in nearly the same attitude as
Mithras/Perseus in Mithraic iconography.[34]

Furthermore, Tarsus was an intellectual center (Strabo 14.5.13) and
in particular a center of Stoic philosophy, for example, Chrysippus
[third century B.C.], considered the second founder of the movement,
was born at nearby Soli; and the Stoic Athenodorus (74 B.C.–A.D. 7),
the teacher of Augustus in Rome, lived in Tarsus in earlier and later
life and was also governor of Tarsus. The stoics were notably active in
cosmological speculations. In all, then, it is entirely likely that southern Asia Minor (especially Lycia, Cilicia, Soli, and Tarsus) was the
region in which in the first century B.C. (the area and time indicated
by Plutarch) these several currents came together in the emergence
of the "mysteries" of Mithras. (Mithras coming from Persia was assimilated with Perseus ancestor of the Persians through Perses; Mith-
ras/Perseus replaces the lion [Leo] in the slaying of the bull [Taurus];
the import of the central iconography is astronomical and cosmic.)

In A.D. 66 Tiridates, king of Armenia, came on a state visit to Rome
and addressed Nero with the words, "I have come to you, my god, to
worship you as I worship Mithras" (Dio 62.5.2). According to Pliny
(A.D. 23–79; *Natural History* 30.6.17) he brought Magi with him and
"initiated Nero into their banquets." We have already seen that the
Magi appear to have become Zoroastrian priests (p. 101), and that
Mithra(s) came to have an important place in Zoroastrianism, thus
with the present reference to initiation some early form of the Mithraic mysteries may have been involved.

At any rate, with the poet Statius (c. A.D. 80), who spent most of his
life in Rome, there is an unmistakable reference, apparently based on
his own personal observation, to the characteristic meeting place (a
subterranean chapel) and central iconography (the bull-slaying scene)
of the mysteries of Mithras as known later in surviving monuments.
In *Thebaid* (1.719–20) Statius writes of "Mithras as beneath the rocks
of the Persian cave he presses back the horns that resist his control."

33. Ernst E. Herzfeld, *Iran in the Ancient East,* 251 and plates xlvii, lxii; Erich F. Schmidt,
*Persepolis,* vol. 1, *Structures, Reliefs, Inscriptions,* 83 and plates 19, 20, 53; Donald N. Wilber, *Persepolis: The Archaeology of Parsa, Seat of the Persian Kings* 25, 87.

34. A. L. Frothingham, "The Cosmopolitan Religion of Tarsus and the Origin of Mithra," *AJA*
22 (1918): 63–64.

In scholia usually attributed to Lactantius Placidus (a grammarian of the fifth century A.D.) it is explained in comment on this portion of the *Thebaid* (1.717ff.) that the Persians worship the sun, called Mithras or Apollo, and that their rites passed from the Persians to the Phrygians and from the Phrygians to the Romans. There follows this elucidation of the words of Statius:

> The expression "resist his control" has reference to the figure of Mithras holding back the horns of a recalcitrant bull, whereby is indicated the sun's illumination of the moon, when the latter receives its rays. . . .
> In these verses the mysteries of the rites of the sun are set forth. For in proof that the moon is inferior and of less power the sun is seated on the bull and grasps its horns. By which words Statius intended the two-horned moon to be understood, not the animal on which he rides.[35]

Extant monuments of the Mithraic mysteries—underground chapels, sculptured scenes, and inscriptions—are found from the borders of the Roman Empire in the east to the British Isles in the west, and are especially numerous on the northern frontier from the Black Sea to the North Sea.[36] None is earlier than the end of the first century A.D. and most belong to the second century and later.[37]

Especially on the frontiers the inscriptions are often connected with military personnel, for example, the dedication at Böckingen on the Neckar River of two altars, one to Mithras and one to Apollo (dated A.D. 148), by a centurion of the Roman Legion VIII Augusta. Thus the cult was evidently favored and spread by the Roman army, although, as many other inscriptions show, it certainly had many civilian adherents as well.[38] Plutarch (*On Isis and Osiris* 369d–e) attributes to Zoroaster the Magian the teaching that Oromasdes (Ahura Mazda) and Areimanios (Ahriman) are opposed to each other as light to darkness, and that Mithras is between the two and called the mediator. If, as this suggests, the Iranian dualism was preserved in the Mithraism of the Roman Empire, this conception of the conflict of light and darkness, of good and evil, could have been among the factors making the cult attractive in military circles.

The typical chapel of the Mithraic mysteries was subterranean (a

35. A. S. Geden, *Select Passages Illustrating Mithraism,* 37.

36. Maarten J. Vermaseren, *Corpus Inscriptionum et Monumentorum Religionis Mithriacae.*

37. Maarten J. Vermaseren, *Mithras: The Secret God,* 29–30; R. L. Gordon, "Mithraism and Roman Society," *Religion* 2 (1972): 92–121, esp. 93 and n. 10; Edwin M. Yamauchi, "The Apocalypse of Adam, Mithraism, and Pre-Christian Gnosticism," in *Études Mithriaques,* 537–63, esp. 550–57.

38. C. M. Daniels, "The Role of the Roman Army in the Spread and Practice of Mithraism," in *Mithraic Studies: Proceedings of the First International Congress of Mithraic Studies,* ed. John R. Hinnells, 2.249–74.

*spelaeum* or *crypta,* i.e., a cavern or crypt; called by Tertullian [*De Corona* 15] a *castra tenebrarum,* a "military camp of darkness"), and of small size, perhaps accommodating only fifty or sixty persons to judge from known examples. Porphyry (*De Antro Nympharum* 5–6) remarks that Zoroaster himself consecrated a natural cave in honor of Mithra in imitation of the world-cave that Mithra fashioned, and so the custom continued of celebrating rites in either natural or artificial caves. Of the cave of Mithra (and of other gods) Porphyry also says (20–21) that it was an image and symbol of the cosmos.

In the subterranean Mithraic chapel the main iconographical feature is usually a representation—for example, in Rome the sculptured relief on the front of the altar in the Mithraeum under the Church of San Clemente; and the stucco group, destroyed and scattered by the Christians but restored, in the main niche in the Mithraeum under and behind Santa Prisca—in which Mithras, in tunic or cloak and Phrygian cap, bestride a bull, seizes it by the nose, and plunges a dagger into its shoulder. As to the interpretation of this central scene, a painted inscription in the Mithraeum at Santa Prisca plainly refers to Mithras: "And you saved us after having shed the eternal blood."[39] On this basis the *tauroctony* (bull-slaying) has been explained as a divine sacrifice, in which the blood of the bull gives life (and to that extent it may be connected with the *taurobolium,* a term described on p. 195 chiefly in respect to the cult of Cybele but also occasionally attested in the cult of Mithras).[40]

The comment of the scholiast on the *Thebaid* of Statius (see p. 206), although relatively late and probably of limited validity, points rather to an astronomical interpretation. In fact the ceiling of a Mithraic chapel is often adorned with stars (e.g., Dura Europos, San Clemente in Rome), while the *tauroctony* itself is usually overarched by the signs of the zodiac (beginning with Aries the Ram, Taurus the Bull, and so on), or sometimes by representations of the seven planets (e.g., a marble relief in the Museo Civico, Bologna, from left to right: Sun, Saturn, Venus, Jupiter, Mercury, Mars, Moon).[41]

Furthermore, in addition to Mithras and the bull, the other figures identifiable in the *tauroctony* are a series of stars and constellations, including scorpion (Scorpio), snake (Hydra), raven (Cervus), cup (Krater), lion (Leo Major), and dog (Canis Minor). The bull is identifiable

39. Maarten J. Vermaseren and C. C. van Essen, *The Excavations in the Mithraeum of the Church of Santa Prisca in Rome,* 217–18.

40. John R. Hinnells, "Reflections on the Bull-Slaying Scene," in *Mithraic Studies,* ed. Hinnells, 2.290–312.

41. *Mithraic Studies,* ed. Hinnells, plate 2, 33c; see plate 21 for a similar motif from the Dura Mithraeum.

with the constellation Taurus, and Mithras with the constellation Perseus (Rescuer, or Champion), who in Greek mythology slew the serpent-entwined Gorgon Medusa, meanwhile looking away—exactly as Mithras usually looks away from the bull—and who as a constellation is just above Taurus in the northern sky. A tall serpent-entwined human figure in the composition can therefore reflect the very Gorgon Medusa of the Perseus myth. Also on either side of the central figures are often two torchbearers, named Cautes and Cautopates, the former holding his torch upward, the latter downward; these may be the spring and fall equinoxes, respectively.[42] An additional detail is the fact that the tail of the bull is usually portrayed as ending in ears of grain, and in view of the equation of Taurus with the spring equinox, these may be understood as standing for the agricultural fertility of the springtime.

In approximately 125 B.C. Hipparchus, the great Bithynian astronomer, discovered the precession of the equinoxes (the gradual change in the points at which the sun crosses the celestial equator, marking the equinoxes). From approximately 4000 to 2000 B.C. the spring equinox was in Taurus, then moved into Aries for the next two thousand years, and into Pisces, the Fishes, in the present era (with Aquarius, the Water Carrier, to come next). So the central scene can show how Mithras/Perseus brought to an end the age of Taurus, the age immediately preceding the Greco-Roman period, and introduced the age of Aries in which the Mithraic mysteries arose.[43] Thus the mysteries of Mithras were set in a cosmic framework of vast proportions and (as will be further evident in the grades of initiation) had to do with nothing less than salvation in the celestial spheres.

As in other Greek and Roman religious associations there were cult meals in Mithraism,[44] and as in other mysteries there were initiations. Of the latter, Justin (c. A.D. 100–165; *First Apology* 66) relates that "bread and a cup of water are set out with certain incantations in the mystic rites of one who is being initiated." Jerome (Epistle 107.2) tells

42. For other explanations of the torchbearers as the morning and evening sun, and of the tall figure as eternal Time (Kronos), see Martin Schwartz, "Cautes and Cautopates: The Mithraic Torchbearers," in *Mithraic Studies,* ed. Hinnells, 2.406–23; and M. J. Vermaseren, "A Magical Time God," in *Mithraic Studies,* ed. Hinnells, 2.446–56.

43. For the astronomical theory, see David Ulansey, "Mithras and Perseus: Mithraic Astronomy and the Anatolian Perseus-Cult"; idem, "Mithras and Perseus," *Helios* 13.1 (Spring 1986): 32–62; and idem, "Mithraic Studies: A Paradigm Shift?" *RSR* 13.2 (April 1987): pp. 104–10. For the earlier theory, which looked more to Iranian than to Greco-Roman backgrounds, see Franz Cumont, *The Mysteries of Mithra*; Maarten J. Vermaseren, "Mithras in der Römerzeit," in *Die orientalischen Religionen im Römerreich,* ed. Vermaseren, 96–120.

44. J. P. Kane, "The Mithraic Cult Meal in Its Greek and Roman Environment," in *Mithraic Studies,* ed. Hinnells, 2.313–51.

of the destruction of a cavern of Mithras by a city official of Rome, and of the "dreadful images" used in the initiation of votaries; the latter are listed in what are apparently seven successive grades: *corax* (raven), *nymphus* (bridegroom), *miles* (soldier), *leo* (lion), *Perses, heliodromus,* and *pater.* The last three are the highest grades: *Perses* is the Persian (originally the name of the son of Perseus and Andromeda, the eponymous ancestor of the Persians), *heliodromus* is the courier of the sun, and *pater,* the father of the community, must represent Mithras himself. The seven grades were also equated with the planets in the sequence Raven/Mercury, Bridegroom/Venus, Soldier/Mars, Lion/Jupiter, Persian/Moon, Courier of the Sun/Sun, and Father/Saturn (the most remote planet known to the ancients). Thus advancement through the grades of the cult symbolized the ascent of the soul after death through the planetary spheres and presumably on to an ultimate destination in the realm of the fixed stars.[45]

Tertullian describes the initiation of a soldier of Mithras in the "camp of darkness" as involving washing with water (*De Baptismo* 5) and ceremonies in which a crown is offered on a naked sword (as if in mimicry of martyrdom), placed on the head, then voluntarily transferred to the shoulder with the declaration by the initiate that Mithras is his crown (*De Corona* 15). Mithras "sets his marks on the foreheads of his soldiers, celebrates an offering of bread, introduces an image of a resurrection [*imago resurrectionis*], and with the sword opens the way to the crown" (*De praescriptione haereticorum* 40), perhaps suggesting that in the initiation there was a simulation of death and experience of life beyond. This interpretation is supported by Porphyry, who says that the Persians initiate the novice into the mysteries by an allegorical descent of the souls to the lower world (for which they use the name *cave; De Antro Nympharum* 5–6) and a return, and that "in all the highest grades the doctrine of metempsychosis is held, which also is apparently signified in the mysteries of Mithra" (*De Abstinentia* 4.16).

## Sol Invictus

It has already been seen that Mitra/Mithra/Mithras has many associations with the sun (Latin, *sol*), and there are iconographical examples in the Mithraeum at Dura Europos where Mithras and Sol are side by side and are identified, respectively, by Phrygian cap and ra-

---

45. Gordon, "Mithraism and Roman Society," 97; and idem, "Reality, Evocation and Boundary in the Mysteries of Mithras," *JMS* 3.1–2 (1980): 21–99.

diate head.[46] In paintings in the Mithraeum at Santa Prisca in Rome, at the head of a procession of the seven grades of the Mithraic community, the Heliodromus (courier of the sun) wears a red robe and a golden radiate crown to represent Sol, and walks toward the Pater (father of the community), who is seated on a throne and identified by a red Phrygian cap as representing Mithras.[47] It was also the case that Mithras was himself often identified with the sun.

As the orb that disappears each evening into the darkness but reappears each morning in brightness, the sun is the eternal victor; and the supreme Being incarnate in the daily presence of the solar sphere is therefore Sol Invictus, the unconquered and unconquerable sun. Thus in the identification of Mithras with the sun, and in the titles used in dedications to Mithras in many inscriptions at Rome and on coins, Mithras is himself called the divine and invincible sun (in full *Deo Soli Invicto Mithrae*).[48]

The emperor Julian (A.D. 361–363), from the viewpoint of the Christians called the "apostate," was a worshiper of the sun as Mithras and Sol Invictus. In a treatise *On the Sovereign Sun* Julian relates that when, even as a boy, he looked upon the solar brightness his soul felt as if it were seized and carried up out of itself, and in his mature belief he points to the transcendent reality that is beyond the visible orb: "I feel how difficult it is for the human mind even to form a conception of that Sun who is not visible to the sense, if our notion of him is to be derived from the Sun that is visible; but to express the same in language, however inadequately, is, perhaps, beyond the capability of man!" And he begs Hermes, "presiding over all knowledge," to assist him in the attempt to speak on this theme (131d–32b).[49]

In *The Caesars* (336c) Julian notes that in his role as the sun Mithras is a savior and a guide for souls in the afterlife:

> "And to you," Hermes said to me [Julian], "I have granted the discovery of father [*pater*] Mithras. Keep his commands, thus preparing a steadfast haven and anchorage for yourself in life, and with good hope establishing that god as your guide when it is necessary to depart from this world."

Again, calling Mithras "the seven-rayed god" (ἑπτάχτινα θεόν, i.e., of solar nature), Julian refers to the Mithraic mysteries and says (*Oration* 172d):

    46. *Mithraic Studies*, ed. Hinnells, 2, plates 26a, 29a.

    47. Vermaseren and van Essen, *Excavations in the Mithraeum*, 155–56.

    48. D. W. MacDowall, "Sol Invictus and Mithra: Some Evidence from the Mint of Rome," in *Mysteria Mithrae*, ed. Ugo Bianchi, 557–71.

    49. Charles William King, *Julian the Emperor*, 219–21. For the view of Christianity by Julian and other Romans, see Robert L. Wilkin, *The Christians as the Romans Saw Them*.

And if I should touch on the ineffable mysteries which the Chaldean celebrated with Bacchic frenzy concerning the seven-rayed god, leading souls upward through that deity, I would be telling things that are not to be known, indeed things that are most not-to-be-known for the rabble, but which are [already] well-known to the blessed performers of divine works. Therefore I will keep silence about these things for now.[50]

Celsus, quoted by Origen (*Against Celsus* 6.22), says that in the mysteries of Mithras the ascent of the soul through the celestial spheres of the fixed stars and the seven planets is represented as on a ladder with lofty gates and, on top, an eighth gate. The first seven gates are characterized by the metals of which they are made and are named for the gods of the planets: lead/Saturn, tin/Venus, copper/Jupiter, iron/Mercury, a mixture of metals/Mars, silver/Moon, and gold/Sun. Salvation with Mithras eventuates in ultimate passage through the solar gate into the boundless beyond.

While the identification of Mithras and Sol Invictus was probably held by most of the Roman worshipers of Mithras, Sol Invictus was also otherwise an independent deity.[51] In particular at Emesa in Syria, Sol Invictus was worshiped with the additional name *Elagabalus* (the name *el-Gabal*, "the god Gabal," is probably related to the Arabic word for mountain, *gebal*). The future Roman emperor Elagabalus (A.D. 218–222) was born at Emesa in 204, where the family of his mother Julia Soaemias were hereditary high priests of the sun-god from whom he took his own name. When Elagabalus went to Rome to assume the throne he took with him from Emesa a black conical meteorite with mysterious signs that symbolized the sun, and in Rome he undertook to place Sol Invictus Elagabalus above even Jupiter himself (Dio 80.11.1). Upon the murder and condemnation of the profligate emperor, the god was banished from Rome (Dio 80.21.2) and the god's symbol sent back to Emesa. But the worship of the sun-god continued widely throughout the empire, and under Aurelian (A.D. 270–275) the cult was restored to its former high estate. In the year 274 Aurelian declared the god—now called Deus Sol Invictus—the official deity of the Roman Empire; he built a splendid temple of the sun in Rome (Zosimus [c. A.D. 450], *Historia Nova* 1.61), and set the sun's birthday celebration (*natalis solis invicti*) on December 25, the date then accepted for the winter solstice (also in his solar character the birthday of Mithras). In the time of Constantine the cult of Deus Sol Invictus was still at its height, and the portrait of the sun-god was on the coins

---

50. Bruce Lincoln, "Mithra(s) as Sun and Savior," in *La soteriologia dei culti orientali nell'Impero Romano*, ed. Ugo Bianchi and Maarten J. Vermaseren, 505–23.

51. Gaston H. Halsberghe, *The Cult of Sol Invictus.*

of Constantine. With his defeat of Licinius in A.D. 323 he became the uncontested ruler of the empire (323–337) and was free to openly accept Christianity, from which time onward his numismatic representations and inscriptions were only such as to be inoffensive to non-Christians and Christians alike. As Arnobius (c. A.D. 290; *Adversus Nationes* 1.29) and his disciple Lactantius (c. 240–320; *De Origine Erroris* 5), the latter the tutor of Constantine's son Crispus, had been saying should be done, henceforward Constantine would worship not the sun but the one who had created the sun. Likewise it must have been in this time and with the intent to transform the significance of an existing sacred date that the birthday of Jesus, which had been celebrated in the East on January 6 (Epiphanius [c. 315–403], *Panarion* 51.22.4),[52] was placed in Rome on December 25, the date of the birthday celebration of Sol Invictus. This date appears in a list of dates probably compiled in A.D. 336 and published in the Roman city calendar, edited by Filocalus, for the year 354 (*VIII kal. Ian. natus Christus in Betleem Iudeae*).[53]

### Emperor Worship

It is also in the East that there are antecedents for the rise of emperor worship in the Roman world.[54] In Mesopotamia the concept of the divine character of the king is found to a limited extent (e.g., the stele of Naram-Sin of Akkad [2291–2255 B.C.] with the king's helmet with horns, the insignia of divinity).[55] In Egypt the idea appears regularly (where the king was the embodiment of Horus and the son of Re). In the Hellenistic world the idea is of wide application; for example, in Athens when Demetrius I Poliorcetes liberated the city from Cassander (307 B.C.) he was said to be "the only true god [θεός], while all the others were asleep or making a journey or nonexistent" (Athenaeus [c. A.D. 200] 6.253); in Egypt Ptolemy II (285–246 B.C.) and his sister-wife Arsinoe II were brother-sister gods (θεοί ἀδελφοί); and in Syria, Antiochus IV (175–164 B.C.) was known as "Epiphanes," that is "the Manifest [god]."

In Rome worship of the ruler began only in the restricted sense that the ruler was regarded as divine after his death, or that worship was centered not directly on the ruler himself but on his Genius or was coupled with reverence for the city, considered as the goddess Roma. In the provinces, and later in Rome too, there was less reticence in the

---

52. Jürgen Dummer, *Panarion haer. 34–64*, 284.
53. Theodor Mommsen, *Chronica minora,* 1.71.
54. *Römischer Kaiserkult,* ed. Antonie Wlosok.
55. *ANEP,* fig. 309.

matter. Appian, writing in the first half of the second century A.D., formulates the prevailing principle: "The Romans now pay honors to each emperor at his death if he has not reigned in a tyrannical manner or made himself odious" (*Civil Wars* 2.148).

Terms that were in the course of time applied to the ruler included *augustus* (Greek, σεβαστός), "august," a word originally belonging to the language of religion, hence "worthy of reverence"; *divus,* as an adjective (Greek, θεῖος), "divine," as a substantive (Greek, θεός), "deity, god, goddess"; *divi filius* (Greek, θεοῦ υἱός), "son of god," used especially when the ruler's predecessor had been posthumously deified; *dominus* (Greek, κύριος, δεσπότης), "master, lord," not necessarily implying divinity, but easily coming to have that connotation; *soter* (Greek, σωτήρ), "savior, deliverer," not necessarily a divine title but gradually gaining a divine sense.

Julius Caesar was assassinated in March 44 B.C.; when an unpredicted comet appeared afterward in July this was believed to be his soul taken to heaven (Suetonius, *Julius* 88). On 1 January 42, by vote of the senate and people, he was declared a god (*Divus Julius*).[56] Octavian, Caesar's adopted son, was therefore the son of a deity (*Divi Juli filius*) and, in 29 B.C. he erected a temple for his deified adoptive father (Dio 51.22.2–4), while he himself was given the title of Augustus by the senate in 27 B.C. On one occasion he was a spectator at a play in which the words "O just and gracious lord" were uttered, and then taken by the audience as applying to himself, but he reproved what he regarded as unseemly flattery (Suetonius, *Augustus* 53.1). In the years 12 to 7 B.C. Augustus reorganized Rome into fourteen regions and 265 districts (*vici*)—each district having a shrine dedicated to two deities of the crossroads (*Lares viales*) and to the Genius of Augustus (Ovid, *Fasti* 5.145). At Athens a temple was dedicated to the Genius of Augustus (Suetonius, *Augustus* 60); at Ancyra (modern Ankara) in Galatia there was a temple of Rome and Augustus, and it still preserves a copy of the long obituary inscription that Augustus composed for himself, beginning, "The achievements of the divine Augustus" (*Res Gestae divi Augusti*).[57]

Tiberius (A.D. 14–37) also resisted direct worship of himself. Once being called "lord" (*dominus*) he warned the speaker not to address him again in such a fashion (Suetonius, *Tiberius* 27). On another occasion he declared plainly that he was a mortal man (Tacitus, *Annals* 4.38.1). In Caesarea in Palestine, however, an inscription of Pontius Pilate, whom he appointed governor, mentions a Tiberieum or temple

56. Stefan Weinstock, *Divus Julius.*
57. P. A. Brunt and J. M. Moore, *Res Gestae Divi Augusti.*

of Tiberius. Gaius Caligula (37–41) was the first emperor to require recognition of his divinity while alive: he punished persons severely for never having sworn by his Genius (Suetonius, *Caligula* 27.3) and, after at first forbidding anyone to set up images of himself, later ordered temples to be erected and sacrifices to be offered to himself as to a god (Dio 59.4.4). Under Claudius (41–54) the title *lord* was evidently increasingly in use, for it occurs in the record of a lawsuit in the Oxyrhynchus Papyri (1.37.6) where a date is given in the seventh year of Tiberius Claudius Caesar the Lord (κύριος). Nero (54–68), the last emperor of the Julian line descended from Aeneas (Dio 62.18.4), was the second of the rulers to actively encourage divine honors for himself. When in 66 Tiridates king of Armenia came with a large entourage to Rome he addressed Nero as "master" (δέσποτα) and said, "I have come to you, my god [θεός], to worship you as I worship Mithras"; thereupon Nero confirmed his rule over Armenia (Dio 62.5.2). In 67 Nero's special military corps, the Augustans, undertook to make a statue of Nero weighing a thousand pounds—presumably for cult worship (Dio 63.18.3). Finally it was said that so many honors were accepted by Nero that almost the whole world under his rule was filled with his images of silver and gold (Dio 67.8.1). Vespasian (69–79), founder of the Flavian house, returning to Rome from the Jewish War, was hailed as "savior" (Josephus, *War* 7.71). Domitian (81–96), the last of the Flavians, climaxed the development by insisting upon being regarded as a god and by taking pride in being called "master" (δεσπότης) and "god" (θεός), which titles were used not merely in speech but also in written documents (Dio 67.5.7).

The factors that contributed to the development and long continuance of such worship of the emperors must have included gratitude for benefits received, a sense of the numinous in the exercise of imperial power, and a realization that the cult was an important element in the scheme of provincial government and a bond of union among the different populations of the empire. It was doubtless the political value of the cult that led to obligatory participation for all people of the empire. In its religious aspect compulsory participation in the cult collided with the exclusive monotheism of the Jews (Deut. 5:7–9; 6:4), and with the position of the Christians who, while they willingly prayed *for* the emperor (1 Tim. 2:2; Polycarp [c. A.D. 69–155], *To the Philippians* 12.2), were not willing to pray *to* the emperor. Judaism, however, was treated as a privileged religion (*religio licita*) and the Jews were exempt from the compulsion,[58] but the Christians became the object of many persecutions.[59]

---

58. Emil Schürer, *A History of the Jewish People in the Time of Jesus Christ*, 2.2.259–60.

59. Ethelbert Stauffer, *Christ and the Caesars*.

Only with the edict of universal toleration by Constantine and Licinius in A.D. 313 was there full permission for the Christians as well as for all others to follow whatever religion any person should choose (Lactantius, *De Mortibus Persecutorum* 48). Finally, however, the other extreme was reached and there was no longer official approval for anything except Christianity. In A.D. 392 a decree of the emperor Theodosius I (379–395) prohibited "pagan" worship as a crime of the same character as treason (Codex Theodosianus 16.10.12).[60] In the course of time "paganism" disappeared as a religious system and the once living faiths of the Roman Empire became religions of the past, leaving, however, their numerous records and monuments.

60. Joseph Cullen Ayer, *A Source Book for Ancient Church History*, 263–64, 346–47.

# 7

# Gnostic Religion

The Greek noun γνῶσις is derived from the verb "to know" (γιγνώσκω) and means "knowledge." The knowledge so named may be of purely secular events or facts, but in the New Testament the word is used particularly for knowledge in the realm of spiritual matters, for example, knowledge as an attribute of God (Rom. 11:33), knowledge about God (1 Cor. 15:34), knowledge of the truth (1 Tim. 2:4), and the like. In one passage, however, there is a warning against the "contradictions of what is falsely called knowledge," literally the "antitheses of pseudonymous gnosis" (1 Tim. 6:20), and here the reference seems to be to a whole system of so-called knowledge that, from the point of view of the writer, is to be avoided. The same words are used by Irenaeus in the title of his main work, *Refutation and Overthrow of the Falsely So-Called Gnosis* (commonly cited by the abbreviated Latin title, *Adversus Haereses,* "Against Heresies"), in which he deals with several such systems.

The modern word, in use from the eighteenth century onward, for *gnosis* as a whole system of "knowledge" is "Gnosticism," and was applied in the first instance to the Christian Gnostic systems of the second and third centuries, in which the "knowledge" was esoteric and aimed at salvation; thus the term has continued to be used for all systems marked by these characteristics. More specifically Gnosticism is definitively characterizable as "anti-cosmic dualism."[1]

## Sources

Most of the information that was previously available concerning Gnosticism came from its opponents, especially the Christian writers

1. Hans Jonas, *The Gnostic Religion,* 33; Kurt Rudolph, *Gnosis: The Nature and History of Gnosticism,* 60

Façade of the Coptic Museum in Old Cairo, repository of the Coptic
Gnostic papyri from Nag Hammadi

Irenaeus (A.D. 130–200), Hippolytus of Rome (170–235), Tertullian
(155–220), Clement of Alexandria (150–215), Origen (185–254), Eusebius of Caesarea (260–340), Epiphanius of Salamis (315–403), and
Augustine (for Manichaeism) and the Neoplatonist Plotinus (*Ennead*
2.9 is entitled "Against the Gnostics; or Against Those That Affirm
the Creator of the Cosmos and the Cosmos Itself to Be Evil"). For the
most part these writers describe the systems with which they are concerned in their own words; in some cases they quote actual excerpts
from Gnostic texts.[2]

Original sources of more or less pronounced Gnostic character already known for some time include the so-called *Corpus Hermeticum*
(Greek texts of the second and third centuries A.D.); Codex Askewianus
with the work known as Pistis Sophia (third century); Codex Brucianus with the two Books of Jeu (third century?); Papyrus Berolinensis
8502 (fifth century) with the Gospel of Mary, the Apocryphon of John,
and the Sophia of Jesus Christ; the Odes of Solomon, preserved in
Coptic and Syriac versions (second century); the Hymn of the Pearl,
contained in the apocryphal Acts of Thomas (second/third century);
some other scattered materials in other apocryphal Acts of Apostles;
and the Mandaean and Manichaean literature (to be described in chaps.
8–9).[3]

2. Robert M. Grant, *Gnosticism: A Source Book of Heretical Writings from the Early Christian
Period*; Werner Foerster, *Gnosis: A Selection of Gnostic Texts*, vol. 1, *Patristic Evidence*.

3. Rudolph, *Gnosis*, 25–30.

The major modern discovery is that of the so-called Nag Hammadi Coptic Gnostic Papyri.[4] The find was made in 1945 by a certain Muhammad Ali Rudolf es-Samman, and the documents became known to the world only gradually over the next several years (at about the same time as the Dead Sea Scrolls, which were found at Qumran in 1947). They were found at the foot of a cliff called Jebel et-Tarif on the right bank of the Nile River, across from the village of Nag Hammadi, from which the texts take their commonly used name. The find was of a pottery jar containing papyrus codices in leather bindings. From paleography and also from some dates preserved in fragments of documents in the bindings,[5] the manuscripts are datable to about the middle of the fourth century A.D. While the texts are in Coptic it is evident that many of them are translations of Greek originals that date back to somewhere in the second and third centuries A.D. Fragments of what are now recognizable as such originals are, for example, Oxyrhynchus Papyri 1, 654, and 655, which contain portions of what is now found more fully in the Coptic Gospel According to Thomas.

## Date

Given the date of the available written sources concerning the Gnostic religion (second century A.D. and later), and the fact that there are many Christian elements, it seems probable that the Gnostic movement originated at about the same time as Christianity. There are, however, some texts that have been thought to be devoid of Christian elements, some texts now with Christian traits but perhaps revealing earlier non-Christian forms,[6] and some that have many Jewish elements (although they are usually strongly anti-Jewish). These are grounds for the theory of the existence of a pre-Christian Gnosticism, presumably originating in a syncretistic Hellenistic environment or on the fringes of Judaism.[7] On the basis of this theory, words of apparently Gnostic type found in the Pauline letters such as fullness

4. *The Facsimile Edition of the Nag Hammadi Codices*; The Coptic Gnostic Library; *The Nag Hammadi Library in English*; Foerster, *Gnosis: A Selection of Gnostic Texts*, vol. 2, *Coptic and Mandean Sources*; Nag Hammadi Studies; Rudolph, *Gnosis*, 44–48; Edwin M. Yamauchi, "The Nag Hammadi Library," *Journal of Library History* 22.4 (1987): 425–41; D. Scholer, *Nag Hammadi Bibliography 1945–1969* (NHS1); idem, "Bibliographia Gnostica Supplementum," *NT* 13– (1971–); Folker Siegert, *Nag-Hammadi-Register*.
    5. J. W. B. Barns, G. M. Browne, and J. C. Shelton, *Nag Hammadi Codices: Greek and Coptic Papyri from the Cartonnage of the Covers* (NHS 16).
    6. Takasi Onuki, "Wiederkehr des weiblichen Erlösers Barbelo-Pronoia; Zur Verhältnisbestimmung der Kurz- und Langversionen des Apokryphon des Johannes," *Annual of the Japanese Biblical Institute* 13 (1987): 85–143.
    7. Rudolph, *Gnosis*, 52, 276ff.

(πλήρωμα, Col. 1:19), principalities (ἀρχαί, Rom. 8:38), depth (βάθος, Rom. 8:39), ruler (ἄρχων, 1 Cor. 2:6, 8), and the like, and ideas of possible Gnostic affinity found in the Gospel According to John, are thought to have been borrowed from already existing Gnosticism. On the other hand, however, the words of Paul and the ideas in John may have been taken from the Pauline letters and from the fourth Gospel by the Gnostics themselves and incorporated in their texts with their own more explicitly Gnostic meanings.[8] Thus as a developed system Gnosticism was probably not pre-Christian, although some forms may have been non-Christian.[9]

## Church Fathers' Reports

One of the varieties of religious experience in early Christianity was a line of development, traceable in the second century and later, which was marked by: (1) the recognition of the authority of a succession of bishops in churches founded by the apostles; (2) the determination of the writings to be regarded as apostolic and thus forming a canon of the New Testament; and (3) the formulation of brief confessions of faith such as the so-called Apostles' Creed. This led to the conception of "orthodoxy" (from Greek ὀρθός, "straight, right, true," and δοκέω, "think, believe") as over against "heresy" (Greek αἵρεσις, "sect, party, school," from αἱρέω, "take, choose for oneself").[10] It is from within the line leading to "orthodoxy" that the Christian authors, dignified in Catholic theology as "Church Fathers," write as they oppose the "heresy" (or "heresies") of Gnosticism.

Eusebius, bishop of Caesarea (c. 325), quotes Hegesippus (c. 180) to the effect that the church was not yet "corrupted by vain discourses" until after the martyrdom of James the Just (61/62), when Symeon the cousin of Jesus was chosen bishop of Jerusalem, and a certain Thebouthis, who was not chosen, began the corruption "by the seven heresies, to which he belonged." Of the heresies that are then named the first is that of Simon, from whom came the Simonians, and the names of many others follow (*Church History* 4.22.4–6). Of these and others we will discuss the following: Simonians, Menandrianists, Basilidians, Carpocratians, Saturnilians, Marcionists, Valentinians,

---

8. R. M. Wilson, *The Gnostic Problem: A Study of the Relations Between Hellenistic Judaism and the Gnostic Heresy,* 77, 81; and idem, *Gnosis and the New Testament,* 144.

9. Edwin M. Yamauchi, *Pre-Christian Gnosticism: A Survey of the Proposed Evidences,* 170–86, 246–49; and idem, "Pre-Christian Gnosticism, the New Testament and Nag Hammadi in Recent Debate," *Themelios* 10.1 (1984): 22–27.

10. Joseph Cullen Ayer, *A Source Book for Ancient Church History,* 109–26.

Ptolemaeus, Marcosians, Barbelo-Gnostics, Sethians, Ophites, and Naassenes.

### Simonians

In Acts 8:9–24 Simon is said to have practiced magic (μαγεύω; compare μάγος, a Magus, originally a member of the Median tribe of the Magi, who interpreted celestial phenomena, used wizards' spells, etc.— Herodotus 1.101; 7.37, 191) in Samaria, where he said that he himself was somebody great and the people said that he was "that power of God which is called Great." Justin Martyr (c. 100–165; *Apology* 1.26) places Simon in Rome in the time of Claudius (A.D. 41–54), where he was associated with a former prostitute, named Helena, of whom it was said that she was "the first thought [ἔννοια] generated by him." Irenaeus (*Adversus Haereses* 1.23.1–4) goes on to say that Simon claimed to have appeared among the Jews as the Son, to have descended in Samaria as the Father, and to have come to other nations in the character of the Holy Spirit. Helena descended to the lower regions of space and generated angels and powers by whom the world was formed, and then she became a captive of the lower powers (the lost sheep, Matt. 18:12; Luke 15:4). Simon, as the Great Power, appeared among men as a man in order to free Helena and others from the rule of those who made the world. Thus it was from Simon and the Simonians that "what is falsely called knowledge" (1 Tim. 6:20) took its beginning.

Epiphanius of Salamis (*Panarion* 1.2.21)[11] claims that Simon considered unnatural sexual relations a matter of moral indifference, and used materials from such in his "mysteries." Describing Simon's system, Epiphanius writes:

> Simon also offers certain names of principalities and authorities, and he speaks of various heavens, describes powers to correspond with each firmament and heaven, and gives outlandish names for these. He says that there is no way to be saved but by learning this mystical doctrine, and offering sacrifices of this kind to the Father of all, through these principalities and authorities. This world has been defectively constructed by wicked principalities and authorities, he says. But he teaches that there is a death and destruction of flesh, and a purification of souls only—and (only) if these are initiated through his erroneous knowledge. And thus the imposture of the so-called Gnostics begins.[12]

11. Frank Williams, *The Panarion of Epiphanius of Salamis: Book I (Sects 1–46)* (NHS 35), 55–62.
12. Ibid., 60.

In Samaria, when Simon offered money to be able to convey the gift
of the Holy Spirit, Peter condemned him (Acts 8:18–24); according to
the so-called Clementine *Homilies* and *Recognitions* (second–third
centuries), there was further contention between Simon and Peter in
various cities, including Rome. At Rome, according to Hippolytus
(*Refutation of Heresies* 6.15) Simon met his end when he had himself
buried alive and instructed his disciples to dig him up again after
three days, but was not raised again to life.

Because what the church fathers say of Simon's doctrine goes beyond what might be anticipated from the record in the Book of Acts,
it may be that these reports reflect later developments among Simon's
followers.

### Menandrianists

According to Justin Martyr (*Apology* 1.26.4) and Irenaeus (*Adversus Haereses* 1.23.5), the successor of Simon was Menander, also a
Samaritan by birth. Like Simon, Menander also taught that the world
was made by angels, but claimed that he himself, rather than Simon,
was the person who was sent as the savior. While the supreme power
remains unknown, the knowledge Menander conveys enables his disciples to overcome the angels that made the world and, being baptized
into himself, to possess immortal youth.

### Basilidians

Clement of Alexandria (*Stromata* 7.17) says that Basilides, from
whom the Basilidians took their name, arose under Hadrian (A.D.
117–138) and continued under Antoninus Pius (138–161); Irenaeus
(*Adversus Haereses* 1.24.1) and Eusebius (*Church History* 4.7.3) place
him in Alexandria. Eusebius in the same passage gives the name of
a certain Agrippa Castor as having written a refutation of the mysteries of Basilides, and quotes this source to the effect that Basilides
wrote twenty-four books on the gospel. The Muratorian Canon also
refers to and repudiates Basilides's works.[13]

Clement (*Stromata* 4.12) quotes from the twenty-third book of the
*Exegetica* of Basilides, which is presumably the same work referred to
by Agrippa Castor. The material quoted has to do with the question
of sin and suffering in the light of divine providence. According to
Clement, the hypothesis advanced by Basilides was that the soul that
has sinned in a previous existence is punished by suffering in this life,

---

13. Ayer, *Source Book*, 120.

with this difference, however: that the elect soul has the honor of martyrdom, while the other soul is purged by punishment appropriate to its misdeeds.

Irenaeus (*Adversus Haereses* 1.24) gives a brief summary of the doctrines of Basilides. According to this presentation Basilides taught that there is an unborn and nameless Father, from whom proceeded by emanation a whole series of principalities and angels, who occupy 365 heavens. The angels who dwell in the lowest heaven, namely, that which is visible to us, formed all the things that are in the world, and made allotments among themselves of the nations that are on earth. The chief of these angels is thought to be the God of the Jews. This God desired to make the other nations subject to his own people; hence the other nations resisted him and were at enmity with his nation. The Father, therefore, sent his first-begotten Nous (νοῦς, "mind")—who is called Christ—to bestow on those who believe in him deliverance from the power of those who made the world. Christ appeared on earth as a man, and wrought miracles. He did not suffer death. Simon of Cyrene, who bore his cross (Matt. 27:32; Mark 15:21; Luke 23:26), was transformed to look like him, and was crucified. Jesus received the form of Simon and, standing by, laughed at them. Then he ascended, invisibly, to him who sent him. Those who know these things are freed from the power of the principalities who formed the world.

Hippolytus (*Refutation of Heresies* 7.8–15) gives a relatively extensive account of the teachings of Basilides and his followers, from which we learn the following. Basilides claimed to have received secret discourses from Matthias, which the latter in turn had heard in the form of special instructions from the Savior. Basilides taught that there was a time when there was nothing. Since there was nothing, God himself was "nonexistent." Then the nonexistent God made a nonexistent universe out of what was nonexistent. He "hypostatized" or caused to subsist a certain single seed that contained in itself the entire mixture of all the seeds of the universe. In the seed was a threefold sonship, in every respect of the same substance with the nonexistent God. Of this threefold sonship, one portion was composed of fine particles, one of coarse particles, and one was in need of cleansing. The fine portion ascended to the nonexistent one, being drawn, as is each being in its own way, by his exceedingly great beauty and loveliness. The coarse portion was not able to hurry upward, and therefore equipped itself with the Holy Spirit like a wing. But the Holy Spirit was not of the same substance as the sonship, and so was eventually left behind by this second ascending portion of sonship. Thereupon the Holy Spirit became a firmament between the hypercosmos and the cosmos, that is, between the supermundane realm and the universe. The third portion of the sonship, which needed cleansing, remained meanwhile in the great heap of the mixture of the seeds of the universe, where it both conferred and received benefits.

At this point there was begotten from the cosmic seed-mixture the Great Archon, the Head of the universe, who is of inexpressible beauty, magnitude, and power. He rose to the firmament, did not suppose that there was anything beyond, and did not know that the sonship remaining in the seed-mixture was wiser than he; therefore he considered himself the wise architect and proceeded to create every part of the universe. He begot a son, wiser than himself, and seated him at his right hand. The Archon may also be called the Demiurge (δημιουργός, "craftsman, maker, creator"), and the place of his throne is called the Ogdoad (the Eight). Another Archon then arose out of the seed-mixture. His place is called the Hebdomad (the Seven). He also made a son who was wiser than himself. The whole universe was now finished, as well as the hypercosmic things, but the third sonship that had been left in the seed-mixture still needed to be reinstated above. So the gospel came into the universe. It came from the sonship, and it came to the Archon in the Ogdoad through the son who sat beside him. The son, known also as the Christ, instructed the Archon, and the Archon learned what the nonexistent is, what the sonship is, what the Holy Spirit is, what the arrangement of all things is, and how these things will be restored. This is the wisdom spoken in a mystery. The Archon was now afraid, and confessed the sin he had committed in magnifying himself. Then the gospel came, in similar fashion and with similar results, to the Archon of the Hebdomad. This Archon was the one who spoke to Moses in Exodus 6:2–3, and the statement in that passage that the name of the Lord was not made known means that the Archon of the Hebdomad did not reveal the principalities and powers and authorities, as well as the 365 heavens whose Archon is Abrasax (the Greek letters of this name correspond with the number 365, which corresponds also with the number of days in the year).

At this point it must be remembered that, even though the gospel had illuminated the Ogdoad and the Hebdomad, the third sonship was still in the seed-mixture. It had been left there, in fact, in order to benefit the souls that were in a state of formlessness, and also to receive benefit. Now the light came down from the Ogdoad and the Hebdomad, and illuminated Jesus the son of Mary. Thereupon the third sonship, which had been left below, followed Jesus and ascended and came above after being cleansed. When the entire sonship comes to be above the boundary that is marked by the Spirit, that is, the boundary between the cosmos and the hypercosmic realm, then the creation will receive mercy. From the Archon of the Ogdoad on down, a great ignorance will come upon the whole universe, so that nothing may desire anything contrary to nature. Concerning things above there will be neither tidings nor knowledge among things below, in order that the souls below may not be tormented by longing after impossibilities, as if a fish were to desire to graze on the mountains with sheep. And thus the restoration of all things will take place. As for Jesus, through whom the third sonship was cleansed, it was his bodily part that suffered, that came from formlessness and reverted into formlessness. The psychic part of his being rose again; it belonged to the Hebdomad, and reverted to the same. The part of his being that belonged to the elevated dwelling-place of the Great Archon, he raised, and it remained with the Great Archon. And the part that belonged to the dividing Spirit, he carried upward, and it remained in the dividing Spirit. In creation the different orders of created things had been confused together. Jesus became the firstfruits of the differentiation of the various orders of created things, and his passion took place for no other reason than to accomplish the differentiation of what had been confused.

### *Carpocratians*

Along with the followers of Basilides, Irenaeus (*Adversus Haereses* 1.28) mentions the followers of Carpocrates, and says of both that they "have introduced promiscuous intercourse and a plurality of wives, and are indifferent about eating meats sacrificed to idols, maintaining that God does not greatly regard such matters." In a separate passage Irenaeus (*Adversus Haereses* 1.25) speaks further about Carpocrates and his followers. They maintain that the world was created by angels greatly inferior to the unbegotten Father. They hold that Jesus was the natural son of Joseph, but received power from the Father above so that he was able to escape from the inferior creators of the world and ascend to the Father; the soul that is like Christ can likewise despise the world rulers and receive power to accomplish the same results. Meanwhile the Carpocratians practice magical arts and incantations, and consider themselves at liberty to practice all things that are irreligious and impious, since, they hold, things are evil or good simply in virtue of human opinion. In fact they think it necessary for souls to experience every kind of life and action, and if this is not done in one incarnation it will have to be accomplished by means of transmigration. Citing the saying of Jesus (Matt. 5:25–26) about agreeing with an adversary lest one be put in prison, they explain that the words, "You will never get out till you have paid the last penny," mean that no one can escape from the power of those angels who made the world, but that one must pass from body to body, until one has experience of every kind of action which can be practiced in this world, and when nothing is longer wanting to him, then his liberated soul should soar upward to that God who is above the angels, the makers of the world. In this way all souls are saved, whether their own which, guarding against all delay, participate in all sorts of actions during one incarnation, or those, again, who, by passing from body to body, are set free, on fulfilling and accomplishing what is requisite in every form of life into which they are sent, so that at length they shall no longer be [shut up] in the body.

### Saturnilians

Along with Basilides, Irenaeus (*Adversus Haereses* 1.24.1–2) also names Saturninus (or Saturnilus), from Antioch in Syria. He taught that there is "one Father unknown to all," who made angels and powers. It was a company of seven angels who made the world, and also said, "Let us make man in our image" (Gen. 1:26). The first man whom they made, however, was unable to stand upright until "the power above" sent the "spark of life" into him. It is this spark of life that, after death, returns above. The God of the Jews was one of the angels, and the prophecies were spoken partly by the angels who made the world, partly by Satan. Christ only had the appearance of a man, but he came to destroy the God of the Jews and to save those who believe in him, that is, those who have the spark of life. It is obviously of the utmost importance to preserve this spark of life from defilement in the evil, angel-created world that the spark may at last return to its proper home above. It is Satan from whom marriage and reproduction come, therefore both are to be completely avoided lest Satan's work be furthered. Requisite also is abstinence from animal food.

### Marcionists

Along with Saturninus, Irenaeus (*Adversus Haereses* 1.28.1) also names Marcion as preaching against marriage, thus, as Irenaeus thinks, "setting aside the original creation of God, and indirectly blaming him who made the male and female for the propagation of the human race." Some of Marcion's associates also "introduced abstinence from animal food, thus proving themselves ungrateful to God, who formed all things." As such, it was from Saturninus and Marcion that the movement of the Encratites sprang. In Greek ἐγκράτεια (from ἐν, "in," and κράτος, "strength"), like Latin *continentia*, means "self-control," hence the Encratites were the "self-controlled" ones, and this was meant in the sense of radical abstinence and continence, aimed at aloofness from the evil world and from all that would tend to continue its evil.

Marcion's system is known further not only from Irenaeus (*Adversus Haereses* 1.27.2–3) but also especially from Tertullian's extensive *Against Marcion*. Marcion himself, originally a shipmaster from Pontus, taught in Rome but was expelled from the church (A.D. 144) and went on to head his own heretical movement (Tertullian, *Praescriptio haereticorum* 30; *Adversus Marcionem* 1.19; 4.4), being active in the time of Justin Martyr (c. 150; *Apology* 1.26, 58) and under the episcopate of Anicetus (154–166; Irenaeus, *Adversus Haereses* 3.4.3).

Basic in the thought of Marcion is his perception of the contrasts between the law and the gospel, which he sets forth in his lost *Antitheses* (discussed in detail by Tertullian). This leads to his doctrine of two gods, in which he also follows his predecessor Cerdo (who lived at Rome in the time of Hyginus, 137–141): "The God proclaimed by the law and the prophets was not the Father of our Lord Jesus Christ. For the former was known, but the latter unknown; while the one also was just, but the other good" (Irenaeus, *Adversus Haereses* 1.27.1–3). It is the former, the Old Testament God of retributive justice, who made the world; it is the latter, the New Testament God of love from whom Jesus came, who is so high above as to be unknown. So Marcion, by the aid of the devils, has caused many of every nation to speak blasphemies, and to deny that God is the maker of this universe, and to assert that some other being, greater than he, has done greater works (Justin, *Apology* 1.26).

While Marcion evidently did not go into such mythological elaborations as are characteristic of most of the Gnostic systems, the foregoing framework of his thought is certainly Gnostic in the distinction of the two gods and the identification of the lower as the Demiurge, the creator of the world.

## Valentinians

Epiphanius (*Panarion* 1.2.31.2–3)[14] was told that Valentinus, founder of the Valentinian school, was born in Egypt and received a Greek education in Alexandria; Tertullian (*Praescriptio haereticorum* 30) describes him as a disciple of Platonism. Irenaeus (*Adversus Haereses* 3.4.3) says that Valentinus came to Rome in the time of Hyginus (137–141), flourished under Pius I (141–154), and remained until An-

14. Williams, *Panarion of Epiphanius*, 153.

icetus (154–166). Thus Valentinus was active in Rome in approximately 138–160. In Rome, Irenaeus says (*Adversus Haereses* 3.4.3), Valentinus took public part in the church but also taught in secret and was, at last, excommunicated. Irenaeus also says (*Adversus Haereses* 1.11) that Valentinus shaped the principles of the Gnostic heresy into a distinctive character in his own school. In addition Irenaeus (*Adversus Haereses* 3.11.9) cites as a "comparatively recent writing" a Valentinian book entitled "The Gospel of Truth"; since *Against Heresies* was written under Eleutherus (174–189) about 180, the book must have appeared not long before that date. The Muratorian Canon also refers to and repudiates a Valentinian writing, saying, "Of Valentinus, the Arsinoite, and his friends, we receive nothing at all, who have also composed a long new book of Psalms."

Tertullian (*Praescriptio haereticorum* 38) contrasts Valentinus with Marcion in regard to treatment of the Scriptures. Whereas Marcion openly used the knife, not the pen, to excise passages at will, Valentinus proceeded with more cunning and skill: he adapted his matter to the Scriptures, yet actually took away more, and added more, by removing the proper meaning of each word and adding fantastic arrangements of nonexistent things. In another work specifically directed *Against the Valentinians* (1), Tertullian describes them as, in his time, a very large body of heretics.

In the *Stromateis,* Clement of Alexandria quotes several passages from letters and homilies by Valentinus. In these Valentinus speaks of the Father who alone is good, of the divine nature of Jesus, and of the living Aeon (αἰών) to which the world is as much inferior as an image is to a living person. In creation, the one put into man the seed of substance from above. Man, however, uttered such great things that he terrified the angels, and they speedily marred the work. The heart of man is the abode of many evil spirits. Only by the presence of the good, in manifestation through the Son, can the heart become pure.[15]

As thus summarized, the fragments quoted by Clement of Alexandria are not extensive enough to give any full idea of the system of thought set forth by Valentinus. As far as they go, they do not suggest as complex a system as Irenaeus and others ascribe to him; these latter may therefore be reporting some later developments as well as the original teaching of Valentinus.

Irenaeus (*Adversus Haereses* 1.11.1) says that Valentinus taught that there is an inexpressible Dyad, whose two parts may be called Arretus (Unspeakable) and Sige (Silence). From this Dyad emanated a second Dyad, namely, Pater (Father) and Aletheia (Truth). From the

---

15. Grant, *Gnosticism: A Source Book*, 143–45.

Tetrad arose another Tetrad, namely, Logos (Word) and Zoe (Life), Anthropos (Man) and Ecclesia (Church), thus constituting in all the primary Ogdoad. From Logos and Zoe ten powers were produced; from Anthropos and Ecclesia came twelve. All that has been described thus far constitutes the Pleroma (πλήρωμα, Fullness), that is, "the fully explicated manifold of divine characteristics . . . forming a hierarchy and together constituting the divine realm."[16]

In the Pleroma a divine being named Horos (Limit) separates the Bythos (Depth), where the uncreated Father is, from the rest of the Pleroma where the created Aeons are. One of the twelve beings who emanated from Anthropos and Ecclesia fell from its original condition, that is, fell quite out of the Pleroma, and produced the remainder of the universe. Another being named Horos (Limit) separates the Pleroma from that which is outside it. The being who fell out of the Pleroma became the mother of Christ, and Christ returned to the Pleroma. Jesus emanated from Christ who returned to the Pleroma (although other ideas of his origin were advanced too), and the Holy Spirit emanated from Ecclesia. The mother, however, was unable to return to the Pleroma, and she brought forth another son, the Demiurge, who is the creator of all things outside the Pleroma, and the ruler of everything under him.[17]

Many more details of the system of Valentinus (and perhaps of its amplification by his followers) are given by Hippolytus (*Refutation of Heresies* 6.24–32), while Epiphanius (*Panarion* 1.31) draws upon both Irenaeus and Hippolytus for his account and also adds material of his own.

### *Ptolemaeus*

Among the followers of Valentinus, the most prominent was Ptolemaeus (Ptolemy). Irenaeus (*Adverses Haereses* 1, preface 2) calls the school of Ptolemaeus a flower picked from that of Valentinus and, in the first eight chapters of *Against Heresies*, gives an extended summary of Valentinian doctrines, which are presumably essentially those of Ptolemaeus. "They say," Irenaeus begins (1.1), "that in the invisible and ineffable heights above there exists a certain perfect, pre-existent Aeon." This Aeon they call Proarche (Fore-Beginning), Propator (Fore-

16. Jonas, *Gnostic Religion,* 181.

17. In comparison at this point it may be noted that in Plato's *Timaeus* (28c; 41a–b) the Maker and Father of this universe is called a Demiurge and entrusts to lesser gods the making of the living creatures of air, water, and earth. There is a section of Plato's *Republic* (588b–589b) in Nag Hammadi Codex VI.5 (see James Brashler, "Plato, *Republic* 588b–589b," in Douglas M. Parrott, *Nag Hammadi Codices V,2–5 and VI with Papyrus Berolinensis 8502,1 and 4* [NHS 11], 325–39).

Father), and Bythus (Depth). Eternal and unbegotten, he remained
through countless ages in profound serenity and quiescence. With him
was Ennoia (Thought), also called Charis (Grace) and Sige (Silence).
When Bythus determined to put forth or cause to emanate from himself the beginning of all things, he put this project into Sige, like seed
into the womb, and she brought forth Nous (Mind). Nous is like and
equal to him who produced him, and alone comprehends the greatness
of the Father. Nous is also called Monogenes (Only-Begotten), Pater
(Father), and Arche (Beginning) of all things. Along with him was
produced the feminine Aletheia (Truth). Thus was constituted the first
Tetrad, namely, Bythus and Sige, then Nous and Aletheia. Nous or
Monogenes also sent forth Logos (Word) and Zoe (Life), and from them
came Anthropos (Man) and Ecclesia (Church). This made the original
Ogdoad, four masculine-feminine pairs, each joined in union (συζυγία)
with the other.

It is obvious that this account is much the same as, only somewhat
more detailed than, that with which we have already become familiar
with respect to Valentinus. Here in Ptolemaeus too, the process of
emanation goes on until there are in all thirty Aeons (8 + 10 + 12),
who constitute the invisible and spiritual Pleroma. It was to set forth
the mystery of these Aeons that the Savior did no public work for
thirty years (see Luke 3:23); while the first, third, sixth, ninth, and
eleventh hours mentioned in the parable of the laborers in the vine-
yard (Matt. 20:1–16) point to the same mystery (1 + 3 + 6 + 9 + 11
= 30). The Aeon who was derived from Anthropos and Ecclesia and
fell out of the Pleroma, mentioned by Valentinus, was the youngest of
that group of twelve, and was named Sophia (Wisdom). Her experiences are narrated at some length, and it is held that she was ultimately restored to her place in the Pleroma. Then, lest any of the
other Aeons should fall into a calamity similar to that of Sophia,
Christ and the Holy Spirit were emitted by Monogenes, in accordance
with the foreknowledge of the Father. Christ proclaimed among the
Aeons the knowledge of the Father, namely, that he cannot be com-
prehended, seen, or heard, but can be known only through Monogenes
(see John 1:18). The Holy Spirit taught the Aeons what is the true rest
(ἀνάπαυσις; κατάπαυσις occurs in Heb. 4:1–10), and everything was
established and brought into a state of perfect repose. Then, acting in
perfect harmony, the Aeons emitted an emanation to the honor and
glory of Bythus, a being of the most perfect beauty, the very star and
perfect fruit of the Pleroma, namely, Jesus. He is called Savior, Christ,
Logos, and All, because he is from all.

What transpired outside the Pleroma is told in detail. While the
First Sophia Aeon returned to the Pleroma, her Desire, which was also

called Achamoth (evidently derived from the Hebrew word for wisdom, חָכְמָה [ḥokmâ]), remained of necessity outside the Light and the Pleroma, in an intermediate place of Shadow and Void called the Middle. She sought for the Light, but Horos hindered her. As he did so, he exclaimed "Iao" (probably from Yahweh), and this was the origin of that name. This Second or Lower Sophia was the Mother who made the Demiurge and he, in turn, made heaven, earth, and man. While man received his psychic nature from the Demiurge, he has his body from the earth, his flesh from matter, and his spiritual man from the Mother Achamoth. Evidently reckoning body and flesh together in one category, it was also said that there are three elements in a person, the material, the psychic, and the spiritual. The material must of necessity perish. The psychic, which is between the material and the spiritual, can go to either side according to its inclination. The spiritual is supposed to be united with the psychic in order to assume shape, and then the two elements can be instructed together in conduct.

The Demiurge also, according to at least one version of the doctrine, emitted Christ as his own son. At the baptism the Savior from the Pleroma descended upon Christ but, since the Savior could not experience suffering, was taken away from him when he was led before Pilate. The passion of the Lord really pointed to what happened to the last of the Aeons, and his cry on the cross, "My God, my God, why hast thou forsaken me?" (Matt. 27:46), simply indicated that Sophia was abandoned by the Light and restrained by Horos from going forward. Although Achamoth was wandering outside the Pleroma, she was sought after by the Savior, as he indicated when he said that he came for the lost sheep (Matt. 18:12; Luke 15:4).

The consummation will take place when all that is spiritual has been shaped and perfected in knowledge. This refers to the spiritual men who have perfect knowledge concerning God, and have been initiated into the mysteries of Achamoth. Everything that is of a material nature must end in decay. That which is of a psychic nature may choose what is worse and end in destruction, or choose what is better and find rest in the place of the Middle. Psychic men do not have perfect knowledge. They get strength through works and "mere" faith. They must practice continence and good conduct if they are to be saved and attain at last to the place of the Middle. For those who are spiritual and perfect, however, such a course of conduct is not at all necessary. They will be entirely and undoubtedly saved, not by means of conduct, but because they are spiritual by nature. It is not conduct that leads one into the Pleroma, but simply the seed that is sent from there like an infant child, and goes back thither when it is perfected. When all the seed shall have come to perfection, then their Mother

Achamoth will leave the Middle and enter the Pleroma. There she and
the Savior will be united as bride and bridegroom. The spirituals also,
putting off their psychic natures and becoming intelligent spirits, will
enter the Pleroma, there to be given as brides to the angels who attend
the Savior. The Demiurge will move into the place of the Mother Sophia, in the Middle, and there the psychic natures of the righteous
will find rest. Then the fire that is hidden in the universe will blaze
forth and burn. It will destroy all matter, and itself as well, and then
have no more existence. "Such," says Irenaeus at the end of the eighth
chapter of *Against Heresies* 1 (at least according to a note preserved
at that point in Latin) "are the views of Ptolemaeus."

A letter of Ptolemaeus addressed to a certain Flora is preserved by
Epiphanius (*Panarion* 1.2.33.3–7).[18] In it Ptolemaeus distinguishes
three parts in the Old Testament law: (1) the ethical precepts that
Jesus came not to destroy but to fulfil (Matt. 5:17), (2) the ordinances
that were interwoven with injustice, and were abrogated by Jesus, and
(3) the symbolic part, such as sacrifices, that were done away with in
literal application, but kept as images of transcendent things. As for
the source of such a law as this, it cannot have come from the perfect
God (as its imperfect nature shows); nor can it have come from the
devil, since that would be an unlawful thought to utter; but it must
have come from the Demiurge, who dwells in the Middle, and is inferior to the perfect God but superior to the adversary.

### Marcosians

Marcus was another Valentinian leader, the teachings and practices
of whom, and of whose followers, Irenaeus describes (*Adversus Haereses*
1.13–22). The Marcosians evidently observed the Eucharist in some
form, and Marcus was reputed to be able to do certain magical tricks
with the wine. Some of the group had a rite in which a bridechamber
was prepared, and a mystical initiation was performed with the pronunciation of certain secret expressions. They affirmed that this was
a spiritual marriage, celebrated after the likeness of the unions above.
Others led candidates to water and baptized them "into the name of
the unknown Father of the universe, into Truth the mother of all, into
him who came down into Jesus, into unity and redemption and fellowship with the Powers" (*Adversus Haereses* 1.21.3). Others repeated
numerous mysterious words. After baptism, the initiated person was
anointed with balsam. Others said that it was superfluous to bring
persons to the water. Instead, they mixed oil and water together, and

18. Williams, *Panarion of Epiphanius*, 198–204; see also Gillies Quispel, *Ptolémée: Lettre à Flora*.

poured the mixture on the heads of those being initiated, using formulas such as those already mentioned. "And this," says Irenaeus, "they want to be the redemption" (*Adversus Haereses* 1.21.4).

Of the activity of the Marcosians in general, Irenaeus (*Adversus Haereses* 1.18.1) says that "every day each one of them, as he is able, invents something new; for no one is considered perfect unless he produces great untruths among them"; and of their literature he says (*Adversus Haereses* 1.20.1) that they have "an unspeakable number of apocryphal and spurious writings."

### Barbelo-Gnostics

Before Irenaeus brings book 1 of *Against Heresies* to a close he names yet the Barbelo-Gnostics, Sethians, and Ophites. Apart from sects deriving from the Simonians, Irenaeus (*Adversus Haereses* 1.29.1–4)[19] says, there has sprung up a multitude of Barbelo-Gnostics, appearing like mushrooms growing out of the ground. Barbelo was a feminine power who emanated from the unnamed Father, and she plays a role much like that of Ennoia (Thought) and Sophia (Wisdom) in some of the other systems. What Irenaeus goes on to tell of the system named for Barbelo corresponds with the cosmological exposition in the first part of the Apocryphon of John (see p. 243).

### Sethians

The Sethians (Irenaeus, *Adversus Haereses* 1.30.1–14) emphasized the role of Ialdabaoth. He was the son of Sophia the Mother, and had a son named Nous (Mind), who was in the form of a serpent (Greek, ὄφις; see pp. 234–35). It was Ialdabaoth who made man in his own image, and breathed his own light-spirit into him, then tried to get this luminous power back again. Adam and Eve became the parents not only of Cain and Abel, but also of Seth and Norea (whereby a wife was provided for Seth). Seth was "another child instead of Abel, for Cain slew him," as Eve said (Gen. 4:25), therefore (it was concluded) of a different generation, superior to Cain and Abel. As Epiphanius (*Panarion* 1.3.39)[20] explains, the Sethians proudly trace their ancestry to Seth and ascribe to him everything that seems virtuous. Because sin persisted, the Mother brought on the flood so that only the pure seed of Seth might be preserved, and of the eight persons (1 Pet. 3:20) who were in the ark, seven were of the pure stock, but one was Ham

---

19. Foerster, *Gnosis*, 1.104–5.
20. Williams, *Panarion of Epiphanius*, 255–61; Foerster, *Gnosis*, 1.293–95.

who was smuggled aboard by the malevolent angels so that the wicked stock that they had created should not perish (Tertullian, *Against All Heresies* 2). Thus the world reverted to its ancient state of disorder, and was filled with evils just as before the flood. After this, however, Christ appeared from the line of Seth, and Christ is Seth himself. When Christ descended on Jesus, Jesus began to work miracles and heal and announce the unknown Father, but when Jesus was crucified Christ departed from him. After eighteen months in which Christ tarried on earth and instructed a few of the disciples, whom he knew to be capable of understanding great mysteries, he was received back up into heaven and sat down at the right hand of his father Ialdabaoth. Finally the consummation of all things will take place when all the light that is scattered here below is gathered together on high, in an incorruptible Aeon.

Hippolytus (*Refutation of Heresies* 5.14–17) gives a quite different account of those he calls Sethians, and cites a book called Paraphrase of Seth for their secret doctrines.

### Ophites

As noted in the foregoing, the son of Ialdabaoth was Nous (Mind), who was in the form of a serpent (Irenaeus, *Adversus Haereses* 1.30.5). Others said that Sophia herself became the serpent (*Adversus Haereses* 1.30.15). It is from the same serpent that the Ophites take their name. Tertullian (*Against All Heresies* 2) says of the Ophites that they magnify the serpent to such a degree that they prefer him even to Christ himself. Epiphanius narrates the Ophite myth (*Panarion* 1.3.37)[21] in these terms: Ialdabaoth (here called the son of Prunicus ["wanton"], another name for Sophia the Mother on high) came into being on a level lower than that of the Aeon on high, and had seven sons who created seven heavens. To keep them from knowing what was higher, Ialdabaoth closed off the area above himself, and it was the seven sons—whether they were aeons or gods or angels—who fashioned man in the image of their father, Ialdabaoth. At first the man was unable to stand, but when Prunicus sent a spark—the soul—into man, the man arose, recognized the Father on high who was above Ialdabaoth, and praised him. Ialdabaoth was distressed, and brought the snake into being as his son; but when the snake taught the man and woman the whole of the knowledge of the mysteries on high, Ialdabaoth was angry and threw the snake down from heaven. Therefore the Ophites call the serpent a king from heaven, and magnify him for such knowl-

21. Williams, *Panarion of Epiphanius*, 241–48.

edge and offer him bread. This they do literally, for they have an actual snake that they keep in a sort of basket, and when it is time for their mysteries they bring the snake out and let it coil up on loaves that are afterward broken and distributed to the recipients.

## Naassenes

Hippolytus (*Refutation of Heresies* 5.1.3ff.) also refers to ones who take their name from the serpent, namely, the Naassenes (from the Hebrew word for serpent, נָחָשׁ [nāḥāš]). The Naassenes, Hippolytus says, derive the principal points of their system out of a great number of discourses that James the Lord's brother is said to have delivered to Mariamne (this name and also Mariham and Mariam are variant forms of the name *Mary,* and presumably refer to one of the Marys of the Gospel tradition, probably Mary Magdalene; see the Gospel of Mary, p. 240 below). The Naassenes also draw upon the Gospel of the Egyptians (5.2.9) and the Gospel According to Thomas (5.2.20).

They have composed their own hymn, Hippolytus says (5.5.1–2), in which they celebrate their mysteries. The hymn declares that the first principle that generated the universe was "first-born Nous [Mind]," the second principle was Chaos, while the third principle fell to the soul, which was evidently derived from both Mind and Chaos. Therefore the soul is in an ambiguous state. Sometimes it sees the light, sometimes it falls into evil, sometimes it weeps, sometimes it rejoices. Thus in its wanderings it has come into a labyrinth of evils and in the end it finds no exit, being the slave of death. But Jesus saw this situation and asked the Father to send him. He will descend, bearing the seals, he will pass through all the Aeons, he will reveal all mysteries, he will impart the secrets of the holy way.[22]

# Greek Papyri

## Oxyrhynchus Papyri 1, 654, and 655

As mentioned above, Oxyrhynchus Papyri 1, 654, and 655 (all probably around A.D. 200)[23] contain texts in Greek that are the equivalent of corresponding texts in the Coptic Gospel According to Thomas; no. 655 contains other portions that are certainly of gnostic flavor, and it was found among the indubitably Gnostic papyri from Nag Hammadi.

---

22. Foerster, *Gnosis,* 1.282.
23. Bernard P. Grenfell and Arthur S. Hunt, *The Oxyrhynchus Papyri,* 1.1; 4.654, 655.

Therefore the three Greek papyri are evidently fragments of Gnostic works, although for the most part what they may have contained that was explicitly Gnostic is no longer extant.

### Rylands Papyrus 463

Rylands Papyrus 463 is probably also from Oxyrhynchus and dates from the early third century.[24] The fragment begins (recto lines 1–5):

> the remainder of the course of the season of the time
> of the Aeon rest in silence. When
> she had said these things Mariamne was
> silent, as thus far the Savior
> had spoken. . . .

Thereafter Andrew and Peter are evidently involved in criticism of Mariamne, but Levi defends her (verso lines 22–25):

> If the Savior believed her worthy,
> who are you to set her at naught?
> For he knew her thoroughly and
> loved her firmly.

The words *Aeon, rest,* and *silence* are all prominent in the Gnostic vocabulary. The title *Savior* (σωτήρ), which is an infrequent designation of Christ in the canonical Gospels (Luke 2:11; John 4:42), is so frequent among the Gnostics that Irenaeus says in his summary of Valentinian doctrines (*Adversus Haereses* 1.1.3) that these Gnostics use the term to the exclusion of "Lord" (κύριος). Thus the fragment appears as a small portion of a Gnostic book, and in fact the present material will be found substantially in the Coptic Gospel of Mary in Papyrus Berolinensis 8502 (see p. 240).

Mariamne's (Mariham, Mariam, Mary) prominence in Gnostic tradition has already been seen in connection with the Naassenes (as per Hippolytus), and is noted here in the statement that Jesus loved her "firmly." Also in the Coptic Gospel of Mary it is said (10.2–3) that the Savior loved her more than the rest of women. All of this is reminiscent of the prominence of Mary Magdalene among the women followers of Jesus in the canonical Gospels, and supports the identification of this Mary with Mary Magdalene.

24. C. H. Roberts, *Catalogue of the Greek and Latin Papyri in the John Rylands Library, Manchester*, vol. 3, *Theological and Literary Texts (Nos. 457–551)*, 18–23.

## Oxyrhynchus Papyrus 1081

Oxyrhynchus Papyrus 1081 was found at Behnesa and probably belongs to the early fourth century.[25] On the recto (lines 36–38) is the statement: "The Master of all is not the father [Pater] but the Fore-Father [Propator]." Exactly such a contrast between the Fore-Father who is the original, eternal Aeon from whom all existence emanated, and the Father who belongs only to the second Dyad in the Pleroma, was a feature of Valentinian thought (Irenaeus, *Adversus Haereses* 1.1.1; 1.11.1). Words typical of the Gnostic vocabulary are also scattered throughout the text: "Savior," "emanation," "thought," "beginning," and "unbegotten." Furthermore, the text such as it is agrees substantially with the corresponding portion of the Coptic text of the Gnostic work, the Sophia of Jesus Christ, in Papyrus Berolinensis 8502 (see p. 241). In the fragmentary opening of the recto (lines 25–27) of the Greek papyrus it is evident that there is a conversation between a person whose name is lost, and the Savior: "Lord, how then. . . . The Savior said. . . ." In the corresponding section of the Berlin Papyrus (88.19ff.) we learn that the one questioning the Savior is none other than Mariham, that is Mariamne (probably Mary Magdalene), who is also prominent in Gnostic tradition as the recipient of special revelations from Christ.

# Coptic Papyri

## The Gospel According to Thomas

As noted above in consideration of the Naassenes, Hippolytus (*Refutation of Heresies* 5.2.20) says that they use the Gospel According to Thomas. Also Origen (*Homily on Luke*),[26] Eusebius (*Church History* 3.25.6–7), and Cyril of Jerusalem (*Catechetical Lectures* 4.36; 6.31) all mention a book of this name and repudiate it. It is probably the very same work that is found as the second tractate of Nag Hammadi Codex II, for the colophon gives the name the Gospel According to Thomas, and the text begins, "These are the secret words which Jesus the living spoke, and Didymus Judas Thomas wrote." Almost the same words, although somewhat broken, are at the beginning of Oxyrhynchus Papyrus 654, and in this text along with Oxyrhynchus Papyri 1 and 655 there are several passages that correspond with passages in the Nag

---

25. Arthur S. Hunt, *Oxyrhynchus Papyri*, 8.1081.
26. Max Rauer, *Die Homilien zu Lukas in der Übersetzung des Hieronymus*, 5.

Hammadi text, hence the latter must go back to a Greek form at least as early as the Greek papyri (i.e., c. A.D. 200).[27]

According to its opening statement, the work was written by Didymus Judas Thomas. In Hebrew and Aramaic the name *Thomas* means "twin"; in Greek likewise Didymus is literally "twin." In John 11:16, 20:24, and 21:2 Thomas called the Twin (Δίδυμος) is one of the twelve disciples of Jesus; in some Syriac manuscripts (sy$^s$ and sy$^c$) Judas (not Iscariot) in John 14:22 has become Thomas or Judas Thomas; in Matthew 13:55 and Mark 6:3 Judas is the name of a brother of Jesus. Evidently from a combination of these data it was concluded that these were all names of one person and that he was none other than the twin brother of Jesus. Thus the apocryphal Acts of Thomas (probably composed in Edessa, Syria, in the first half of the third century; probably written originally in Syriac, but with an extant Greek text that is better than such Syriac as is still available) has to do with "Judas Thomas who is also [called] Didymus" (§ 1), and he is described as "twin brother of Christ, apostle of the Most High and fellow-initiate into the hidden word of Christ, who dost receive his secret sayings" (§ 39).[28]

The Coptic text of the Gospel According to Thomas consists of 114 (according to the usual reckoning) passages (λόγια, "sayings"), each introduced with the words, "Jesus said"—thus constituting the most extensive collection of sayings attributed to Jesus outside of the New Testament tradition.[29] Other named speakers are Simon Peter, Matthew, and Thomas (all in Logion 13), Mariham (i.e., Mary; Logion 21), and Salome (Logion 61). One passage (Logion 12) refers to James the Just (brother of Jesus and head of the Jerusalem church) as the proper leader after the departure of Jesus.

The largest amount of material in the Coptic gospel is parallel to texts in the canonical Gospels. In some cases the texts are virtually identical (e.g., Logion 54 and Luke 6:20); in some cases the Coptic version is shorter (e.g., Logion 63 and Luke 12:16–21); in some cases longer (e.g., Logion 47 and Matt. 6:24; Luke 16:13). The exact nature of the relationships is difficult to determine.

In another case Logion 2 and its parallel in Oxyrhynchus Papyrus 654 (lines 6–9) read:

27. Edgar Hennecke, *New Testament Apocrypha*, 1.278–307.

28. Ibid., 2.425–531.

29. A. Guillaumont et al. *The Gospel According to Thomas*; Robert M. Grant and David N. Freedman, *The Secret Sayings of Jesus: The Gospel of Thomas*; R. M. Wilson, "The Gospel of Thomas," in Hennecke, *New Testament Apocrypha*, 1.511–22.

Let him who seeks, not cease seeking until he finds, and when he finds,
he will be troubled, and when he has been troubled, he will marvel and
he will reign over the All.

The same saying is quoted by Clement of Alexandria (*Stromata* 2.9;
5.14) and attributed to the Gospel According to the Hebrews (first half
of the second century, a work that also gives a prominent place to
James the Just):

He who seeks will not cease until he finds; and having found he will be
astounded, and being astounded he will reign, and reigning he will rest.

Again in Logion 37 (and Oxyrhynchus Papyrus 655, lines 17–23)
the disciples ask Jesus, "When will you reveal yourself to us, and when
will we see you?" Jesus replies:

When you take off your clothing and are not ashamed, and take your
clothes and put them under your feet like little children, and tread on
them, then [you will be] sons of the Living One and you will not be
afraid.

A somewhat similar saying is quoted by Clement of Alexandria (*Stromata* 3.13) from Julius Cassianus (a Valentinian teacher of the late
second century) and attributed to the Gospel of the Egyptians (a work
that Hippolytus [*Refutation of Heresies* 5.2.20] says was used by the
Naassenes). Here the introductory question is asked by Salome:

When Salome asked when what she had inquired about would be known,
the Lord said: "When you have trampled on the garment of shame and
then the two become one and the male with the female [is] neither male
nor female."

In the foregoing there are already items suggestive of Gnostic emphasis, for example, the place of Didymus Judas Thomas, Mariham
(Mary), and Salome, otherwise known as recipients of secret teachings
from Christ. Also the Greek word ἐκδύω in Oxyrhynchus Papyrus 655
(line 22) and Logion 37, meaning "strip" or "take off (clothing)," is the
same word used figuratively in 2 Corinthians 5:4 for stripping off the
earthly body in death. Here it can accord with the Gnostic hope of
stripping off the fleshly garment of the present corruptible existence,
although the words "and are not ashamed" can also point back to
Genesis 2:25 when Adam and Eve "were not ashamed," and indicate
the hope to recover such innocence of life.

At any rate there are other passages in the Coptic gospel surely to be understood in the Gnostic sense, most notably Logion 50, in which both the Gnostic's origin in the world of light and ultimate destiny in "rest" are recognized:

> Jesus said: "If they say to you: 'From where have you originated?,' say to them: 'We have come from the Light, where the Light originated through itself. It stood and it revealed itself in their image.' If they say to you: '[Who] are you?,' say: 'We are his sons and we are the elect of the Living Father.' If they ask you: 'What is the sign of your Father in you?,' you say to them: 'It is a movement and a rest.' "

### The Gospel of Mary

The Gospel of Mary is the first of three plainly Gnostic works in Papyrus Berolinensis 8502, with a fragment in Rylands Papyrus 463 (see p. 240).[30] The title is given in the colophon, where the name is spelled Marihamm, otherwise in the body of the text, Mariham (the name is a variant form of the name *Mary,* and of the Marys in the Gospel tradition it is probably Mary Magdalene who is meant).

Of the numbered pages of the work in the Coptic codex the first six pages and also pages 11–14 are missing. At the broken beginning of the Coptic text it appears that a question is being asked about the time of the end of the world and whether matter will be destroyed or saved. To this the Savior replies, not with complete clarity, that all natures will be resolved again into their own roots; and then admonishes, as frequently in the synoptic Gospels (Matt. 11:15; etc.), "He who has ears to hear, let him hear." Then Peter, acknowledging that Christ has now explained all things to them, nevertheless goes on and asks a further question about sin, which the Savior answers. After that the Blessed One, as Christ is now called, gives a farewell salutation and commission to preach the gospel of the kingdom, which is woven together out of words that echo a number of canonical Gospel sayings. From this and from the fact that the Savior goes away immediately afterward, we gather that the setting is in the postresurrection period, a setting frequently found in Gnostic works.

So the Savior departs, and the disciples grieve and give fearful consideration to their commission to preach to the Gentiles, saying, "If they did not spare him, how will they spare us?" Thereupon Mariham stands up and admonishes them to overcome their irresolution, saying,

---

30. Walter C. Till, *Die gnostischen Schriften des koptischen Papyrus Berolinensis 8502,* 62–79; R. M. Wilson and George W. MacRae, "The Gospel According to Mary," in Parrott, *Nag Hammadi Codices V, 2–5 and VI,* 453–71.

"But rather let us praise his greatness, for he has prepared us and made us into men" (9.10–12, 18–20). Peter then says to her, "Sister, we know that the Savior loved you more than the rest of women," and asks her to tell them the words of the Savior she knows but that they have not heard. Mary then begins to tell them how she saw the Lord in a vision (10.1ff.).

At this point pages 11–14 are lost; on page 15 Mary is evidently continuing to recount the revelation that the Savior gave her, and is describing the ascent of the enlightened soul past various powers. To the powers the soul speaks triumphantly: "My desire has been ended, and ignorance has died. . . . From this time on will I attain to the rest [ἀνάπαυσις] of the time [χρόνος] of the season [καιρός] of the aeon, in silence" (16.19–21; 17.4–7). This is the point at which Rylands Papyrus 463 begins, and from here to the end the Coptic and the Greek texts are substantially parallel, and both close with the disciples going forth to preach.

## The Sophia of Jesus Christ

The third Gnostic work in Papyrus Berolinensis 8502 is the Sophia of Jesus Christ (77.8–127.12),[31] of which there is an unpublished but substantially parallel text in Nag Hammadi Codex III, the fourth tractate, and a short parallel portion in Greek (corresponding to Papyrus Berolinensis 8502, 88.19–91.14) in Oxyrhynchus Papyrus 1081 (see p. 237). The word *sophia* in the title may be either translated as "wisdom" or left untranslated as Sophia, since in Gnosticism we hear both about "the wisdom spoken in a mystery" (Hippolytus, *Refutation of Heresies* 7.14, in a passage against the Basilidians) and about Sophia who is a great Aeon (e.g., Irenaeus, *Adversus Haereses* 1.1.2; 1.2.2; etc., in a passage against Ptolemaeus).

As in many Gnostic works, the setting is on a mountain, after the resurrection, and Christ appears in an indescribable form, like a great angel of light, to his twelve disciples and seven women. Some of them ask him questions, and he gives a long series of doctrinal expositions, then concludes in part with these words:

> "Behold, I have taught you the name of the Perfect One, the whole will of the holy angels and of the Mother, that the manly host may here be made perfect, that they may appear in all Aeons from the Unlimited up to those which have arisen in the unsearchable riches of the great in-

31. Till, *Die gnostischen Schriften,* 194–295.

visible Spirit; that they all may receive of his goodness and of the riches
of his place of rest, above which there is no dominion. . . ."
Thus said the blessed Redeemer and vanished from their sight. . . .
From that day on his disciples began to preach the Gospel of God, the
eternal Father of him who is immortal for ever. [124.9–125.9; 126.17;
127.10][32]

## The Apocryphon of John

Of the Apocryphon of John, which is the second Gnostic work in
Papyrus Berolinensis 8502 (19.6–77.7) no earlier Greek text is presently known, but a Greek original may be assumed as was demonstrably the case for the Gospel According to Thomas, the Gospel of
Mary, and the Sophia of Jesus Christ. There are, however, three other
copies of the Apocryphon in the Nag Hammadi literature, namely, the
first tractate in each of the Codices II, III, and IV, suggesting the
special importance attached to this work in the circles from which this
collection comes. The texts in Papyrus Berolinensis and in Codex III
represent a shorter version of the book, while the texts in Codices II
and IV are a longer version. Each text has the same colophon, desig-
nating the work as the "secret wisdom" (ἀπόκρυφον) of John.[33]
As the work opens (19.6 in Papyrus Berolinensis and parallels in
the Nag Hammadi texts), John the brother of James—these being the
sons of Zebedee—goes up to the temple one day and meets a Pharisee
who asks him where his master is. John replies that he has returned
to the place from which he came, whereupon the Pharisee declares
that he was a deceiver. John goes away to a mountain, in a desert
place, and with grief in his heart, asks (20.8–14):

How then was the Savior appointed, and why was he sent into the world
by his Father who sent him? And who is his Father? And of what nature
is that Aeon to which we will go?

Then John sees a vision. A child appears to him, who at the same
time has the luminous form of an old man. This one, who is eventually
(45.6) called Christ, promises (22.3ff.) to reveal all things to John, and

---

32. Other books of various degrees of Gnostic character, often classified as gospels under the
name of Jesus, are the two Books of Jeu in Codex Brucianus (Carl Schmidt and Violet MacDermot,
*The Books of Jeu and the Untitled Text in the Bruce Codex* [NHS 13]); Pistis Sophia in Codex Askewianus (Carl Schmidt and Violet MacDermot, *Pistis Sophia* [NHS 9]); and the Dialogue of the
Savior (Stephen Emmel, Helmut Koester, and Elaine Pagels, *Nag Hammadi Codex III,5: The Dialogue of the Savior* [NHS 26]); see also Hennecke, *New Testament Apocrypha*, 1.243–63.
33. Till, *Die gnostischen Schriften*, 79–195; Hennecke, *New Testament Apocrypha*, 1.314–31.

proceeds to do so in a long discourse that continues without interruption until (45.6) John breaks in with a question.

The Father of All, it is explained (22.20ff.), is an incomprehensible Spirit, describable mainly in negatives, and his imperishable Aeon exists in rest and reposes in silence (26.7–8). The Spirit saw its own image, however, in the pure water of light that surrounded it, and its thought (Ennoia) became active (27.1ff.). So Barbelo came into existence, who is the First Thought, the Image, and the Virginal Spirit (27.18ff.). From Barbelo was born Monogenes (Only-Begotten), or Christ (30.1ff.). Out of the light that is Christ came four emanations (32.19ff.), namely, Charis (Grace), Synesis (Understanding), Aesthesis (Perception), and Phronesis (Prudence). Charis is connected with the first great light, Harmozel (33.8ff.), where the perfect man, Adam, is established (35.5ff.). In the second light, Oroiael, is the abode of Seth, the son of Adam (35.20ff.). In the third light, Daueithe, are the seeds of the saints, who are the descendants of Seth (36.2ff.). In the fourth light, Eleleth, are the souls who repented only belatedly and thus finally came to know their fulfilment (36.7ff.). Connected with the fourth light, also, was Sophia, the Aeon who in ignorance gave birth to an imperfect work, a monster, whom she named Ialdabaoth (36.16ff.). This is the First Archon (38.14–15). He joined himself with Unreason and created the firmament and material world and the powers and angels who rule over it (39.5ff.). When he saw all this creation and all these angels beneath him, Ialdabaoth, now (41.6–7; 42.10–11) called also Saklas, became boastful and, using the words of Exodus 20:5 and Isaiah 45:5, said, "I am a jealous God; besides me there is no other" (44.14–15). Thereupon the Mother, that is, Sophia, began to be "moved" because she recognized her deficiency (45.1–5).

Up to this point the doctrines in the Apocryphon of John (22.17–45.5) are very much the same as those reported by Irenaeus in his account of the Barbelo-Gnostics (*Adversus Haereses* 1.29). Summarizing the teachings of this group of Gnostics (see p. 233), Irenaeus tells about the Father who cannot be named, the Aeon called Barbelo, and the four emanations, Charis, Synesis, Phronesis, and (varying one name) Thelesis (Will), who are associated with the four great lights. Also he tells about Sophia, and the work of the First Archon, and closes the account with the arrogant declaration of the latter: "I am a jealous God; and besides me there is no other." Also in his account of the Sethians and Ophites Irenaeus (*Adversus Haereses* 1.30) tells about the great role of Ialdabaoth. Thus these main teachings of the present tractate must have existed before approximately A.D. 180, the date of Irenaeus's *Against Heresies*.

At this point in the Apocryphon of John (45.6) John breaks in with

a question to Christ concerning the significance of the word *moved,*
which had just been used (45.1) with respect to the Mother, Sophia.
From here on through the end of the book John asks more and more
questions. As the revelation progresses we are told of the creation of
man (49.2ff.). Like the perfect man, Adam, in whose image he was
made, he too was called Adam. Although seven powers and 360 angels
took part in making him, this creature remained unmoving (50.15ff.)
until Ialdabaoth breathed into him his spirit, which was the power he
had from the Mother, Sophia (51.17ff.). Then a formation was made
out of earth, water, fire, and wind (actually matter, darkness, desire,
and the opposing spirit). This material body became the fetter and the
tomb of the man (55.3ff.). The man was then (55.20ff.) placed in Paradise, but the delight of this place was only a deceit. The blessed
Father, however, is a compassionate benefactor and had sent the
Thought of Light, called Life (Zoe, the name of Eve in the Septuagint
version of Gen. 3:20), as a helper (Gen. 2:18) for the man (52.17ff.). At
the present juncture this power (i.e., the Thought of Light) was brought
forth out of the man and made into a female form (59.6ff.), Eve. Ialdabaoth realized that these two creatures withdrew from him, and his
angels drove them out of Paradise (61.7ff.). Then Ialdabaoth looked
upon the virgin who stood at the side of Adam, and with her he begot
two sons (62.3ff.). These were Yahweh (*iaue*) and Elohim (*eloeim*).
Yahweh had a face like a bear, and was unrighteous; Elohim had a
face like a cat, and was righteous; these two have been known ever
since as Cain and Abel.

Then (63.2ff.) Adam begot Seth, who had the same substance. Therefore the Mother sent the spirit to Seth and his descendants to awaken
them out of lack of perception and out of the wickedness of the grave
(i.e., of the body), so that they may attain to holy perfection (63.16ff.).
Concerning these Christ says (65.3–66.12):

> Those upon whom the spirit of life descends, after they have bound them-
> selves together with the power, will be saved and will become perfect;
> and they will become worthy to ascend to those great lights; for they
> will become worthy to purify themselves with them from all wickedness
> and from the temptations of iniquity, in that they aim at nothing but
> the incorruptible assembly, and they strive for it without wrath, envy,
> fear, desire, and satiation. They will not be affected by all of these things
> nor by anything except only the flesh, which they make use of while
> they wait in expectation for the time when they will be led forth and
> will be received by the Receiver into the dignity of the eternal, imper-
> ishable life and calling; whereby they endure all things and bear all
> things, so that they may pass through the contest for the prize and
> inherit eternal life.

So they will attain to the place of rest of the Aeons (68.11–13). But those souls that have not known the All will have to be placed repeatedly in fetters, that is, undergo new incarnations, until at last they attain knowledge and are saved (68.12–69.13). With certain other disquisitions the revelation concludes. Then (76.7ff.) John is told to write down what he has received, and a curse is expressed upon anyone who gives out this information in exchange for a gift or food or drink or clothing or anything else. "He [i.e., Christ] gave him [i.e., John] this mystery and forthwith disappeared from him. And he [i.e., John] came to his fellow disciples and began to tell them what had been said to him by the Savior" (76.15–77.5). So the apocryphon comes to its end in Papyrus Berolinensis (and similarly in the Nag Hammadi texts), and the colophon follows (77.6–7) with the title of the book. Such is a full-scale example of the Gnostic answer to the questions of how this evil world came into being, and of how the soul may rise out of it to salvation.[34]

### The Gospel of Truth

As noted above in connection with the Valentinians, Irenaeus (*Adversus Haereses* 3.11.9) speaks of a Valentinian book named the Gospel of Truth, which was published not long before his own work (c. A.D. 180):

> The Valentinians . . . boast that they possess more Gospels than there really are. Indeed, they have arrived at such a pitch of audacity as to entitle their comparatively recent writing "the Gospel of Truth," though it agrees in nothing with the Gospels of the apostles, so that they have really no Gospel which is not full of blasphemy.

In Nag Hammadi Codex I (known as the Jung Codex, because most of it was for a time in the Jung Institute in Zurich) the third tractate is untitled but begins with the words, "The gospel of truth is joy." Since an ancient book was often known by its opening words, it is quite possible that this is the very work (in a Coptic translation of the Greek original) to which Irenaeus referred and, from the nature of its teaching, it is surely the work of a Valentinian teacher, some think even of Valentinus himself. It does not, however, set forth the details

---

34. The fourth and last tractate in Papyrus Berolinensis 8502 (Till, *Die gnostischen Schriften*, 478–93) is the Act of Peter, a part of the apocryphal Acts of Peter (Hennecke, *New Testament Apocrypha*, 2.276–78), which is not Gnostic but apparently valued reading matter in Gnostic circles.

of a theological system as some of the other Valentinian works, but is essentially a homily or meditation.[35]

Beginning with the affirmation that "the gospel of truth is joy" (Codex I, 16.31), the author goes on to say that this joy is experienced by those who have grace from the Father of truth to know him who came forth from the Pleroma, who is immanent in the thought and mind of the Father, and who is called the Savior. On the other hand, those who are ignorant of the Father experience anguish and terror and live, as it were, in a fog in which no one can see (17.10ff.). In that fog, error prepares its works and forgettings or oblivions (17.30ff.). But in Jesus Christ (thus named for the first time in 18.16) knowledge appeared in order that oblivion might be destroyed and the Father be known (18.4ff.). For that reason error became angry with him and he was nailed to a tree (18.21ff.). This is, of course, a reference to the crucifixion and, a little further along (20.25–27), the author quite unmistakably echoes Colossians 2:4 when he says of Jesus: "He was nailed to a tree; he published the edict of the Father on the cross."

Referring evidently to the public ministry of Jesus, the author says (19.17ff.) that he (i.e., Jesus) made himself a guide and appeared in schools, where he spoke the word as a teacher. Then (19.21ff.) there came those who were wise in their own opinion, and put him to the test (see Matt. 16:1; Mark 8:11; etc.), but he confounded them and they hated him because they were not truly wise. Over against the wise came "the little children . . . to whom the knowledge of the Father belongs" (19.28ff.), and they, like the babes who are contrasted with the wise in Matthew 11:25 and Luke 10:21, receive the revelation. As it is put here (19.34ff.), there is revealed in their heart the book of the living, which was written in the thought and mind of the Father. Indeed (22.3ff.) if a person has knowledge it is shown that he is a being from on high. If he is called, he hears, responds, and turns to him who calls him, in order to ascend to him. To those who are such the author says, "You are the children of the understanding of the heart" (32.38–39), and, with many echoes of the language of the canonical New Testament, he urges them (33.1–8) to strengthen those who have stumbled, reach out to the sick, feed the hungry, give rest to the weary, lift up those who wish to arise, and awaken those who are asleep. "If strength does this way," the author adds (33.9–11), "it becomes even stronger."

Continuing this theme and incorporating many allusions to the ca-

---

35. Jacques-É. Ménard, *L'Évangile de Vérité* (NHS 2); Harold W. Attridge and George W. MacRae, "The Gospel of Truth," in Harold W. Attridge, *Nag Hammadi Codex I (The Jung Codex)* (NHS 22), 55–122; Hennecke, *New Testament Apocrypha*, 1.233–41. There is also a fragmentary portion of the Gospel of Truth in Nag Hammadi Codex XII.2.

nonical New Testament in his language, the author admonishes (33.30ff.) his readers to do the will of the Father, for the Father is kind and his will is good. The kindness and mercy of the Father is also stressed in connection with an anointing with ointment, which is described at a later point (36.17ff.). This anointing is for those who "receive a bringing back," and "the ointment is the mercy of the Father." "Those whom he has anointed are the ones who have become perfect." He is good, it is reiterated (36.35ff.), and he knows his plantings and has planted them in his paradise, which is his place of rest. It is, in fact (42.21ff.), in him who is at rest that they rest, and the Father is in them and they are in the Father.

Finally (42.41ff.), using the first-person singular for the first time, the author testifies that he himself has come to be in the place of rest and, having had this experience, it is not fitting for him to speak of anything else. What is fitting (43.2ff.) is to be concerned at all times with the Father of the All and the true brothers upon whom the love of the Father is poured out. Thus, with only a few more words, the author brings to a close this homily or meditation in which language so frequently allusive to the canonical New Testament expresses a Gnostic view of life, the view that through knowledge of where one has come from and is going, one may have joy and rest in union with the loving Father.[36]

### The Gospel According to Philip

In Pistis Sophia (chap. 42) Jesus charges Philip (whom he calls blessed), Thomas, and Matthew to write down what he says and does, this being explained by Mariam/Mary (chap. 43) as intended to fulfil the requirement of Deuteronomy 19:15 for two or three witnesses to provide adequate evidence.[37] Epiphanius (*Panarion* 1.2.26.13)[38] attests the existence of a "fictitious" gospel in the name of Philip, which was in use among the Gnostics, and gives a short excerpt from it. According to this excerpt, Philip said that the Lord had revealed to him what the soul must say in its ascent to heaven and what answer it must give to each of the powers above, namely, that it has come to know itself and has gathered itself together from every quarter, has sown no children for the Archon, knows who the Archon is, and is itself of those who are from above. So, the soul is set free. But if it has become the parent of a son it must be held below until it is able to retrieve its own children and bring them back to itself.

36. Jan Helderman, *Die Anapausis im Evangelium Veritatis* (NHS 18).
37. Schmidt and MacDermot, *Pistis Sophia*, 71–72.
38. Williams, *Panarion of Epiphanius*, 94.

In Nag Hammadi Codex II a work identified in its colophon as the Gospel According to Philip is the third tractate and follows immediately after the Gospel According to Thomas.[39] For the most part the work consists of a series of sayings of varying length and in little recognizable order. From a saying early in the text (100.21–24) it would appear that the author and perhaps his readers, had come out of a Jewish background: "When we were Hebrews, we were orphans and had [only] our mother, but when we became Christians we obtained a father and a mother." Apart from his name in the colophon, the apostle Philip appears only once, and this is in a passage where it is not clear how much is the saying of Philip and how much is the further comment of the author (121.8–19):

> Philip the apostle said: "Joseph the carpenter planted a garden [παράδεισος, literally "paradise"] because he needed the wood for his trade. It was he who made the cross from the tree which he planted. . . . His seed was Jesus, but the planting was the cross. But the tree of life is in the midst of the garden and the olive tree from which the anointing is made by him for the resurrection.["]

As touched upon already in this passage, the most distinctive emphasis of the Gospel According to Philip is upon the sacraments and upon what is evidently a Gnostic interpretation of the same. There are five sacraments (115.27–30): "The Lord did everything in a mystery: a baptism and an anointing and a eucharist and a redemption and a bridechamber."

The baptism (βάπτισμα) is evidently an immersion in running water, called "living water," and this is a "body," so when a man is about to go down to the water for the baptism he unclothes himself in order that he may put this one on (123.21–25). The Greek verb for the act of baptism means "to dip under," and also has one specific meaning frequently found, "to dye." In a figure of speech probably originating in a play on these words, it is noted that good dyes perish only with the things that are dyed in them, that is, the dyes last as long as the goods; but God's dyes are immortal, therefore those who are dyed with them are immortal. "But God baptizes those whom he baptizes with water" (109.12–20). "If," however, "anyone goes down to the water and comes up without receiving anything and says, 'I am a Christian,' he has taken the name at interest [i.e., he has just borrowed it, and is subject to having it demanded of him]. But if he receive the Holy

---

39. R. M. Wilson, *The Gospel of Philip*; C. J. de Catanzaro, "The Gospel According to Philip," *JTS* 13 (1962): 35–71; Walter C. Till, *Das Evangelium nach Philippos* (we cite the gospel according to Till's enumeration).

Spirit he has the gift of the name, [and] he who has received a gift is not deprived of it (112.22–29).

The anointing (χρῖσμα; described also in the Gospel of Truth) is with olive oil (as noted in Philip's [?] saying in 121.17) and presumably follows the baptism. In fact there can be said to be two baptisms, in light and in water, and "the light is the anointing" (117.12–14). Indeed the anointing can be said to be superior to the baptism, for it is on account of the anointing (χρῖσμα) that we have been called Christians (Χριστιανοί) and that he has been called Christ (Χριστός; 122.12–16).

The Eucharist (εὐχαριστία) involves the bread and the cup (see 1 Cor. 11:23–25; etc.). Of the latter it is said, "The cup of prayer contains wine and water, since it is appointed as the type of the blood for which thanks is given. And it is full of the Holy Spirit, and it belongs to the wholly perfect man. When we drink this, we shall receive for ourselves the perfect man" (123.14–21).

The redemption (Greek ἀπολύτρωσις, as in Rom. 3:24; etc.), as a sacrament, is not otherwise dealt with in the Gospel According to Philip. It may be remembered that Irenaeus (*Adversus Haereses* 1.21.4) tells how some of the Marcosians, in place of water baptism, pour oil and water on the heads of initiates, and maintain that this is "the redemption," but that practice hardly corresponds with the indications in the present gospel where "redemption" is separate from both baptism and anointing.

The bridechamber (νυμφών) appears to be accorded the highest place among the five sacraments, and is a frequent topic throughout the book, especially toward the climactic end of the work. Alluding to an alleged three houses for places of offering in Jerusalem, into the third of which the high priest entered alone, it is said: "Baptism is the holy house. [Anointing?] is the holy of the holy one [singular]. But the holy of the holy ones [plural] is the bridechamber" (117.21–25). There is also "the great bridal chamber" (παστός, a variant for νυμφών), which must be above in the Pleroma, since it was revealed by the Father of the All, who united with the virgin who came down (119.3–11). The bridal chamber that is above must therefore be the archetype of its counterpart, the bridechamber on earth, and the earthly ceremony must be intended to celebrate and prefigure what is to be enjoyed in ultimate entry into the spiritual realm. Presumably the sacrament is much like what Irenaeus (*Adversus Haereses* 1.21.3) describes among the Marcosian Valentinians:

For some of them prepare a bridechamber [νυμφών] and perform a mystical rite with those who are being perfected [i.e., initiated], pronouncing

certain invocations, and they affirm that it is a spiritual marriage which
is celebrated by them, after the likeness of the unions above.

It is also explained that if anyone becomes a son of the bridechamber, he will receive the light, but if anyone does not receive it while
he is in this world, he will not receive it in the other place; he who
does receive the light will not be seen and cannot be detained by the
hostile powers on his ascent to the world above (134.4–7; see also
118.5–9; 124.22–30).

Otherwise also the Gospel According to Philip is composed within
the general framework of Gnostic thought. The world, it is said, came
into being through a transgression (παράπτωμα, the word used of
Adam's trespass in Rom. 5:15–17, but here evidently referring to the
Gnostic Demiurge). "For," it is explained, "he who created it wanted to
create it indestructible and immortal, [but] he fell away and did not
attain to his hope" (123.3–6). As for the soul of the individual person,
"it is a precious thing, and it came into being in a despised body"
(104.25–26). Therefore it is fitting for us to acquire the resurrection
for ourselves while we are still in this world (presumably through
knowledge and the sacraments), "in order that when we strip off the
flesh we may be found in the Rest and not walk in the Middle [the
intermediate place between darkness and light, where the Demiurge
and the psychic natures will remain while the spirituals go on into the
Pleroma—Irenaeus, *Adversus Haereses* 1.7.1]" (114.18–20).

Remembering the representation in Pistis Sophia 42 of Jesus as
charging Philip, Thomas, and Matthew to write down what he said
and did, and given the Gospel According to Thomas and the Gospel
According to Philip in the Nag Hammadi Codex II (nos. 2 and 3), it
might be expected that the same codex might contain a "Gospel According to Matthew," but no work of such title appears there. Eusebius
(*Church History* 3.25.6) in fact mentions a "Gospel According to Matthias," and Clement of Alexandria (*Stromata* 2.9; 3.4; 7.13; 4.6) mentions "Traditions of Matthias the apostle" and gives several quotations,
but these are not of any marked Gnostic character. There is, however,
in Nag Hammadi Codex II (no. 7) a Book of Thomas the Contender,
and it begins with the words, "The secret words that the Savior spoke
to Judas Thomas which I, even I Matthias, wrote down,"[40] and it is
possible that this work could be considered the Gnostic Gospel According to Matthias (Matthew).[41]

40. John D. Turner, "A New Link in the Syrian Judas Thomas Tradition," in Martin Krause,
*Essays on the Nag Hammadi Texts in Honour of Alexander Böhlig* (NHS 3), 109–19.
41. Hennecke, *New Testament Apocrypha*. 1.312.

## The Gospel of the Egyptians

The work here under consideration is found in two versions in Nag Hammadi Codices III (no. 2) and IV (no. 2). In the colophon in Codex III (69.6–19) it is called both the Gospel of the Egyptians (by which title it is commonly known) and also the Holy Book of the Great Invisible Spirit.[42] The book is not related to an apocryphal Gospel of the Egyptians (known chiefly from quotations by Clement of Alexandria in his *Stromata*), although the apocryphal gospel also exhibits some Gnostic traits and is said by Hippolytus (*Refutation of Heresies* 5.2.8–9) to have been used by the Naassenes.[43]

The first section of the work (40.12–55.16a; citing the text of the Coptic Codex III.2) tells of the origin of the heavenly world. From the supreme God, who is the Great Invisible Spirit, there evolves a trinity made up of Father, Mother (Barbelo), and Son, and yet many more heavenly beings come into existence, arranged in many ogdoads. Most important in the climax of this first section is the heavenly Adam ("Adamas, the shining light"; 49.8), who asked for a son who might become the father of an incorruptible race (51.6–9). There came forth "the four great lights; Harmozel, Oroiael, Davithe, Eleleth, and the great incorruptible Seth, the son of the incorruptible man Adamas" (51.18–22).

The second section (55.16b–66.8a) has to do with the earthly race of Seth and with the work of Seth on their behalf. After five thousand years the great light Eleleth thinks it appropriate that a ruler over chaos and the underworld should come into being, and we hear now of Sophia and of how, from her, comes forth the great angel Saklas. Together with the great demon Nebruel, Saklas creates twelve angelic powers and sends them to become the rulers of the world. He then boasts of his work: "I, I am a [jealous] god, and apart from me nothing has [come into being]" (57.1–58.26).

The seeds of Seth are planted in this world, and in it are exposed to dangers of flood, conflagration, famine, and plague—afflictions that are originated by the devil (διάβολος). When Seth sees all of this he prays for the protection of his children, and four hundred ethereal angels come forth to guard them, and will do so until the consummation of the present aeon, when its Archons will be judged (61.1–62.24). But also by the will of the whole Pleroma Seth himself

---

42. Alexander Böhlig and Frederik Wisse, *Nag Hammadi Codices III,2 and IV,2: The Gospel of the Egyptians (The Holy Book of the Great Invisible Spirit)* (NHS 4). On the colophon, see also P. Bellet, "The Colophon of the *Gospel of the Egyptians*: Concessus and Macarius of Nag Hammadi," in R. M. Wilson, *Nag Hammadi and Gnosis* (NHS 14), 44–65.

43. Hennecke, *New Testament Apocrypha*, 1.166–78.

comes down into the midst of the perils of the world, puts on the living Jesus as a garment, and accomplishes a work of salvation on behalf of his children; those who are worthy of the baptism that he brings "will by no means taste death" (62.24–66.8a).

The third section of the book (66.8b–67.26) consists of hymns, including this word of praise near the end: "O God of silence! I honor thee completely. Thou art my place of rest." Finally the fourth section (68.1–69.17) designates the great Seth himself as the author of the book and, although the concluding colophon and title give the names for the work noted above, it would seem that it might well be called the Gospel According to Seth. As such it has some points of contact with what Irenaeus says about the Sethians (p. 233), and Epiphanius (*Panarion* 1.2.26.8.1) says that some of the Gnostics have books "in the name of Seth."[44]

### The Apocalypse of Adam

Along with books in the name of Seth, Epiphanius (*Panarion* 1.2.26.8.1) mentions Apocalypses of Adam,[45] and the fifth and final tractate in Nag Hammadi Codex V is a work named, both at the beginning and at the end of the text, the Apocalypse of Adam.[46] The book describes itself (64.2–4) as the revelation that Adam delivered to his son Seth in the seven hundredth year, which is presumably a reference to the Septuagint rendering of Genesis 5:4, in which Adam is said to have lived seven hundred years (not eight hundred as in the Hebrew text) after the birth of Seth. Therefore the revelation must have been passed on by Adam just before his own death. It seems that when Adam was first created out of the earth, along with Eve, they both possessed glory and knowledge of the eternal God, but the ruler (*archon*) of the Aeons and the powers acted against them and they lost the glory and the knowledge, were enslaved by the creator-god, and came under the domination of death (64.6–65.12; 67.10–13). Three men (65.26), however—obviously heavenly visitors—brought a revelation of future events to Adam, and this is what he transmitted to Seth, and Seth passed on to his seed (85.19–22).

The creator-god of the world will try to destroy humankind by flood, but Noah will be preserved and divide the earth among his sons, Shem, Ham, and Japheth (70.20–23; 72.15–17). Again fire and sulphur and asphalt (compare the account of Sodom and Gomorrah in Gen. 19:24)

---

44. Williams, *Panarion of Epiphanius*, 88.

45. Ibid.

46. George W. MacRae, "The Apocalypse of Adam," in Parrott, *Nag Hammadi Codices V.2–5 and VI*, 151–95.

will be cast upon the descendants of Ham and Japheth, but the three angels—Abrasax (the Greek letters correspond to the number 365, the days of the solar year), Sablo, and Gamaliel—will come to deliver them (75.9–11, 22–25). Then once again, for the third time (in sequence to the flood and the fire), the Illuminator (φωστήρ, "light-giver") of knowledge will come to bring salvation (76.8–22):

> And he will redeem their souls from the day of death. For the whole creation . . . will be under the authority of death. But those who reflect upon the knowledge of the eternal God in their heart[s] [i.e., the Gnostics] will not perish.[47]

In his work, however, even though he performs signs and wonders (77.1–2), the Illuminator will be attacked by the powers who rule the world. They cannot see the Illuminator himself, but "they will punish the flesh of the man upon whom the holy spirit has come" (77.14–18).

A long section (77.27–83.4) has to do with the origin of the Illuminator, and it concludes with the recognition by the Gnostics that God chose the Illuminator from all the Aeons to bring his knowledge to men.

Finally "the peoples" bless those who have known God with a knowledge of the truth, and declare that they will live forever, but of themselves they say that because they have served the "powers" their souls will die (83.9–84.3). Here three angelic powers are named, Micheu, Michar, and Mnesinous. They are described as "over the holy baptism and the living water," but are said to have defiled the water of life and to have drawn it within the will of the (evil) powers. For this, these three powers are obviously condemned, and the baptism they represent is repudiated. But in the very last lines of the text (85.30–31), as in the Gospel of the Egyptians (Nag Hammadi Codex III.2, 64.10–12), three more names are given—Yesseus, Mazareus, Yessedekeus—and these are called "imperishable illuminators" and are equated with "the living water." Thus these must be powers that dispense salvation,[48] and the living water is presumably the baptism approved by the Gnostics (presumably equated with the reception of *gnosis*) in contrast with the water baptism presided over by Micheu, Michar, and Mnesinous.

It is plain that this work depends heavily upon Jewish traditions— Adam, Noah, the flood, Sodom and Gomorrah, and the like—and it has been held by some that the book is quite lacking in anything that recalls Christianity and hence is to be taken as an example of non-

47. Ibid., 177.
48. Böhlig and Wisse, *Nag Hammadi Codices III,2 and IV,2*, 30.

Christian and probably pre-Christian Gnosticism. The repudiation of one type of baptism, however, may very well be understood as directed against the practice of the orthodox church,[49] and along with that could go avoidance of mention of other matters likewise connected with the orthodoxy from which the Gnostics separated themselves.[50] Furthermore, the figure of the Illuminator, who comes to redeem from death, upon whom the Holy Spirit descends, who works signs and wonders, and who is punished in the flesh, is surely a reflection of Jesus Christ, here interpreted as the Gnostic redeemer.[51]

### Other Works

The Paraphrase of Shem (Seem), which is the first tractate in Nag Hammadi Codex VII, has also been held by some to be both non-Christian and pre-Christian. Like the Apocalypse of Adam, however, this work also speaks against a water baptism that is imperfect, erroneous, and impure (30.25; 31.16; 37.14–38.9), and this is again probably the practice of the orthodox church as viewed by the Gnostics. Likewise the figure of the heavenly redeemer, here named Derdekeas, whose origin was in the light (8.24–25), who endured the wrath of the world, and who was victorious (36.13–14), is probably, like the Illuminator in the Apocalypse of Adam, patterned after Jesus Christ.[52]

Further in relation to Seth and his descendants, a work in Nag Hammadi Codex VII (no. 5) is entitled in its colophon "The Three Steles of Seth." In the opening of the text it is set forth as a revelation of Dositheos (presumably the little-known heretical leader named along with Simon and others by Hegesippus in Eusebius, *Church History* 4.22.5), who saw and understood the three steles. In content the text gives words of praise and prayer that appear to be those of the soul in some kind of ascent and descent in worship. The idea of the three steles may have developed out of a legend reported by Josephus (*Antiquities* 1.68–71) to the effect that the descendants of Seth discovered the science of the heavenly bodies and in order to prevent the loss of these discoveries—since Adam had predicted that the universe would be destroyed at one time by fire and at another by flood—inscribed

49. Klaus Koschorke, *Die Polemik der Gnostiker gegen das kirchliche Christentum* (NHS 12), 146–47.

50. Françoise Morard, "L'*Apocalypse d'Adam* de Nag Hammadi," in Martin Krause, *Gnosis und Gnosticism* (NHS 8), 35–42.

51. G. M. Shellrude, "The Apocalypse of Adam: Evidence for a Christian Gnostic Provenance," in Martin Krause, *Gnosis and Gnosticism* (NHS 17), 82–91.

52. Koschorke, *Die Polemik der Gnostiker*, 146; Karl M. Fischer, "Die Paraphrase des Seem," in Martin Krause, *Essays on the Nag Hammadi Texts in Honour of Pahor Labib* (NHS 6), 261, 266.

them on two pillars, one of brick that would survive the fire and one of stone that would survive the flood.

There is also a work called in its colophon the "Second Treatise of the Great Seth" (Nag Hammadi Codex VII.2). Other than in the colophon the name of Seth is not found in the text, which consists of a revelation discourse of Christ, but it is possible that Christ is meant to be identified with Seth as in the Gospel of the Egyptians, where Seth puts on the living Jesus as a garment. The docetic view that is probably implied in that representation is here made explicit as Christ says (55.10–56.19): "I did not die in reality but in appearance. . . . It was another, Simon, who bore the cross on his shoulder. . . . But I was rejoicing in the height. . . . And I was laughing at their ignorance"— exactly the view that is attributed by Irenaeus (*Adversus Haereses* 1.24.4) to the Basilidians.[53]

The same view is also in the Apocalypse of Peter (Nag Hammadi Codex VII.3, 81.15–23) where the Savior says to the apostle Peter: "He whom you saw on the tree, glad and laughing, this is the living Jesus. But this one into whose hands and feet they drive the nails is his fleshly part, which is the substitute being put to shame, the one who came into being in his likeness."[54]

On the other hand in a tractate (Nag Hammadi Codex IX.1) in which Melchizedek is apparently identified with Jesus Christ and in which there is favorable reference to the congregation of the children of Seth, there is an antidocetic view, and those are opposed who say that "he is unfleshly, though he has come in the flesh, [and that] he did not come to suffering [though] he came to suffering" (5.7–8).

## Common Elements in the Gnostic Systems

From the above materials it is evident that there is much variety in the Gnostic systems, and even antithetical positions are found. There are also, however, not a few elements that recur frequently and may be taken as defining the common outlines of Gnosticism.

In philosophy the basic concept is that of anticosmic dualism. In the Gathas of Zarathushtra, the holy spirit of the Wise Lord, the Architect of the world, is opposed by the hostile spirit; and in the *Manual of Discipline* from Qumran (1QS 3.13–4.26), God, from whom all exists, assigned man two spirits, the one of truth and light, the other of perversion and darkness, between whom to choose. But in both Zo-

53. *Nag Hammadi Library in English,* 332.
54. Ibid., 344.

roastrianism and Judaism the world itself, the work of God, is essentially good. The Gnostic dualism, however, although it may be influenced by both of the foregoing, is distinguished by its negative assessment of the visible universe as a realm of evil and of darkness.

In theology, therefore, the creation and rule of an evil universe cannot be assigned to a good God. Rather the maker of what is seen must have been an intermediate power (a Demiurge) and likewise the associates of the Demiurge (the Archons, who are the powers and rulers operative in the various spheres of being) must be of less than good character. So the supreme God, who is the ultimate lord of the universe, must reside far above, so far, indeed, as to be the "unknown" God. Here there is a sense of an ineffable spiritual reality, which goes even beyond the saying of Ecclesiastes 5:2, "God is in heaven, and you upon earth; therefore let your words be few," for the Gnostic God dwells in the silence and is describable, if at all, in negatives.

In cosmology, the Gnostic picture of the universe is not necessarily different in externals from that of the ancient world in general. As there, here too we hear of the earth, the underworld, the planetary spheres, and so on. What is distinctive is the dualistic view already described, according to which the origin of this universe goes back to lower powers, and that these, although often called angels, are hostile to God and to humanity.

In anthropology, the same dualistic view sees human beings as presently entrapped in the material universe and, unless enlightened, even ignorant that there is anything other than this dark and evil place. The dualism also extends, however, to the picture of the human being, whose inmost nature is seen as a spark of light from the world of light and goodness above, itself presently entrapped in a material body (σῶμα, sometimes in parallel with σῆμα, "tomb"). As well as "spark" (σπινθήρ), the innermost self is called "spirit" (πνεῦμα) and "soul" (ψυχή). Persons may also be divided into two or three classes, the "spiritual" (πνευματικός), the "psychic" (ψυχικός, usually meaning unspiritual), and the "fleshly" (σαρκικός), "earthly" (χοικός), or "hylic" (from Greek ὕλ, "matter," meaning sinful, hostile to God).

In soteriology, therefore, that which is fundamentally necessary is "knowledge" (γνῶσις) of the true nature of the self, that is, of its heavenly origin and proper heavenly home, to which, given this knowledge, it can hope to return. The "knowledge" can also include information needed about the spheres between earth and heaven, the powers that control these spheres, and the procedures and passwords necessary for passing there in the final ascent of the soul after death. While the transcendent God is unknown and unknowable, he commissions the Savior, and it is the essential work of the Savior to bring this knowledge. Revelations of saving knowledge come also from other heavenly beings, in visions and dreams, and the like.

In Christology (a term properly applicable, since the picture of the Gnostic Savior is at least usually and perhaps always patterned after Christ), there are docetic views, that is, the Savior who is a light-being from above only "seems" (from Greek δοκέω) to be in the person of Jesus, and departs before suffering (thus, e.g., in the Second Treatise of the Great Seth and in the Apocalypse of Peter), but also antidocetic views, contradicting the former (e.g., in the Melchizedek tractate).

In ethics, the view of the present world as inherently evil can also lead to contradictory positions. Since the world is evil anyway, it does not matter what is done in it, and libertinism can follow (e.g., Basilides and Carpocrates, along with Ptolemaeus's allowance for any conduct by the "spirituals"). On the other hand it can be deemed necessary to withdraw from and stay aloof from the evil world in every way possible, and the ascetic call to renounce the body and its desires can follow (e.g., Saturninus, Marcion, and Ptolemaeus's teaching for the "psychics").

Finally, in eschatology, the Gnostic systems envision not only the end-experience of the individual, for whom death is liberation from entanglement in matter and the beginning of the ascent of the soul to its proper heavenly home, but also the end-goal for the whole cosmos. This cosmic end-goal is the bringing back or the "restoration" (ἀποκατάστασις) of all things (e.g., Nag Hammadi Codices I.5, Tripartite Tractate 123.19–23; and VI.8, Asclepius 74.7–11; Irenaeus, Adversus Haereses 1.14.1). The purified and returned sparks of light will come back to the Father and be gathered together in the Pleroma, whereby the "deficiency" (ὑστέρημα) in the Pleroma, due to the fall of Sophia and all that ensued (e.g., Nag Hammadi Codex III.2, Gospel of the Egyptians 59.18) will be made good, and the original complete state of "rest" (ἀνάπαυσις; Irenaeus, Adversus Haereses 1.2.6) be re-established.[55] On the other side of the matter the whole natural order, with all the evil and darkness by which it has been characterized, will be brought to an end (Nag Hammadi Codex VII.1, Paraphrase of Shem 45.8–31; 48.8–27):

Then Nature [φύσις] will have a final opportunity. And the stars will cease from the sky. The mouth of error will be opened in order that the evil Darkness may become idle and silent. And in the last day the forms of Nature will be destroyed with the winds and all their demons; they will become a dark lump [βῶλος, i.e., sealed up and rendered harmless],

55. Helderman, Die Anapausis im Evangelium Veritatis, 179.

just as they were from the beginning. And the sweet waters which were
burdened by the demons will perish. . . . The other works of Nature will
not be manifest. They will mix with the infinite waters of darkness. And
all her forms will cease from the middle region. . . .

Blessed are they who guard themselves against the heritage of death,
which is the burdensome water of darkness. . . . When the consummation
has come and Nature has been destroyed, then their minds will separate
from the Darkness. Nature has burdened them for a short time. And
they will be in the ineffable light of the unbegotten Spirit without a
[bodily] form [any more].[56]

## Relationships with Orthodoxy

From the Coptic Gnostic papyri (and their Greek originals) it is
evident that the Christian Gnostic systems developed for some centuries alongside the orthodox forerunner of the main Christian church,
and were distinguished by such matters as giving priority to immediate experience rather than ecclesiastical structure, teaching that
ignorance rather than sin is the cause of suffering, recognizing a feminine as well as a masculine element in the divine, explaining the
resurrection of Christ as spiritual rather than bodily, and pointing to
self-knowledge as knowledge of God.[57]

Whereas orthodoxy contended for "the faith which was once for all
delivered to the saints" (Jude 3), a faith that is "ever one and the same"
(Irenaeus, Adversus Haereses 1.10.2), and did not look with favor on
other options, the Gnostics could be considered open to the expectation
that the Holy Spirit would continue to "teach . . . all things" (John
14:26). Thus they came to alternative thoughts and practices that were
plainly meaningful to many, and that have continued to be of influence
in various forms of religious tradition, including the esoteric.

56. The Nag Hammadi Library in English, 327–28.
57. Elaine H. Pagels, The Gnostic Gospels; and idem, The Gnostic Jesus and Early Christian
Politics.

# 8

# Mandaean Religion

The Mandaean religion takes its name from the Mandaean word *mandaia*, which means "having knowledge." The language in which the sacred books of the religion are written is also known as Mandaean or Mandaic, and is a dialect of Eastern Aramaic.[1] In this language the noun *manda* means "knowledge" (corresponding to Greek γνῶσις), and the adjective *mandaia* (corresponding to Greek γνωστικός, "a gnostic, one having knowledge") designates a Mandaean (layman), while the plural *mandaiia* (masc.) and *mandaiata* (fem.) are used for both priests and lay Mandaeans.[2]

There is also a verb *naṣar*, which means "to keep back or keep secret," and from this is derived the noun *naṣiruta* (or *naṣaruta*), which means "secret knowledge" and is used to refer to the esoteric knowledge communicated only to initiates. From this usage a select group among the priests who have received this knowledge are called *naṣuraiia* or Nasoraeans, but the term is also used in the broad sense as parallel to Mandaean, for example, in the *Right Ginza*: "Instruct the Nasoraeans and Mandaeans [*naṣuraiia umandaiia*] and chosen ones whom thou hast chosen out of the world."[3]

The traditional home of the Mandaeans as known in relatively modern times is in the marshy region of the lower Tigris and Euphrates (in the heart of old Sumer) in Iraq, and along the Karun River in Khuzistan in southwestern Iran. Now a dwindling remnant, the Mandaeans have been largely displaced in the Mesopotamian marshes by the Marsh Arabs but, known as the Sabbaeans or Subba, they are still scattered in small numbers between Amara, Qurna, Nasiriyah, and

---

1. Rudolf Macuch, *Handbook of Classical and Modern Mandaic*.
2. E. S. Drower and R. Macuch, *A Mandaic Dictionary*, 247.
3. Mark Lidzbarski, *Ginzā: Der Schatz; oder, Das Grosse Buch der Mandäer*, 296.17–18; Drower and Macuch, *Mandaic Dictionary*, 285–86; references to *Right Ginza* and *Left Ginza* follow Lidzbarski's page and line numbers.

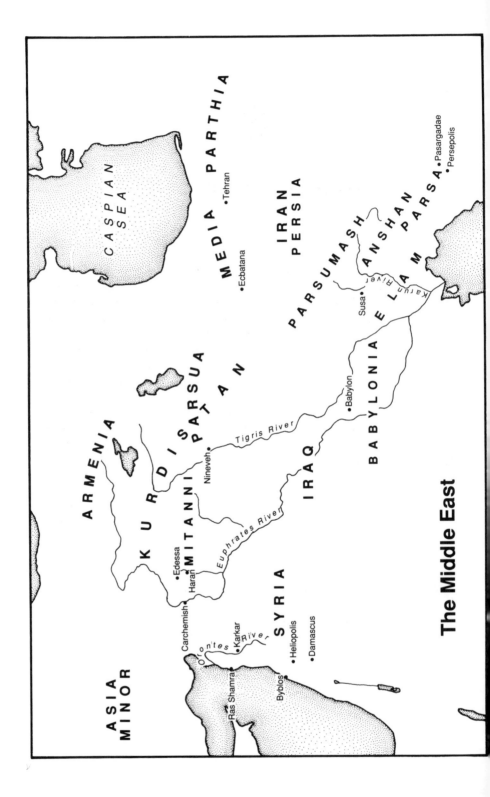

The Middle East

Suq esh-Shiukh and are also found in Basra, Baghdad, and other cities, as well as in Ahwaz in Khuzistan.[4]

Explorers and inquirers began to provide information about the Mandaeans in works published in Europe from 1560 onward, and at that time they were said to number about fifteen thousand. The first Mandaean manuscript (the *Diwan Abatur*) was brought to Europe in 1622. Now an extensive Mandaean literature is available and has been the subject of many studies.[5]

## Literature

The available Mandaean literature is almost entirely religious in character.[6] The chief work, which amounts to the Bible of the Mandaeans, is the codex known as the *Ginza* or "Treasure," also called the *Sidra Rabba* or "Great Book," and the "Book of Adam."[7] The first part is the "right hand [*iamina*]" *Ginza,* and comprises a collection of eighteen theological, mythological, cosmological, and moral treatises;[8] the second and smaller part is the "left hand [*smala*]" *Ginza,* and contains hymns and songs of the soul on its ascent after death to the heavenly realm of light.

Another relatively large work is the "Book of John," also called the "Book of the Kings."[9] This is a collection of thirty-seven named tractates (divided in Mark Lidzbarski's edition into seventy-six chapters), largely mythological and legendary in content. The name *John* (Jahja/Johana) refers to John the Baptist, of whom there are narratives and sermons in the tractate that bears his name (chaps. 18–33). As for this being also a book of "Kings," the latter is a Mandaean title of heavenly light-beings, many of whom have a place in the book: one, the great light-spirit, Joshamin, gives his name to an early tractate in the book (chaps. 3–10).

The largest assemblage of ritual texts is the *Qolasta* ("Collection") or "The Canonical Prayerbook of the Mandaeans." Probably existing

4. E. S. Drower, *The Mandaeans of Iraq and Iran*; Gavin Young, *Return to the Marshes*; and idem, *Iraq: Land of Two Rivers,* 173–74.

5. For Mandaean bibliography, see Svend Aage Pallis, *Essay on Mandaean Bibliography 1560–1930*; Macuch, *Handbook of Classical and Modern Mandaic,* 467–77; and idem, *Zur Sprache und Literatur der Mandäer,* 245–50.

6. Kurt Rudolph, *Mandaeism,* 2; and idem, in Macuch, *Zur Sprache und Literatur der Mandäer,* 147–70.

7. Lidzbarski, *Ginzā.*

8. Wilhelm Brandt, *Mandäische Schriften.*

9. Mark Lidzbarski, *Das Johannesbuch der Mandäer*; references to the "Book of John" follow Lidzbarski's chapter numbers.

The marshes of Lower Mesopotamia, former home of the Mandaeans

originally as separate scrolls, the texts here contained include prayers, hymns, and songs for various ceremonies, especially for baptism, the mass of the soul, and so on.[10]

Other texts are known as "secret scrolls," being accessible only to the Mandaean priests. These include a rite of marriage called "The Marriage Ceremony of the Great Shishlam," and a rite for the consecration or "coronation" of priests called "The Coronation of the Great Shishlam." As the titles indicate, the ceremony is in each case that of Shishlam Rba. The name *Shishlam* means "perfected perfection," and is the Mandaean name for the Divine Man, who personifies perfected and perfect humanity. His title *rba* means "great," and is also the word for a teacher, master, and initiator. Thus in the rites here described the Great Shishlam is regarded as the personification or prototype of the bridegroom and of the priest in their respective cases.[11]

A very lengthy scroll known as "The Thousand and Twelve Questions" contains secret ritual and moral instructions, which are never imparted to the laity and are only given to the young priest at his initiation into the priesthood. The seven texts that compose the scroll deal with the mass of the soul, the ceremonies of marriage, burial, baptism, and the like.[12]

Two other "secret scrolls," short commentaries that have to do chiefly with the ceremony for the dead, are called "The Great First World"

10. Mark Lidzbarski, *Mandäische Liturgien*; E. S. Drower, *The Canonical Prayerbook of the Mandaeans.*

11. E. S. Drower, *Šarḥ ḏ Qabin ḏ Šišlam Rba (D.C. 38): Explanatory Commentary on the Marriage-Ceremony of the Great Šišlam*; and idem, *The Coronation of the Great Šišlam.*

12. E. S. Drower, *The Thousand and Twelve Questions.*

and "The Lesser First World."[13] Both are illustrated with relatively crude drawings of holy trees and plants, probably pictures of spiritual worlds and beings.[14]

Another category of works is that of the so-called *Diwan*s, a term that usually means a miscellaneous collection from various authors. The *Diwan*s are said to number twenty-four, all in the form of scrolls, some with illustrations. The *Diwan Abatur* or "Progress Through the Purgatories" is preserved in a scroll about twenty feet long and is named for the light-being (Abatur) who weighs the soul in the beyond. Along with the text the illustrations, in an almost cubist and evidently conventionalized art style, depict the purgatories and their demons, the moon ship, the sun ship, the ship that ferries the souls of the righteous from the earth to the world of Abatur, the scales for the weighing of the soul, the heavenly baptizers in the world of Abatur who baptize the souls in the heavenly Jordan, and so on.[15]

The "Diwan of the Baptism of Hibil Ziwa" describes a baptism (*maṣbuta*) that a Mandaean priest must undergo if he has suffered pollution by infringement, even accidental or involuntary, of ritual rules. As the prototype of such happening, it seems that the light-being Hibil Ziwa ("Light Giver") was sent into the seven worlds of darkness to perform certain tasks and incurred such pollution that he could not return to the world of light until he underwent a ritual meal (*zidqa brika*, "blessed oblation") and a baptism, and these happenings are related and pictured in the work in question.[16]

Hibil Ziwa also figures in the "Book of the Zodiac" (*Sfar Malwasha*), which he is said to have given to Adam Paghra (the physical Adam) so that Adam might be able to foresee coming events. The work is indeed consulted by Mandaean priests for all sorts of astronomical knowledge in respect of the naming of a child, the choice of auspicious days, and the like.[17]

In all the Mandaean literature, only one work professes to give information about the early history of the Mandaeans. This is a fragmentary scroll of 248 lines that bears the title *Haran Gawaita* ("Inner Haran") and is also called the "Diwan of the Great Revelation." The text is very broken and obscure.[18]

13. E. S. Drower, *A Pair of Naṣoraean Commentaries (Two Priestly Documents): The Great First World and the Lesser First World*.

14. Rudolph, *Mandaeism*, plates xib, xiib.

15. E. S. Drower, *Diwan Abatur; or, Progress Through the Purgatories*; Rudolph, *Mandaeism*, plates vi–x.

16. E. S. Drower, *The Haran Gawaita and the Baptism of Hibil-Ziwa*, 27–96; Rudolph, *Mandaeism*, plate xia.

17. E. S. Drower, *The Book of the Zodiac*.

18. Drower, *Haran Gawaita*, 3–23.

There are also many Mandaean texts engraved on lead tablets or rolls and inscribed on clay bowls (usually on the interior of the bowls). These are predominantly of magical import, intended as incantations, exorcisms, and the like; as such they name many spiritual beings, both beneficent and maleficent.[19] An example is a lead amulet, usually dated about A.D. 400. Along with much about the evil influence of the planets, the misfortunes that beset the city, and the affliction that is on the threshold, there is this appeal (lines 115–18):

> In the name of Life! May there be protection, and health to the house, to the wife, and to the sons and daughters, to the door, and to the threshold, and to the body of Per Nukraya, son of Abandukt![20]

## Date

The extant Mandaean literature is relatively late, the oldest dated manuscript bearing a date in the year 936 of the Muslim reckoning, equivalent to A.D. 1529/1530.[21] Nevertheless the present manuscripts certainly contain much earlier materials.

In the "Book of John" (chap. 22) the Muslims press the Mandaeans to say who their prophet is, what their holy book is, and to whom they pray, the intent of the questioning evidently being to establish whether the Mandaeans should be included along with the Jews and the Christians in the tolerated status of "peoples of the book" (ahl al-kitab). In this respect Muhammad says in the Quran (5.68–69; see also 2.62; 22.17):

> O People of the Book, you follow no good till you observe the Torah and the Gospel and that which is revealed to you from your Lord. . . . Surely those who believe and those who are Jews and the Sabeans and the Christians—whoever believes in Allah and the Last Day and does good—they shall have no fear nor shall they grieve.[22]

Here the Sabeans are evidently considered to possess written scriptures even as the Jews have the Torah and the Christians have the Gospel (in Quran 22.17 the Magians, i.e., the Zoroastrians, are named

---

19. Edwin M. Yamauchi, *Mandaic Incantation Texts*; Fulvio Franco, "A Mandaic Lead Fragment from Tell Baruda (Choche)," *Mesopotamia* (Florence) 17 (1982): 147–50.

20. Yamauchi, *Mandaic Incantation Texts,* 2, 6–7, 235–55.

21. Macuch, *Handbook of Classical and Modern Mandaic,* lvi.

22. Maulana Muhammad Ali, *The Holy Qur'ān,* 262; see also 31 n. 103.

along with the Sabeans, Jews, and Christians as people with a "book," namely the Avesta).

In a work called *Kitab al-Fihrist* ("Catalogue of the Sciences"), written by al-Nadim in A.D. 988, there is mention of the Mughtasilah ("those who wash themselves," i.e., practice ablutions), described as very numerous in the marshlands of southern Iraq and called the "Sabeans of the Marshes"; "they observe ablution as a rite and wash everything which they eat."[23] These Mughtasilah/Sabeans are probably Mandaeans or include the Mandaeans and, as noted above, it is by the name of Sabeans (Sabbaeans/Subba) that the present-day Mandaeans are still known in Iraq.

Therefore the Sabeans in the Quran are probably also to be identified as the Mandaeans or as including the Mandaeans, thus indicating that Mandaean written texts must already have been brought together in some collected form so as to constitute a "book" and to authenticate the Mandaeans as "people of the book" by the time of Muhammad and the time when the Arabs brought Islam to Mesopotamia in the seventh century A.D. Very possibly it was in order to substantiate further their position in this very regard that the Mandaean *Ginza* was also called the "Book of Adam," and their "Book of the Kings" was also named for John (the Baptist)—both Adam and John the Baptist being prominent in the Quran.[24]

In colophons in the "Canonical Prayerbook of the Mandaeans" (71, 171) and other books the copying of the manuscript is traced in reverse sequence through a long series of copyists all the way to a certain Zazai d-Gawazta in the year 272 of the present era. If these references may be trusted we are carried back to the second half of the third century A.D. for the writing down of at least part of the "Canonical Prayerbook" and other works.[25]

It has also been shown that some of the poems in the Coptic "Psalms of Thomas," ascribed to Thomas, one of the first disciples of Mani (A.D. 216–277), are virtual adaptations of some of the Mandaean poetry (especially in the *masiqta*-hymns); thus again it is indicated that Mandaean texts existed in written form already in the third century A.D.[26]

Exact dating of the magical texts mentioned above is difficult: those on lead tablets or rolls are attributed to the third to the fifth centu-

---

23. Bayard Dodge, *The Fihrist of al-Nadim*, 2.811, 922, see under Sabians(2).

24. Kurt Rudolph, *Die Mändäer*, 1.23, 36–44, 70; and idem, *Mandaeism*, 2.

25. Macuch, *Handbook of Classical and Modern Mandaic*, lxv–lxvi. References to the "Canonical Prayerbook of the Mandaeans" are given according to page numbers in Drower, *Canonical Prayerbook of the Mandaeans*.

26. Torgny Säve-Söderbergh, *Studies in the Coptic Manichaean Psalm-Book*.

ries A.D. Although their specialized content is of limited value with respect to the religion as a whole, they are seen as the earliest datable original Mandaean documents. The similar texts on clay bowls are attributed to the fifth to the seventh centuries A.D.[27]

In spite of the relatively late date of the Mandaean literature, it is held by some that the Mandaean religion, as well as Gnosticism in general, is pre-Christian and is indeed presupposed in early Christianity. Thus it is argued, for example, that the Gnostic/Mandaean redeemer myth is the basis of the presentation of Jesus as the heavenly revealer and redeemer in the fourth Gospel.[28] The only first-century evidence for this view, however, has to be taken from the New Testament itself (where other explanations of background are possible); therefore the theory remains speculative.[29]

It is also to be noted that Epiphanius (*Panarion* 1.18.1.1ff.; 1.29.6.1ff.)[30] mentions "a sect of the Nasaraeans [αἵρεσις τῶν Νασαραῖων]," which "was before Christ, and did not know Christ," and distinguishes them from the Jewish-Christian Nazoraeans (Ναζωραῖοι), the latter so named because of the city of Nazareth (see Matt. 2:23). Since the Mandaeans called themselves Nasoraeans, the statement of Epiphanius could be evidence for the Mandaean movement as pre-Christian in date. Epiphanius, however, describes the Nasaraeans as practicing Judaism "in all respects" (which the Mandaeans did not do) and does not describe the Nasaraeans as practicing baptism (which the Mandaeans did). Thus it hardly appears likely that these pre-Christian Nasaraeans are the Mandaeans, even though the Mandaeans later used much the same name.[31]

Accordingly, on the basis of the concrete evidence of the dates for the actual Mandaean literature adduced above, extending from the Islamic period (seventh century A.D.) back to the third century A.D., the origin of the Mandaean movement may more probably be placed in the third or perhaps in the second century A.D.[32]

## World History

In no less than seven of the eighteen tractates of the *Right Ginza* (1, 2, 3, 10, 13, 15, 18) there are accounts, not always consistent, of

27. Kurt Rudolph, in Macuch, *Zur Sprache und Literatur der Mandäer,* 162–63.

28. Rudolph, *Die Mandäer,* 1.19, 101 and n. 4.

29. Raymond E. Brown, *The Gospel According to John,* 1.liv–lvi.

30. Karl Holl, *Ancoratus und Panarion haer. 1–33,* 215ff., 321ff.; Frank Williams, *The Panarion of Epiphanius of Salamis: Book I (Sects 1–46),* 42ff., 112ff.; Henry M. Shires, "The Meaning of the Term 'Nazarene,'" *ATR* 28 (1947): 19–27, esp. 22–23.

31. Edwin M. Yamauchi, *Gnostic Ethics and Mandaean Origins,* 60–62.

32. Ibid., 71.

the creation and history of the world.[33] In the first tractate, (5ff.) the account begins with the supreme Being, who is called the great King of Light (*Malka d-Nhura*), and whose dwelling (like that of El in the Ras Shamra texts, see p. 138) is in the high North (7.3). He is also called the Great Soul (*Mana Rabba*) and the Lord of Greatness (*Mara d-Rabutha*).

The world of the King of Light is a world of light and brilliance, of goodness and truth, and of eternity without death (10.35ff.). There is another world, however, and it is full of evil and falsehood, a world of darkness without light, and of death without life in eternity (14.30ff.). Into this latter world the King of Light sent Hibil Ziwa ("the Light Giver"; see p. 263), here identified with Gabriel, with the command that heaven and earth, plants and animals, and the man Adam and his wife Hawwa should come into being (15.1ff.). In the second tractate the same events transpire, but while Hibil Ziwa forms the world of light, it is another spirit-being, Ptahil (the name possibly derived from the Egyptian Ptah),[34] who is the Demiurge and actual creator of the physical universe (33.31).

In the third tractate we hear of a primal "fruit," out of which everything was derived, and of *mana* ("spirit, intelligence"), out of which came the "First Life" (*Hiia Qadmaiia*). By the prayer of the First Life, the Second Life, named Joshamin, arose, and also the Uthras, which are subsidiary life-giving and life-sustaining spirits (66.14ff.). The Uthras are innumerable; three bear the names of Hibil (i.e., Abel), Shitil (i.e., Seth), and Anos (i.e., Enoch); and they are incarnate in *Manda d-Hiia* who is the personification of knowledge (*gnosis*) and the outstanding savior-spirit of the Mandaean religion.[35]

At this point in the third tractate *Manda d-Hiia* descends into the underworld where he encounters the evil spirits of the darkness, with Ruha at their head. In Hebrew the corresponding word רוּחַ (*rûaḥ*) simply means "spirit," but here Ruha is an evil female demon. Her son Ur is the king of the darkness (81.3ff.). Ruha is also the mother of the Seven (planets, including the sun and the moon) and the Twelve (signs of the zodiac). Ur is a great serpent or dragon who lies upon "the black water" under the earth, with seven underworlds of darkness below him and seven firmaments above him.[36] In the outcome of the confrontation *Manda d-Hiia* is able to overcome and bind the king of the darkness and enclose his entire dwelling with an iron wall (87.13ff.).

---

33. Drower, *Mandaeans of Iraq and Iran*, 73.

34. Drower and Macuch, *Mandaic Dictionary*, 383–84.

35. Ibid., 247.

36. Wilhelm Brandt, *Die mandaïsche Religion,* 61–62; Drower, *Mandaeans of Iraq and Iran,* 252–56.

In further respect of the creation, in the third tractate we learn that from the origin of the earth to Adam was 360,000 years; from Adam to the end of the world will be 480,000 years (107.3ff.). Ptahil the Demiurge called upon the planets to assist in the creation of Adam, but when the planets made Adam there was no soul in him and he was unable to stand upon his feet (108.4ff.). Thereupon the First Life sent Hibil, Shitil, and Anos as helpers to infuse soul, brought from the world of light, into Adam; they also gave him Hawwa (Eve) as his wife (108.4ff.).[37] The human being is, therefore, a composite creature with the spirit enclosed in a material body; with knowledge of its celestial origin the spirit may, at death, ascend to its proper home above.

Another version of the creative work of Ptahil the Demiurge is in the fifteenth tractate of the *Right Ginza* (351.16–31). Here Ptahil utters seven cries: with the first cry he composed the earth, called Tibil, and stretched out the firmament; with the second cry he distributed the Jordans and canals in the earth; with the third cry he created the fish in the sea and the feathered birds of every sort; with the fourth cry he created all vegetables and seeds; through his fifth cry all evil vermin and reptiles came into being; through the sixth cry the whole formation of the darkness arose; and through his seventh cry there arose the female demon Ruha and her seven sons, the planets.

After Adam the history of the world unfolds (in the first, second, and eighteenth tractates of the *Right Ginza*; 27.19–28.15; 45.22–46.12; 408.24–410.13) in four periods. These periods are marked by three catastrophes and by the names of their survivors, and in the fourth place by the founding and existence of Jerusalem, the periods of time being stated in terms both of generations and of thousands of years. The world was "swept away" the first time by sword and pestilence, the survivors being the otherwise unknown Ram and his wife Rud, thirty generations and 216,000 years after Adam; the second time by fire, the survivors being the also otherwise unknown Shurbai and his wife Sharhabel, twenty-five generations and 156,000 years after Ram and Rud; the third time by flood, the survivors being the biblical Noah and his son Shem, fifteen generations and 100,000 years after Shurbai and Sharhabel. Then, six generations and 6,000 years after Noah, Jerusalem was built, to stand 1,000 years in "blossom" and 1,000 years in "devastation," when the whole earth (*tibil*) shall be destroyed

---

37. At a place where the text is broken (109.29; see also 245.9–10) there is the name Adakas-Mana; this name (also Adam Kasia) is that of the spiritual Adam, while Adam Paghra is the physical Adam; the spiritual Adam and Hawwa (Eve) dwell in Mshunia Kushta, a spiritual world in which the prototypes of all earthly things and beings exist (Svend Aage Pallis, *Mandaean Studies*, 108; Drower, *Diwan Abatur*, 41; Drower and Macuch, *Mandaic Dictionary*, 7, 280).

(410.13). The total of the years is 480,000, already noted as the total time from Adam to the end of the world (107.4–5).[38]

As for the founding of Jerusalem, it was "Jorabba, whom the Jews name Adonai, he, his companion Ruha and the seven planets," who took this under consideration, and at the command of Adonai they built the city (410.8–11; see also 25.10–11). Adonai (*adunai*) is of course the Hebrew word *Lord* (אֲדֹנָי [*'ădōnāy*]); Jorabba (*iurba*) appears elsewhere in the *Right Ginza* as the keeper of one of the purgatories (188.25), and is probably a sun-spirit, since elsewhere it is Shamash (*shamish*), the sun itself, who is said to be the same as Adonai (25.7; 135.9–10); Ruha we have already met as the female demon who is the mother of the seven planets.[39] It was therefore under evil influences, according to this representation, that Jerusalem came into being, and the added characterization of the Jewish people, who are evidently considered sun worshipers, is extremely unflattering (25.11–19; 43.8–15).

After this we hear of Abraham and Moses, both of whom are described as prophets of the evil Ruha (43.21–23; 46.10; 410.14ff.). As for King Solomon, of whom we hear too, the demons were subject to him until he glorified himself and became unthankful for the goodness of his Lord; then the demons turned away from him and he lost his rule; "whoever glorifies himself must then cause shame for himself" (28.16–21; 46.13–18).

When four hundred years went by in Jerusalem, Jesus, son of Mary (*Miriam*) and head of the Christians, was born; he created a church for himself and gathered a community to himself (410.31ff.). Jesus Christ was baptized by John (*Johana*) and became wise through the wisdom of John, but then distorted the words of John, altered the baptism in the Jordan, and preached sacrilege and deceit in the world (51.14–17). His name is Immanuel (*Amunel*) and he called himself Jesus the Savior, but he is a false Messiah (29.19; 47.16–19). He was the son of Ruha (248.8–9) and is one of the seven angels who lead people astray: (1) the Sun, (2) Venus, (3) "Christ, the falsifier, who falsifies the original doctrine," (4) the Moon, (5) Saturn, (6) Jupiter, and (7) Mars (46.29–35). *Ginza* tells its readers to not fear Christ the Roman (i.e., Byzantine, presumably so-called in reflection of the hostility between the Byzantine church and the Mandaeans), who alters the genuine revelation, nor to allow the planets, Ruha, and Christ to exercise lordship over them (49.14–15; 437.12–13). One of the purgatories is that of Jesus Christ, in which are found those who denied the

38. Brandt, *Die mandäische Religion,* 123.
39. Drower and Macuch, *Mandaic Dictionary,* 7, 191, 428–29, 443.

life and confessed Christ (186.40ff.). On the day when heaven and earth end, Ruha, Christ, the sun, the moon, and the planets, and those who have made confession to them, will fall to the king of darkness and to the final fire (203.11ff.; 255.22ff.). Thus the Mandaeans, in spite of some knowledge of biblical data, express as violent opposition to Christianity as to Judaism.

In addition to the mention of John the Baptist in the *Ginza* 51.12–52.14, there is another section in the *Right Ginza* (190.22–196.23) about John, in which we are told of the baptism of *Manda d-Hiia* by John and of John's death and ascent to the world of light. Also there is a long section about Jahja/Johana in the book that bears his name ("Book of John" 75–123). In all, however, except for John's baptismal work in the Jordan River (including the baptism of Jesus), and a few details such as the names (Zakhria and Enishbai) and advanced age of his parents, there is very little contact between the Mandaean tradition and the New Testament narratives concerning John; rather John appears fully as a prophet of the Mandaean religion (so also in the *Haran Gawaita*).

After a final reference to Jesus the head of the Christians in the eighteenth tractate of the *Right Ginza,* the text continues (411.6ff.) with further respect to world history with a listing of early Iranian kings including the Kayanians Luhrasp and Gushtasp (Vishtaspa), of others including Solomon son of David, and of Sandar (Alexander) the Greek. Somewhat thereafter we come to the name of King Ardban, and are therefore evidently in the time of the Parthian (Arsacid) dynasty (c. 250 B.C.–A.D. 226), for there were no less than five kings of that dynasty named Artabanus, with dates as follows: I (211–191 B.C.), II (128–123 B.C.), III (A.D. 12–38), IV (A.D. 80–81), and V (A.D. 212–226).[40] This Ardban, who is the only one named in the *Ginza,* must be Artabanus V, for after attributing to him a reign of fourteen years, it is said that "after him were Persian kings," with Ardshir at their head. The latter were the Sasanians or Neo-Persians, with Ardashir I (A.D. 226–241) as the founder of the Sasanian Empire.[41] Then, after the "Persian kings," come the "Arabian kings," and of them it is said that they will reign for seventy-one years (414.18). Seventy-one years after the first Arab forces entered Persia (A.D. 632) and the last Sasanian king was killed (Yazdegerd III, d. 651) would reach only into the early eighth century. Since the Arabs actually ruled much longer, this tractate must have been compiled sometime around the middle of the seventh century (407).

40. Jacob Neusner, *A History of the Jews in Babylonia*, 1.164; *CHI* 3.1.98–99; 3.2.783.
41. Neusner, *History of the Jews in Babylonia*, 2.1, 4; *CHI* 3.1.119.

## Mandaean History

The broken text of the *Haran Gawaita,* which alone in the Mandaean literature professes to give historical information about the early history of the Mandaeans (whom it calls Nasoraeans), begins in the middle of a sentence with reference to an anonymous "him" whose identity has been lost:

> and Haran Gawaita receiveth him and that city in which there were Nasoraeans, because there was no road for the Jewish rulers. Over them was King Ardban. And sixty thousand Nasoraeans abandoned the Sign of the Seven and entered the Median hills, a place where we were free from domination by all other races. [3][42]

In the continuation of the text we are told that the Nasoraeans loved the Lord, that is, Adonai, until Mary, "a daughter of Moses," became the mother of the "False Messiah," who dwelt on Mount Sinai with his brother, and gathered to himself a people called Christians (3–4). Jahja/Johana (John the Baptist) was born too, and he was "a healer whose medicine was Water of Life" and an "envoy of the High King of Light" (5–7). Sixty years after his death the Jews persecuted the Nasoraeans (7–8). Apparently in divine reprisal for this hostile action, Jerusalem was destroyed and made "like heaps of ruins"; also the Jews in Baghdad (Babylonia), where four hundred of their rulers had reigned for eight hundred years, were brought to an end (9). In succession to the descendants of King Ardban (the Parthian rulers, the Arsacid dynasty), the Hardabaean dynasty (evidently the Sasanians, since their rule followed that of the Parthians) ruled for 360 years (14–15). "Then the Son of Slaughter, the Arab [Muhammad and his successors]," took the sovereignty (15). After four hundred years of Arab rule, the False Messiah will return and perform miracles by fraud and sorcery during a reign of six thousand years (19–20). Thereafter, for some unexplained reason, "fifty thousand years will pass in calm ease . . . and ill-will shall be removed from the minds of all peoples, nations, and tongues" (20). But finally there will be decadence and the end of the world will come (21).

Returning to the opening sentences of the text, the Nasoraeans are described as abandoning "the Sign of the Seven [planets]." This is surely a reference to Jerusalem, for we have already seen that in the *Right Ginza* it was the seven planets with Ruha their mother who built Jerusalem at the command of Adonai (410.8–11), and Christ

---

42. References to *Haran Gawaita* are given according to page numbers in Drower, *Haran Gawaita.*

"the falsifier" is named as one of the seven planets whose evil influence is warned against (46.24–35), while in another text the Seven are brought into connection with the law in Jerusalem.[43] Also the statement in the *Haran Gawaita* (3) that the Nasoraeans "loved the Lord, that is, Adonai," until the birth of Jesus and the rise of Christianity, suggests that originally they had some relationship to the Jewish environment, although, as we have seen, they are later violently opposed to Judaism. The dating also seems to be very confused, for Mary the mother of Jesus is called a daughter of Moses, and Jesus is associated with Mount Sinai.

Abandoning Jerusalem, then, we are told that the Nasoraeans were received in Haran Gawaita and entered the Median hills. Haran Gawaita means "the inner Haran," and is possibly a reference to Haran in northwestern Mesopotamia. The Median hills (*Tura d-Madai*) must be the mountainous regions of southwestern Iran, ancient Media. In the *Haran Gawaita* (10) it is said that the Median mountains are called Haran Gawaita. Therefore perhaps it was the whole territory from northwestern Mesopotamia to southwestern Iran into which the Nasoraeans moved.

The ruler who was "over them," presumably meaning the one under whom they had a favorable reception and received protection, was King Ardban. As we have already seen, there is only one Ardban mentioned in the *Ginza* and this is most probably the Parthian king Artabanus V; as thus apparently the most well-known king of that name in Mandaean tradition, it is probably he who is also meant here. The empire of the Parthians (c. 250 B.C.–A.D. 226) included Babylonia, and from the second century B.C. their major capital was Ctesiphon on the left bank of the Tigris (opposite Seleucia). With the defeat and death of Artabanus V in A.D. 226 and the occupation of the palace of Ctesiphon by the victorious Ardashir, the Parthians were succeeded by the Sasanians. If the identification of King Ardban with Artabanus V is correct, the main movement of the Nasoraeans from the west into Parthian territories in the east was in the early third century A.D.

That in the course of time the Nasoraeans/Mandaeans lived both in the west and in the east is also suggested by other general references in their literature.[44] As to the west, there is much information given about the Palestinian region, the Jews, and Judaism. For example, the *Jardna* (i.e., the Jordan River) is of great importance and is the name for all "living" (i.e., flowing) water, in which it is requisite that the numerous Mandaean baptisms and ablutions be performed. This fact is most convincingly explained by the supposition that their

43. Lidzbarski, *Mandäische Liturgien*, 211.7–8; Rudolph, *Die Mandäer*, 1.55, 100–101.

44. Rudolph, *Die Mandäer*, 1.59ff.; Geo Widengren, *Der Mandäismus*, 56ff.

original baptismal practice was in the Jordan River in Palestine, near where they lived, and that when they were compelled to leave their homeland they went on calling each flowing water which they used in this way the ".Jordan."[45]

As to the east, there are many reflections of life in Mesopotamia and Iran. Linguistically, some eighty loanwords from the Akkadian and some 125 loanwords from the Iranian languages have been counted in the Mandaic language. Geographically, the Euphrates and the Tigris rivers are frequently mentioned (e.g., *Right Ginza* 61.25; 414.7; etc.). The emphasis upon the seven planets may reflect a Babylonian background, while the contrast of light and darkness is much like the same contrast in Persia.

Continuing in the *Haran Gawaita* and in respect to the life of the Nasoraeans in the east, we gather that their situation was relatively favorable under the Parthians. In this time in Baghdad (Babylonia), it is reported, the Nasoraeans "multiplied and became many," and they had as many as 400 temples (*maŝknas*; 10). Under the Sasanians, however, the number of their temples shrank to 170 (14). This corresponds with the known fact that the Sasanians (Neo-Persians) were strong Zoroastrians and suppressed other faiths: the inscription of their high priest Kartir at Naqsh-i Rustam (see p. 110), for example, tells how he persecuted Jews, Buddhist ascetics, Brahmans, Nasoraeans, and Christians.[46] As for "the Son of Slaughter, the Arab," when he "emerged" (as the *Haran Gawaita* puts it), "he drew the sword and converted people to himself by the sword." By then only sixty Nasoraean sanctuaries remained in Babylonia (12, 15).

On the other side we have seen that when the *Right Ginza* speaks harshly against Christ it may call him a "Roman" (49.14; see also 51.26, 28; 52.5, 8, 22; 416.19), doubtless meaning a Byzantine and reflecting the hostility of the Byzantine church. Thus in the long run it was probably pressure both from the Byzantine world on the one hand and from Islam on the other that pushed the Mandaeans more and more into the swampy regions of southern Mesopotamia where their chief centers were found in modern times.[47]

## Cult

### Baptism

In the Mandaean cult[48] baptism is of central importance, and was obviously that which earned for the Mandaeans the name of "those

45. Lidzbarski, *Das Johannesbuch der Mandäer*, xix.
46. Martin Sprengling, *Third Century Iran: Sapor and Kartir*, 51.
47. Rudolph, *Die Mändäer*, 1.252, 254.
48. Ibid., vol. 2, *Der Kult*.

who wash themselves" (*mughtasilah*). It was requisite that this washing be done in "living" (i.e., flowing) water, which was called the Jordan even when it was no longer the actual river of that name in Palestine. It was also believed that these waters were descended from the heavenly Jordan, or Jordans (plural), which exist in the worlds of light. "All the world attests that the living water comes forth from beneath the throne of God" (*Right Ginza* 281.21–22). There is also a "Light-Euphrates" (*prash ziua*), which is the heavenly prototype of the earthly Euphrates River, the latter in many ways taking the place of the original Jordan for the Mesopotamian Mandaeans, and the two rivers (Jordan and Euphrates) being mingled in their view. "Let us ascend to the mouth of the Light-Euphrates, to the bank of the great Jordan of Life, and to the great edifice of our Father" (*Left Ginza* 425.35–36). The water of Mandaean baptism has, therefore, both the natural sense of cleansing and making pure, and also the sense of communicating life because, in the Mandaean view, it comes from the world of heavenly life.

The Mandaean baptism is called *maṣbuta,* a word that signifies immersion.[49] In the "Diwan of the Baptism [*maṣbuta*] of Hibil Ziwa," in which the story is told of the cleansing of the great "Light Giver" after his descent into the darkness, we hear of the essential elements in the ceremony:

1. *Immersion.* "Then Hibil Ziwa . . . descended into the Jordan and submerged himself thrice in the name of Yawar Rabba [a light-spirit, serving as the divine baptizer, overseeing the event]" (53).
2. *Signing.* "Ayar Rabba [a light-spirit, serving as the priest conducting the ceremony] signed him thrice with his forefinger, beside the thumb, upon the forehead from the right ear to the left ear. . . . For thus is the Sign of the Father, that is the Right, distinguished from the Sign of the Left, which is the Mother [at death the soul passes into Mother Earth, then must put on the Father, i.e., assume the spiritual and immaterial]" (53; see also 39 n. 5).
3. *Drinking.* "When you gave him [three] palmfuls of water to drink, you lifted him out of all his pollutions and re-established the mystery of spirit and soul" (54).
4. *Investiture with a myrtle wreath.* "And when you recited 'Let Light shine forth' over the wreath and he set it upon his head,

---

49. Eric Segelberg, *Maṣbūtā: Studies in the Ritual of the Mandaean Baptism.* References to the "Diwan of the Baptism of Hibil Ziwa" are given according to page numbers in Drower, *Haran Gawaita.*

the wreath shone; from celestial worlds it came to him and you set it upon his head" (54).

5. *Ritual handclasp* (*kushta,* the word also means right, right-dealing, truth, pact, and the like, and is often personified as a celestial being;[50] in the ceremony each of two persons clasps the right hand of the other, then carries his own hand to his lips and kisses it). "And when you lift him up and take his right hand in the *kushta,* you have mingled the Jordan with your raiment and his raiment and have set his mind at peace. And make him this response while his hand is in your hand, say to him: '*Kushta* strengthen you and raise you up! Seek and find, speak and be heard.' And say to him: 'Your *kushta* shall be your witness and your baptism shall be established, and not be in vain. The *kushta* [pact] which you have made . . . will deliver you from all involuntary offenses and from pollutions of the darkness which occur in the abode of mortality' " (54–55; see also 17 n. 5).

6. *Anointing with oil.* "And when you take the oil and say: 'Healing, purity, and forgiving of sins be there for this the soul of Hibil Ziwa son of Manda d-Hiia who descended to the Jordan and was baptized and received the pure sign,' then each takes oil in his bowl. . . . And take oil with the finger next the thumb of your right hand and sign from the right ear to the left ear" (55).

7. *Sacred meal.* "And (when) they recite (prayers for) the *pihta* [sacramental bread] and *mambuha* [sacramental water], each shall stand up, with his own bowl, and they shall recite the eight *pihta* prayers and the two *mambuha* prayers. . . . And they shall eat and drink" (58).

Such was the baptism of Hibil Ziwa, the original pattern rite of the *mashbuta.* "And Hibil Ziwa said: 'Everyone that is baptized with my baptism, Hibil Ziwa's, shall be set up beside me and shall resemble me, and shall dwell in my world, Hibil Ziwa's' " (59). In fact, according to the "Canonical Prayerbook of the Mandaeans," Hibil Ziwa himself baptized the first man Adam; Ptahil, it will be remembered, created Adam's body but was unable to give it life; only upon this baptism did Adam arise and live (29, 32).

### Mass of the Soul

The second main ceremony in the Mandaean cult is the so-called mass of the soul (*masiqta*). With respect to death, we have seen that

---

50. Drower and Macuch, *Mandaic Dictionary,* 209–11.

the basic Mandaean belief is that, although now enclosed in a material body, the soul is of heavenly origin and, given "knowledge," can hope at death to return to the worlds of light from which it came.[51] From this point of view the angel of death, named Shaurel, is known as the Releaser for he comes to release the soul from the body; in the world he is called "Death," but to those who have knowledge about him, he is *kushta* (*Left Ginza* 424.30–425.1). Grief for the departed is therefore unseemly and is strictly forbidden: if anyone is separated from his body in death, do not weep, mourn, and raise lamentation over him (*Right Ginza* 21.6–7, 14–16).

Various rites of burial, of remembrance of the dead, and the like, are appropriate, however, and most important of all is the *masiqta*. The word means literally the "ascent" or the "raising up" of the soul, and the ceremony involves a sacramental meal, equivalent to a mass, accompanied by hymns and prayers, all intended to assist the soul to rise after death to heaven. At least as known in modern times the *masiqta* begins on the third evening after death, because by then it is believed the soul has left its body and begun its journey (of forty-five days) to the celestial world.[52] Here, as in the baptismal meal, the elements are *pihta* and *mambuha*, but somewhat differently prepared, and here the priest partakes as proxy for the deceased.[53]

In its ascent, the soul of the departed must rise through superterrestrial spheres and pass a number of stations. These stations are known by the term *matarta*,[54] which means watch or vigil, and also place of detention or purgatory, the connotation being that if all is not well the soul may be held there for punishment and cleansing before being allowed to go further. These stations are sometimes called "the watch-houses of the planets," and they are kept and ruled by various supernatural beings. The passage of the soul through the *matarta*s is described according to almost the same scheme, but with somewhat varied content, in a tractate of the *Right Ginza* (183–90) and another of the *Left Ginza* (443–52); other descriptions with many variations in details are found in the *Right Ginza* in the tractate that tells of the death and ascent of John the Baptist (190–96), and in the tractate that has the name of the legendary Dinanukt (205–12; also in the *Qolasta,* in the *Diwan Abatur,* etc.).

In the scheme in the *Left Ginza* (443–52) there are seven purgatories and the identification of their keepers and rulers is as follows:

51. Wilhelm Brandt, *Das Schicksal der Seele nach dem Tode nach mandäischen und parsischen Vorstellungen.*

52. Drower, *Mandaeans of Iraq and Iran,* 198.

53. Drower, *Canonical Prayerbook of the Mandaeans,* 58 n. 1.

54. Drower and Macuch, *Mandaic Dictionary,* 241–42.

(1) "Nbaz, the strength of heaven" (444.34); (2) "the wise scribe Nbu [the Babylonian Nabu/Nebo, identified with the planet Mercury]" (446.1);[55] (3) "the seven figures whom Ptahil called forth [the seven planetary spirits that came into being at the seventh cry of the Demiurge Ptahil; *Right Ginza* 351.31]" (446.41); (4) here (448.12) the name of the keeper is missing, but in 188.25 Jorabba (*iurba*) is a keeper of a purgatory, and perhaps should be named here; (5) "this watch-house is that of the sorcerer Christ, the son of the Spirit of the Lie [Ruha], who has set himself up as god [*alaha*] of the Nasoraeans" (449.4–6);[56] (6) "Ewath, the Holy Spirit" (450.8–9); and (7) here the name of the keeper is again missing; since the ones found in fetters here are "evil ones whom Ptahil called forth" (451.10), Ptahil may be the keeper.

Above the seven purgatories the soul comes to the eighth station, which is the watch-house of "the old, lofty, hidden, safeguarded Abatur" (451.25–26). As the keeper of the last watch-house, between the purgatories and the worlds of light, Abatur presides over the weighing in the balance of the souls that come. He weighs works and recompense; he determines who are already worthy, who must be consigned to further purification, weighed again, and then pronounced worthy to go on to the worlds of light. Whereas in the first seven purgatories idolaters, murderers, and unrighteous of all sorts are being punished, here are only adherents of the true religion who have failed in some of their duties and thus been unworthy of the name of Nasoraean.

In the "Book of John" (xxvii) Abatur is derived from Joshamin, the Second Life, and he is himself the Third Life and Ptahil is his son (see *Right Ginza* 173.36ff.). In the "Canonical Prayerbook of the Mandaeans" (105 n. 4, 199 n. 2) Abatur has two forms: as Abatur *rama* (the Lofty Abatur) he occupies a high throne; as a lower counterpart he is Abatur *d-muzania* (the Abatur of the Scales), a change in status from the higher position with which he is not pleased.

In the "Book of John," Hibil Ziwa, the Light Giver, announces the appointment of Abatur to be in charge of the scales: "I have made smooth a way from the darkness to the dwelling of light. I have set up witnesses in the watch-house of Abatur. I have brought Abatur here and installed him as judge of the world. I have placed him in charge of the balance, and given him authority over the works of the world" (198.20ff.; see also 232.1ff. for Abatur's displeasure with the position). Similarly in the *Diwan Abatur* (1ff.), Hibil Ziwa says to Abatur:

> "Arise! set up your throne in the House of Boundaries and take over sovereignty. And sublimate that which is sound from that which is base

55. Ibid., 287.
56. Brandt, *Die mandäische Religion*, 211–12.

when man's measure is full and he comes and is baptized in the Jordan, is weighed in your scales, is sealed with your seal, and rises up and dwells in your world."[57]

And when Abatur is displeased Hibil Ziwa bids him be calm, and proceeds to instruct him about the sins that deserve punishment and about the several purgatories. As the *Diwan Abatur* (8–9) further explains and also illustrates in its pictures, in the scales of Abatur the soul is weighed against the soul of Shitil, the latter being Adam's son (Seth), who reputedly gave his life for his father and was thus the purest of all human souls.[58]

In the "Canonical Prayerbook" (45–46), after the soul is weighed in the House of Abatur and found worthy, it must go on and cross the Waters of Death (*hafiqis mia*), which are the frontier of the worlds of light. The mention of a bridge in one passage (80) must reflect the Zoroastrian Cinvat Bridge (see pp. 88–89); in the *Diwan Abatur* a ship ferries the soul.

So the final destination of the approved soul is the House of Life ("Canonical Prayerbook" 46). It is also called the Place of Light, and described as all light and all brilliance. When the savior-spirit *Manda d-Hiia* leads John thither John directs his prayer to the First Life, the Second Life, and the Third Life: "Corresponding to this hour in which I stand here, and corresponding to this ascent in which I have ascended, may it be the same for all true and believing persons, who are signed with the sign of life and baptized with the pure baptism, and over whom the name of the mighty First Life is spoken." The passage concludes: "Praised be the Life, the Life is victorious, and victorious is the person who has come hither" (*Right Ginza* 196.17–23).

In a hymn of the soul in the *Left Ginza* (525–27) there is rejoicing over the prospect of the ascent: "How much I rejoice, how much my heart rejoices . . . in anticipation of the day when my adjudication will be settled . . . and my journey will be to the Place of Life!" (525.24–29). And a hymn of the mass of the soul ("Canonical Prayerbook" 53–54) likewise anticipates:

With him, with the Deliverer [Shaurel, the angel of death]
The souls of this *masiqta* will ascend.
They will behold the Place of Light
And the Everlasting Abode.
On their road the Seven will not detain them,

57. References to *Diwan Abatur* are given according to page numbers in Drower, *Diwan Abatur*.
58. Pallis, *Mandaean Studies*, 86–87, 111–14.

Nor will the Judge of the False question them.
The Life will count you in his reckoning
And the good will set you up in their midst.
To the place to which the good go they will guide you
And in the place in which they stand they will set you up;
Lamps of radiance are found before you,
Beams of light behind you.
*Kushta* will come at your right
And Piety will smoothen your path.
. . . . . . . . . . . . .

the ferry which ferries over the Elect
Will set out toward you and take you across.
(Then) from Abatur of the Scales
A savior will come forth toward you.
The savior that comes toward you
Is all radiancy and light from head to foot.
. . . . . . . . . . . . . . .

(So) rise up, behold the Place of Light!
And Life is victorious.

Besides baptism and the mass of the soul, other religious ceremonies include the rite of marriage and the consecration of a priest; for both the bridegroom and the priest the Great Shishlam was the prototype, as described in the books bearing his name. A daily ritual ablution in "living" water is called a "sign" (*rushma*); daily devotions (*rahmia*) are prescribed for three prayer-times (at sunrise, at noon, and before sunset); for both *rushma* and *rahmia* appropriate texts are contained in the *Qolasta* ("Canonical Prayerbook" 102–4, 106ff.).

# Ethics and Gnostic and Biblical Relationships

The basic concept of Mandaean ethics is *kushta*, which has the manifold meanings of truth, right, right-dealing, good faith, faithfulness, plighted word, pact, promise, and also the action of giving the right hand (see p. 275).[59] What is true and right is what is required of believers in relation to the highest beings and in relation to one another.

Major collections of Mandaean ethical precepts are found in a "moral codex" in the *Right Ginza* (16.5–27.18),[60] and in a series of "admonitions" in the "Book of John" (169–81); other injunctions are found in

---

59. Drower and Macuch, *Mandaic Dictionary*, 209–11; Lidzbarski, *Das Johannesbuch der Mandäer*, xvii.
60. Brandt, *Mandäische Schriften*, 24–43.

portions of the "Thousand and Twelve Questions" (195ff.),[61] and elsewhere.

We have seen that the first tractate in the *Right Ginza* begins with praise of the highest Being and a description of his world of Light, then goes on with an account of the creation through Hibil Ziwa, the Light Giver, of the world and of Adam and his wife Hawwa. It is immediately following this account of creation that the "pure Sent One" (i.e., Hibil Ziwa) addresses to Adam and all his kin the long series of injunctions and warnings that comprise the "moral codex" and instruct all Mandaeans in their ethical and cultic obligations.

In some typical citations in *Right Ginza* (16ff.; numbers in parentheses refer to paragraph numbers in *Right Ginza* 16–26), the instructions run as follows. They should praise the Lord of all beings thrice in the day and twice in the night (91). Adam should take a wife and build a family (92). Do not break the marriage, do not steal, do not kill (94). Do not love lie and falsehood, nor gold and silver and worldly possession, for the world passes away and your possession and works will be left behind (95). Do not reverence Satan, false deities, and idols (96). Honor father and mother and the elder brothers as the father (99). Give alms to the poor and be a guide to the blind (104). If you see one who hungers, feed him; one who thirsts, give him to drink; one who is naked, clothe him (105). All that is hateful to you, do not to your neighbor (150). Clothe yourselves in white and wear a white turban like the heavenly beings (175).

In the "Book of John" the admonitions are in much the same spirit as in the *Right Ginza* and in not a few cases are repetitions of the same sayings, including the "negative Golden Rule" (47.177). In the same "Book of John" (31.110–11) in the earlier tractate concerning Jahja/Johana (John the Baptist) the same instruction that was given to Adam in the *Right Ginza* is given also to John (and of course also therewith to all the believers) to take a wife and build a family. Otherwise John will be a false prophet and like a dried-up stream on which one raises no plants. When John fears that he would then neglect his devotions, he is assured that he can be true both to his wife and to his religious duty.

The regulations in the "Thousand and Twelve Questions" relate to the priesthood, but in one case, for example, have to do with the problem of murder. If a man commits murder he is not to receive the crown of a priest, but upon repentance and baptism he may be readmitted to the Mandaean community, but only as a layman (197.7).

---

61. References to "The Thousand and Twelve Questions" are given according to page numbers in Drower, *Thousand and Twelve Questions*.

It may now be remembered that with the derivation of their name from *manda* (= *gnosis*) the Mandaeans are aligned with other "Gnostic" groups in their emphasis on knowledge, and in their cosmology and mythology we have seen such ideas as are also elsewhere recognizable in the Gnostic framework of thought as those of the opposition of light and darkness, of the making of the inferior world by a Demiurge, of the return of the soul to its homeland, and the like.[62]

In the Gnostic world in general, because of the perception that the present world is inferior or evil, there was a tendency on the one hand to antinomianism, that is, since the world is evil anyway, whatever is done in it is a matter of indifference, and license is both natural and permissible; and a tendency on the other hand to asceticism, that is, since the world is evil, self-denial is necessary as a means of extrication from its meshes. Concretely, for example, on the one hand, Irenaeus (*Adversus Haereses* 1.31.2) quotes the Cainites as saying, "This is 'perfect knowledge,' to undertake without fear such actions as should not even be mentioned"; and, on the other hand, Menander's disciple, Saturninus, called for complete abstention from marriage and from meat.[63]

The examples from Mandaean texts given just above, however, have shown in the Mandaean *gnosis* a high moral earnestness: instead of promoting a sense of freedom from law, there is a codification of rigorous requirements; instead of denying natural human relationships, marriage itself is held to be a sacred duty. In these respects Mandaean ethics stand closer to the law of Moses and the teachings of Jesus, than to the teachings otherwise generally known as Gnostic.[64]

---

62. Gilles Quispel, "Gnosis," in *Die orientalischen Religionen im Römerreich,* ed. Maarten J. Vermaseren, 423–24.

63. R. M. Grant, *Gnosticism and Early Christianity,* 107.

64. Yamauchi, *Gnostic Ethics and Mandaean Origins,* 24ff.

# 9

# Manichaean Religion

## Sources

The sources of information concerning Mani and his movement are numerous and fall into various categories:[1] First are the writings of Mani himself. Mani considered it important to put his teachings into written form. One work, the *Shabuhragan* ("Shapur Book"), written in Middle Persian, was addressed to the Sasanian king Shapur I (reigned A.D. 241–273). Seven works, written in Aramaic, constituted a canon; their titles were Living Gospel, Treasure of Life, Pragmateia (i.e., Tractate), Book of the Mysteries, Book of the Giants, Epistles, Psalms and Prayers. Along with these books there were also a commentary and a book of pictures to assist the understanding of the doctrines. Mani himself was a painter, and his picture book was called *Arzhang,* or "Book of the Drawing." All of these materials, however, survive only in fragmentary texts and quotations by other writers.

There are also writings by followers of Mani. At the beginning of the twentieth century, expeditions to Central Asia found (chiefly in Turfan [now Turpan] and in Tunhuang [now Dunhuang]) many manuscripts and fragments of manuscripts containing Manichaean texts written in Middle Persian, Parthian, Sogdian, Uygur, and Chinese,[2] and also manuscripts with pictures, dating from around A.D. 750–850.[3] In 1930 extensive Coptic papyri were found in Egypt with Manichaean

1. L. J. R. Ort, *Mani: A Religio-Historical Description of His Personality,* 20ff.
2. Werner Sundermann, *Mittelpersische und parthische kosmogonische und Parabeltexte der Manichäer*; Jes P. Asmussen, *Manichaean Literature: Representative Texts Chiefly from Middle Persian and Parthian Writings*; Werner Sundermann, *Mitteliranische manichäische Texte kirchengeschichtlichen Inhalts.*
3. Albert von Le Coq, *Die buddhistische Spätantike in Mittelasien,* vol. 2, *Die manichaeischen Miniaturen.*

Ruins of Kaochang, city on the Ancient Silk Road, near Turfan in the Xinjiang Uygur Autonomous region of China

texts: a book of *Homilies* from the end of the third century A.D.,[4] a book of *Kephalaia* (*kephalaion* means head, main point, summary) from the beginning of the fourth century,[5] and a book of *Psalms* from the fourth century.[6] In 1969 a very small parchment codex (192 pages, 1¾ inches × 1⅜ inches) in Cologne was opened and deciphered and found to contain biographical accounts of Mani; the work was translated from a Syriac original and was written in Greek in probably the fifth century A.D.[7]

Finally, there are writings by others about Mani and Manichaeism. A number of early Christian authors speak of Mani and his religion, but ordinarily from a polemical point of view. The most important is Augustine (A.D. 354–430), the son of a non-Christian father and a Christian mother, who was himself for nearly nine years (376–384) a member of a Manichaean community in North Africa, in which he held the position of a Hearer. After becoming a Christian in 386 he wrote against Manichaeism in many of his works, both composing

4. H. J. Polotsky, *Manichäische Homilien*, vol. 1, *Manichäische Handschriften der Sammlung A. Chester Beatty.*

5. H. J. Polotsky and A. Böhlig, *Kephalaia.*

6. C. R. C. Allberry, *A Manichaean Psalm-Book.*

7. Ron Cameron and Arthur J. Dewey, *The Cologne Mani Codex (P. Colon. inv. nr. 4780): "Concerning the Origin of His Body."*

polemical essays and recording personal disputations with Manichaean opponents.

Arab authors also tell about Mani and his religion, notably al-Nadim and al-Biruni, and although as representatives of Islam these two regard Mani as heretical they provide not a little objective information. The book *Kitab al-Fihrist* ("Catalogue of the Sciences") was written by al-Nadim in the year A.D. 988, and in chapter 9 he describes a number of sects and tells of their scholars and the books they composed; among these he deals at some length with Mani's life, doctrines, and books.[8] The *Chronology of Ancient Nations*[9] was written by al-Biruni in A.D. 1000 and his *India*[10] was written thirty years later. In the *Chronology* there is a section on Mani and the Manichaeans; in the *India* there are scattered references and quotations.

## The Life of Mani

As related in the *Fihrist* of al-Nadim,[11] the parents of Mani, his father Futtuq Patek and his mother Mays or Marmaryam, were both descendants of the Ashkanian or Arsacid royal family. They were originally from Hamadan in Iran, but moved to Babylon (i.e., Babylonia) and lived at al-Mada'in, comprised of the city of Seleucia on the west bank of the Tigris and the Persian capital of Ctesiphon on the east bank. There, during three days in a temple of idols that Patek used to frequent, he heard repeatedly a voice that admonished him, "Oh, Futtuq, do not eat meat! Do not drink wine! Do not marry a human being!" After that Patek became connected with a group of people in the environs of Dastumisan (in lower Babylonia between Wasit and Basra) known as the Mughtasilah ("those who wash themselves"). The Mughtasilah are described by al-Nadim (see p. 265) as very numerous in the marshlands of southern Iraq and as known as the "Sabeans of the Marshes"; they were probably Mandaeans or included the Mandaeans.[12]

It was at this time that Mani was born. In his *Chronology*[13] al-Biruni says that according to Mani's own statement in the *Shabuhragan* Mani was born in the village of Mardini on the upper canal of

8. Bayard Dodge, *The Fihrist of al-Nadīm*, 2.773–805.

9. C. Edward Sachau, *The Chronology of Ancient Nations*, 207–9 (London ed.; pp. 189–92 in Lahore reprint).

10. C. Edward Sachau, *Alberuni's India*, 1.48, 54–55, 264, 381; 2.105, 169.

11. Dodge, *Fihrist of al-Nadīm*, 2.773ff.; see also Geo Widengren, *Mani and Manichaeism*, 23ff.

12. Dodge, *Fihrist of al-Nadīm*, 2.811, 922, see under Sabians (2).

13. Sachau, *Chronology of Ancient Nations*, 208 (reprint p. 190).

Kutha, and the date of his birth was in the year 527 of the era of the
Babylonian astronomers, that is, the era of Alexander (by which the
Muslim chronographers mean the Seleucid era). The Seleucid year
indicated was equivalent to A.D. 216/217, and the exact date of Mani's
birth was probably Nisanu 8, equivalent to April 14, A.D. 216.[14]

After that, as the *Fihrist* continues the account,[15] Mani's father
brought Mani to him so that Mani was reared in accordance with the
cult to which his father belonged. When Mani was twelve years old
(A.D. 228/229) he received a revelation from an angel called Tawm, a
name explained by al-Nadim as meaning the "Companion," but probably a rendering of the Syriac *tauma,* the "Twin." The angel was sent
from "the King of the Gardens of Light" (explained by al-Nadim as
"God Exalted"). The message to Mani was: "Leave this cult, for thou
art not one of its adherents. Upon thee are laid purity and refraining
from bodily lusts, but it is not yet time for thee to appear openly,
because of thy tender years."

When Mani was twenty-four years old (A.D. 240/241) the same heavenly messenger came again and told him: "The time is fulfilled for
thee to come forth and to give the summons to thy cause." The angel
also assured Mani that the Lord had chosen him for his mission, which
was "to preach the gospel of truth as from his presence, and to carry
on in this [mission] with all . . . perseverance." Accordingly Mani now
came forth publicly, and the day when he did so was the day of the
coronation of the Sasanian king Shapur I in 241: "It was Sunday, the
first day of Nisanu, when the sun was in Aries." With Mani on this
occasion were two disciples, Simeon and Zakko, and also his own father, who evidently wished to see the developments in his son's cause.

The *Cologne Mani Codex*[16] also discusses (2–14) Mani from the age
of four to twelve years, and the revelations he received. Here Mani
himself speaks of his youthful participation in "the teachings of the
baptists," and reports that the angel, the Twin, said to him on two
occasions: "Strengthen your power, make your mind firm, and receive
all that is about to be revealed to you," and "submit to all that is about
to come upon you" (13.4–12). Again in its third section (72–99) the
codex describes Mani's life among and eventual break with the baptists, whose sect is here said to have been founded by Elchasai (Origen,
in Eusebius, *Church History* 6.38, mentions the Elchasaites and their
book, which appears to have been a chief authority for the Jewish-
Christian Gnostic sects).[17] Instead of their ever-repeated washings of

---

14. S. H. Taqizadeh, "The Dates of Mani's Life," *AM,* n.s. 6 (1957): 106–21, esp. 108.
15. Dodge, *Fihrist of al-Nadīm,* 2.774ff.
16. Cameron and Dewey, *Cologne Mani Codex,* 8–17, 57–79.
17. Wilhelm Brandt, *Elchasai: Ein Religionsstifter und sein Werk.*

themselves and their food, Mani told the sectarians that genuine purity "is that which comes through knowledge, a separation of light from darkness, of death from life, of living waters from turbid" (84.12–16). When he said these things to them, Mani reports that some regarded him as a prophet and teacher, but others were filled with jealousy and rage. Some even voted for his death.

So Mani went forth into the world to preach his message. In a Parthian text (M 4,2 V)[18] he summarizes his earlier life and his sending forth:

> I am a grateful pupil who originated from the country Babylon. I originated from the country Babylon and at the gate of truth I am placed. I am a singer, a pupil who was led away out of the country Babylon so that I should call out a call in the world.

In his journeying Mani went first to the east, even sailing to India, perhaps meaning the Makran coast and Gandhara. In the *Kephalaia* Mani records:

> At the close of King Ardashir's years [Ardashir I, founder of the Sasanian dynasty, reigned A.D. 226–241] I set out to preach. I sailed to the land of the Indians. I preached to them the hope of life and I chose there a good selection.
> In the year that King Ardashir died and his son Shapur [reigned 241–273] became king, I sailed from the land of the Indians to the land of the Persians, and from the land of Persia I came to the land of Babylon, Maisan [Mesene, the district of Basra], and Susiana.[19]

The trip to India was evidently brief, but the mention of a "good selection" chosen there must mean that followers were won and perhaps some organization instituted for the continuation of the work. It was a very important point when Mani gained the support of Shapur I, as it was earlier for Zarathushtra when he obtained the allegiance of Vishtaspa (see p. 82).

In the *Fihrist*[20] al-Nadim says that Mani traveled in the land for about forty years before he met with Shapur, which can of course not be correct since the entire reign of Shapur I (241–273) was not that long; Mani's meeting with the king must have been sooner. On the other hand there is no reason to doubt the statement of the *Fihrist* that it was Firuz, the brother of Shapur, who brought Mani into the

18. Ort, *Mani*, 74.
19. Polotsky and Böhlig, *Kephalaia*, 15.24–31.
20. Dodge, *Fihrist of al-Nadīm*, 2.776.

presence of the king. The Manichaeans say, al-Nadim continues, that when Mani came before the king there were on his shoulders what resembled two lamps of light, and Shapur, although having originally intended to kill Mani, was awed by him. Accordingly Mani was able to request the king's favor for his adherents and the right for them to travel wherever they might wish throughout the land. Shapur granted all that Mani requested. With such approval for his mission, "Mani carried his propaganda to India, China, and the peoples of Khorasan [the large eastern province of Iran], appointing a disciple of his for each region."

In an autobiographical fragment written on both sides in the Parthian language (M 566 I)[21] Mani tells of his meeting with a king, most probably his meeting with Shapur I. On the recto the king asks, "Whence are you?" and Mani replies, "I am a physician from the land of Babylon." On the verso there is reference to the healing of a girl by Mani, in response to which she salutes him as her "god and life-giver." Thus Mani presented himself to the king as one who, in at least one of his functions, was a healer of the sick, a profession with religious connotations.

In the *Kephalaia* Mani also tells of his meeting with Shapur and of the favorable reception he received, and states that he stayed in the ruler's following for a number of years (the exact number lost in the text): "I came before King Shapur. He received me with great honor and granted that I should wander in [his territories and] preach the word of life. I spent further years . . . [with] him in his retinue."[22] As already noted, it was also for King Shapur that Mani composed *Shabuhragan*.

Since it was Firuz, the brother of Shapur I, who introduced Mani to the king, it may be presumed that Firuz had already been converted by Mani, although we lack any record of such an event. Another brother of the king was also converted by Mani, presumably also before the meeting with Shapur, and of this event we have a record in a Parthian text (M 47).[23] This brother's name was Mihrshah, the governor of Meshun (i.e., Maisan or Mesene, the district of Basra), where Mani came on his way back from India. At the moment of Mani's arrival Mihrshah was feasting in his garden, which was very large and lovely, and of which he was very proud. Being extraordinarily hostile to the religion of Mani, Mihrshah said to him: "In the paradise which you proclaim will there be such a garden as this garden of mine?" Mani heard this

21. Sundermann, *Mitteliranische manichäische Texte*, 23–24, text 2.2.
22. Polotsky and Böhlig, *Kephalaia*, 15.31–34.
23. Sundermann, *Mitteliranische manichäische Texte*, 102–3, text 10.

utterance of disbelief, then by his miraculous power showed Mihrshah the celestial Paradise of Light, with all the divine beings, the immortal breath of life, every kind of garden, and other splendid things. Mihrshah was overcome and fell to the ground unconscious for three hours, during which time the beautiful vision presumably continued, and he still remembered it afterward, when Mani laid his hand on Mihrshah's head and brought him back to consciousness. Thereupon Mihrshah was so filled with awe that he knelt before Mani, and was thus evidently converted to Mani's teaching.

The last days and the death of Mani are related in detail in the *Homilies* (1.42–67), although the extant text is broken.[24] Shapur I was followed on the throne by an older son Hormizd I, who reigned only a few months (A.D. 273/274), and then by a younger son Bahram I (274–277). Hormizd I was still friendly to Mani as his father had been (*Homilies* 1.48.9–10), but Bahram I was not. At the point of the death of Hormizd and the accession of Bahram, Mani was evidently in his native Babylonia. Then—perhaps with a premonition already of danger to his life and a desire to reach what might be safer territory—Mani traveled down the Tigris and went on as far as Hormizd-Ardashir in the province of Susiana, intending to push on into the Kushan realm with its centers at Kabul and Gandhara. But at this juncture he was evidently no longer free to go where he wished, and a royal edict commanded him not to go on. The Coptic text states: "Thereupon he turned back in anger and distress." He was in fact beginning his last journey. He came back to Mesene and then up the Tigris by boat to Ctesiphon. As he traveled Mani made allusions to his coming death and said to his adherents: "Look upon me and satisfy yourselves, my children, for I shall bodily withdraw from you" (*Homilies* 1.44.12–13, 18–20).

From Ctesiphon Mani went to the royal residential city of Belapat (in Susiana), and there the Zoroastrian priests, the Magi (*magousaios*), took the initiative against him. They formulated an accusation and brought it to a certain Kardel, from whom it was passed up through higher officials to the king himself, who ordered Mani to come to the palace.

A very fragmentary Parthian text (M 6031),[25] which deals with the same events, says: "Thereupon Kerder the *magbad* [*mobad*] planned with his friends who served before the king, and . . . jealous and cunning." This personage, Kerder, is probably the same as the priest named

---

24. Polotsky, *Manichäische Homilien,* 1.42–67; W. B. Henning, "Mani's Last Journey," *BSOAS* 10 (1942): 941–53.

25. Sundermann, *Mitteliranische manichäische Texte,* 71, text 4a.13; Ort, *Mani,* 55.

Kardel in the *Homilies,* and also the same as the influential priest in Zoroastrianism (see p. 110), Kartir the *magbad* (*mobad*).

The audience of Mani with Bahram I is described both in the *Homilies* and in a Middle Persian text (M 3).[26] According to the Middle Persian text, Mani was accompanied by an interpreter named Nuhzadag (who is probably the author of the text M 3) and two other men. The king was at dinner and had not yet washed his hands (i.e., had not yet finished his meal). Courtiers came in and said: "Mani has come and is standing at the door." The king bade Mani wait, then came out to him together with the Queen of the Sakas (the wife of his grandson the satrap of Sakastan, who later reigned as Bahram III, A.D. 293), and with Kerder the son of Ardawan (the latter must be the same as Kartir son of Ardawan who is named in the inscription of Shapur I on the Ka'bah-i Zardusht at Naqsh-i Rustam; see p. 110), and is to be clearly distinguished from Kartir the *mobad*).[27] The queen and Kartir the son of Ardawan, although present, took no recorded part in the proceedings.

As the Parthian text (M 6031) continues the account, the king addressed Mani and said at once ominously: "You are not welcome." Then he went on to criticize Mani because Mani participated neither in fighting nor in hunting, nor was even, the king said, a good physician. It may be remembered that when Mani first came before Shapur I he presented himself as "a physician from Babylon," and had in fact just healed a sick girl. At this point Mani declared to Bahram that even among the king's servants he had freed many from demons and healed many of diseases. Bahram, however, remained unmoved.

In the *Homilies* (1.47.22–48.24)[28] Bahram also asks why revelation should have come to Mani and not to himself, and to this Mani can only reply that God reveals truth to whom he will. He then says, "Do with me what you will." As a last appeal Mani also refers to the favor that Shapur and Hormizd showed to him, but all was of no avail, and the king ordered Mani chained and imprisoned.

In prison Mani was evidently able to see and talk with his disciples. A Middle Persian fragment written on both sides (M 454 I)[29] probably represents this period. On the recto Mani instructs his disciples as to their conduct after his death. Each should train a disciple ("a helper to the religion") of his own. All must be brave "to endure the suffering of the lord [i.e., the same suffering as that of Mani himself]," in order to "find pious reward and honor and eternal life in the highest." On

---

26. Sundermann, *Mitteliranische manichäische Texte,* 130–31, text 23; Ort, *Mani,* 52–54.
27. Martin Sprengling, *Third Century Iran: Sapor and Kartir.*
28. Polotsky, *Manichäische Homilien,* 1.47–48.
29. Sundermann, *Mitteliranische manichäische Texte,* 135–36, text 24.3.

the verso Mani is described as sending instructions to his whole following through a teacher named Mar Ammo, and as blessing his disciples. Then, while a teacher named Uzzi and two others stay behind
with him, the others go out weeping, anticipating the sad events to
follow.

In the continuing recital of events in the *Homilies* (1.54.11–67.21)[30]
there is an enumeration of specific days (1.60.2–15): On Sunday Mani
came to Belapat. On Monday he was accused. On Tuesday—here what
followed is missing, but there is mention of how Mani reassured his
church (ἐκκλησία) up until Saturday. Then he was put in chains and
placed in prison. The date of the imprisonment was the eighth day of
Emschir. It was twenty-six days before he "went on high" (i.e., died).
His death, which ensued at eleven o'clock in the morning, undoubtedly
took place in prison, and is attributed to the hardships of his life and
the sufferings of his last days.

A fragmentary Parthian text (M 5569 verso)[31] gives the date and
place of Mani's death: "On the fourth day of the month Shahrevar,
Monday, and at the eleventh hour . . . in the provincial capital Belapat." Two Coptic *Psalms* (225, 226)[32] also put the death on a Monday
(which means the twenty-six days of imprisonment must have begun
in midweek), but give the date as the fourth day of Phamenoth. Since
both sources agree on Monday the fourth, it has been surmised that
neither the Persian nor the Coptic month name originally formed part
of the date; perhaps it was the Babylonian month Addaru (February–March) for which the translators substituted approximately corresponding month names from their own calendars. It was only in the
year A.D. 277 that the fourth day of Addaru fell on a Monday; therefore
it is surmised that 277 was the year of the death of Mani, which is in
agreement with the information provided in a Parthian fragment[33]
and other sources that Mani was sixty years old when he died. In the
year 277 the date indicated would have been equivalent to February 26,
and this date—February 26, A.D. 277—may be taken as probable for
the death of Mani.[34]

As to the disposition of the body of Mani, the *Homilies* (1.67.13–14)
state that the remains were obtained by Mani's followers and taken to
Ctesiphon for burial. In the *Fihrist*,[35] however, al-Nadim says that,

---

30. Polotsky, *Manichäische Homilien*, 1.54–67.
31. Ort, *Mani*, 61.
32. Allberry, *Manichaean Psalm-Book*, 17.24–27, 18.6–7.
33. W. Henning, "Neue Materialien zur Geschichte des Manichäismus," *ZDMG* 90 (1936): 1–18,
esp. 60 (Henning's date here for the death is 276; later he gives March 2, 274—see *CHI* 3.1.119).
34. Taqizadeh, "Dates of Mani's Life," 107, 113.
35. Dodge, *Fihrist of al-Nadīm*, 2.794.

after executing Mani, Bahram gibbeted two halves of his body at two gateways of the city of Jundi-Shapur (a city a little to the east of ancient Susa). These two gateways were afterward called the Upper and Lower *Mar* (Saint) or the Upper and Lower *Man* (Mani) Gates. Somewhat differently, al-Biruni says in his *Chronology*[36] that Bahram stripped off the skin of the corpse, filled it with grass, and hung it up at the gate of Jundi-Shapur. This place was thereafter known as the *Bab Mani* (Gate of Mani).

Although Mani must surely have died in chains in prison, his followers, presumably borrowing Christian terminology, called the death of their master a "crucifixion" (e.g., *Homilies* 1.45.9; 1.60.5). Likewise in the Parthian text M 5569 verso the death is called by a term equivalent to the Buddhist *parinirvana*. But from the point of view of the Manichaean faith the death of Mani is most characteristically seen as the exchange of the worldly dress of the body for royal garb, and as an ascension with joy to the regions of light. This description of the event is on the recto of the same Parthian text (M 5569):[37]

> Like a lord, who lays aside his weapons and his clothes and puts on another royal garment, thus the apostle of light laid aside the warlike dress of the body, and took place in a ship of light, and he took the divine garment, the diadem of light and the beautiful garland. And in great happiness he flew with the light gods, who went on [his] right hand and on [his] left, with harp and song of happiness; he flew by divine, miraculous power like a swift lightning and a bright sight hastening to the radiant path of light and to the moon chariot, the assembly of the gods, and he remained with the Father, the god Ohrmazd. And he left orphaned and sad the whole flock of the community of the just, because the master of the house had died.

## Teachings of Mani and Relations with Buddha, Zoroaster, and Jesus

Both al-Nadim in the *Fihrist* and al-Biruni in the *Chronology of Ancient Nations* declare that Mani was acquainted with the doctrines of the Magians and the Christians. Al-Biruni also notes in his *India* that Mani learned the doctrine of reincarnation from the Hindus and put it into his own system. Also in quoting in his *Chronology* from

---

36. Sachau, *Chronology of Ancient Nations*, 208 (reprint p. 191).

37. Sundermann, *Mitteliranische manichäische Texte*, 30–31, text 2.10; Ort, *Mani*, 59–62. For the garment of light and other picture-terms in Manicheism, see Victoria Arnold-Döben, *Die Bildersprache des Manichäismus*, 151ff., etc.

Mani's *Shabuhragan,* al-Biruni says that Mani held that from time to time various "apostles of God" came to earth to bring wisdom and works: at one time this took place through the Buddha in India, again through Zoroaster in Persia, yet again through Jesus in the country of the west, and finally in the person of Mani himself in the country of Babylon.[38] Thus Mani affirmed that the Buddha, Zoroaster, Jesus, and he himself all derived their inspiration from the same divine source; this is why his doctrines were related to those of his predecessors.

Likewise in a Parthian hymn (M 42) there is the same sequence of teachers, coming to a climax with Mani.[39] The text is in the form of a dialogue between a deity (probably Jesus in his divine nature as "the Splendor") and a youth (probably the human soul in its need of re-demption). Here Zarathushtra is (properly) the first of the series of teachers to be named. Zarathushtra, it is said, came down to the realm of Persia and showed truth, but Satan sent out the demons of wrath to do harm. In turn Shakyamuni Buddha "opened the door of redemp-tion for the fortunate souls which he redeemed from the Indians," but he went into *nirvana* and told his followers to wait for the coming of a future redeemer, namely, Maitreya. Then Jesus came and destroyed Jerusalem together with the places of the demons of wrath, but the actions of (Judas) Iscariot and the sons of Israel put an end to his work. Finally came Mani and, as the text breaks off, the youth is saying, "They sent to me the Lord Mani [*Mar Mani*] as savior, who led me out of the slavery in which I served the enemies, against my wish [and] in fear."

In line with the climactic position of Mani in the sequences of teach-ers in the foregoing texts, in a Middle Persian text (M 5794 I)[40] Mani maintains unequivocally that the religion he has chosen is superior to previous religions, and that this is so in no less than ten points (of which only the first four points are preserved in the fragmentary doc-ument): (1) the former religions were in one country and one language, but Mani's will be in every country and every language; (2) the former religions existed only as long as they had pure leaders, but Mani's will remain until the end; (3) the souls that in their own religion did not make proper accomplishment will come (presumably through reincar-nation) to Mani's religion, which will be the door of redemption for them; and (4), to quote Mani's words, "this revelation of mine of the

38. Dodge, *Fihrist of al-Nadīm,* 2.776; Sachau, *Chronology of Ancient Nations,* 207 (reprint p. 189); and idem, *Alberuni's India,* 1.54–55.

39. Ort, *Mani,* 120.

40. F. C. Andreas and Walter Henning, *Mitteliranische Manichaica aus Chinesisch-Turkestan,* 295–96 (T II D 126 = M 5794).

two principles and my living books, my wisdom and knowledge are more and better than those of the earlier religions."

In relation to Buddhism it has already been noted that the death of Mani is described in the Parthian text M 5569 by a word equivalent to *parinirvana,* and the same Parthian term (or cognate forms) is used again for the death of Mani (in M 5), for the death of the Buddha (in M 42), and for the death of Jesus (in M 104). There is also (in M 8171) mention of "the district of the transmigration of souls."[41] In Buddhist terminology the Sanskrit *parinirvana* signifies entry into the state of final release from the cycles of birth and rebirth,[42] and the concepts of rebirth and of ultimate release must therefore have been a part of Manichaean belief. It is not unlikely that Mani became familiar with such terminology and concepts when he was in India (as al-Biruni says), and used the same in his own preaching.

In relation to Jesus and Christianity, both al-Nadim and al-Biruni report that Mani declared himself to be the παράκλητος (promised by Jesus in John 14:16).[43] Not a few Manichaean texts also reflect acquaintance with and use of Christian literature, much of which acquaintance and use may go back to Mani himself.[44] In his own *Shabuhragan,* as known in Middle Persian fragments (M 473, M 475, M 477, M 482),[45] Mani employs and cites at length the account of the last judgment from Matthew 25:31–46. In a Parthian text (M 4570)[46] about the trial of Jesus before the Jewish authorities there are quotations from Matthew 26–27, Mark 14, and Luke 22, which probably come from Tatian's *Diatessaron.* In another text (M 18),[47] which tells of the trial of Jesus before Pilate and of the women at the tomb, there is use not only of the canonical Gospels (probably from a harmony like that of Tatian) but also of the apocryphal Gospel of Peter. There is also demonstrable use of other apocryphal gospels, including the Gospel According to Philip and the Gospel According to Thomas. For example, Logion 5 in the Gospel According to Thomas reads: "Know what is before your face, and what is hidden from you will be revealed to you." This saying is incorporated in *Kephalaia* in an extended dis-

---

41. Ort, *Mani,* 61 (M 5569 verso), 240 (M 5), 120 (M 42), 151 (M 104), 242 (M 8171).

42. *Nirvana* is the state of release, *parinirvana* is the attaining of the state (at death). See E. J. Thomas, "Nirvāṇa and Parinirvāṇa," in *India Antiqua: A Volume of Oriental Studies Presented by His Friends and Pupils to Jean Philippe Vogel,* 249–50.

43. Dodge, *Fihrist of al-Nadīm,* 2.776; Sachau, *Chronology of Ancient Nations,* 207 (reprint p. 189).

44. H.-C. Puech, "The Gospel of Mani," in Edgar Hennecke, *New Testament Apocrypha,* 1.350–61.

45. Asmussen, *Manichaean Literature,* 103–6.

46. Ibid., 101; Sundermann, *Mitteliranische manichäische Texte,* 76–79, text 4a.18.

47. Puech, "Gospel of Mani," 1.352.

quisition on the sun (chap. 65).[48] The sun, it is remarked at this point, is high over all, corresponding to the mystery of the Father of Greatness. "[See], my beloved," the text continues, "I have instructed you in two mysteries, the mystery of the night and the mystery of the day. . . . Now the mystery of the Light and the mystery of the Darkness are daily revealed in the creation." The sun, the text goes on to explain, represents the mystery of the Light, as it comes daily into the world and reveals the wonders of its free gifts (χάρισμα); the fearful night, on the other hand, corresponds to the mystery of the Darkness, and reveals itself in evil deeds. In their error (πλάνη), however, the sects do not understand this (and here comes the quotation from the Gospel According to Thomas):

> They do not distinguish the mystery of the Light and that of the Darkness. Concerning this mystery, which to the sects is hidden, the Savior [Σωτήρ] gave an intimation to his disciples: "Know what is before your face, and what is hidden from you will be revealed to you."

There are also two direct quotations and one indirect reference that, according to al-Biruni in his *India*,[49] Mani attributed to Jesus, but are otherwise unknown. In the case of the second of these quotations al-Biruni says the passage was in Mani's "Book of Mysteries"; perhaps the other two passages were in the same book. The three passages read as follows:

> The apostles asked Jesus about the life of inanimate nature, whereupon he said: "If that which is inanimate is separated from the living element which is comingled with it, and appears alone by itself, it is again inanimate and is not capable of living, while the living element which has left it, retaining its vital energy unimpaired, never dies."

> Since the apostles knew that the souls are immortal, and that in their migrations they array themselves in every form, that they are shaped in every animal, and are cast in the mould of every figure, they asked Messiah what would be the end of those souls which did not receive the truth nor learn the origin of their existence. Whereupon he said: "Any weak soul which has not received all that belongs to her of truth perishes without any rest or bliss."

> The other religious bodies blame us because we worship sun and moon, and represent them as an image. But they do not know their real natures; they do not know that sun and moon are our path, the door whence

48. Polotsky and Böhlig, *Kephalaia*, 163.1–164.8.
49. Sachau, *Alberuni's India*, 1.48, 54; 2.169.

we march forth into the world of our existence [into heaven], as this has been declared by Jesus.

It becomes evident, however, in the Manichaean literature that although Mani and the Manichaeans refer to many events in the life of Jesus, especially those connected with his suffering and death, they hold a docetic view, as is also familiar in Christian Gnosticism. In Manichaean terminology the true Son of God is "Jesus the Splendor"; as a divine being he cannot really participate in a world that is material and evil; he can only manifest an apparent corporeality in the form of Jesus the son of Mary. It was only Mary's son who suffered and died, not the Son of God. Along this line of thought a Parthian fragment (M 24) states that the secret truth of Christ is that he changed his form and his appearance; and a Middle Persian fragment (M 25 I) holds the Christians guilty of blasphemy because they call upon the son of Mary (bar Maryam) as the Son of the Lord (Adonai).[50]

Thus it is to the divine figure, to Jesus the Splendor (or the Glorious), that many Manichaean hymns are addressed, for example, the Middle Persian M 28 II, which calls upon Jesus as the physician who heals spiritual sicknesses:[51]

We will open the mouth to call upon thee, and make the tongue ready for praise. We call upon thee, [who art] entire life. We praise thee, Jesus the Splendor, the New Kingdom.

Thou art, thou art . . . a Healer, the most beloved Son. . . . Come for salvation . . . Helper of the tender and conqueror of the attacker! Freer of those who are bound and Healer of the wounded! Awakener of the sleeping and Arouser of the drowsy!

We will fill our eyes with praise and open our mouth for invocation. And we will bring reverence to thy Greatness, to thee, Jesus the Splendor.

In relation to Zoroastrianism, in the Middle Persian fragment M 28 I Mani speaks as forcibly against the Zoroastrians as against the Christians:[52]

And do not also those that worship the blazing fire know by this very fact that their end belongs to fire? And they assert that Ohrmazd and Ahrman [Ahriman] are brothers. It is consistent with such ideas that they will come to an evil end.

50. Asmussen, *Manichaean Literature*, 14, 103, 106–7.

51. Andreas and Henning, *Mitteliranische Manichaica*, 312–18. For "Jesus the Splendor," see "Jesus der Ruhmreiche" in the index of Eugen Rose, *Die manichäische Christologie*.

52. W. B. Henning, *Zoroaster: Politician or Witch-Doctor?*, 50.

It is plain that the central assertion here regarded as utterly wrong is that of Zurvanism, which, on the basis of the Gathic description of Ahura Mazda (Ohrmazd) and Angra Mainyu (Ahriman) as "twins" (see p. 88), theorized that they were in fact both the sons of a more ultimate reality, namely, Zurvan or Time.[53] The vehemence of Mani's denunciation supports the supposition that this form of Zoroastrianism was especially prominent in Sasanian Iran, and the fact that Magian priests at the court of Bahram I were instrumental in bringing about the death of Mani suggests likewise that these priests were Zurvanites. Obviously to Mani to say that the powers of good and evil were brothers was to relegate the good god to an utterly unworthy position.

Fundamental ideas of Zoroastrianism are, however, unmistakably basic to the religion of Mani. It has already been noted that Mani considered his "revelation of the two principles" to be one of the points of superiority of his religion over previous religions, and the two principles are no doubt the two opposing principles of light and darkness, so important also in the teaching of Zarathushtra. Along with the two principles, Mani's thought also involves the recognition of three "times," and the conception of great epochs in the course of world history—climaxing in a final separation of good and evil in the end-time renovation of the universe—is likewise crucial in Zoroastrian doctrine. Thus, as far as Manichaeism is concerned, in chapter 17 of *Kephalaia*[54] the history of the whole cosmos is described in terms of three "times" (*kairos*); and in the *Homilies* (1.7.11–13)[55] the followers of Mani say:

He [i.e., Mani] taught us everything and he spread out everything for us. He gave us knowledge about the beginning; he taught us the mysteries of the middle, and also the separation of the end.

## Mythology

The two principles and the three times provide the underlying structure of Manichaean myth, at least the essentials of which presumably derive from Mani himself. For the reconstruction of the myth it is possible to turn to reports of Manichaean teaching by al-Nadim, al-Biruni, and Augustine, and to materials scattered throughout extant Manichaean literature.[56] Without considering many ramifications and variations, the main outline is in brief as follows.

53. R. C. Zaehner, *Zurvan: A Zoroastrian Dilemma*.
54. Polotsky and Böhlig, *Kephalaia*, 55.16–57.32.
55. Polotsky, *Manichäische Homilien*, 1.7.
56. Widengren, *Mani and Manichaeism*, 43–73; Alexander Böhlig, "Der Manichäismus," in *Die orientalischen Religionen im Römerreich*, ed. Maarten J. Vermaseren, 438–42.

In the beginning of things, the First Epoch, there were in existence the two principles: light, which was good, and darkness, which was evil. In the realm of light and in a sense identical with the light was God, called Father of Greatness, Father of Light, King of the Gardens of Light, God Zurvan, and other names. With the Father of Greatness were his twelve sons, the twelve Aeons. In the realm of darkness, which was also the realm of matter, were the Prince of Darkness, named Ahrman, and his demons, called Archons. As the powers of darkness became aware of how desirable the realm of light was, it became their intention to break into that realm. In order to provide resistance to this danger the Father of Greatness "called" into being the Mother of Life, and she in turn "called" forth the Primal Man, whose name was Ohrmazd.

With a view to the combat to come, Orhmazd clad himself in his "ingredients," the five light elements (air, wind, light, water, fire), while the Prince of Darkness, Ahrman, also equipped himself with five contrary "ingredients" (smoke, flame, obscurity, pestilential wind, clouds). In the battle that ensued Ohrmazd was defeated and lay helpless far down in the abyss of matter and darkness, while the ingredients of light became mixed with the ingredients of darkness, thus constituting the state of "mixture" that marked the Second Epoch.

In order to rescue the Primal Man the Father of Greatness "called" into being the Friend of Light, who "called" the Great Builder, who "called" the Living Spirit. The Living Spirit is sometimes identified with Mithra,[57] and sometimes (in Greek sources) named the Demiurge, as the creator of the visible universe. At this point the Living Spirit proceeded to the boundary of darkness and hailed the Primal Man with a "summons," to which the Primal Man answered with a "response." Accompanied by the Mother of Life, the Living Spirit extended his right hand to the Primal Man and the latter was drawn up out of the depths of darkness and returned to his celestial home. The Living Spirit also smote the demons of darkness, the Archons, and out of their bodies made the world. Further, from some of the particles of light that had not been contaminated by darkness the Living Spirit made the sun and moon, and from some only partially damaged particles he made the stars.

There remained behind, however, the third part of the particles of light, those apparently hopelessly contaminated, and for their recovery, in the Third Epoch, the Father of Greatness "called" the Third Messenger (also sometimes identified with Mithra). The place of the Third Messenger is in the sun, which is his chariot or ship. As for the

---

57. Mary Boyce, "On Mithra in the Manichaean Pantheon," in *A Locust's Leg: Studies in Honour of S. H. Taqizadeh,* ed. W. B. Henning and E. Yarshater, 44–54.

moon, it is the place of Jesus the Splendor. In the first half of the month, while the moon waxes, the rescued particles of light rise in a pillar of light, called the "column of glory," to the moon; in the second half of the month, while the moon wanes, the light particles are conducted to the sun, and from there are finally returned to the realm of light.

The actual rescue of the particles of light, however, involved many more events. In an attempt to keep some of the light under their control the powers of darkness created the first human couple, Gehmurd and Murdiyanag (Adam and Eve). In Adam was gathered the remaining light, but his body was derived from the powers of evil, and he was sunk in a deep sleep, unaware of the light within him (and the same state of affairs continued ever after in the descendants of Adam and Eve). In parallel with the rescue of the Primal Man by the Living Spirit, a Redeemer came to rescue Adam. The Redeemer was a manifestation of the Third Messenger, and is variously called Ohrmazd (i.e., the Primal Man himself) or Jesus the Splendor. He woke Adam from the sleep of death and brought to him the knowledge (*gnosis*) of what he was and of how the light within him might return to the celestial realm of light.[58] So also the later series of teachers, of whom Mani was the last and the climax, continued to bring redemptive knowledge to human souls.

Before all souls are redeemed, however—and there are particles of light throughout nature, in plants and trees and fruits as well as in animals and humans—the world will experience a "great war," after which the worldwide triumph of the Manichaean religion will follow. Then the last judgment will take place.

As noted above, the description of the last judgment given by Mani in his *Shabuhragan* (represented in the fragments M 473, M 475, M 477, M 482 R)[59] draws heavily upon Matthew 25:31–46. Jesus (here in Mani's account called the god Khradeshahr) will stand and a great call will go out, of which the whole world will be aware. Angels will go to the east and to the west, and the righteous and the evildoers will come together before Khradeshahr. As in Matthew 25:31ff. the judge will separate the evildoers from the righteous and place them on his left hand and condemn them for their failure, and place the righteous on his right hand and praise them for giving their service.

Thereafter the divine beings will leave the world to be engulfed in a fire that will burn for 1,468 years. The last elements of light that it is still possible to rescue will form a "statue," which will rise to heaven like a pillar of light, and the earth will be annihilated. The demons

58. On Gnosticism, see chap. 7.
59. Asmussen, *Manichaean Literature*, 103–6.

of darkness and such souls as are unredeemed will be thrown together in a clump (*bolos*), a prison already made by the Great Builder, and thus the final separation of the two principles of light and darkness will be completed.

## Manichaean Community

In the *Fihrist* al-Nadim uses the Muslim term *imam* (the one claiming the right to rule) for the head of the Manichaean community (called *sardar* in Parthian and *sarat* in Middle Persian):[60]

> As Mani was ascending to the Gardens of Light, but before [he completed] his ascension, he established as the *imam* after him Sis [Sisinnios], who upheld the faith of God and its purity until he died. Then the *imam*s received the faith one from another.

As al-Nadim goes on to tell, the continuing succession of heads of the Manichaean church, inaugurated by Mani's appointment of his presumably chief disciple as his direct successor, was centered in Babil (Babylon, probably meaning the region rather than the city, since Ctesiphon was the chief center), and was uncontested until in the eighth century (in the reign of the Caliph al-Walid, A.D. 705–715), when a schismatic group (the Dinawwariyah, the eastern branch of the Manichaean church) arose, which claimed that the *imam* might reside elsewhere, and was itself centered on the other side of the river of Balkh (the Amu Darya).

The choice of Sisinnios as the first head of the church after Mani is also spoken of in the *Psalms* (241),[61] where there is mention of teachers (apostles) and bishops. Although Mani was in prison and spending "twenty-six days and the nights of them in irons," he was nevertheless able to order the affairs of the church before he died: "Thou didst appoint the twelve teachers and the seventy-two bishops. Thou didst make Sisinnios leader over thy children." In all, to complete five classes in the hierarchy of the Manichaean church, there were not only (1) 12 teachers or apostles, and (2) 72 bishops, but also (3) 360 "house masters," that is, priests or presbyters, as well as the large classes of (4) the elect, and (5) the hearers (see Middle Persian M 36).[62] In choosing the numbers of 12 apostles and 72 (sometimes 70) bishops Mani was undoubtedly following a Christian pattern (Matt. 10:1 for the twelve; Luke 10:17 where the texts vary between 70 and 72).

60. Dodge, *Fihrist of al-Nadīm*, 2.791–92.
61. Allberry, *Manichaean Psalm-Book*, 44.10.
62. Andreas and Henning, *Mitteliranische Manichaica*, 324.

As to the manner of life in the religion, again al-Nadim provides information.[63] For the elect and for the hearers (both of which classes may include both male and female members) there were different requirements.

> He [Mani] said: "He who would enter the religion must examine his soul. If he finds that he can subdue lust and covetousness, refrain from eating meats, drinking wine, as well as from marriage, and if he can also avoid [causing] injury to water, fire, trees, and living things, then let him enter the cult.

The foregoing plainly applies to those who will enter upon the life of the elect. The restrictions under which they must live mean that they must depend upon others to provide for their daily needs, and to do that is the service of the hearers, who are permitted to lead secular lives. The hearers also, however, are under obligations, for Mani prescribed for them ten ordinances, calling for renunciation of worship of idols, telling of lies, avarice, killing, adultery, stealing, teaching of defects, magic, upholding of two opinions about the faith, and neglect and lassitude in action.

The end results of the two ways of life are also different, as al-Nadim elucidates.[64] When death comes to one of the elect, "a light shining deity in the form of the Wise Guide" comes and leads the soul safely, even in spite of any devil's attacks, in ascent to the celestial Gardens of Light. The hearer, however, must pass through intermediary experience—probably rebirth or rebirths—"until his light and spirit are rescued," and he is fit to enter paradise. As for the evil man who is quite outside the church, at death the devils attend him and the good deities reproach him, and thus "he continues to vacillate in the world and in torment, until the time for punishment, when he is cast down to the underworld." In the beyond there is a great structure that is the new Garden of Paradise; on the wall the elect will stand in the light and look down upon the evildoers in hell. "Thus shall the wicked have an increase of regret, grief, and affliction, which will be their lot forever and ever."

As to practices in the church, there were prescribed prayers and fastings, differing between the elect and the hearers (e.g., seven prayers for the elect, four for the hearers), and there was a weekly day of observance, Sunday for the hearers, Monday for the elect.[65]

There was also an important annual festival in memory of Mani, celebrated at the end of a month of fasting and on the day of his death.

63. Dodge, *Fihrist of al-Nadīm*, 2.788–89.
64. Ibid., 795–97.
65. Ibid., 790–91.

This was called the Bema, because a throne or seat (βῆμα) was placed in the meeting room, presumably as a symbol of the presence of Mani. In a description in the *Homilies* (1.27.19–22; 33.17–20; see also 71.4ff.)[66] of the future triumph of the Manichaean religion after the "great war," there are several references to the Bema and along with it references to the "Drawing" and also the "Gospel" and other books—for example, "Then the Bema will be glorified. . . . The great Drawing . . . the Gospel and the books . . . will be glorified." And again, "He, who has revealed . . . his is this exalted Bema. . . . His is this Drawing," which suggests that on the Bema or along with it may have been exhibited Mani's "Book of the Drawing" and perhaps other books too as further tokens of his presence.

In a fragmentary Sogdian text (T II D 123)[67] there is a portion of a Bema liturgy, and it mentions confession, a meal, and the singing of several hymns (the titles of which are given in Parthian and Middle Persian) as elements in the observance. Many of the *Psalms* (219–41)[68] are called "Psalms of the Bema," and were no doubt employed in the Bema celebration when this took place in the area of the Coptic language. In view of the nature of the occasion it is natural that in these psalms there are many references to the last days and death of Mani, and also that Mani is saluted by many of his exalted titles. In one psalm (225),[69] for example, he is hailed as "my lord Mani, the judge of this universe," and in another (227)[70] it is said, "We worship thee, the judge, the Paraclete, we bless thy Bema whereon thou art seated."

As for references to the last days and death of Mani, Bema Psalm 225 asks: "Who will give me word of my shepherd and teach me how he was slain in the godless city by the lawless sects, the beasts that were maddened by the poison of their flames of fire?" With further reference to the priests of the fire, the Magians, the text tells how they asked the king to do away with Mani, as one who was leading all people astray. So the king "commanded them to fetter the righteous one that he might please the Magians, the teachers of Persia, the servants of fire." For twenty-six days Mani was in prison and in chains. In his last hours he prayed, then ascended to the heights. Evidently to make sure that Mani was really dead, the king "commanded the physicians . . . to examine the body, thy holy body, which he mocked and plotted against." The date of Mani's death is stated: "On the second day of the

66. Polotsky, *Manichäische Homilien,* 1.27, 33.
67. Asmussen, *Manichaean Literature,* 68.
68. Allberry, *Manichaean Psalm-Book,* 1–45.
69. Ibid., 17.1.
70. Ibid., 20.19–20.

week [i.e., Monday], thou didst receive the glory of victory, thou didst bind the diadem upon thee, for thou didst kill the race of darkness, in the month Phamenoth, on the fourth day, Monday, thou didst receive thy garland."[71]

Bema Psalm 226 likewise tells of the imprisonment and death of Mani and gives the same date for his death. At the end Mani addresses his "Familiar" or "Twin-Spirit," who has evidently been with him ever since the first revelation at the age of twelve and throughout his ministry and is still with him now. Mani says:

> I was gazing at my Twin-Spirit with my eyes of light, beholding my glorious Father, him who waits for me ever, opening before me the gate unto the height. I spread out my hands, praying unto him; I bent my knees, worshiping him also, that I might divest myself of the image of the flesh and put off the vesture of manhood.

After Mani's death his "body was brought forth in the city, when they had cut off his head and hung it up amid the whole multitude."[72] Such are some of the remembrances of the sufferings and death of Mani that were brought to mind afresh in the observance of the Bema festival.

In addition to Manichaean hymns and psalms already cited, there are in Parthian two long texts that contain whole cycles of hymns. These are the *Huwidagman* and the *Angad Roshnan*. In line with the fundamental ideas of Manichaeism the chief themes are the desire for the liberation of the light from its imprisonment in material existence, and the hope for a wonderful destination for the redeemed. In the *Huwidagman* the speaker asks in part:

> Who will take me over the flood of the tossing sea—
> the zone of conflict in which there is no rest?
>
> Who will lead me beyond rebirths, and free me from
> [them] all—and from all the waves, in which there is no rest?

And the beneficent King says in part:

> [I shall release thee] from all deceit and turbulence . . .
> [and] the torment of death.
>
> Thou shalt put on a radiant garment, and gird on
> Light; and I shall set on thy head the diadem of sovereignty.

71. Ibid., 15.5–8, 16.20–22, 17.14–16, 24–27.
72. Ibid., 19.22–31.

The *Angad Roshnan* has been tentatively attributed to Mar Ammo (who was with Mani at the end and became the great missionary to the east), and is addressed to the deity, the Friend of the Lights. It includes these lines:

> Rich Friend of the beings of Light! In mercy grant
> me [strength and] succour me with every gift!
>
> My soul weeps within, and cries out [at each] distress
> and stab.
>
> This carrion-form is ended for me, and the hour of
> life, with [its] turbulent days.
> It was tossed and troubled as a sea with waves.
> Pain was heaped on pain, whereby they ravage my soul.
>
> Who shall save me . . . and make for me a path . . .?
>
> Who shall take off from me this . . . body, and clothe
> [me] in a new body . . .?
>
> When I had said these words, with soul a-tremble,
> I beheld the Savior as he shone before me.
>
> In joy unbounded he spoke with me, raising up my soul
> from deep affliction.
>
> To me he sayeth, Come, spirit! fear not. I am thy
> Mind, thy glad tidings of hope.
>
> I shall take [thee] with might, and enfold [thee] with
> love, and lead [thee] to [thy] home, the blessed abode.
>
> Come, spirit, fear no more! Death has fallen, and
> sickness fled away.
>
> Hence, spirit, come! . . . I shall lead [thee] to the height,
> [to thy native abode].[73]

## Extension and Extinction of Manichaeism

That Mani himself traveled widely, even to India (perhaps the Makran coast and Gandhara), we have noted in the survey above of his life. In the *Kephalaia* Mani summarizes his work:

> [I spent] many years in Persia, in the land of the Parthians, as far as
> [the kingdom of] Adiabene and the borderlands of the Roman Empire. . . .

73. Mary Boyce, *The Manichaean Hymn-Cycles in Parthian*, 81–159.

I have [sown] the seed of Life. . . . [My] hope has gone to the east of the world and [to all] the regions of the inhabited earth [οἰκουμένη], to the north and to the [south].[74]

In the *Fihrist*[75] al-Nadim likewise gives a summary of the missionary work initiated by Mani: "Mani carried his propaganda to India, China, and the peoples of Khorasan, appointing a disciple of his for each region." As to the commissioning of disciples by Mani for missionary work, there is a Middle Persian text the first part of which (M 2 recto I–II, verso I[76]) is on "The Coming of the Apostle into the Countries." Here we learn that Manichaean missionaries went to the Roman Empire, where they experienced doctrinal disputes with the other religions. They chose many elect and hearers. One emissary in particular, named Patek (hardly Mani's father of the same name), was there for one year. Mani sent scribes and books to a certain Adda and instructed him to preach in the area where he was. Adda labored hard, founded monasteries, chose many elect and hearers, and wrote. He came as far as Alexandria. He chose Nafsha for the religion, presumably a leader to continue the work. When Mani was in Holwan (a provincial capital on the road between Ctesiphon and Hamadan) he chose Mar Ammo (the teacher who was with him at the end of his life, and who knew the Parthian language), a Parthian prince named Ardawan, and scribes and a painter of miniatures, and sent them to Abarshahr, a province in Khorasan, the great eastern province that was the homeland of the Parthians. At the border of Khorasan, Mar Ammo met a spirit who was the frontier guard of the province. The spirit asked what Mar Ammo intended and whence he came. When Mar Ammo replied that he was a disciple of Mani, the spirit bade him return whence he came. Mar Ammo stood, fasting for two days, in praise in front of the sun, and Mani appeared to him and told him to read to the spirit from a book called *The Treasure of the Living*, which he carried. When the spirit returned, the spirit asked what his religion was, and Mar Ammo replied, "We do not eat flesh nor drink wine, from [women] we keep far away," and read to him from the designated book. The spirit then acknowledged that Mar Ammo was not just a "man of religion" but a "true bringer of religion," and evidently welcomed him, for he said, "When I receive you, then the gate of the whole East will be opened in front of you."

Wherever they went, however, the Manichaeans were subject to opposition and persecution. In their homeland the action of Bahram I

74. Polotsky and Böhlig, *Kephalaia*, 15.34–16.9.
75. Dodge, *Fihrist of al-Nadīm*, 2.776.
76. Andreas and Henning, *Mitteliranische Manichaica*, 301–5.

that led to the death of Mani was only the beginning of many persecutions directed thereafter against Mani's followers. As al-Nadim records in the *Fihrist*,[77] after Bahram I "had executed and gibbeted Mani and forbidden the people of his kingdom to dispute about the religion, he began to slay the followers of Mani wherever he found them. So they did not stop fleeing from him until they had crossed the river of Balkh [Amu Darya] and entered the realm of the Khan [ruler of Turkish tribes of Asia], with whom they remained." In the *Homilies* (1.76.11ff.; 1.81.8ff.)[78] we also learn of new persecutions initiated by Bahram II (A.D. 277–293), son and successor of Bahram I, and we hear Sisinnios, Mani's chosen successor, pray to Mani for help: "Since the day when you chose me . . . my children have been killed in every land. . . . O my Father, send thy power that it bear up those who have been crucified. . . . In the years of King Bahram son of Bahram this took place." In what followed Sisinnios was brought into the presence of the king and, after answering the king bravely, was killed, and was succeeded by Innaios as the next head of the church (*Homily* 1.82.3ff.).[79]

After the Arab conquest of Babylonia and Iran (A.D. 651) in the time of the Umayyad rulers (661–750), as al-Nadim continues the account,[80] the Manichaeans returned and were for a time treated well by such governors of Iraq as al-Hajjaj (694–714) and his successor Khalid (d. 738), and the head of the church lived again in Babil (the region of Babylon). The Abbasids (750–1258), however, founded their new capital of Baghdad ("gift of God") near the old capital of Seleucia-Ctesiphon and, when both the Zoroastrians and the Manichaeans were perceived as possible rebels against the Arab rule, called all of them and their sympathizers by the general term for "heretic" (*zandiq*), and subjected them to much persecution. For example, as al-Nadim relates, a certain Muhammad ibn 'Ubayd Allah, secretary to al-Mahdi (the third Abbassid caliph who ruled at Baghdad in 775–785), confessed to being a *zandiq,* and so al-Mahdi had him executed. Under these circumstances the leaders of the Manichaean church no longer remained in Babil but sought out any place where they could be safe, and the last time any of them appeared was during the days of the caliph al-Muqtadir (908–932), for they feared for their lives and kept their identity secret as they moved about the region. For the most part the Manichaeans went again into the eastern province of Khorasan and Central Asia, with only a few remaining in the Islamic regions. In the

77. Dodge, *Fihrist of al-Nadīm,* 2.802.
78. Polotsky, *Manichäische Homilien,* 76, 81.
79. Ibid., 82–83.
80. Dodge, *Fihrist of al-Nadīm,* 2.802–5.

days of Mu'izz al-Dawlah (who ruled at Baghdad, 946–967) al-Nadim knew of three hundred Manichaeans in Baghdad. A quarter of a century later when he wrote the *Fihrist* there were not as many as five of them there.

In the east there were Manichaeans at a number of cities, which al-Nadim mentions, including Samarkand "and especially Tunkath," the latter probably being the modern Tashkent, formerly called Binkath. From there they went on along the "silk road,"[81] as we know from the manuscripts and paintings found among the Turkish Uygurs at Turfan (Turpan), and on into China. In China, however, already in A.D. 732 an imperial edict was issued against Manichaeism, which prohibited further missionary work although allowing the faith to "western barbarians." The edict read:

> The doctrine of Mar Mani is through and through a perverted creed. Falsely it takes the name of Buddhism and deceives the people. This must be formally prohibited. But since it is the indigenous faith of the western barbarians and other people, it shall not be accounted a crime for them to practice it on their own behalf.[82]

Again in A.D. 842/843, with the collapse of the Uygurs who had supported the Manichaeans in China, Manichaean monasteries were closed, their leaders exiled or slain, their property confiscated, and the religion proscribed.[83]

In the west the wide diffusion of Manichaeism is attested by the writings, ordinarily polemical, of Christian authors. The church historian Eusebius (c. A.D. 325), for example, writes in violent criticism of Mani (*Church History* 7.31):

> His very speech and manners proclaimed him a barbarian in mode of life, and, being by nature devilish and insane, he suited his endeavors thereto and attempted to pose as Christ: at one time giving out that he was the Paraclete and the Holy Spirit himself, conceited fool that he was, as well as mad; at another time choosing, as Christ did, twelve disciples as associates in his new fangled system. In short, he stitched together false and godless doctrines that he had collected from the countless, long-extinct, godless heresies, and infected our empire with, as it were, a deadly poison that came from the land of the Persians; and from him the profane name of Manichaean is still commonly on men's lips to this day.

81. For the "silk road," see Irene M. Franck and David M. Brownstone, *The Silk Road: A History.*
82. Widengren, *Mani and Manichaeism,* 133.
83. *EB* 5.581.

So also Augustine (A.D. 354–430) gives this description of the Manichaeans, which, although also violently critical of them, nevertheless provides some accurate information (Letter 236.2):

> The Hearers eat meat and cultivate lands, and, if they wish, have wives, none of which things is allowed to the Elect. The Hearers go on their knees before the Elect, humbly begging the imposition of their hands. They join them in adoring and praying to the sun and the moon. They fast with them on Sundays, and along with them they believe all the blasphemous tenets which make the Manichaean heresy so detestable. Thus they deny Christ's birth of a virgin, and say that his flesh was not true flesh, but false, that his passion accordingly was mere pretense, and his resurrection null. They speak evil of the patriarchs and the prophets. They say that the law, given by God's servant Moses, was not given by the true God, but by the Prince of Darkness. They consider all souls, not only of men, but even of beasts, to be of the substance of God, and altogether parts of God. Finally, they say that the good and true God entered into conflict with the race of Darkness, and mingled a part of himself with the Princes of Darkness, which part is defiled all the world over, but is purified by the meals of the Elect and by the sun and moon; while any portion of deity which it has been found impossible thus to purify is bound with an everlasting bond of punishment at the end of the world. Thus God is believed to be not only liable to violation and contamination and corruption, seeing that a portion of him is reducible to such misery, but to be unable even at the end of the world to get himself wholly cleansed from that so great defilement and uncleanness and misery.

We also learn from Augustine the names of several prominent Manichaeans against whom he spoke, namely, Faustus, Fortunatus, Felix, and Secundinus.

Opposition in the West to Manichaeism came not only from Christianity but also from the Roman Empire itself. Thus in A.D. 297 the emperor Diocletian issued an edict, addressed to the African proconsul Julianus, in which Diocletian initiated outright persecution of the Manichaeans (even as in 303 the same emperor began his persecution of the Christians). The Manichaeans, Diocletian said, were exciting otherwise peaceful communities, and their Persian customs might contaminate as with a baleful poison the innocent Roman people and indeed the whole world. Therefore the Manichaean writings and their authors as well as their leaders were to be burned, and their followers were to lose their lives and to have their property confiscated by the state. Others infected by the Manichaean doctrines were condemned to compulsory labor in the mines and confiscation of their property.[84]

---

84. Widengren, *Mani and Manichaeism*, 118.

Under such hostile pressures, which sooner or later fell upon the followers of Mani wherever they went, his religion, which was once known from the Pillars of Hercules in the west to China in the east, and was in existence from the third century A.D. to the fifteenth, came to an end as a continuing community of faith, leaving only the memory and fragmentary records of the man and his followers, the man who himself stood, as he believed, in succession to Zoroaster, the Buddha, and Jesus, and was surely one of the great personages in the history of religions.[85]

85. *CHI* 3.2.990.

# Reflective Postscript

And so . . . the myth . . . will save us if we believe it, . . . and so we shall hold ever to the upward way and pursue righteousness with wisdom always and ever, . . . and thus . . . we shall fare well.

—Plato, *Republic* 621b–d

In that day Israel will be the third with Egypt and Assyria, a blessing in the midst of the earth, whom the LORD of hosts has blessed, saying, "Blessed be Egypt my people, and Assyria the work of my hands, and Israel my heritage."

—Isaiah 19:24–25

In past generations he allowed all the nations to walk in their own ways; yet he did not leave himself without witness.

—Acts 14:16–17

# Bibliography

In addition to the main books listed here, see also other detailed studies cited at relevant points in the notes. All references are to personally used and verified materials. In addition to the present work other relevant books by Jack Finegan are:

*Light from the Ancient Past.* Princeton: Princeton University Press, 1946; rev. ed. 1959; paperback repr., 2 vols., 1969.

*The Archeology of World Religions.* Princeton: Princeton University Press, 1952; paperback repr., 3 vols., 1965.

*Handbook of Biblical Chronology.* Princeton: Princeton University Press, 1964.

*Hidden Records of the Life of Jesus.* Philadelphia/Boston: Pilgrim, 1969.

*The Archeology of the New Testament: The Life of Jesus and the Beginning of the Early Church.* Princeton: Princeton University Press, 1969; paperback repr., 1978.

*The Archeology of the New Testament: The Mediterranean World of the Early Christian Apostles.* Boulder, Colo.: Westview/London: Croom Helm, 1981.

*Archaeological History of the Ancient Middle East.* Boulder, Colo.: Westview, 1979; repr. New York: Dorset, 1986.

## Introduction

Bleeker, C. J. *Egyptian Festivals: Enactments of Religious Renewal.* Studies in the History of Religions 13. Leiden: E. J. Brill, 1967.

Eliade, Mircea. *Traité d'histoire des religions.* Rev. ed. Paris: Payot, 1964.

Frankfort, Henri, et al. *The Intellectual Adventure of Ancient Man.* Chicago: University of Chicago Press, 1946.

Jacobsen, Thorkild. *The Treasures of Darkness: A History of Mesopotamian Religion.* New Haven: Yale University Press, 1976.

van der Leeuw, G. *Religion in Essence and Manifestation.* 2 vols. New York: Harper & Row, 1963.

## Chapter 1

Barton, George A. *The Royal Inscriptions of Sumer and Akkad.* London: Oxford University Press, 1929.

Beek, Martin A. *Atlas of Mesopotamia.* New York: Nelson, 1962.

Deimel, Antonius. *Pantheon Babylonicum.* Rome: Pontificium Institutum Biblicum, 1914.

Falkenstein, A. *Die Inschriften Gudeas von Lagaš.* Vol. 1, *Einleitung.* Analecta Orientalia 30. Rome: Pontificium Institutum Biblicum, 1966.

————. *Das Sumerische.* Handbuch der Orientalistik 1.2.1–2.1. Edited by B. Spuler. Leiden: E. J. Brill, 1964.

————. *Sumerische Götterlieder.* 2 vols. Heidelberg: Carl Winter, 1959–1960.

Farber-Flügge, Gertrud. *Der Mythos "Inanna und Enki" unter besonderer Berücksichtigung der Liste der m e.* Studia Pohl 10. Rome: Biblical Institute, 1973.

Forbes, R. J. *Studies in Ancient Technology.* 9 vols. Leiden: E. J. Brill, 1955–1964.

Frankfort, Henri. *Kingship and the Gods.* Chicago: University of Chicago Press, 1948.

Gray, John. *Near Eastern Mythology.* London: Hamlyn, 1969.

Hallo, William W., and J. J. A. Van Dijk. *The Exaltation of Inanna.* New Haven: Yale University Press, 1968.

Heidel, Alexander. *The Babylonian Genesis.* 2d ed. Chicago: University of Chicago Press, 1951.

————. *The Gilgamesh Epic and Old Testament Parallels.* 2d ed. Chicago: University of Chicago Press, 1963.

Jacobsen, Thorkild. *Toward the Image of Tammuz and Other Essays on Mesopotamian History and Culture.* Edited by William L. Moran. Harvard Semitic Series 21. Cambridge: Harvard University Press, 1970.

————. *The Treasures of Darkness: A History of Mesopotamian Religion.* New Haven: Yale University Press, 1976.

*Kramer Anniversary Volume: Cuneiform Studies in Honor of Samuel Noah Kramer.* Edited by Barry L. Eichler. Alter Orient und Altes Testament 25. Neukirchen-Vluyn: Neukirchener Verlag, 1976.

Kramer, Samuel Noah. *From the Poetry of Sumer: Creation, Glorification, Adoration.* Berkeley: University of California Press, 1979.

————. *History Begins at Sumer.* 3d ed. Philadelphia: University of Pennsylvania Press, 1981.

————. *The Sacred Marriage Rite: Aspects of Faith, Myth, and Ritual in Ancient Sumer.* Bloomington: Indiana University Press, 1969.

————. *Sumerian Culture and Society: The Cuneiform Documents and Their Cultural Significance.* Cummings Module in Anthropology 58. Menlo Park, Calif.: Cummings, 1975.

————. *Sumerian Mythology.* Rev. ed. New York: Harper, 1961.

————. *The Sumerians: Their History, Culture, and Character.* Chicago: University of Chicago Press, 1963.

Lambert, W. G., and A. R. Millard. *Atraḥasīs: The Babylonian Story of the Flood.* Oxford: Clarendon, 1969.

Moortgat, Anton. *Tammuz: Der Unsterblichkeitsglaube in der altorientalischen Bildkunst.* Berlin: Walter de Gruyter, 1949.

Moscati, Sabatino, ed. *An Introduction to the Comparative Grammar of the Semitic Languages.* Porta Linguarum Orientalium, n.s. 6. Wiesbaden: Otto Harrassowitz, 1964.

Parrot, André. *The Tower of Babel.* Studies in Biblical Archaeology 2. New York: Philosophical Library, 1955.

*The Place of Astronomy in the Ancient World: A Joint Symposium of the Royal Society and the British Academy.* Edited by F. R. Hodson. London: Oxford University Press, 1974.

Riemschneider, Kaspar K. *Lehrbuch des Akkadischen.* 2d ed. Leipzig: VEB Verlag Enzyklopädie, 1973.

Roberts, J. J. M. *The Earliest Semitic Pantheon.* Baltimore: Johns Hopkins University Press, 1972.

*Studies in Honor of Benno Landsberger on His Seventy-Fifth Birthday.* Edited by H. G. Guterbock and T. Jacobsen. Assyriological Studies 16. Chicago: University of Chicago Press, 1965.

Tigay, Jeffrey H. *The Evolution of the Gilgamesh Epic.* Philadelphia: University of Pennsylvania Press, 1982.

Ungnad, Arthur. *Grammatik des Akkadischen.* 5th ed. Edited by Lubor Matouš. Munich: C. H. Beck, 1969.

Van Buren, E. Douglas. *Symbols of the Gods in Mesopotamian Art.* Analecta Orientalia 23. Rome: Pontificium Institutum Biblicum, 1945.

Weiher, Egbert von. *Der babylonische Gott Nergal.* Alter Orient und Altes Testament 11. Neukirchen-Vluyn: Neukirchener Verlag, 1971.

Wohlstein, Herman. *The Sky-God An-Anu.* Jericho, N.Y.: Paul A. Stroock, 1976.

Wolkstein, Diane, and Samuel Noah Kramer. *Inanna: Queen of Heaven and Earth.* New York: Harper & Row, 1983.

## Chapter 2

Aldred, Cyril. *Akhenaten and Nefertiti.* New York: Viking, 1973.

————. *Akhenaten, Pharaoh of Egypt: A New Study.* New York: McGraw-Hill, 1968.

Allen, Thomas George. *The Book of the Dead; or, Going Forth by Day.* Studies in Ancient Oriental Civilization 37. Chicago: University of Chicago Press, 1974.

Baines, John, and Jaromír Málek. *Atlas of Ancient Egypt.* New York: Facts on File, 1982.

Bleeker, Claas Jouco. *Egyptian Festivals: Enactments of Religious Renewal.* Studies in the History of Religions 13. Leiden: E. J. Brill, 1967.

————. *Hathor and Thoth: Two Key Figures of the Ancient Egyptian Religion.* Studies in the History of Religions 26. Leiden: E. J. Brill, 1973.

Breasted, James Henry. *The Dawn of Conscience.* New York: Scribner, 1933.

Brunton, Paul. *A Search in Secret Egypt.* New York: Dutton, 1935. Reprint, New York: Samuel Weiser, 1977.

Buck, Adriaan de, and Alan H. Gardiner. *The Egyptian Coffin Texts.* 7 vols. Oriental Institute Publications 34, 49, 64, 67, 73, 81, 87. Chicago: University of Chicago Press, 1935–1961.

Budge, E. A. Wallis. *The Gods of the Egyptians.* 2 vols. London: Methuen, 1904.

Chandler, Tertius. *Moses and the Golden Age.* Bryn Mawr, Pa.: Dorrance, 1986.

David, Ann Rosalie. *A Guide to Religious Ritual at Abydos.* Warminster: Aris & Phillips, 1981.

Desroches-Noblecourt, Christiane. *The Great Pharaoh Ramses II and His Time.* Montreal: Canada Exim Group, 1985.

————. *Tutankhamen.* New York: New York Graphic Society, 1963.

Erman, Adolf. *Die Religion der Ägypter.* Berlin: Walter de Gruyter, 1934.

Faulkner, Raymond Oliver. *The Ancient Egyptian Coffin Texts.* 3 vols. Warminster: Aris & Phillips, 1973–1978.

————. *The Ancient Egyptian Pyramid Texts.* Oxford: Clarendon, 1969.

Frankfort, Henri. *Ancient Egyptian Religion.* New York: Columbia University Press, 1948.

Freud, Sigmund. *Moses and Monotheism.* New York: Knopf, 1939.

Goedicke, Hans. *The Protocol of Neferyt (The Prophecy of Neferti).* Johns Hopkins Near Eastern Studies. Baltimore: Johns Hopkins University Press, 1977.

Griffiths, John Gwyn. *The Origins of Osiris and His Cult.* Studien in the History of Religions 40. Leiden: E. J. Brill, 1980.

Gundel, Wilhelm. *Dekane und Dekansternbilder.* Studien der Bibliothek Warburg 19. Glückstadt and Hamburg: J. J. Augustin, 1936.

Hari, Robert. *New Kingdom Amarna Period: The Great Hymn to Aten.* Iconography of Religions 16.6. Leiden: E. J. Brill, 1985.

Hornbostel, Wilhelm. *Sarapis.* EPRO 32 Leiden: E. J. Brill, 1973.

Hornung, Erik. *Der ägyptische Mythos von der Himmelskuh*. Orbis Biblicus et Orientalis 46. Freiburg, Switzerland: Universitätsverlag/Göttingen: Vandenhoeck & Ruprecht, 1982.

_____. *Altägyptische Höllenvorstellungen*. Abhandlungen der Sächsischen Akademie der Wissenschaften zu Leipzig, Philologisch-historische Klasse 59.3. Berlin: Akademie-Verlag, 1968.

_____. *Conceptions of God in Ancient Egypt: The One and the Many*. Ithaca, N.Y.: Cornell University Press, 1982.

_____, and Elisabeth Staehelin. *Studien zum Sedfest*. Aegyptiaca Helvetica 1. Geneva: Editions de Belles-Lettres, 1974.

Ions, Veronica. *Egyptian Mythology*. 2d ed. London: Hamlyn, 1968.

Karst, Josef. *Die Chronik aus dem armenischen übersetzt mit textkritischem Kommentar*. Eusebius Werke 5. GCS 20. Leipzig: J. C. Hinrichs, 1911.

Lamy, Lucie. *Egyptian Mysteries: New Light on Ancient Spiritual Knowledge*. New York: Crossroad, 1981.

*Lexikon der Ägyptologie*. Edited by Wolfgang Helck and Eberhard Otto. 6 vols. to date. Wiesbaden: Otto Harrassowitz, 1972–.

Lurker, Manfred. *The Gods and Symbols of Ancient Egypt*. New York: Thames & Hudson, 1980.

Mercer, Samuel A. B. *The Pyramid Texts in Translation and Commentary*. 4 vols. New York: Longmans, Green, 1952.

Morenz, Siegfried. *Egyptian Religion*. Ithaca, N.Y.: Cornell University Press, 1973.

_____. *Gott und Mensch im alten Ägypten*. Heidelberg: Lambert Schneider, 1965.

Myśliwiec, Karol. *Eighteenth Dynasty before the Amarna Period*. Iconography of Religions 16.5. Leiden: E. J. Brill, 1985.

Nims, Charles F. *Thebes of the Pharaohs: Pattern for Every City*. New York: Stein & Day, 1965.

Otto, Eberhard. *Egyptian Art and the Cults of Osiris and Amon*. London: Thames & Hudson, 1968.

_____. *Osiris und Amun: Kult und heilige Stätten*. Munich: Hirmer, 1966.

Parker, Richard A. *The Calendars of Ancient Egypt*. Studies in Ancient Oriental Civilization 26. Chicago: University of Chicago Press, 1950.

Piankoff, Alexandre. *Le livre du jour et de la nuit*. Bibliothèque d'étude 13. Cairo: Institut français d'archéologie orientale, 1942.

*The Place of Astronomy in the Ancient World: A Joint Symposium of the Royal Society and the British Academy*. Edited by F. R. Hodson. London: Oxford University Press, 1974 (= *Royal Society Philosophical Transactions* A.276, no. 1257).

Redford, Donald B. *Akhenaten: The Heretic King*. Princeton: Princeton University Press, 1984.

Reymond, Eve A. E. *The Mythical Origin of the Egyptian Temple*. Manchester: Manchester University Press/New York: Barnes & Noble, 1969.

Sander-Hansen, Constantin Emil. *Das Gottesweib des Amun*. Kongelige Danske Videnskabernes Selskab, Historisk-filologiske Skrifter 1.1. Copenhagen: Munksgaard, 1940.

Schäfer, Heinrich. *Die Mysterien des Osiris in Abydos unter König Sesostris III*. Untersuchungen zur Geschichte und Altertumskunde Ägyptens 4.2. Leipzig: J. C. Hinrichs, 1904.

Schlögl, Hermann Alexander. *Der Gott Tatenen*. Orbis Biblicus et Orientalis 29. Freiburg, Switzerland: Universitätsverlag/Göttingen: Vandenhoeck & Ruprecht, 1980.

Schuré, Édouard. *The Great Initiates*. Translated by Gloria Rasberry. West Nyack, N.Y.: St. George, 1961.

_____. *The Mysteries of Ancient Egypt: Hermes/Moses*. Blauvelt, N.Y.: Rudolf

Steiner, 1971 (= chaps. 3 and 4 of *The Great Initiates*).

Schwaller de Lubicz, R. A. *Symbol and the Symbolic: Ancient Egypt, Science, and the Evolution of Consciousness*. New York: Inner Traditions, 1981.

Smith, Ray Winfield, and Donald B. Redford. *The Akhenaten Temple Project*. Vol. 1, *Initial Discoveries*. Warminster: Aris & Phillips, 1976.

Stambaugh, John E. *Sarapis under the Early Ptolemies*. EPRO 25. Leiden: E. J. Brill, 1972.

Steiner, Rudolf. *Christianity as Mystical Fact and the Mysteries of Antiquity*. New York: Putnam, 1914. Reprint, West Nyack, N.Y.: Rudolf Steiner, 1961.

Te Velde, H. *Seth: God of Confusion*. Probleme der Ägyptologie 6. Leiden: E. J. Brill, 1967.

Van den Broek, Roelof. *The Myth of the Phoenix According to Classical and Early Christian Tradition*. EPRO 24. Leiden: E. J. Brill, 1972.

West, John Anthony. *Serpent in the Sky: The High Wisdom of Ancient Egypt*. New York: Harper & Row, 1979.

## Chapter 3

Afnán, Ruhi Muhsen. *Zoroaster's Influence on Greek Thought*. New York: Philosophical Library, 1965.

*The Babylonian Talmud*. Edited by Isidore Epstein. 18 vols. London: Soncino, 1978.

Bailey, Harold Walter. *Zoroastrian Problems in the Ninth-Century Books*. Oxford: Clarendon, 1971.

Barbier de Meynard, C. *Dictionnaire géographique, historique et littéraire de la Perse et des contrées adjacentes, extrait du Mo'djem el-Bouldan de Yaqout*. Paris: L'Imprimerie impériale, 1861. Reprint, Amsterdam: Philo, 1970.

Behrooz, Zabih. *Taghvim va Tarikh dar Iran* (Calendar and Chronicle in Iran). Tehran, 1952.

Benveniste, Émile. *The Persian Religion According to the Chief Greek Texts*. Paris: P. Geuthner, 1929.

Boyce, Mary. *A History of Zoroastrianism*. Handbuch der Orientalistik 1.8.1.2. 2 vols. Leiden: E. J. Brill, 1975, 1982.

————. *The Letter of Tansar*. Serie Orientale Roma 38. Rome: Istituto Italiano per il Medio ed Estremo Oriente, 1968.

————. *A Persian Stronghold of Zoroastrianism*. Oxford: Clarendon, 1977.

————. *Textual Sources for the Study of Zoroastrianism*. Totowa, N.J.: Barnes & Noble, 1984.

————. *Zoroastrians: Their Religious Beliefs and Practices*. London: Routledge & Kegan Paul, 1979.

Christensen, Arthur Emanuel. *L'Iran sous les Sassanides*. Copenhagen: Levin & Munksgaard/Paris: P. Geuthner, 1936. Reprint, Osnabrück: Otto Zeller, 1971.

————. *Les Kayanides*. Kongelige Danske Videnskabernes Selskab, Historisk-filologiske Meddelelser 19.2. Copenhagen: Høst, 1931.

*Christianity, Judaism and Other Greco-Roman Cults: Studies for Morton Smith at Sixty*. Edited by Jacob Neusner. 4 vols. Studies in Judaism in Late Antiquity 12. Leiden: E. J. Brill, 1975.

Clemen, Carl. *Fontes historiae religionis Persicae*. Bonn: A. Marci & E. Weber, 1920.

Dhalla, Maneckji Nusservanji. *History of Zoroastrianism*. New York: Oxford University Press, 1938. Reprint, New York: AMS, 1977.

————. *The Nyaishes; or, Zoroastrian Litanies*. Columbia University Indo-Iranian Series 6. New York: Columbia University Press, 1908. Reprint, New York: AMS, 1965.

————. *Zoroastrian Theology*. New York: N.p., 1914. Reprint, New York: AMS, 1972.

Duchesne-Guillemin, Jacques. *The Hymns of Zarathustra*. Boston: Beacon, 1963.

Reprint, Westport, Conn.: Hyperion, 1979.

————. *Symbolik des Parsismus*. Symbolik der Religionen 5. Stuttgart: Anton Hiersemann, 1961.

————. *Symbols and Values in Zoroastrianism*. Religious Perspectives 15. New York: Harper & Row, 1966.

————. *The Western Response to Zoroaster*. Oxford: Clarendon, 1958. Reprint, Westport, Conn.: Greenwood, 1973.

Erdmann, Kurt. *Das iranische Feuerheiligtum*. Sendschrift der Deutschen Orient-Gesellschaft 11. Leipzig: J. C. Hinrichs, 1941. Reprint, Osnabrück: Otto Zeller, 1969.

*Festschrift für Wilhelm Eilers*. Edited by Gernot Wiessner. Wiesbaden: Otto Harrassowitz, 1967.

Frye, Richard Nelson. *The History of Ancient Iran*. Munich: C. H. Beck, 1984.

*General Atlas of Afghanistan*. Tehran: Sahab Geographic & Drafting Institute, 1970.

Gershevitch, Ilya. *The Avestan Hymn to Mithra*. University of Cambridge Oriental Publications 4. Cambridge: Cambridge University Press, 1959.

Gnoli, Gherardo. *Zoroaster's Time and Homeland*. Istituto Universitario Orientale, Seminario di Studi Asiatici, Series Minor 7. Naples: Istituto Universitario Orientale, 1980.

Gonda, Jan. *The Vedic God Mitra*. Orientalia Rheno-Traiectina 13. Leiden: E. J. Brill, 1972.

————. *The Vision of the Vedic Poets*. Disputations Rheno-Traiectina 8. The Hague: Mouton, 1963.

Hartman, Sven S. *Parsism: The Religion of Zoroaster*. Iconography of Religions 14.4. Leiden: E. J. Brill, 1980.

Haug, Martin. *Essays on the Sacred Language, Writings, and Religion of the Parsis*. Edited by E. W. West. 2d ed. London: Trübner, 1878.

————, and Edward William West. *The Book of Arda Viraf*. Bombay: Government Central Book Depot, 1872. Amsterdam: Oriental Press, 1971.

Herzfeld, Ernst. *Am Tor von Asien: Felsdenkmale aus Irans Heldenzeit*. Berlin: D. Reimer, 1920.

————. *Archaeological History of Iran*. Schweich Lectures 1934. London: Oxford University Press, 1935. Reprint, Munich: Kraus, 1980.

————. *Iran in the Ancient East*. London: Oxford University Press, 1941.

————. *The Persian Empire: Studies in Geography and Ethnography of the Ancient Near East*. Edited by Gerald Walser. Wiesbaden: Franz Steiner, 1968.

Hinnells, John R. *Persian Mythology*. London: Hamlyn, 1973.

Hinz, Walther. *Zarathustra*. Stuttgart: W. Kohlhammer, 1961.

*Historical Atlas of Iran*. Tehran: Tehran University, 1971.

*Historical Atlas of the Religions of the World*. Edited by Isma'īl Rāgī al-Fārūqī. New York: Macmillan, 1974.

Insler, S. *The Gāthās of Zarathustra*. Acta Iranica 3.8. Leiden: E. J. Brill, 1975.

Kent, Roland G. *Old Persian: Grammar, Texts, Lexicon*. 2d ed. American Oriental Series 33. New Haven: American Oriental Society, 1953.

King, L. W., and R. C. Thompson. *The Sculptures and Inscription of Darius the Great on the Rock of Behistûn in Persia*. London: British Museum, 1907.

Lauer, Max. *Des Moses von Chorene Geschichte Gross-Armeniens*. Regensburg: Georg Joseph Manz, 1869.

Markwart, Josef. *Wehrot und Arang: Untersuchungen zur mythischen und geschichtlichen Landeskunde von Ostiran*. Leiden: E. J. Brill, 1938.

al-Mas'ūdī, Abū al-Ḥasan 'Alī. *Les Prairies d'Or*. Translated by C. Barbier de Meynard and A. Pavet de Courteille. Revised by Charles Pella. 3 vols. Paris: Société Asiatique, 1962–1971.

Mayer, Rudolf. *Die biblische Vorstellung vom Weltenbrand: Eine Untersuchung über die Beziehungen zwischen Parsismus und Judentum.* Bonner Orientalistische Studien, n.s. 4. Bonn: Orientalischen Seminars der Universität Bonn, 1956.

*Mémorial Jean de Menasce.* Edited by P. Gignoux and A. Tafazzoli. Louvain: Imprimerie Orientaliste, 1974.

Neusner, Jacob. *A History of the Jews in Babylonia.* Vol. 1, *The Parthian Period.* Studia Post-Biblica 9. Leiden: E. J. Brill, 1965. Reprint, Chico, Calif.: Scholars Press, 1984.

_____. *Judaism, Christianity, and Zoroastrianism in Talmudic Babylonia.* Studies in Judaism. Lanham, Md.: University Press of America, 1986.

*Oriental Studies in Honour of Cursetji Erachji Pavry.* Edited by Jal Dastur Cursetji Pavry. London: Oxford University Press, 1933.

Oxtoby, Willard Gurdon. *Ancient Iran and Zoroastrianism in Festschriften.* Waterloo, Canada: Council on the Study of Religions, 1973.

Pangborn, Cyrus R. *Zoroastrianism: A Beleaguered Faith.* New York: Advent, 1983.

Sachau, C. Edward. *Alberuni's India: An Account of the Religion, Philosophy, Literature, Geography, Chronology, Astronomy, Customs, Laws and Astrology of India about A.D. 1030.* 2 vols. London: Trübner, 1887–1888. Reprint, Delhi: S. Chand, 1964.

_____. *The Chronology of Ancient Nations: An English Version of the Arabic Text of the Athâr-ul-Bâkiya of Albîrûnî, or "Vestiges of the Past," Collected and Reduced to Writing by the Author in A.H. 390–1, A.D. 1000.* London: William H. Allen, 1879. Reprint, Lahore: Hijra International, 1983.

*Sacred Books of the East.* Edited by F. Max Müller. 51 vols. Oxford: Clarendon, 1879–1910.

Scheftelowitz, Isidor. *Die altpersische Religion und das Judentum: Unterschiede, Übereinstimmungen und gegenseitige* Beeinflussungen. Giessen: Alfred Töpelmann, 1920.

Schippmann, Klaus. *Die iranischen Feuerheiligtümer.* Religionsgeschichtliche Versuche und Vorarbeiten 31. Berlin: Walter de Gruyter, 1971.

Schmidt, Erich F. *Persepolis.* 3 vols. Oriental Institute Publications 68–70. Chicago: University of Chicago Press, 1953–1970.

Schoff, Wilfred H. *Parthian Stations, by Isidore of Charax.* Philadelphia: Commercial Museum, 1914. Reprint, Chicago: Ares, 1976.

Shahzadi, Mobed Bahram. *Message of Zarathushtra.* Vol. 1, *Religious Instruction.* 2d. ed. Westminster, Calif.: California Zoroastrian Center, 1986.

Spencer, Hormusjee Shapoorjee. *Are the Gathas Pre-Vedic? and, The Age of Zarathushtra.* Poona, India: H. R. Vaswani, 1965.

Sprengling, Martin. *Third Century Iran: Sapor and Kartir.* Chicago: Oriental Institute, University of Chicago, 1953.

Stronach, David. *Pasargadae: A Report on the Excavations Conducted by the British Institute of Persian Studies from 1961 to 1963.* Oxford: Clarendon, 1978.

Taraporewala, Irach J. S. *The Divine Songs of Zarathushtra: A Philological Study of the Gathas of Zarathushtra.* Bombay: D. B. Taraporevala Sons, 1951. Reprint, New York: AMS, 1977.

*The Teacher's Yoke: Studies in Memory of Henry Trantham.* Edited by Jerry E. Vardaman and James Leo Garrett, Jr. Waco, Tex.: Baylor University Press, 1964.

Tilak, Bal Gangadhar. *The Orion; or, Researches into the Antiquity of the Vedas.* Poona, India: Tilak, 1893.

Warner, Arthur G., and Edmond Warner. *The Sháhnáma of Firdausi Done into English.* Trübner's Oriental Series. 9 vols. London: Paul, Trench, Trübner, 1905–1915.

Zaehner, Robert Charles. *The Dawn and Twilight of Zoroastrianism.* New York:

Putnam, 1961. Reprint, London: Weidenfeld & Nicolson, 1975.

————. *Zurvan: A Zoroastrian Dilemma.* Oxford: Clarendon, 1955. Reprint, New York: Biblo & Tannen, 1972.

## Chapter 4

Aharoni, Yohanan. *The Archaeology of the Land of Israel: From the Prehistoric Beginnings to the End of the First Temple Period.* Philadelphia: Westminster, 1982.

Albright, William Foxwell. *From the Stone Age to Christianity: Monotheism and the Historical Process.* Baltimore: Johns Hopkins University Press, 1940.

————. *Yahweh and the Gods of Canaan: A Historical Analysis of Two Contrasting Faiths.* University of London: Athlone, 1968.

Anati, Emmanuel. *Palestine before the Hebrews: A History, from the Earliest Arrival of Man to the Conquest of Canaan.* New York: Alfred A. Knopf, 1963.

Barton, George A. *The Royal Inscriptions of Sumer and Akkad.* New Haven: Yale University Press, 1929.

Bermant, Chaim, and Michael Weitzman. *Ebla: A Revelation in Archaeology.* New York: Times Books, 1979.

Cassuto, Umberto. *The Goddess Anath: Canaanite Epics of the Patriarchal Age.* Jerusalem: Magnes, 1971.

Clifford, Richard J. *The Cosmic Mountain in Canaan and the Old Testament.* Harvard Semitic Monographs 4. Cambridge: Harvard University Press, 1972.

Coogan, Michael David. *Stories from Ancient Canaan.* Philadelphia: Westminster, 1978.

Craigie, Peter C. *Ugarit and the Old Testament.* Grand Rapids: Eerdmans, 1983.

Cross, Frank Moore. *Canaanite Myth and Hebrew Epic: Essays in the History of the Religion of Israel.* Cambridge: Harvard University Press, 1973.

Dalley, Stephanie. *Mari and Karana: Two Old Babylonian Cities.* London: Longman, 1984.

Driver, Godfrey Rolles. *Semitic Writing from Pictograph to Alphabet.* 3d ed. Edited by S. A. Hopkins. London: Oxford University Press, 1976.

*Eblaitica: Essays on the Ebla Archives and Eblaite Language,* ed. Cyrus H. Gordon, Gary A. Randsburg, and Nathan H. Winter. Vol. 1. Winona Lake, Indiana: Eisenbrauns, 1987.

Eissfeldt, Otto. *Baal Zaphon: Zeus Kasios und der Durchzug der Israeliten durchs Meer.* Beiträge zur Religionsgeschichte des Altertums 1. Halle: Max Niemeyer, 1932.

Engberg, Robert Martin. *The Hyksos Reconsidered.* Studies in Ancient Oriental Civilization 18. Chicago: University of Chicago Press, 1939.

Gibson, J. C. L. *Canaanite Myths and Legends.* 2d ed. First edition by G. R. Driver. Edinburgh: T. & T. Clark, 1978.

Gottwald, Norman K. *The Tribes of Israel: A Sociology of the Religion of Liberated Israel, 1250–1050 B.C.E.* Maryknoll, N.Y.: Orbis, 1979.

Gray, John. *The Krt Text in the Literature of Ras Shamra: A Social Myth of Ancient Canaan.* 2d ed. Documenta et Monumenta Orientis Antiqui 5. Leiden: E. J. Brill, 1964.

*Harper Atlas of the Bible.* Edited by James B. Pritchard. New York: Harper & Row, 1987.

Helck, Wolfgang. *Die Beziehungen Ägyptens zu Vorderasien im 3. und 2. Jahrtausend v. Chr.* Ägyptologische Abhandlungen 5. Wiesbaden: Otto Harrassowitz, 1962.

Herm, Gerhard, *The Phoenicians: The Purple Empire of the Ancient World.* London: Victor Gollancz/New York: Morrow, 1975.

Kapelrud, Arvid S. *Baal in the Ras Shamra Texts.* Copenhagen: G. E. C. Gad, 1952.

—————. *The Violent Goddess: Anat in the Ras Shamra Texts.* Oslo: Universitetsforlaget, 1969.

Kenyon, Kathleen M. *Amorites and Canaanites.* Schweich Lectures 1963. London: Oxford University Press, 1966.

—————. *Digging Up Jericho: The Results of the Jericho Excavations, 1952–1956.* New York: Frederick A. Praeger, 1957.

Kitchen, Kenneth A. *Ancient Orient and Old Testament.* London: Tyndale Press/Chicago: InterVarsity, 1966.

*Lexikon der Ägyptologie.* Edited by Wolfgang Helck and Eberhard Otto. Wiesbaden: Otto Harrassowitz, 1972–.

Loud, Gordon. *The Megiddo Ivories.* Oriental Institute Publications 52. Chicago: University of Chicago Press, 1939.

Macqueen, James G. *The Hittites and Their Contemporaries in Asia Minor.* Ancient Peoples and Places 83. Boulder, Colo.: Westview, 1975.

Margalit, Baruch. *A Matter of "Life" and "Death": A Study of the Baal-Mot Epic (CTA 4-5-6).* Alter Orient und Altes Testament 206. Neukirchen-Vluyn: Neukirchener Verlag/Kevelaer: Butzon und Bercker, 1980.

Matthiae, Paolo. *Ebla: An Empire Rediscovered.* Garden City, N.Y.: Doubleday, 1981.

Moscati, Sabatino. *The World of the Phoenicians.* London: Weidenfeld & Nicolson. New York: Frederick A. Praeger, 1968.

Mullen, E. Theodore, Jr. *The Divine Council in Canaanite and Early Hebrew Literature.* Harvard Semitic Monographs 24. Chico, Calif.: Scholars Press, 1980.

Naveh, Joseph. *Early History of the Alphabet.* Jerusalem: Magnes/Leiden: E. J. Brill, 1982.

Negbi, Ora. *Canaanite Gods in Metal: An Archaeological Study of Ancient Syro-Palestinian Figurines.* Tel Aviv: Tel Aviv University, Institute of Archaeology, 1976.

Oldenburg, Ulf. *The Conflict Between El and Ba'al in Canaanite Religion.* Numen Supplement: Dissertationes 3. Leiden: E. J. Brill, 1969.

Pettinato, Giovanni. *The Archives of Ebla: An Empire Inscribed in Clay.* Garden City, N.Y.: Doubleday, 1981.

Pope, Marvin H. *El in the Ugaritic Texts.* Vetus Testamentum Supplement 2. Leiden: E. J. Brill, 1955.

Pritchard, James B. *Palestinian Figurines in Relation to Certain Goddesses Known Through Literature.* American Oriental Series 24. New Haven: American Oriental Society, 1943.

*Recent Archaeology in the Land of Israel.* Edited by Hershel Shanks and Benjamin Mazar. Washington, D.C.: Biblical Archaeology Society/Jerusalem: Israel Exploration Society, 1984.

Ringgren, Helmer. *Religions of the Ancient Near East.* Philadelphia: Westminster, 1973.

Roberts, J. J. M. *The Earliest Semitic Pantheon: A Study of the Semitic Deities Attested in Mesopotamia before Ur III.* Baltimore: Johns Hopkins University Press, 1972.

Schaeffer, Claude F. A. *The Cuneiform Texts of Ras Shamra–Ugarit.* Schweich Lectures 1936. London: Oxford University Press, 1939. Reprint, Munich: Kraus, 1980.

Sellin, Ernst. *Tell Ta'annek.* Vienna: Akademie der Wissenschaften, 1904.

Shiloh, Yigal. *Excavations at the City of David.* Vol. 1, *1978–1982.* Qedem 19. Jerusalem: Institute of Archaeology, Hebrew University, 1984.

*Symposia Celebrating the Seventy-fifth Anniversary of the Founding of the American Schools of Oriental Research (1900–1975).* Edited by Frank Moore Cross. Cambridge, Mass.: American Schools of Oriental Research, 1979.

*The Syrian Goddess (De Dea Syria); Attributed to Lucian.* Edited by Harold W. Attridge and Robert A. Oden. Missoula, Mont.: Scholars Press, 1976.

*Ugarit in Retrospect: Fifty Years of Ugarit and Ugaritic.* Edited by Gordon Douglas Young. Winona Lake, Indiana: Eisenbrauns, 1981.

*Ugaritica.* Edited by Claude F.-A. Schaeffer et al. 7 vols. Mission de Ras Shamra 3, 5, 8, 15–18. Paris: Paul Geuthner, 1939–1978.

*Ur Excavations: Texts.* Part 1, *Royal Inscriptions.* Edited by C. J. Gadd and L. Legrain. 2 vols. London: British Museum/Philadelphia: Museum of the University of Pennsylvania, 1928.

Van Seters, John. *The Hyksos: A New Investigation.* New Haven: Yale University Press, 1966.

Weippert, Manfred. *The Settlement of the Israelite Tribes in Palestine: A Critical Survey of Recent Scholarly Debate.* Studies in Biblical Theology, 2.21. Naperville, Ill.: Allenson, 1971.

Yadin, Yigael. *Hazor: The Rediscovery of a Great Citadel of the Bible.* New York: Random, 1975.

# Chapter 5

*Atlas of the Classical World.* Edited by A. A. M. van der Heyden and H. H. Scullard. New York: Nelson, 1959.

*Ausführliches Lexikon der griechischen und römischen Mythologie.* Edited by Wilhelm Heinrich Roscher. 6 vols. in 9, + 4 sup. vols. Leipzig: Teubner, 1884–1937. Reprint, Hildesheim: G. Olms, 1977; 7 vols. in 10.

Barthell, Edward E., Jr. *Gods and Goddesses of Ancient Greece.* Coral Gables, Fl.: University of Miami Press, 1971.

Beckman, James. *The Religious Dimension of Socrates' Thought.* Symbolik der Religionen Supplement 7. Waterloo, Canada: Wilfrid Laurier University Press, 1943.

Bleeker, C. J. *Egyptian Festivals: Enactments of Religious Renewal.* Studies in the History of Religions 13. Leiden: E. J. Brill, 1967.

Brady, Thomas Allan. *The Reception of the Egyptian Cults by the Greeks (330–30 B.C.).* University of Missouri Studies 10.1. Columbia, Mo.: University of Missouri Press, 1935.

Buck, R. S. *Plato's Meno.* Cambridge: Cambridge University Press, 1961.

Devambez, Pierre, et al. *The Praeger Encyclopedia of Ancient Greek Civilization.* New York: Frederick A. Praeger, 1967.

Dietrich, Bernard C. *The Origins of Greek Religion.* Berlin: Walter de Gruyter, 1974.

Dillon, John M. *Iamblichi Chalcidensis in Platonis dialogos commentariorum fragmenta.* Leiden: E. J. Brill, 1973.

Dionysios Areopagita. *Mystische Theologie und andere Schriften.* Edited by Walter Tritsch. Weisheitsbücher der Menschheit. Munich: Otto Wilhelm Barth, 1956.

Dodds, Eric R. *Proclus: The Elements of Theology.* 2d ed. Oxford: Clarendon Press, 1963.

Foucart, Paul. *Les mystères d'Éleusis.* Paris: Auguste Picard, 1914. Reprint, New York: Arno, 1975.

Freeman, Kathleen. *Ancilla to the Pre-Socratic Philosophers: A Complete Translation of the Fragments in Diels, Fragmente der Vorsokratiker.* Oxford: Basil Blackwell/Cambridge: Harvard University Press, 1948.

Friedländer, Paul. *Plato.* Bollingen Series 59. 3 vols. New York: Pantheon/Princeton: Princeton University Press, 1958–1969.

Godwin, Joscelyn, *Mystery Religions in the Ancient World.* San Francisco: Harper & Row, 1981.

Guthrie, W. K. C. *Orpheus and Greek Religion: A Study of the Orphic Movement.* 2d ed. New York: W. W. Norton, 1966.

Kerényi, Karl. *The Gods of the Greeks.* London: Thames and Hudson, 1951.

————. *The Heroes of the Greeks*. London: Thames and Hudson, 1959.

Kern, Otto. *Orphicorum Fragmenta*. 2d ed. Berlin: Weidmann, 1963.

Kirk, G. S. *The Nature of Greek Myths*. Woodstock, N.Y.: Overlook, 1975.

MacKenna, Stephen. *Plotinus: The Enneads*. 4th ed. London: Faber & Faber, 1969.

Meineke, August. *Ioannis Stobaei Florilegium*. 4 vols. Leipzig: Teubner, 1852–1857.

Mikalson, Jon D. *Athenian Popular Religion*. Chapel Hill: University of North Carolina Press, 1983.

Moody, Raymond A., Jr. *Life after Life: The Investigation of a Phenomenon—Survival of Bodily Death*. Atlanta: Mockingbird, 1975.

Mylonas, George E. *Eleusis and the Eleusinian Mysteries*. Princeton: Princeton University Press, 1961.

————. *The Hymn to Demeter and Her Sanctuary at Eleusis*. Washington University Studies: Language and Literature, n.s. 13. St. Louis: Washington University Press, 1942.

*Die orientalischen Religionen im Römerreich*. Edited by Maarten J. Vermaseren. EPRO 93. Leiden: E. J. Brill, 1981.

Palmer, Leonard R. *Mycenaeans and Minoans: Aegean Prehistory in the Light of the Linear B Tablets*. 2d ed. New York: Alfred A. Knopf, 1965.

Pater, Walter. *Plato and Platonism*. 2d ed. London: Macmillan, 1910. Reprint, New York: Greenwood, 1969; New York: Johnson, 1973.

Patterson, Robert Leet. *Plato on Immortality*. University Park, Pa.: Pennsylvania State University Press, 1965.

Philip, J. A. *Pythagoras and Early Pythagoreanism*. Phoenix Supplement 7. Toronto: University of Toronto Press, 1966.

Pinsent, John. *Greek Mythology*. London: Hamlyn, 1969.

Raine, Kathleen, and George Mills Harper. *Thomas Taylor, the Platonist: Selected Writings*. Bollingen Series 88. Princeton: Princeton University Press, 1969.

Rice, David G., and John E. Stambaugh. *Sources for the Study of Greek Religion*. Missoula, Mont.: Scholars Press, 1979.

Ring, Kenneth. *Life at Death: A Scientific Investigation of the Near-Death Experience*. New York: Coward, McCann & Geoghegan, 1980.

Rosán, Laurence Jay. *The Philosophy of Proclus: The Final Phase of Ancient Thought*. New York: Cosmos, 1949.

Schuré, Édouard. *From Sphinx to Christ: An Occult History*. Blauvet, N.Y.: R. Steiner, 1970. Reprint, San Francisco: Harper & Row, 1982.

Schwaller de Lubicz, R. A. *Symbol and the Symbolic: Ancient Egypt, Science, and the Evolution of Consciousness*. New York: Inner Traditions, 1981.

*The Significance of Neoplatonism*. Edited by R. Baine Harris. Studies in Neoplatonism 1. Norfolk, Va.: International Society for Neoplatonic Studies, Old Dominion University, 1976.

Snell, Bruno. *The Discovery of the Mind: The Greek Origins of European Thought*. Cambridge: Harvard University Press, 1953. Reprint, New York: Harper, 1960; New York: Dover, 1982.

Stapleton, Michael. *A Dictionary of Greek and Roman Mythology*. London: Hamlyn, 1978.

Steiner, Rudolf. *Between Death and Rebirth*. London: Rudolf Steiner Press, 1975.

Taylor, Thomas. *Iamblichus' Life of Pythagoras*. London: A. J. Valpy, 1818. Reprint, London: John M. Watkins, 1965.

————. *Iamblichus on the Mysteries of the Egyptians, Chaldeans, and Assyrians*. 2d ed. London: Bertram Dobell and Reeves and Turner, 1895. Reprint, London: Stuart & Watkins, 1968.

————. *The Mystical Hymns of Orpheus*. 2d ed. Chiswick: C. Whittingham, 1824.

_____. Sallust: On the Gods and the World. London: E. Jeffrey, 1793. Reprint, Los Angeles: Philosophical Research Society, 1976.

Vidman, Ladislav. Sylloge inscriptionum religionis Isiacae et Sarapiacae. Religionsgeschichtliche Versuche und Vorarbeiten 28. Berlin: Walter de Gruyter, 1969.

Vogel, Cornelia J. de. Pythagoras and Early Pythagoreanism. Assen: Van Gorcum, 1966.

Warren, Edward W. Isagogue: Porphyry the Phoenician. Toronto: Pontifical Institute of Mediaeval Studies, 1975.

Wasson, R. Gordon, Albert Hofmann, and Carl A. P. Ruck. The Road to Eleusis: Unveiling the Secret to the Mysteries. Ethno-mycological Studies 4. New York: Harcourt Brace Jovanovich, 1978.

Weber, Karl-Otto. Origenes der Neuplatoniker. Zetemata: Monographien zur klassischen Altertumswissenschaft 27. Munich: C. H. Beck, 1962.

West, M. L. Early Greek Philosophy and the Orient. Oxford: Clarendon, 1971.

_____. The Orphic Poems. Oxford: Clarendon, 1983.

Wilamowitz-Moellendorff, Ulrich von. Platon: Sein Leben und seine Werke. Edited by Bruno Snell. Berlin: Weidmann, 1948.

Wilson, John A. Herodotus in Egypt. Scholae Adriani de Buck Memoriae Dicatae 5. Leiden: Nederlands Instituut voor het Nabije Oosten, 1970.

## Chapter 6

Akşit, İlhan. Ancient Civilisations of Anatolia and Historical Treasures of Turkey. Istanbul: Ali Riza Baskan, 1982.

Ayer, Joseph Cullen. A Source Book for Ancient Church History. New York: Scribner, 1913. Reprint, New York: AMS, 1970.

Brunt, P. A., and J. M. Moore. Res Gestae Divi Augusti. London: Oxford University Press, 1967.

Chambers, John D. The Divine Pymander, and Other Writings of Hermes Trismegistus. Edinburgh: T. & T. Clark, 1882. Reprint, New York: Samuel Weiser, 1972.

Cornell, Tim, and John Matthews. Atlas of the Roman World. New York: Facts on File, 1982.

Creuzer, Georg Friedrich. Das Mithreum von Neuenheim bei Heidelberg. Heidelberg: C. F. Winter, 1838. Reprint, 1969.

_____. Symbolik und Mythologie der alten Völker, besonders der Griechen. 4 vols. Leipzig: Heyer und Leske, 1810–1812. Reprint, New York: Arno, 1978.

Cumont, Franz. The Mysteries of Mithra. Chicago: Open Court, 1903. Reprint, New York: Dover, 1956.

Dumézil, Georges. Archaic Roman Religion. 2 vols. Chicago: University of Chicago Press, 1970.

Dummer, Jürgen. Panarion haer. 34–64. 2d ed. Epiphanius 2. GCS 31. Berlin: Akademie-Verlag, 1980.

Duthoy, Robert. The Taurobolium: Its Evolution and Terminology. EPRO 10. Leiden: E. J. Brill, 1969.

Études Mithriaques: Actes du 2e Congrès International, Téhéran, du 1er au 8 septembre 1975. Teheran-Liège: Bibliothèque Pahlavi, 1978.

Geden, A. S. Select Passages Illustrating Mithraism. London: Society for Promoting Christian Knowledge, 1925.

Gonda, Jan. The Vedic God Mitra. Orientalia Rheno-Traiectina 13. Leiden: E. J. Brill, 1972.

Griffiths, J. Gwyn. Apuleius of Madauros: The Isis-Book (Metamorphoses, Book XI). EPRO 39. Leiden: E. J. Brill, 1975.

_____. Plutarch's De Iside et Osiride. Cardiff: University of Wales Press, 1970.

Halsberghe, Gaston H. The Cult of Sol Invictus. EPRO 23. Leiden: E. J. Brill, 1972.

Helm, Rudolf. *Die Chronik des Hierony- mus.* 2d ed. Eusebius Werke 7. GCS 47. Berlin: Akademie-Verlag, 1956.

Herzfeld, Ernst E. *Iran in the Ancient East.* London: Oxford University Press, 1941.

King, Charles William. *Julian the Em- peror.* London: G. Bell, 1888.

Köberlein, Ernst. *Caligula und die ägyp- tischen Kulte.* Beiträge zur klassischen Philologie 3. Meisenheim am Glan: An- ton Hain, 1962.

Le Corsu, France. *Isis: Mythe et Mystères.* Collection d'Études mythologiques. Paris: les Belles Lettres, 1977.

Lewy, Hans. *Chaldaean Oracles and Theurgy: Mysticism, Magic, and Plato- nism in the Later Roman Empire.* 2d ed. Edited by Michel Tardieu. Paris: Études Augustiniennes, 1978.

Malaise, Michel. *Les conditions de péné- tration et de diffusion des cultes égyp- tiens en Italie.* EPRO 22. Leiden: E. J. Brill, 1972.

————. *Inventaire préliminaire des documents égyptiens découverts en Italie.* EPRO 21. Leiden: E. J. Brill, 1972.

Mead, G. R. S. *Thrice-Greatest Hermes: Studies in Hellenistic Theosophy and Gnosis.* 3 vols. London: Theosophical Publishing Society, 1906. Reprint, Lon- don: John M. Watkins, 1964; Detroit: Hermes, 1978.

*Mithraic Studies: Proceedings of the First International Congress of Mithraic Studies.* Edited by John R. Hinnells. 2 vols. Manchester: Manchester Univer- sity Press, 1975.

Mommsen, Theodor. *Chronica minora.* 3 vols. Monumenta Germaniae historica 9, 11, 13. Berlin: Weidmann, 1892–1898.

Münch, Marc-Mathieu. *La "Symbolique" de Friedrich Creuzer.* Association des Publications près les Universités de Strasbourg 155. Paris: Éditions Ophrys, [1976].

*Mysteria Mithrae.* Edited by Ugo Bianchi. Proceedings of the International Semi- nar on the "Religio-Historical Character of Roman Mithraism, with Particular Reference to Roman and Ostian Sources," Rome and Ostia 28–31 March 1978. EPRO 80. Leiden: E. J. Brill, 1979.

Nock, A. D., and A.-J. Festugière, *Corpus Hermeticum.* 4 vols. Paris: Société d'Édition "Les Belles Lettres," 1945–1954.

*Die orientalischen Religionen im Römer- reich.* Edited by Maarten J. Vermaseren. EPRO 93. Leiden: E. J. Brill, 1981.

Parrott, Douglas M., et al. *Nag Hammadi Codices V,2–5 and VI, with Papyrus Ber- olinensis 8502,1 and 4.* NHS 11. Leiden: E. J. Brill, 1979.

Perowne, Stewart. *Roman Mythology.* London: Paul Hamlyn, 1969.

Peter, Hermann. *Historicorum Romano- rum Reliquiae.* 2 vols. Leipzig: Teubner, 1870. Reprint, Stuttgart: Teubner, 1967.

Ramsay, William M. *The Cities of St. Paul: Their Influence on His Life and Thought.* London: Hodder and Stoughton, 1907. Reprint, Grand Rapids: Baker, 1967.

Richardson, Emeline. *The Etruscans: Their Art and Civilization.* Chicago: Univer- sity of Chicago Press, 1964. Reprint, 1976.

*Römischer Kaiserkult.* Edited by Antonie Wlosok. Wege der Forschung 372. Darmstadt: Wissenschaftliche Buchge- sellschaft, 1978.

*Sacred Books of the East.* Edited by F. Max Müller. 51 vols. Oxford: Clarendon, 1879–1910.

Schmidt, Erich F. *Persepolis.* Vol. 1, *Struc- tures, Reliefs, Inscriptions.* Oriental In- stitute Publication 68. Chicago: University of Chicago Press, 1953.

Schürer, Emil. *A History of the Jewish People in the Time of Jesus Christ.* 5 vols. Edinburgh: T. & T. Clark, 1885–1891.

Scott, Walter. *Hermetica: The Ancient Greek and Latin Writings . . . Ascribed to Hermes Trismegistus.* 4 vols. Oxford: Clarendon, 1924–1936. Reprint, Lon- don: Dawsons of Pall Mall, 1968.

*La soteriologia dei culti orientali nell'Impero Romano.* Edited by Ugo Bianchi and Maarten J. Vermaseren.

Atti del Collòquio Internazionale su la soteriologia dei culti orientali nell'Impero Romano, Roma 24–29 settembre 1979. EPRO 92. Leiden: E. J. Brill, 1982.

Stauffer, Ethelbert. *Christ and the Caesars*. Philadelphia: Westminster/London: SCM, 1955.

Ulansey, David. "Mithras and Perseus: Mithraic Astronomy and the Anatolian Perseus-Cult." Ph.D. dissertation, Princeton University, 1984.

Vermaseren, Maarten J. *Corpus Inscriptionum et Monumentorum Religionis Mithriacae*. 2 vols. The Hague: Martinus Nijhoff, 1956–1960.

————. *Cybele and Attis: The Myth and the Cult*. London: Thames and Hudson, 1977.

————. *Mithras: The Secret God*. London: Chatto and Windus/New York: Barnes and Noble, 1963.

————, and C. C. van Essen. *The Excavations in the Mithraeum of the Church of Santa Prisca in Rome*. Leiden: E. J. Brill, 1965.

Vidman, Ladislav. *Isis und Sarapis bei den Griechen und Römern. Religionsgeschichtliche Versuche und Vorarbeiten* 29. Berlin: Walter de Gruyter, 1970.

————. *Sylloge inscriptionum religionis Isiacae et Sarapiacae. Religionsgeschichtliche Versuche und Vorarbeiten* 28. Berlin: Walter de Gruyter, 1969.

Warmington, E. H. *Remains of Old Latin*. 4 vols. LCL. Cambridge: Harvard University Press/London: William Heinemann, 1935–1940.

Weinstock, Stefan. *Divus Julius*. Oxford: Clarendon, 1971.

Wilber, Donald N. *Persepolis: The Archaeology of Parsa, Seat of the Persian Kings*. New York: Thomas Y. Crowell, 1969.

Wilkin, Robert L. *The Christians as the Romans Saw Them*. New Haven: Yale University Press, 1984.

Witt, Reginald E. *Isis in the Graeco-Roman World*. Aspects of Greek and Roman Life. London: Thames and Hudson/Ithaca, N.Y.: Cornell University Press, 1971.

Yamauchi, Edwin M. *Pre-Christian Gnosticism: A Survey of the Proposed Evidences*. 2d ed. Grand Rapids: Baker Book House, 1983.

## Chapter 7

Ayer, Joseph Cullen. *A Source Book for Ancient Church History*. New York: Scribner, 1913. Reprint, New York: AMS, 1970.

Coptic Gnostic Library. Leiden: E. J. Brill, 1975–. (A subseries of English translations within Nag Hammadi Studies.)

*The Facsimile Edition of the Nag Hammadi Codices*. 12 vols. Leiden: E. J. Brill, 1972–1984.

Foerster, Werner. *Gnosis: A Selection of Gnostic Texts*. Vol. 1, *Patristic Evidence*; vol. 2, *Coptic and Mandean Sources*. Oxford: Clarendon, 1972, 1974.

Grant, Robert M. *Gnosticism: A Source Book of Heretical Writings from the Early Christian Period*. New York: Harper, 1961. Reprint, New York: AMS, 1978.

————, and David N. Freedman. *The Secret Sayings of Jesus: The Gospel of Thomas*. Garden City, N.Y.: Doubleday, 1960.

Grenfell, Bernard P., and Arthur S. Hunt. *The Oxyrhynchus Papyri*. Vols. 1 and 4. London: Egypt Exploration Fund, 1898, 1904.

Guillaumont, A., H.-C. Puech, G. Quispel, W. Till, and Yassah 'Abd al Masīḥ. *The Gospel According to Thomas*. Leiden: E. J. Brill/New York: Harper, 1959.

Hennecke, Edgar. *New Testament Apocrypha*. Vol. 1, *Gospels and Related Writings*; vol. 2, *Writings Relating to the Apostles; Apocalypses and Related Subjects*. Edited by Wilhelm Schneemelcher. Philadelphia: Westminster, 1963, 1965.

Hunt, Arthur S. *The Oxyrhynchus Papyri*.

Vol. 8. London: Egypt Exploration Fund, 1911.

Jonas, Hans. *The Gnostic Religion: The Message of the Alien God and the Beginnings of Christianity.* 2d ed. Boston: Beacon, 1963.

*The Nag Hammadi Library in English.* San Francisco: Harper & Row/Leiden: E. J. Brill, 1977.

Nag Hammadi Studies. Leiden: E. J. Brill, 1971–. (The following volumes are cited in the text.)

1. David M. Scholer. *Nag Hammadi Bibliography 1948–1969.* 1971.
2. Jacques-É. Ménard. *L'Évangile de Vérité.* 1972.
3. Martin Krause (ed.). *Essays on the Nag Hammadi Texts in Honour of Alexander Böhlig.* 1972.
4. Alexander Böhlig and Frederik Wisse. *Nag Hammadi Codices III,2 and IV,2: The Gospel of the Egyptians (The Holy Book of the Great Invisible Spirit).* 1975.
6. Martin Krause (ed.). *Essays on the Nag Hammadi Texts in Honour of Pahor Labib.* 1975.
8. Martin Krause (ed.). *Gnosis and Gnosticism: Papers Read at the Seventh International Conference on Patristic Studies (Oxford, September 8th–13th 1975).* 1977.
9. Carl Schmidt and Violet Mac-Dermot. *Pistis Sophia.* 1978.
11. Douglas M. Parrott (ed.). *Nag Hammadi Codices V,2–5 and VI, with Papyrus Berolinensis 8502,1 and 4.* 1979.
12. Klaus Koschorke. *Die Polemik der Gnostiker gegen das kirchliche Christentum.* 1978.
13. Carl Schmidt and Violet Mac-Dermot. *The Books of Jeu and the Untitled Text in the Bruce Codex.* 1978.
14. R. M. Wilson (ed.). *Nag Hammadi and Gnosis: Papers Read at the First International Congress of Coptology (Cairo, December 1976).* 1978.
16. J. W. B. Barns, G. M. Browne, and J. C. Shelton (eds.). *Nag Hammadi Codices: Greek and Coptic Papyri from the Cartonnage of the Covers.* 1981.
17. Martin Krause (ed.). *Gnosis and Gnosticism: Papers Read at the Eighth International Conference on Patristic Studies (Oxford, September 3rd–8th 1979).* 1981.
18. Jan Helderman. *Die Anapausis im Evangelium Veritatis.* 1984.
22. Harold W. Attridge (ed.). *Nag Hammadi Codex I (The Jung Codex).* 1985.
26. Stephen Emmel, Helmut Koester, and Elaine Pagels. *Nag Hammadi Codex III,5: The Dialogue of the Savior.* 1984.
35. Frank Williams. *The Panarion of Epiphanius of Salamis: Book I (Sects 1–46).* 1987.

Pagels, Elaine H. *The Gnostic Gospels.* New York: Random, 1979.

———. *The Gnostic Jesus and Early Christian Politics.* Tempe, Ariz.: Department of Religious Studies, Arizona State University, 1982.

Quispel, Gillis. *Ptolémée: Lettre à Flora.* SC 24. Paris: Cerf, 1949.

Rauer, Max. *Die Homilien zu Lukas in der Übersetzung des Hieronymus und die griechischen Reste der Homilien und des Lukas-Kommentars.* 2d ed. Origenes Werke 9. GCS 49. Berlin: Akademie-Verlag, 1959.

Roberts, C. H. *Catalogue of the Greek and Latin Papyri in the John Rylands Library, Manchester.* Vol. 3, *Theological and Literary Texts (Nos. 457–551).* Manchester: Manchester University Press, 1938.

Rudolph, Kurt. *Gnosis: The Nature and History of Gnosticism.* San Francisco: Harper & Row, 1983.

Siegert, Folker. *Nag-Hammadi-Register: Wörterbuch zur Erfassung der Begriffe in den koptisch-gnostischen Schriften von Nag Hammadi.* Wissenschaftliche Untersuchungen zum Neuen Testament 26. Tübingen: J. C. B. Mohr (Paul Siebeck), 1982.

Till, Walter C. *Das Evangelium nach Philippos.* Patristische Texte und Studien 2. Berlin: Walter de Gruyter, 1963.

_____. *Die gnostischen Schriften des koptischen Papyrus Berolinensis 8502.* 2d ed. Edited by Hans-Martin Schenke. TU 60. Berlin: Akademie-Verlag, 1972.

Wilson, Robert M. *Gnosis and the New Testament.* Philadelphia: Fortress/Oxford: Blackwell, 1968.

_____. *The Gnostic Problem: A Study of the Relations Between Hellensitic Judaism and the Gnostic Heresy.* London: A. R. Mowbray, 1958. Reprint, New York: AMS, 1980.

_____. *The Gospel of Philip.* New York: Harper & Row/London: A. R. Mowbray, 1962.

Yamauchi, Edwin M. *Pre-Christian Gnosticism: A Survey of the Proposed Evidences.* 2d ed. Grand Rapids: Baker, 1983.

## Chapter 8

Ali, Maulana Muhammad. *The Holy Qur'ān.* 6th ed. Lahore: Ahmadiyyah Anjuman Isha'at Islam, 1973.

Brandt, Wilhelm. *Die mandäische Religion.* Leipzig: J. C. Hinrichs, 1889. Reprint, Amsterdam: Philo, 1973.

_____. *Mandäische Schriften.* Göttingen: Vandenhoeck und Ruprecht, 1893. Reprint, Amsterdam: Philo, 1973.

_____. *Das Schicksal der Seele nach dem Tode nach mandäischen und parsischen Vorstellungen.* Libelli 152. Darmstadt: Wissenschaftliche Buchgesellschaft, 1967.

Brown, Raymond E. *The Gospel According to John.* 2 vols. Anchor Bible 29, 29A. Garden City, N.Y.: Doubleday, 1966, 1970.

Dodge, Bayard. *The Fihrist of al-Nadīm.* 2 vols. New York: Columbia University Press, 1970.

Drower, E. S. *The Book of the Zodiac = Sfar Mulwašia: D. C. 31.* Oriental Translation Fund 36. London: Royal Asiatic Society, 1949.

_____. *The Canonical Prayerbook of the Mandaeans.* Leiden: E. J. Brill, 1959.

_____. *The Coronation of the Great Šišlam.* Leiden: E. J. Brill, 1962.

_____. *Diwan Abatur; or, Progress Through the Purgatories.* Studi e Testi 151. Vatican City: Biblioteca Apostolica Vaticana, 1950.

_____. *The Haran Gawaita and the Baptism of Hibil-Ziwa.* Studi e Testi 176. Vatican City: Biblioteca Apostolica Vaticana, 1953.

_____. *The Mandaeans of Iraq and Iran: Their Cults, Customs, Magic, Legends, and Folklore.* Oxford: Clarendon, 1937. Reprint, Leiden: E. J. Brill, 1962.

_____. *A Pair of Naṣoraean Commentaries (Two Priestly Documents): The Great First World and the Lesser First World.* Leiden: E. J. Brill, 1963.

_____. *Šarḥ ḍ Qabin ḍ Šišlam Rba (D.C. 38): Explanatory Commentary on the Marriage-Ceremony of the Great Šišlam.* Biblica et Orientalia 12. Rome: Pontificio Istituto Biblico, 1950.

_____. *The Thousand and Twelve Questions (Alf Trisar Šuialia).* Deutsche Akademie der Wissenschaften zu Berlin, Institut für Orientforschung 32. Berlin: Akademie-Verlag, 1960.

_____, and R. Macuch. *A Mandaic Dictionary.* Oxford: Clarendon, 1963.

Grant, R. M. *Gnosticism and Early Christianity.* 2d ed. New York: Columbia University Press, 1966.

Holl, Karl. *Ancoratus und Panarion haer. 1–33.* Epiphanius 1. GCS 25. Leipzig: J. C. Hinrichs, 1915.

Lidzbarski, Mark. *Ginzā: Der Schatz; oder, Das Grosse Buch der Mandäer.* Quellen der Religionsgeschichte 4.13. Göttingen: Vandenhoeck und Ruprecht/Leipzig: J. C. Hinrichs, 1925.

_____. *Das Johannesbuch der Mandäer.* Giessen: Alfred Töpelmann, 1915.

―――――. *Mandäische Liturgien*. Berlin: Weidmann, 1920.

Macuch, Rudolf. *Handbook of Classical and Modern Mandaic*. Berlin: Walter de Gruyter, 1965.

―――――. *Zur Sprache und Literatur der Mandäer*. Studia Mandaica 1. Berlin: Walter de Gruyter, 1976.

Neusner, Jacob. *A History of the Jews in Babylonia*. 5 vols. Studia Post-Biblica 9, 11, 12, 14, 15. Leiden: E. J. Brill, 1965–1970.

*Die orientalischen Religionen im Römer-reich*. Edited by Maarten J. Vermaseren. EPRO 93. Leiden: E. J. Brill, 1981.

Pallis, Svend Aage. *Essay on Mandaean Bibliography 1560–1930*. London: Oxford University Press, 1933. Reprint, Amsterdam: Philo, 1974.

―――――. *Mandaean Studies*. London: Oxford University Press, 1926. Reprint, Amsterdam: Philo, 1974.

Rudolph, Kurt. *Die Mandäer*. 2 vols. Forschungen zur Religion und Literatur des Alten und Neuen Testaments 74, 75. Göttingen: Vandenhoeck und Ruprecht, 1960–1961.

―――――. *Mandaeism*. Iconography of Religions 21. Leiden: E. J. Brill, 1978.

Säve-Söderbergh, Torgny. *Studies in the Coptic Manichaean Psalm-Book*. Arbeten Utgivna med Understöd av Vilhelm Ekmans Universitetsfond 55. Uppsala: Almquist & Wiksells, 1949.

Segelberg, Eric. *Maṣbūtā: Studies in the Ritual of the Mandaean Baptism*. Uppsala: Almquist & Wiksells, 1958.

Sprengling, Martin. *Third Century Iran: Sapor and Kartir*. Chicago: Oriental Institute, University of Chicago, 1953.

Widengren, Geo. *Der Mandäismus*. Wege der Forschung 167. Darmstadt: Wissenschaftliche Buchgesellschaft, 1982.

Williams, Frank. *The Panarion of Epiphanius of Salamis: Book I (Sects 1–46)*. NHS 35. Leiden: E. J. Brill, 1987.

Yamauchi, Edwin M. *Gnostic Ethics and Mandaean Origins*. Harvard Theological Studies 24. Cambridge: Harvard University Press, 1970.

―――――. *Mandaic Incantation Texts*. American Oriental Series 49. New Haven: American Oriental Society, 1967.

Young, Gavin. *Iraq: Land of Two Rivers*. London: Collins, 1980.

―――――. *Return to the Marshes: Life with the Marsh Arabs of Iraq*. London: Collins, 1977.

# Chapter 9

Allberry, C. R. C. *A Manichaean Psalm-Book*. Manichaean Manuscripts in the Chester Beatty Collection 2. Stuttgart: W. Kohlhammer, 1938.

Andreas, F. C., and Walter B. Henning. *Mitteliranische Manaichaica aus Chinesisch-Turkestan*. Sitzungsberichte der Preussischen Akademie der Wissenschaften zu Berlin, philosophisch-historische Klasse, 1933: 7. Berlin: Akademie der Wissenschaften, 1933.

Arnold-Döben, Victoria. *Die Bildersprache des Manichäismus*. Arbeitsmaterialien zur Religionsgeschichte 3. Cologne: E. J. Brill, 1978.

Asmussen, Jes P. *Manichaean Literature: Representative Texts Chiefly from Middle Persian and Parthian Writings*. Persian Heritage Series 22. Delmar, N.Y.: Scholars' Facsimiles & Reprints, 1975.

Boyce, Mary. *The Manichaean Hymn-Cycles in Parthian*. London Oriental Series 3. London: Oxford University Press, 1954.

Brandt, Wilhelm. *Elchasai: Ein Religionsstifter und sein Werk*. Leipzig: J. C. Hinrichs, 1912. Reprint, Amsterdam: Philo, 1971.

Cameron, Ron, and Arthur J. Dewey. *The Cologne Mani Codex (P. Colon. inv. nr. 4780): "Concerning the Origin of His Body."* Society of Biblical Literature: Texts and Translations 15; Early Christian Literature Series 3. Missoula, Mont.: Scholars Press, 1979.

Dodge, Bayard. *The Fihrist of al-Nadīm.* 2 vols. New York: Columbia University Press, 1970.

Franck, Irene M., and David M. Brownstone. *The Silk Road: A History.* New York: Facts on File, 1986.

Hennecke, Edgar. *New Testament Apocrypha.* 2 vols. Edited by Wilhelm Schneemelcher. Philadelphia: Westminster, 1963, 1965.

Henning, W. B. *Zoroaster: Politician or Witch-Doctor?* London: Oxford University Press, 1951.

*India Antiqua: A Volume of Oriental Studies Presented by His Friends and Pupils to Jean Philippe Vogel.* Leiden: E. J. Brill, 1947.

Le Coq, Albert von. *Die buddhistische Spätantike in Mittelasien.* Vol. 2, *Die manichaeischen Miniaturen.* Ergebnisse der königlichen preussischen Turfan-Expeditionen. Berlin: D. Reimer, 1923.

*A Locust's Leg: Studies in Honour of S. H. Taqizadeh.* Edited by W. B. Henning and E. Yarshater. London: Percy Lund, Humphries, 1962.

*Die orientalischen Religionen im Römerreich.* Edited by Maarten J. Vermaseren. EPRO 93. Leiden: E. J. Brill, 1981.

Ort, L. J. R. *Mani: A Religio-Historical Description of His Personality.* Numen Supplement: Dissertationes 1. Leiden: E. J. Brill, 1967.

Polotsky, H. J. *Manichäische Homilien.* Vol. 1, *Manichäische Handschriften der Sammlung A. Chester Beatty.* Stuttgart: W. Kohlhammer, 1934.

————, and A. Böhlig. *Kephalaia.* Manichäische Handschriften der Staat-

lichen Museen Berlin 1. Stuttgart: W. Kohlhammer, 1940.

Rose, Eugen. *Die manichäische Christologie.* Studies in Oriental Religions 5. Wiesbaden: Otto Harrassowitz, 1979.

Sachau, C. Edward. *Alberuni's India: An Account of the Religion, Philosophy, Literature, Geography, Chronology, Astronomy, Customs, Laws and Astrology of India about A.H. 1030.* 2 vols. London: Trübner, 1887–1888. Reprint, Delhi: S. Chand, 1964.

————. *The Chronology of Ancient Nations: An English Version of the Arabic Text of the Athâr-ul-Bâkiya of Albîrûnî, or "Vestiges of the Past," Collected and Reduced to Writing by the Author in A.H. 390–1, A.D. 1000.* London: William H. Allen, 1879. Reprint, Lahore: Hijra International, 1983.

Sprengling, Martin. *Third Century Iran: Sapor and Kartir.* Chicago: Oriental Institute, University of Chicago, 1953.

Sundermann, Werner. *Mitteliranische manichäische Texte kirchengeschichtlichen Inhalts.* Schriften zur Geschichte und Kultur des Alten Orients: Berliner Turfantexte 11. Berlin: Akademie-Verlag, 1981.

————. *Mittelpersische und parthische kosmogonische und Parabeltexte der Manichäer.* Schriften zur Geschichte und Kultur des Alten Orients: Berliner Turfantexte 4. Berlin: Akademie-Verlag, 1973.

Widengren, Geo. *Mani and Manichaeism.* London: Weidenfeld & Nicolson/New York: Holt, Rinehart and Winston, 1965.

Zaehner, R. C. *Zurvan: A Zoroastrian Dilemma.* Oxford: Clarendon, 1955. Reprint, New York: Biblo and Tanner, 1972.

# Index